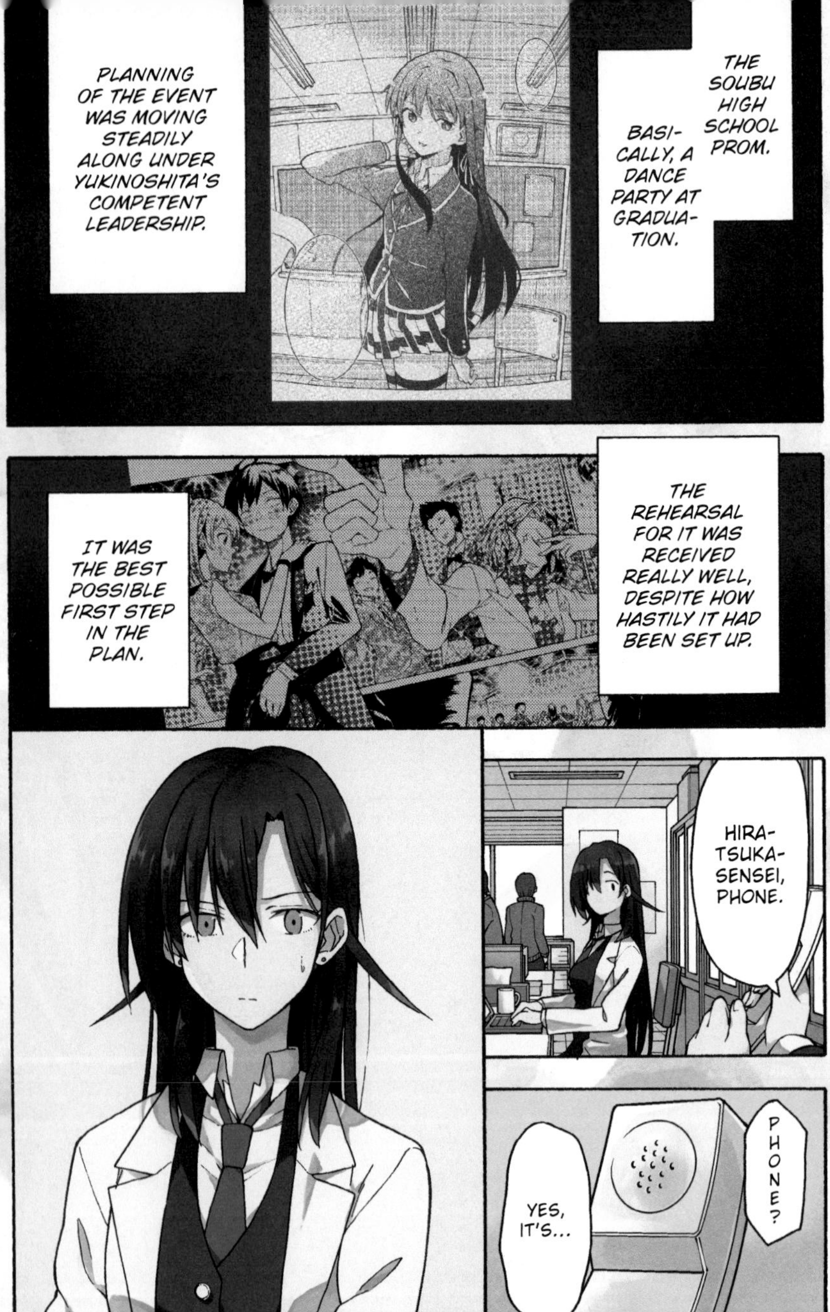
THE SOUBU HIGH SCHOOL PROM.
BASI-CALLY, A DANCE PARTY AT GRADUA-TION.
PLANNING OF THE EVENT WAS MOVING STEADILY ALONG UNDER YUKINOSHITA'S COMPETENT LEADERSHIP.
THE REHEARSAL FOR IT WAS RECEIVED REALLY WELL, DESPITE HOW HASTILY IT HAD BEEN SET UP.
IT WAS THE BEST POSSIBLE FIRST STEP IN THE PLAN.
HIRA-TSUKA-SENSEI, PHONE.
PHONE?
YES, IT'S...

CHAPTER 92 ··· YUI YUIGAHAMA'S THOUGHTS HAPPEN TO TURN TO THE FUTURE.

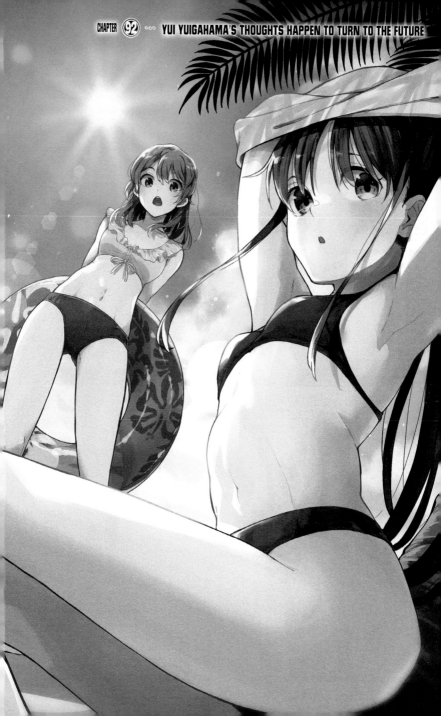

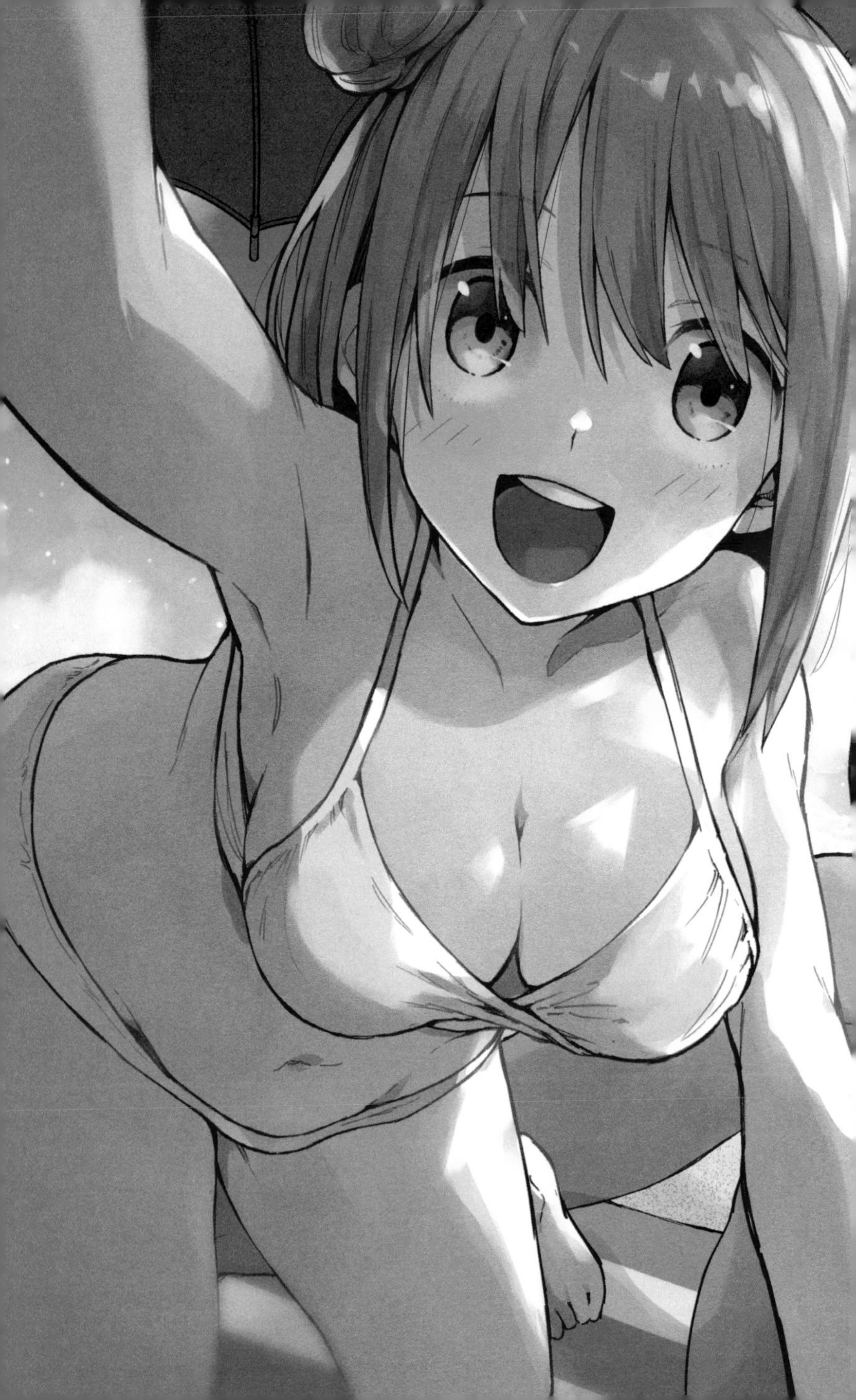

Cover illustration for *Monthly Sunday GX*, October 2020 issue

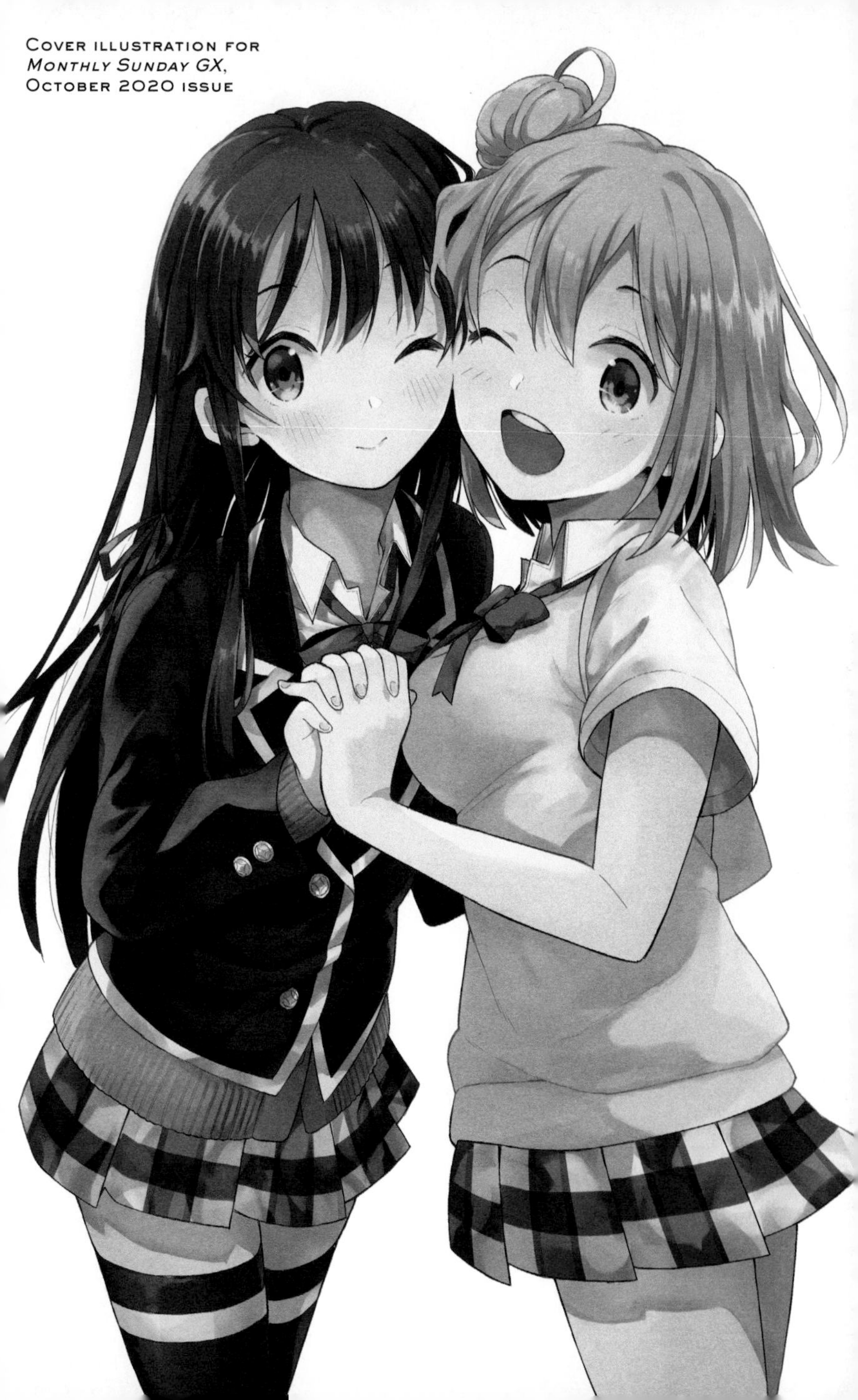

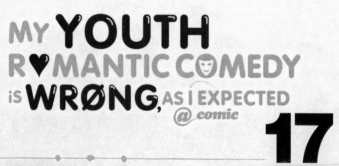

MY YOUTH ROMANTIC COMEDY is WRONG, AS I EXPECTED @comic

17

■ Original Story
Wataru Watari
■ Art
Naomichi Io
■ Character Design
Ponkan ⑧

MY YOUTH ROMANTIC COMEDY IS WRONG, AS I EXPECTED @COMIC

CHARACTERS + STORY SO FAR

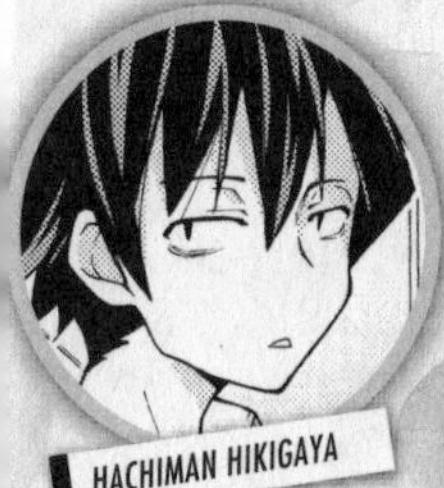

HACHIMAN HIKIGAYA

LONER AND A TWISTED HUMAN BEING. FORCED TO JOIN THE SERVICE CLUB. ASPIRES TO BE A HOUSEHUSBAND.

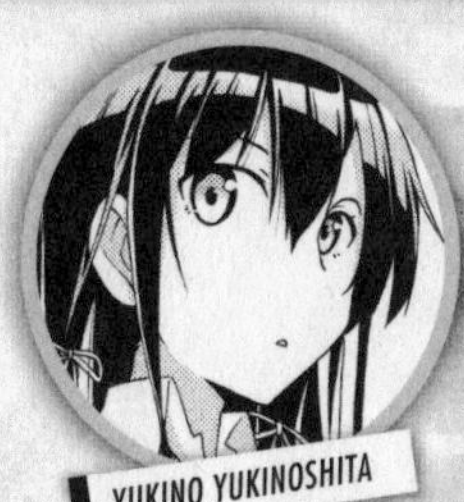

YUKINO YUKINOSHITA

PERFECT SUPERWOMAN WITH TOP GRADES AND FLAWLESS LOOKS, BUT HER PERSONALITY AND BOOBS ARE A LETDOWN. PRESIDENT OF THE SERVICE CLUB.

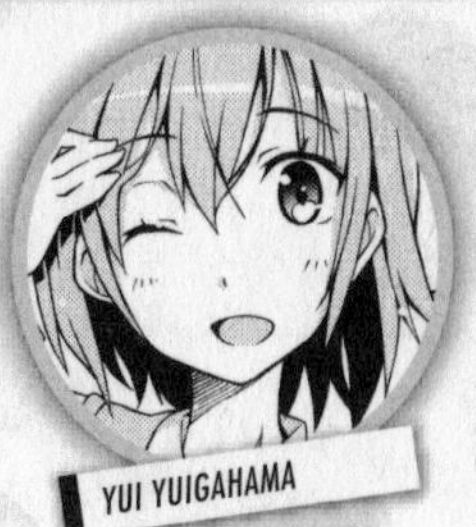

YUI YUIGAHAMA

LIGHT-BROWN HAIR, MINISKIRT, LARGE-BOOBED SLUTTY TYPE. BUT SHE'S ACTUALLY A VIRGIN!? MEMBER OF THE SERVICE CLUB.

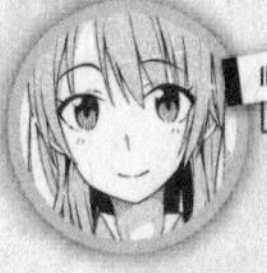

IROHA ISSHIKI

SOCCER CLUB ASSISTANT. FIRST-YEAR.

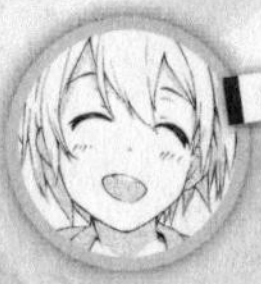

SAIKA TOTSUKA

THE SINGLE FLOWER BLOOMING IN THIS STORY. BUT...HAS A "PACKAGE."

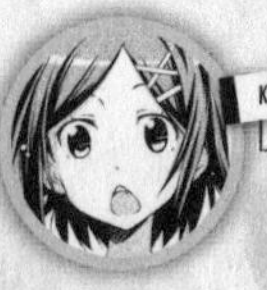

KOMACHI HIKIGAYA

HACHIMAN'S LITTLE SISTER. IN MIDDLE SCHOOL. EVERYTHING SHE DOES IS CALCULATED!?

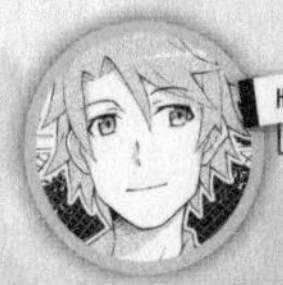

HAYATO HAYAMA

TOP RANKED IN THE SCHOOL CASTE. HANDSOME MEMBER OF THE SOCCER TEAM.

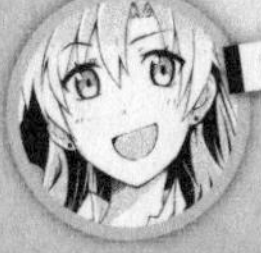

YUMIKO MIURA

THE HIGH EMPRESS NONE CAN OPPOSE.

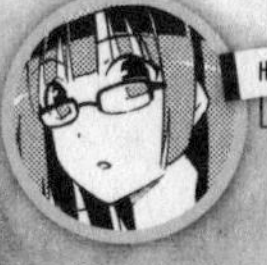

HINA EBINA

A MEMBER OF MIURA'S CLIQUE BUT A RAGING FUJOSHI ON THE INSIDE.

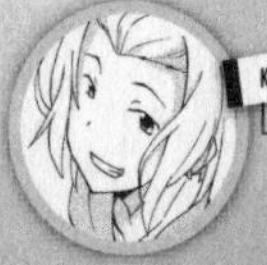

KAKERU TOBE

ALWAYS OVEREXCITED. MEMBER OF HAYAMA'S CLIQUE.

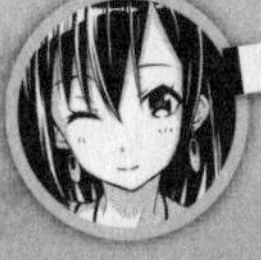

HARUNO YUKINOSHITA

YUKINO'S SISTER. UNIVERSITY UNDERGRADUATE. IS QUITE INTERESTED IN HACHIMAN.

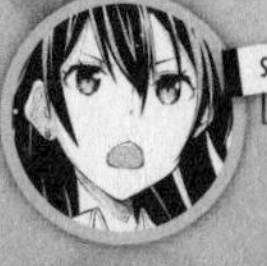

SHIZUKA HIRATSUKA

GUIDANCE COUNSELOR. ATTEMPTING TO FIX HACHIMAN BY FORCING HIM INTO THE SERVICE CLUB.

SO FAR

HACHIMAN AND THE SERVICE CLUB HAVE ACCEPTED THE REQUEST TO HOLD A SCHOOL PROM. BUT WHEN THEY HEAR YUKINO IS DETERMINED TO TAKE PERSONAL RESPONSIBILITY FOR THE EVENT AND MANAGE IT ON HER OWN, HACHIMAN AND YUI DECIDE TO STAY OUT. PRIOR TO THE EVENT, YUKINO AND IROHA STAGE A REHEARSAL, FILMING A PROMO VIDEO WHILE THEY'RE AT IT, TO POPULARIZE THE IDEA WITH THE STUDENTS. THEY ALL LOVE IT, AND NOW THERE ARE JUST A FEW MORE TWEAKS NEEDED FOR THE DAY OF THE EVENT. BUT THEN SOMEONE SHOWS UP TO THROW THE EVENT IN PERIL...

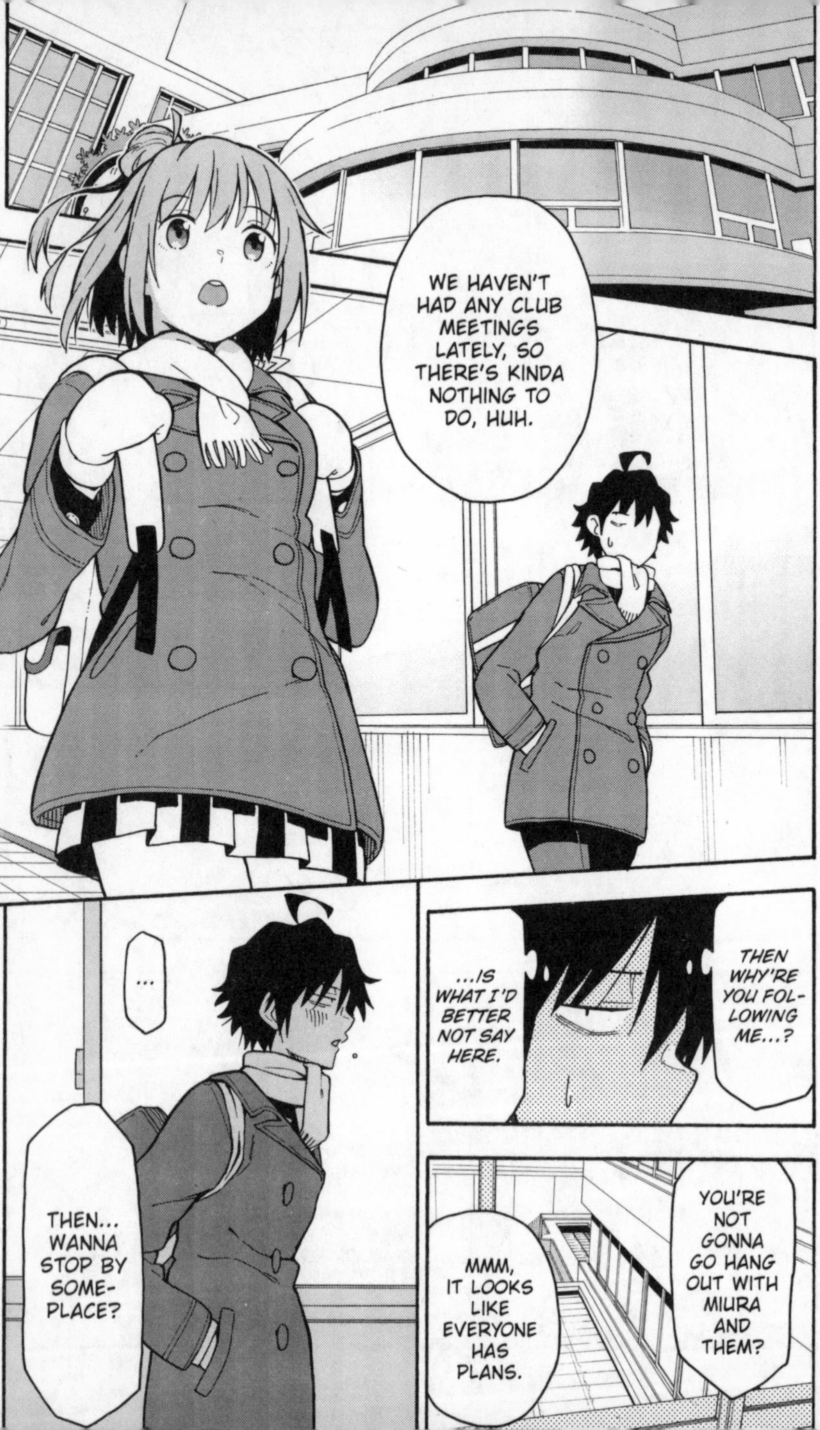
WE HAVEN'T HAD ANY CLUB MEETINGS LATELY, SO THERE'S KINDA NOTHING TO DO, HUH.
THEN WHY'RE YOU FOL-LOWING ME...?
...IS WHAT I'D BETTER NOT SAY HERE.
YOU'RE NOT GONNA GO HANG OUT WITH MIURA AND THEM?
MMM, IT LOOKS LIKE EVERYONE HAS PLANS.
...
THEN... WANNA STOP BY SOME-PLACE?

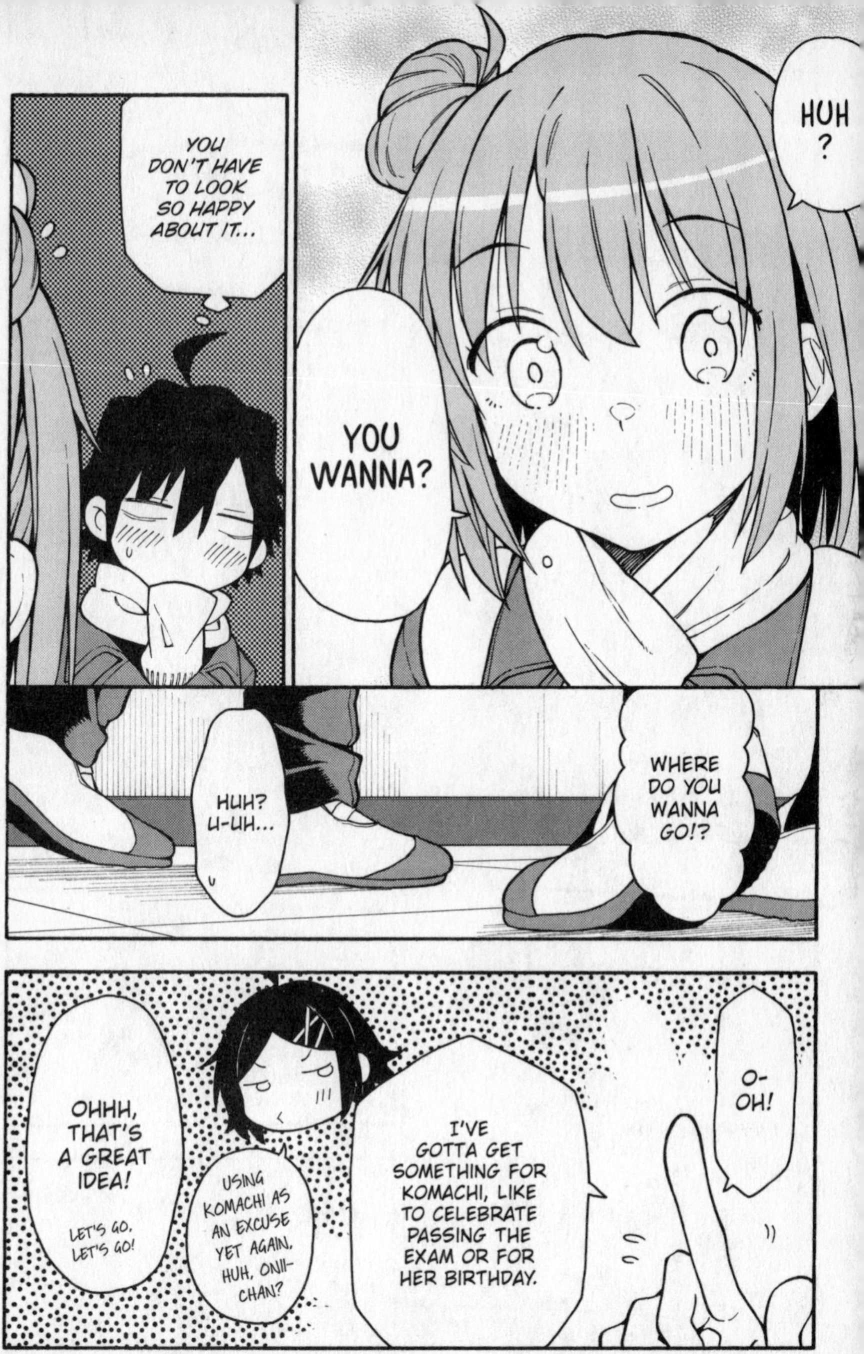
HUH?
YOU WANNA?
YOU DON'T HAVE TO LOOK SO HAPPY ABOUT IT...
WHERE DO YOU WANNA GO!?
HUH? U-UH...
O-OH!
I'VE GOTTA GET SOMETHING FOR KOMACHI, LIKE TO CELEBRATE PASSING THE EXAM OR FOR HER BIRTHDAY.
USING KOMACHI AS AN EXCUSE YET AGAIN, HUH, ONII-CHAN?
OHHH, THAT'S A GREAT IDEA!
LET'S GO, LET'S GO!

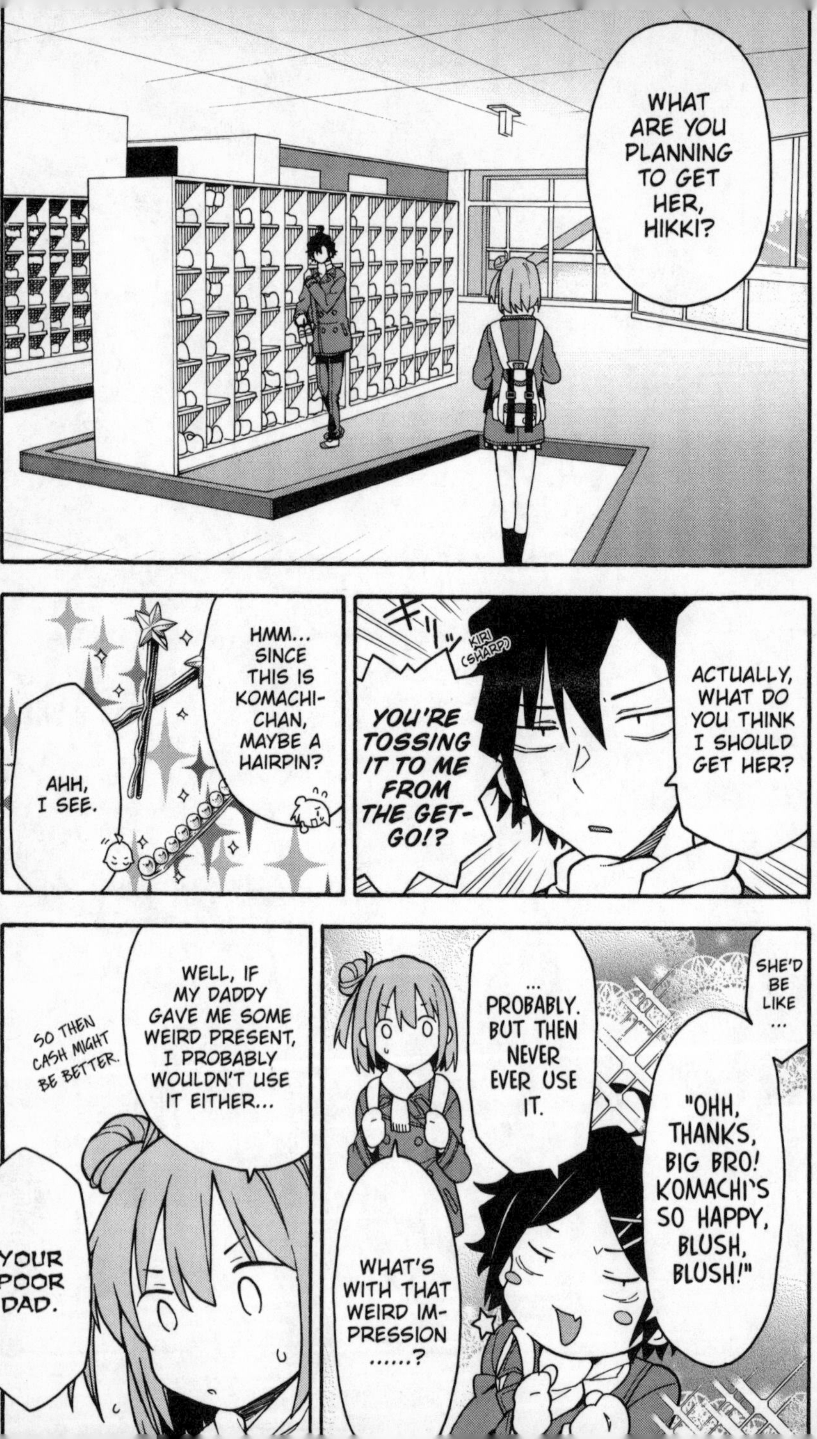
WHAT ARE YOU PLANNING TO GET HER, HIKKI?
ACTUALLY, WHAT DO YOU THINK I SHOULD GET HER?
KIRI (SHARP)
YOU'RE TOSSING IT TO ME FROM THE GET-GO!?
HMM... SINCE THIS IS KOMACHI-CHAN, MAYBE A HAIRPIN?
AHH, I SEE.
SHE'D BE LIKE ...
"OHH, THANKS, BIG BRO! KOMACHI'S SO HAPPY, BLUSH, BLUSH!"
... PROBABLY. BUT THEN NEVER EVER USE IT.
WHAT'S WITH THAT WEIRD IMPRESSION ......?
WELL, IF MY DADDY GAVE ME SOME WEIRD PRESENT, I PROBABLY WOULDN'T USE IT EITHER...
SO THEN CASH MIGHT BE BETTER.
YOUR POOR DAD.

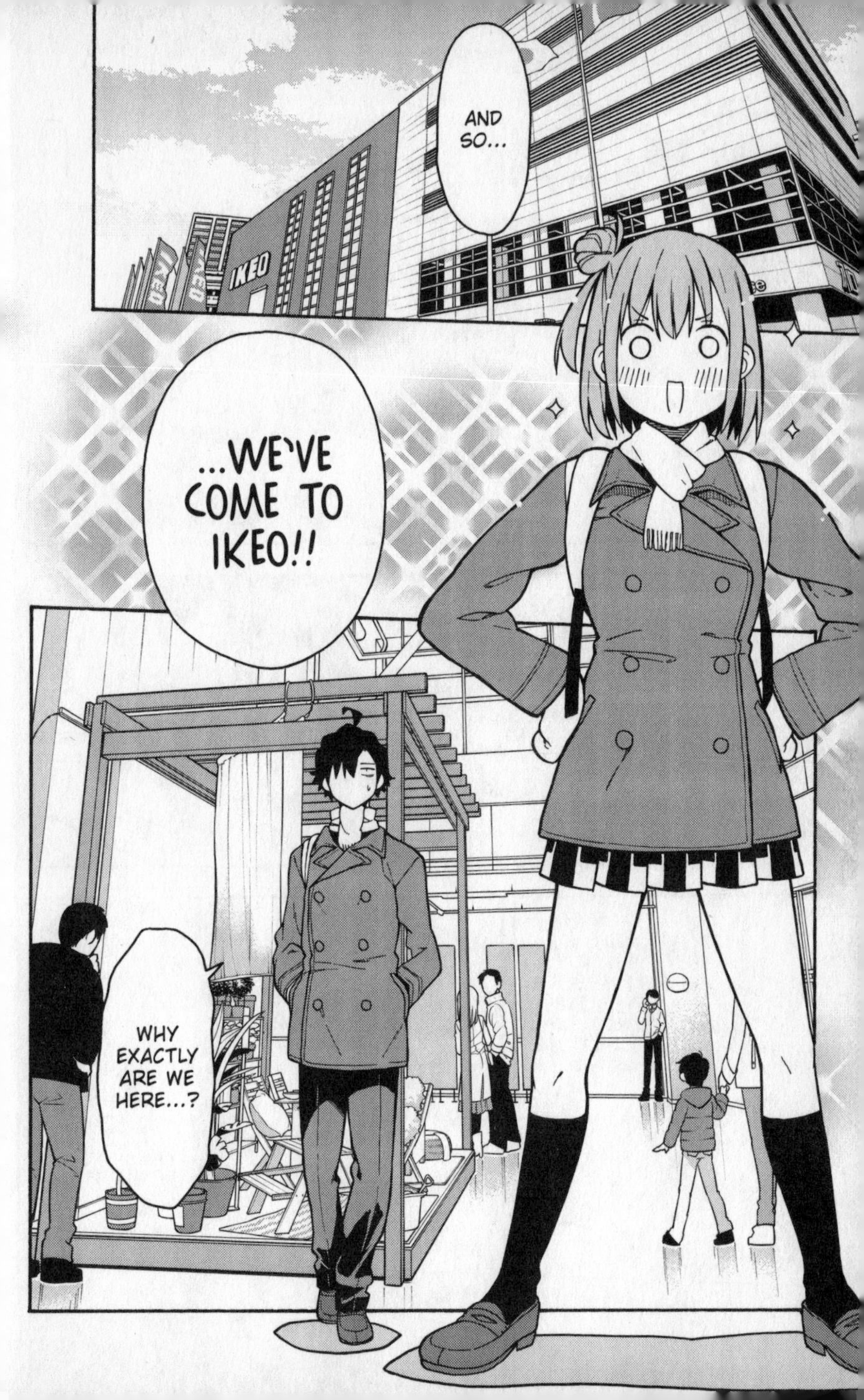

IKEO
AND SO...
...WE'VE COME TO IKEO!!
WHY EXACTLY ARE WE HERE...?

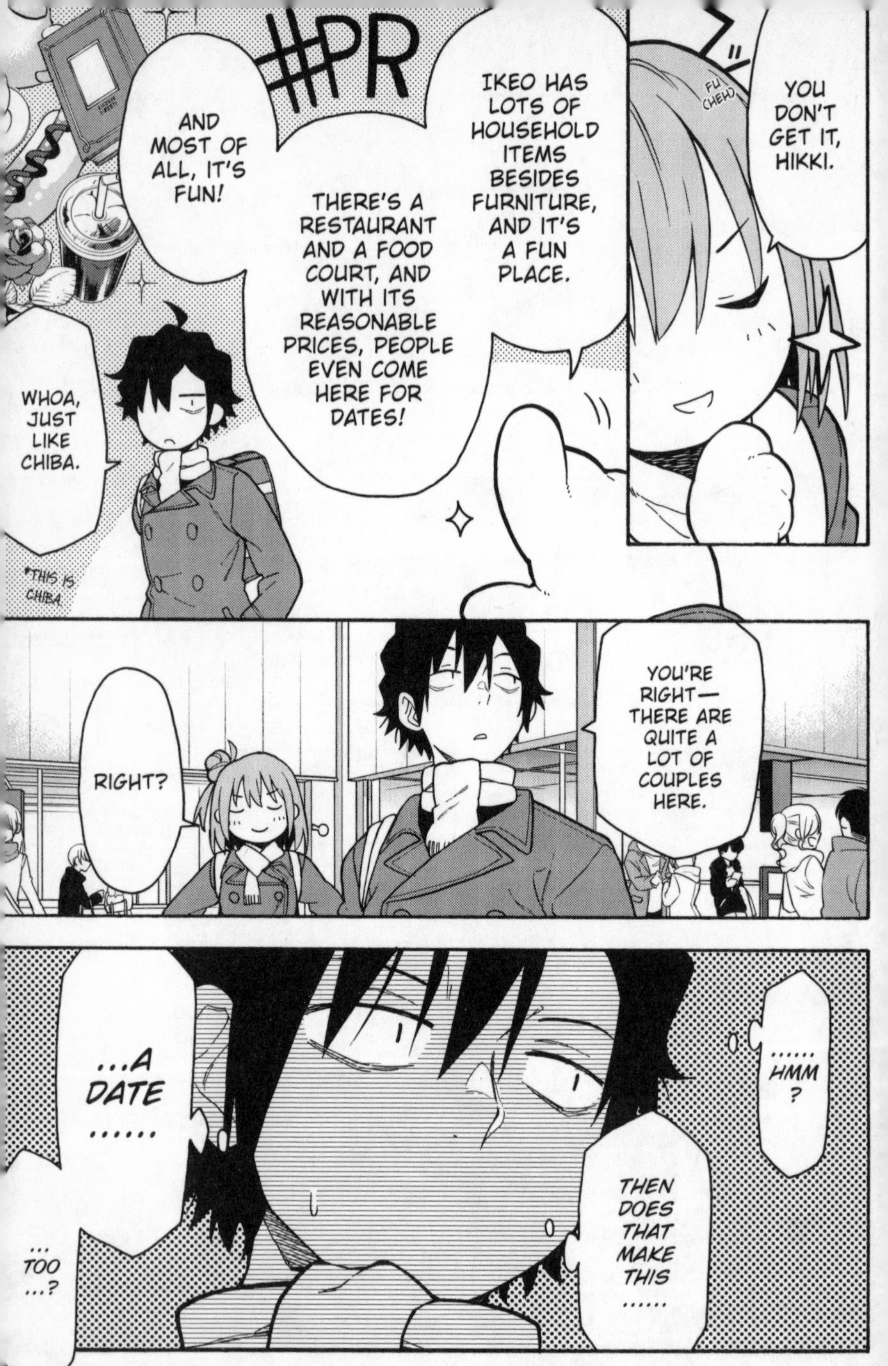
FU (HEH)
YOU DON'T GET IT, HIKKI.
IKEO HAS LOTS OF HOUSEHOLD ITEMS BESIDES FURNITURE, AND IT'S A FUN PLACE.
THERE'S A RESTAURANT AND A FOOD COURT, AND WITH ITS REASONABLE PRICES, PEOPLE EVEN COME HERE FOR DATES!
AND MOST OF ALL, IT'S FUN!
#PR
WHOA, JUST LIKE CHIBA.
*THIS IS CHIBA.
YOU'RE RIGHT—THERE ARE QUITE A LOT OF COUPLES HERE.
RIGHT?
......HMM?
THEN DOES THAT MAKE THIS......
...A DATE......
...TOO...?

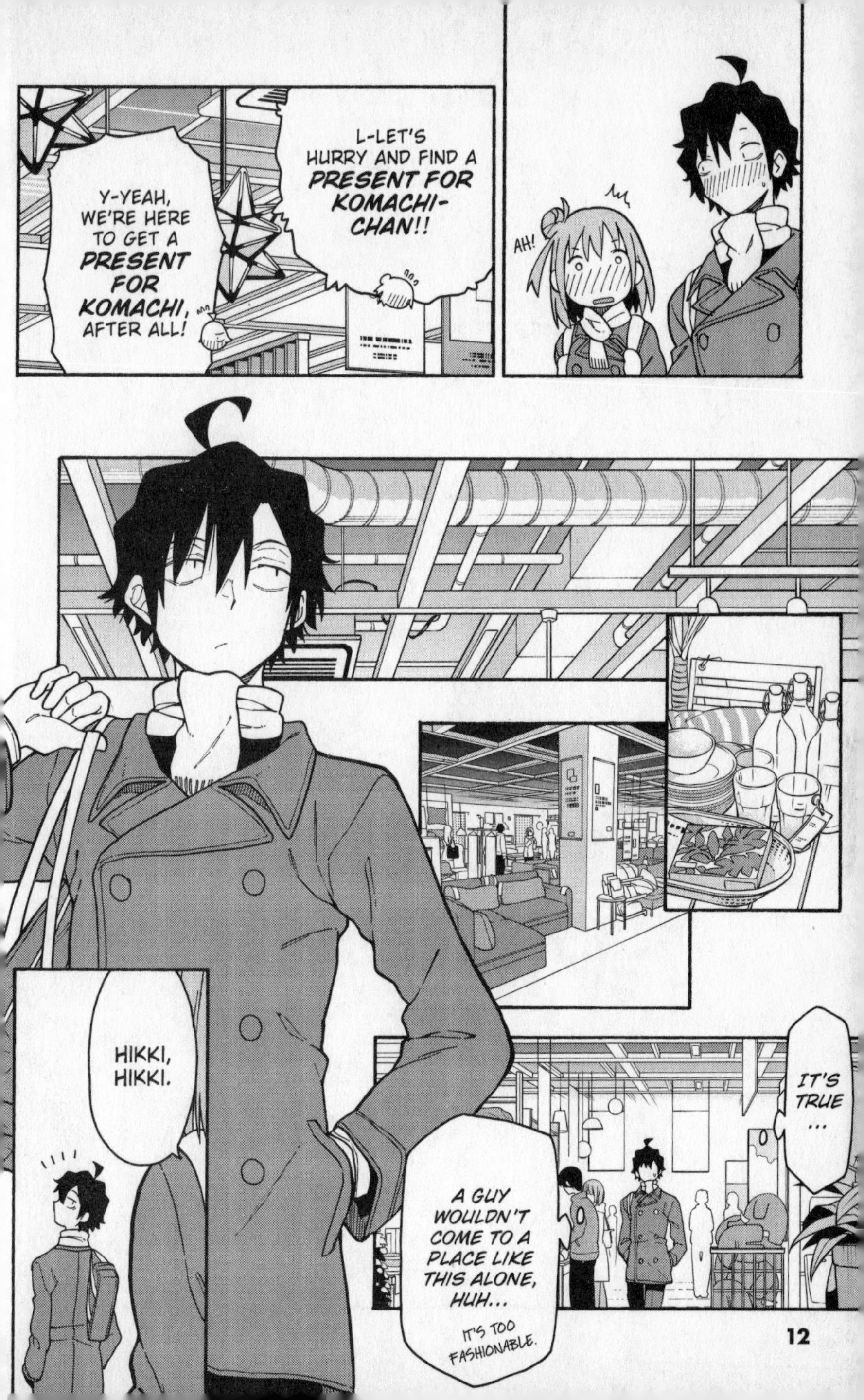
AH!
L-LET'S HURRY AND FIND A PRESENT FOR KOMACHI-CHAN!!
Y-YEAH, WE'RE HERE TO GET A PRESENT FOR KOMACHI, AFTER ALL!
IT'S TRUE...
A GUY WOULDN'T COME TO A PLACE LIKE THIS ALONE, HUH...
IT'S TOO FASHIONABLE.
HIKKI, HIKKI.

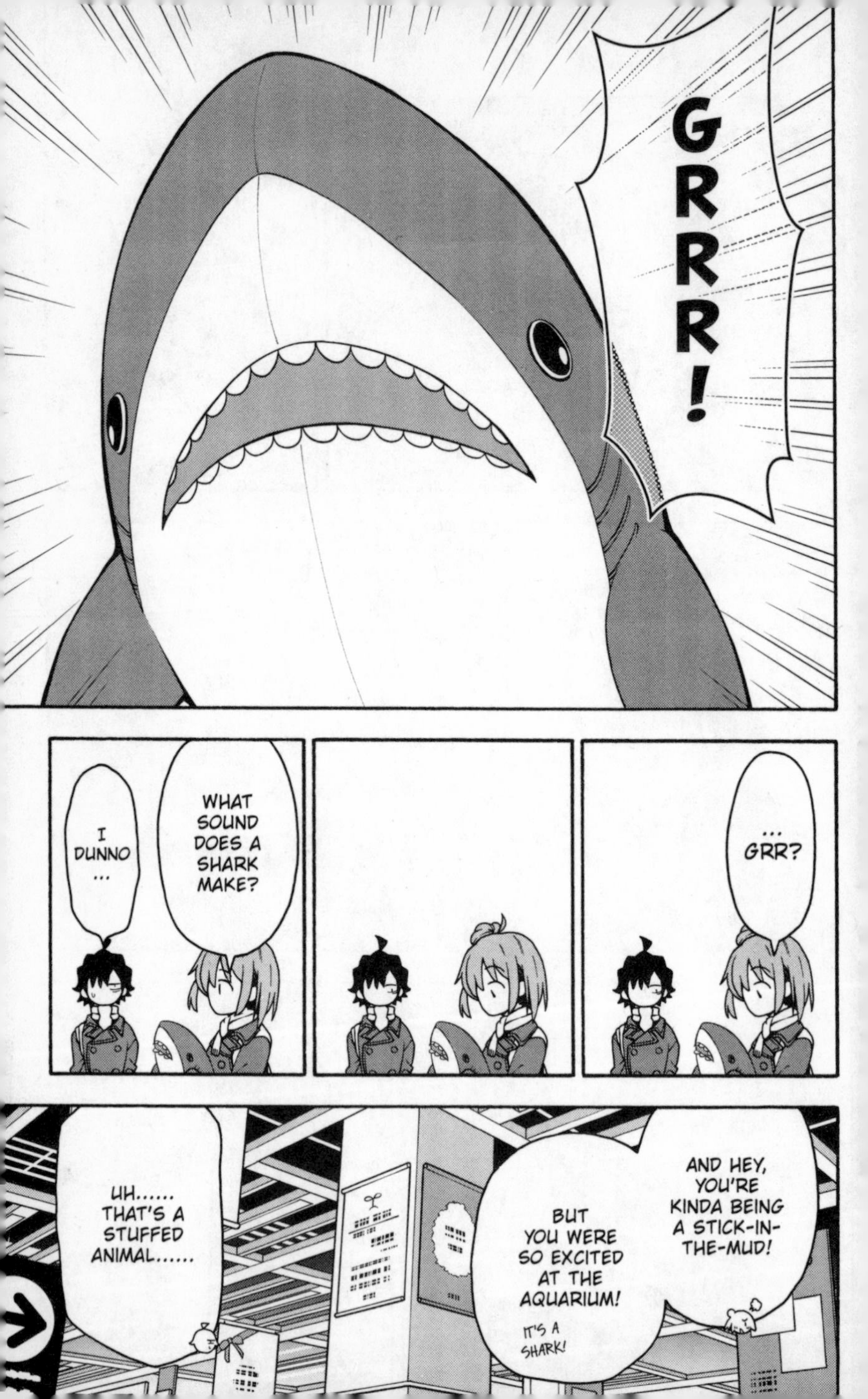
GRRR!
... GRR?
WHAT SOUND DOES A SHARK MAKE?
I DUNNO ...
AND HEY, YOU'RE KINDA BEING A STICK-IN-THE-MUD!
BUT YOU WERE SO EXCITED AT THE AQUARIUM!
IT'S A SHARK!
UH...... THAT'S A STUFFED ANIMAL......

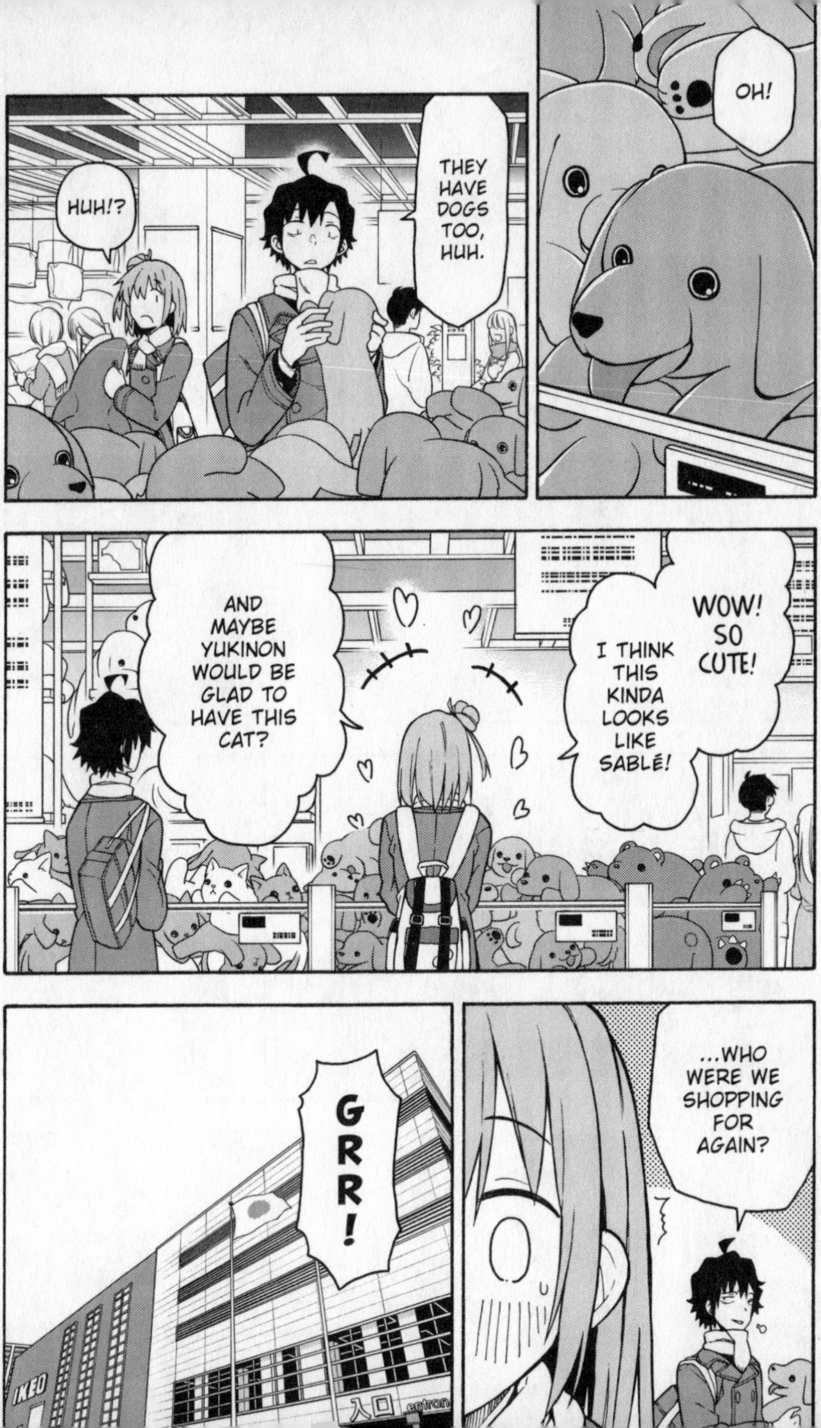
OH!
THEY HAVE DOGS TOO, HUH.
HUH!?
WOW! SO CUTE!
I THINK THIS KINDA LOOKS LIKE SABLÉ!
AND MAYBE YUKINON WOULD BE GLAD TO HAVE THIS CAT?
...WHO WERE WE SHOPPING FOR AGAIN?
GRR!
IKEO
入口

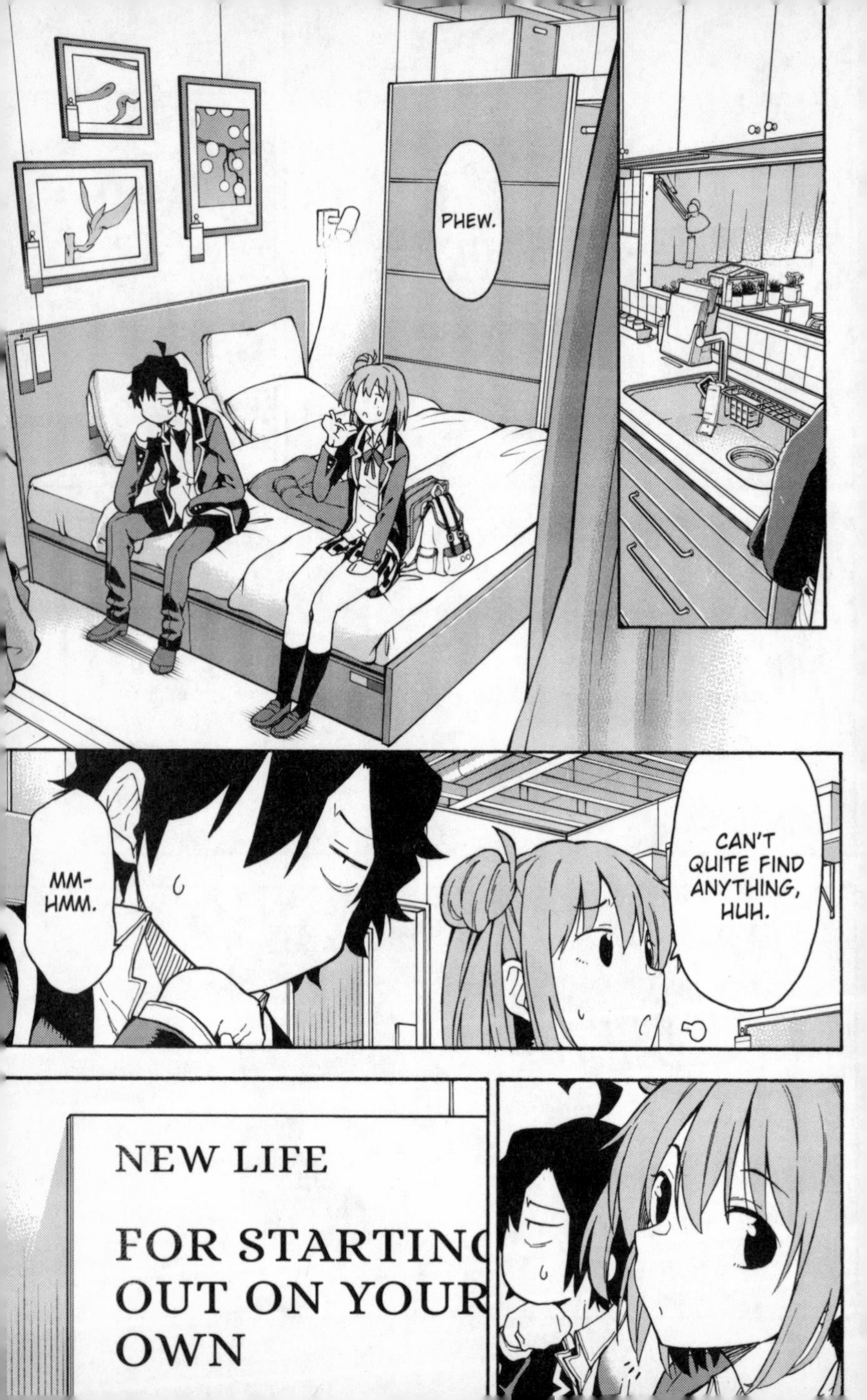
PHEW.
CAN'T QUITE FIND ANYTHING, HUH.
MM-HMM.
NEW LIFE
FOR STARTING OUT ON YOUR OWN

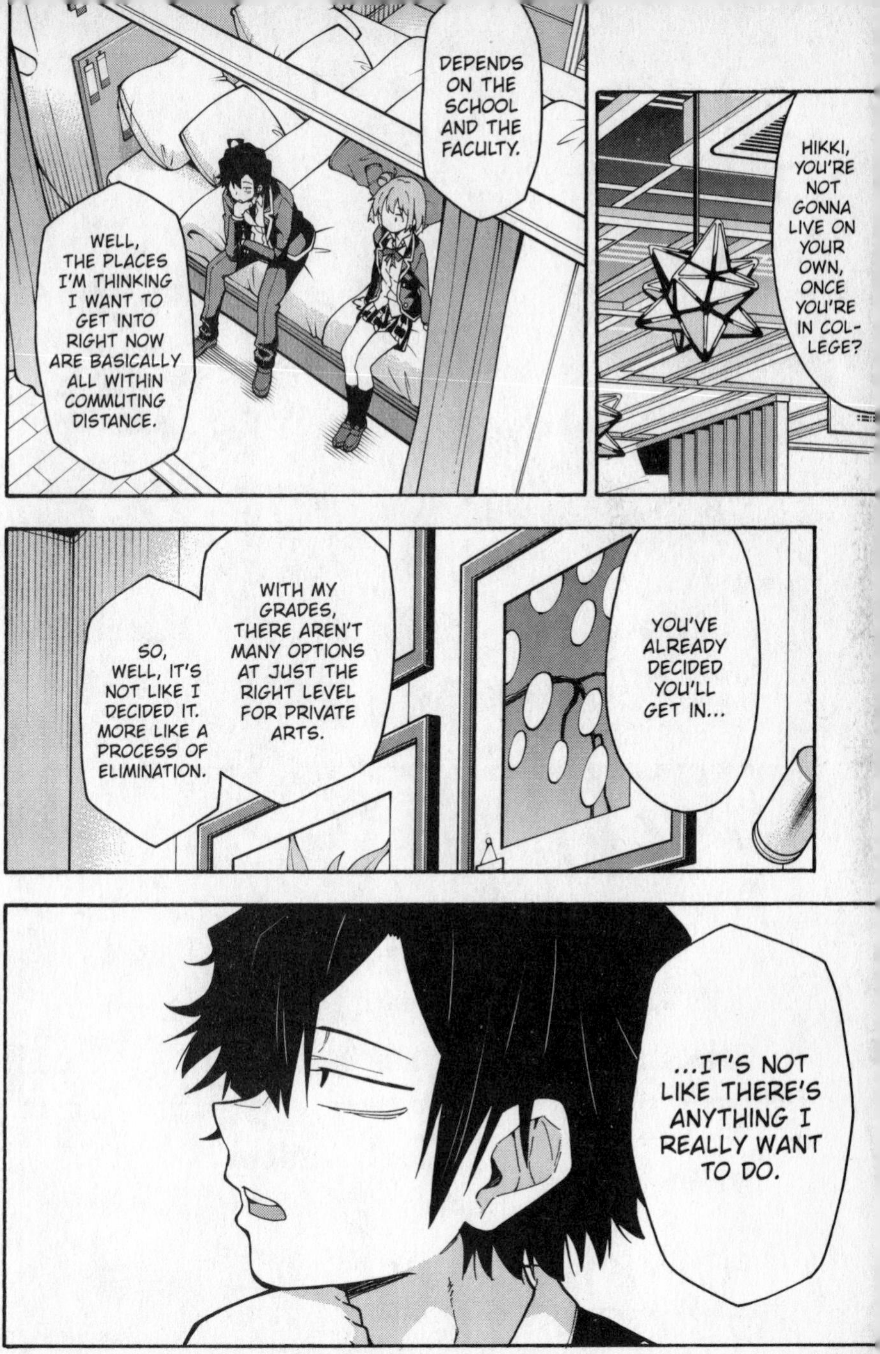
HIKKI, YOU'RE NOT GONNA LIVE ON YOUR OWN, ONCE YOU'RE IN COL-LEGE?
DEPENDS ON THE SCHOOL AND THE FACULTY.
WELL, THE PLACES I'M THINKING I WANT TO GET INTO RIGHT NOW ARE BASICALLY ALL WITHIN COMMUTING DISTANCE.
YOU'VE ALREADY DECIDED YOU'LL GET IN...
WITH MY GRADES, THERE AREN'T MANY OPTIONS AT JUST THE RIGHT LEVEL FOR PRIVATE ARTS.
SO, WELL, IT'S NOT LIKE I DECIDED IT. MORE LIKE A PROCESS OF ELIMINATION.
...IT'S NOT LIKE THERE'S ANYTHING I REALLY WANT TO DO.

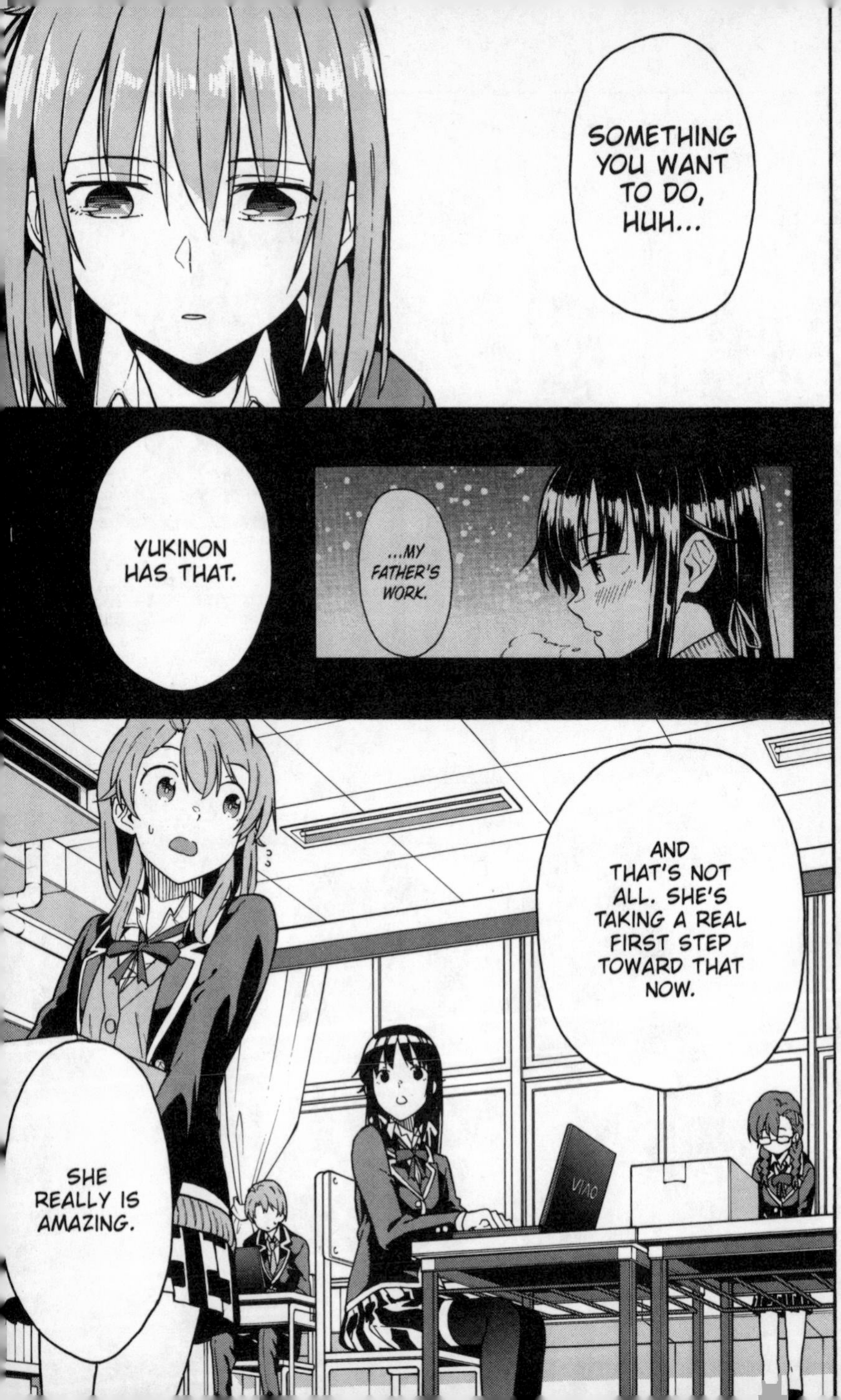
SOMETHING YOU WANT TO DO, HUH...
...MY FATHER'S WORK.
YUKINON HAS THAT.
AND THAT'S NOT ALL. SHE'S TAKING A REAL FIRST STEP TOWARD THAT NOW.
SHE REALLY IS AMAZING.

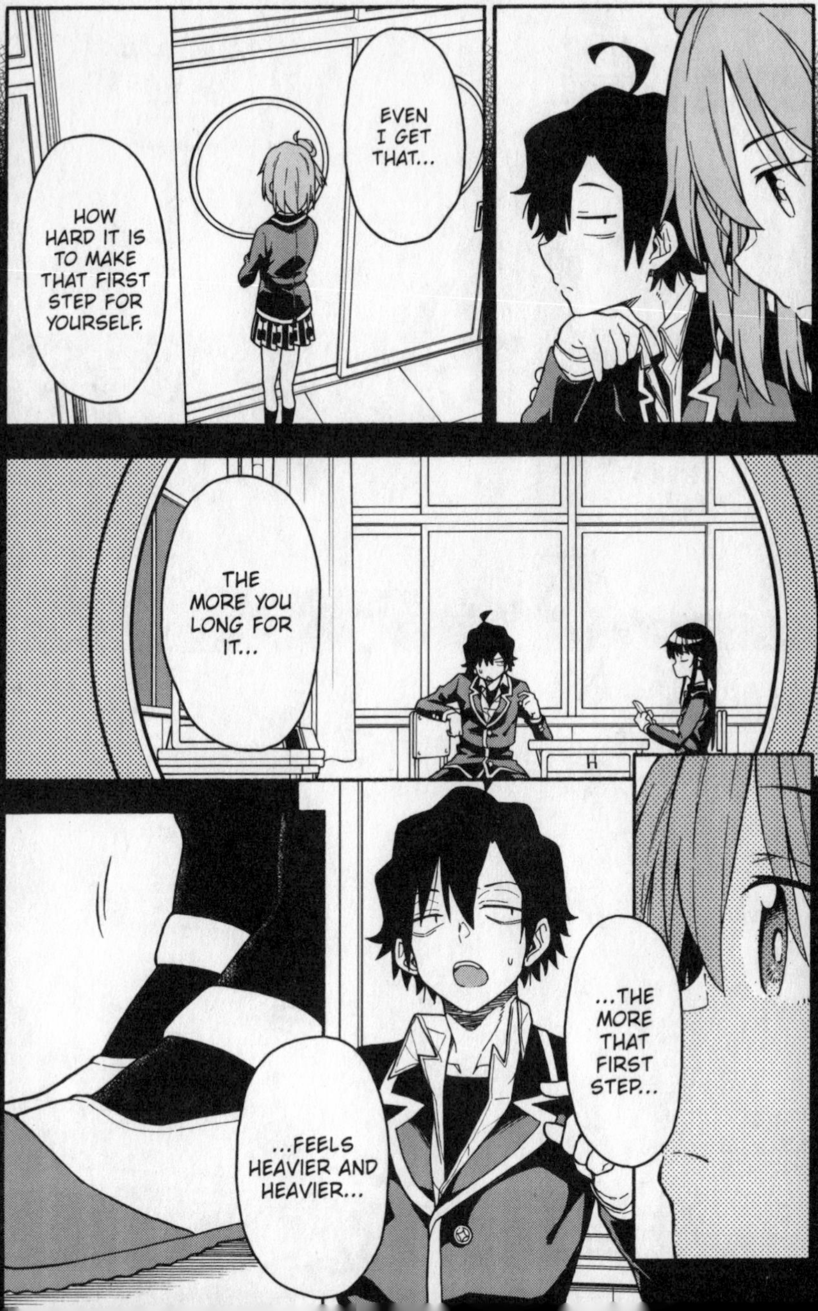
EVEN I GET THAT...
HOW HARD IT IS TO MAKE THAT FIRST STEP FOR YOURSELF.
THE MORE YOU LONG FOR IT...
...THE MORE THAT FIRST STEP...
...FEELS HEAVIER AND HEAVIER...

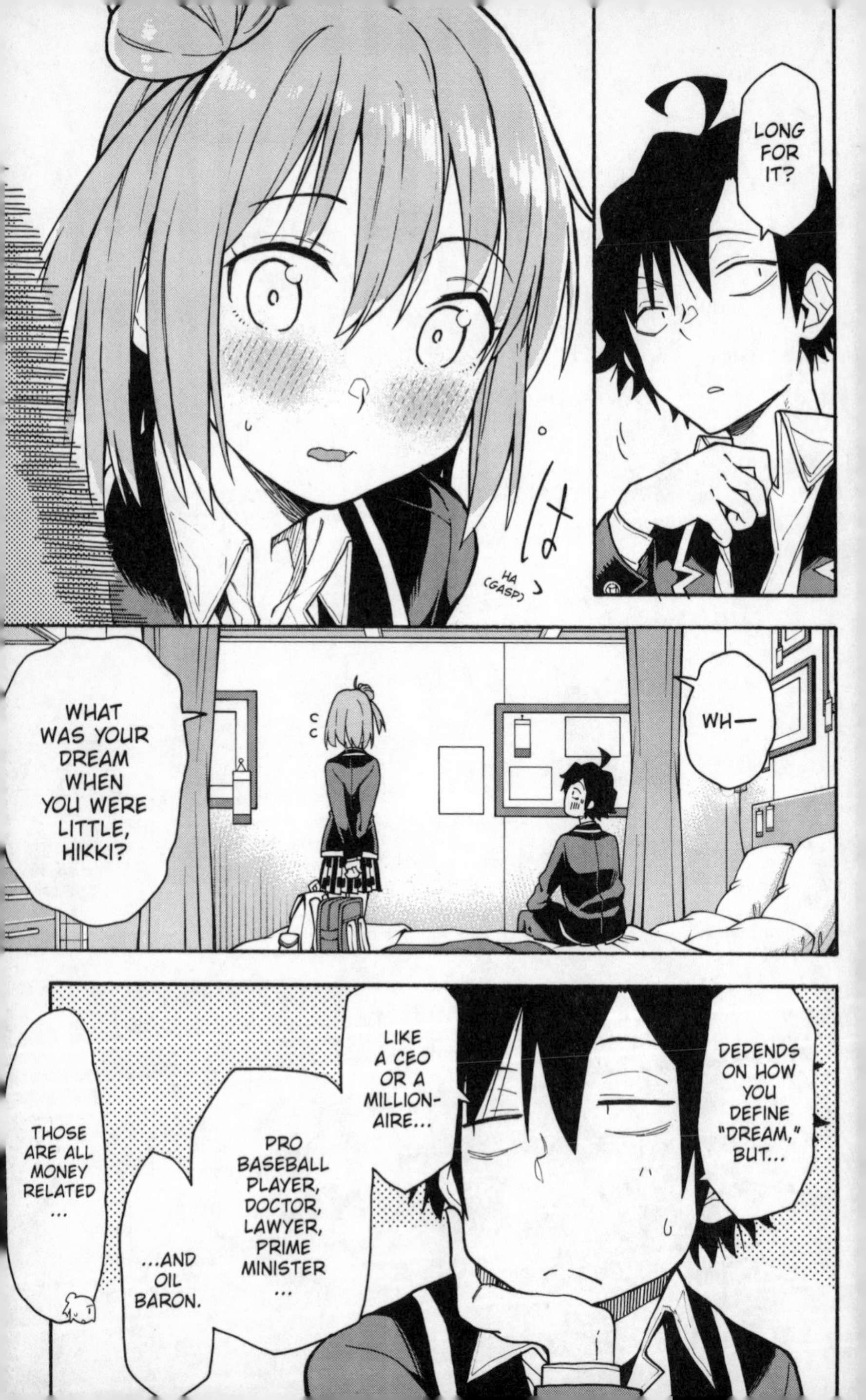
LONG FOR IT?
は
HA (GASP)
WH—
WHAT WAS YOUR DREAM WHEN YOU WERE LITTLE, HIKKI?
DEPENDS ON HOW YOU DEFINE "DREAM," BUT...
LIKE A CEO OR A MILLION-AIRE...
PRO BASEBALL PLAYER, DOCTOR, LAWYER, PRIME MINISTER...
...AND OIL BARON.
THOSE ARE ALL MONEY RELATED...

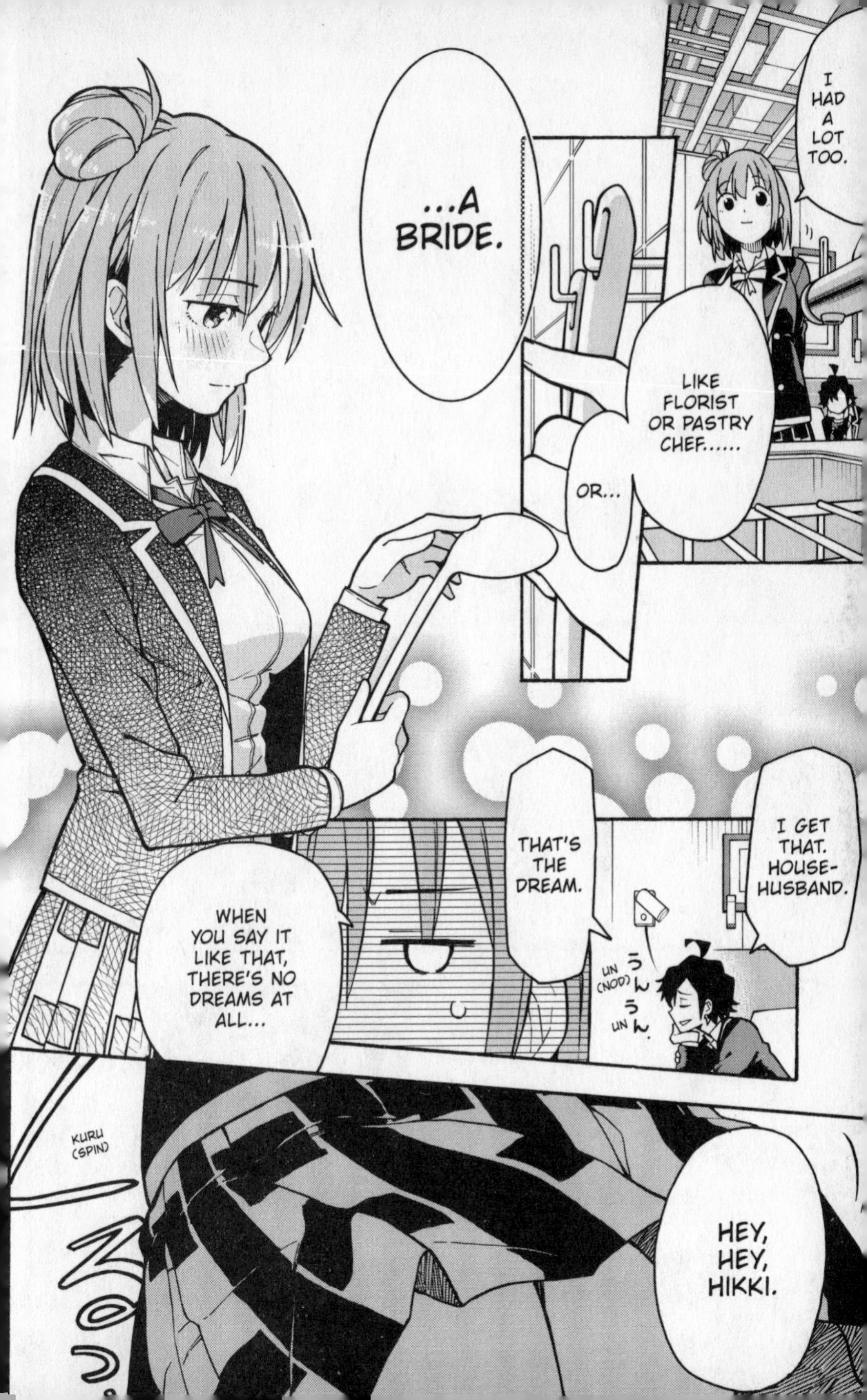
I HAD A LOT TOO.
LIKE FLORIST OR PASTRY CHEF......
OR...
...A BRIDE.
I GET THAT. HOUSE-HUSBAND.
THAT'S THE DREAM.
うん UN (NOD)
うん UN
WHEN YOU SAY IT LIKE THAT, THERE'S NO DREAMS AT ALL...
HEY, HEY, HIKKI.
KURU (SPIN)

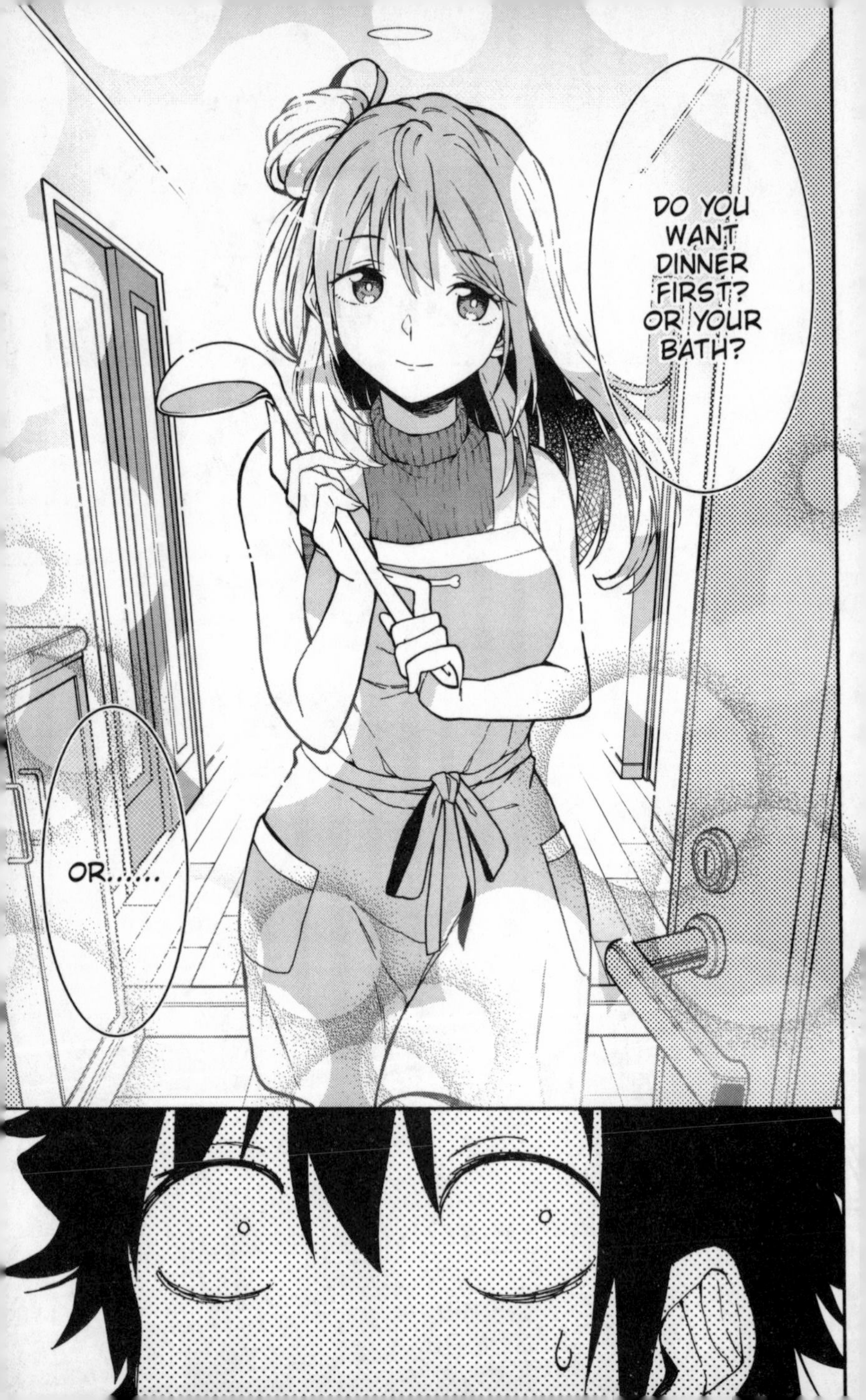
DO YOU WANT DINNER FIRST? OR YOUR BATH?
OR......

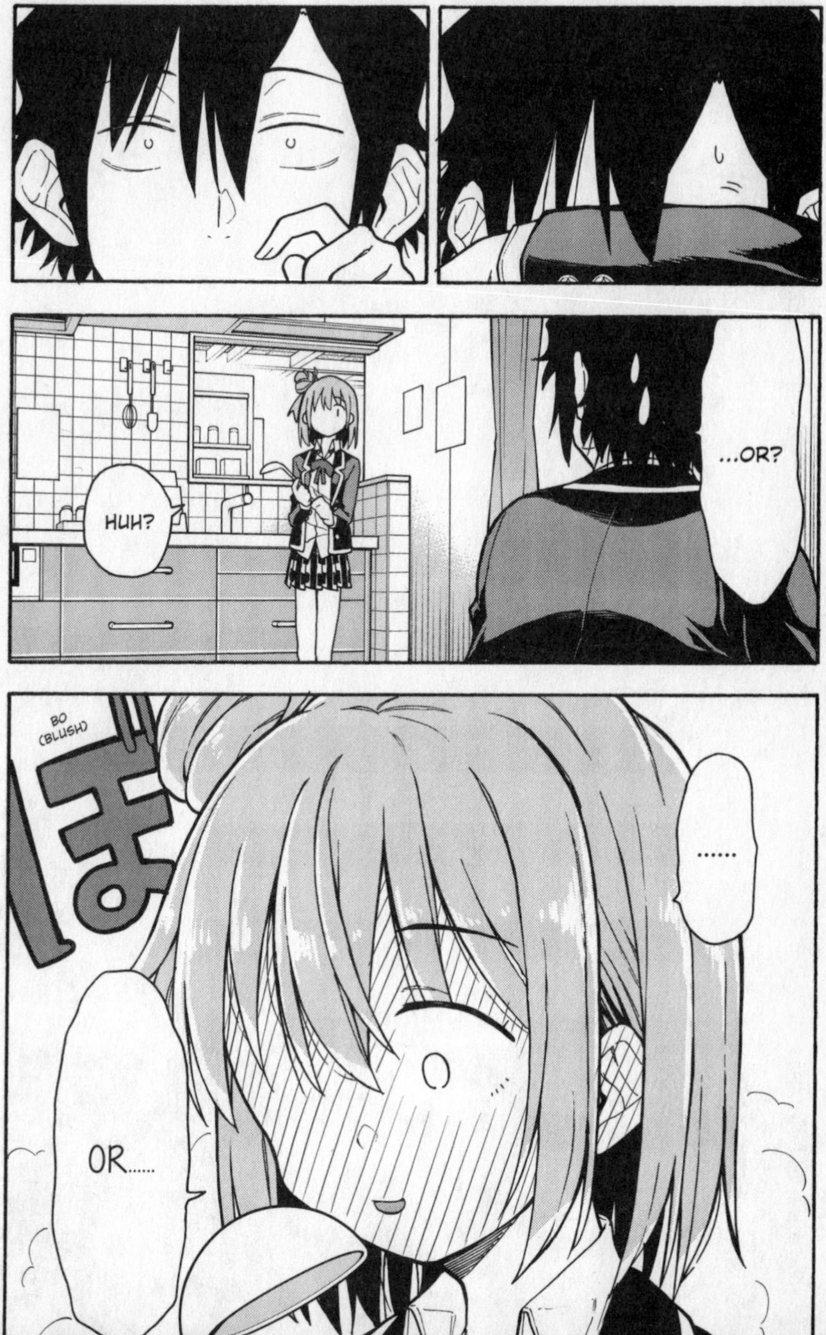
...OR?
HUH?
BO (BLUSH)
......
OR......

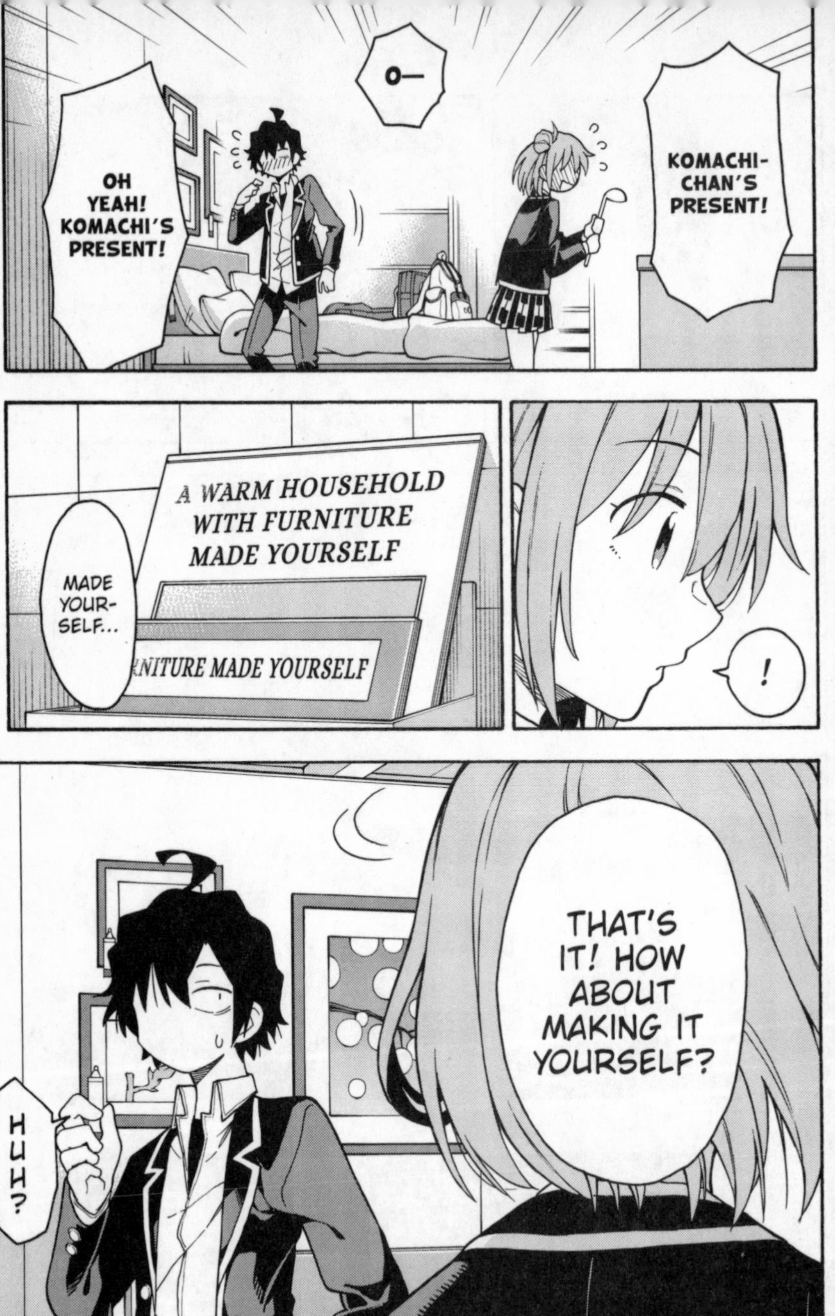
O—
KOMACHI-CHAN'S PRESENT!
OH YEAH! KOMACHI'S PRESENT!
!
A WARM HOUSEHOLD WITH FURNITURE MADE YOURSELF
MADE YOURSELF...
NITURE MADE YOURSELF
THAT'S IT! HOW ABOUT MAKING IT YOURSELF?
HUH?

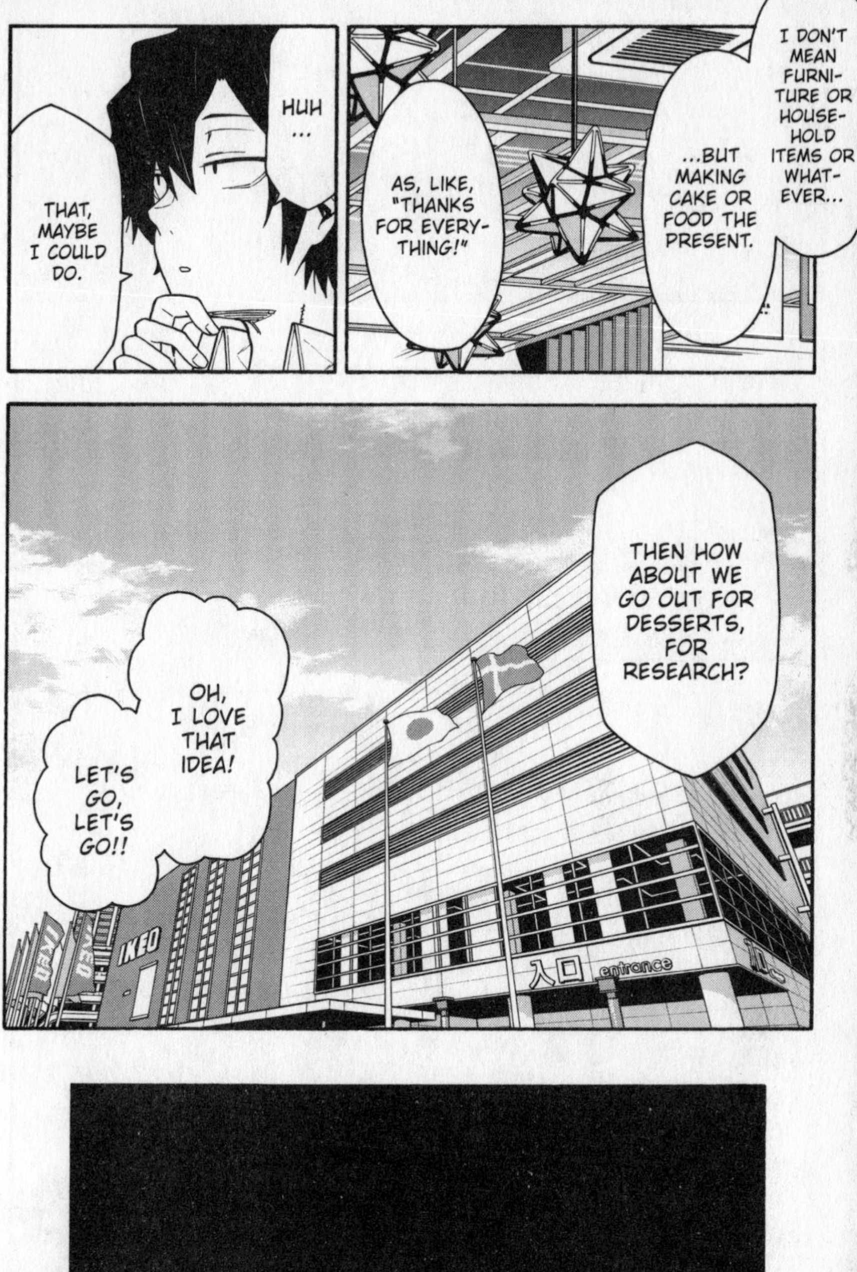
I DON'T MEAN FURNITURE OR HOUSEHOLD ITEMS OR WHATEVER...
...BUT MAKING CAKE OR FOOD THE PRESENT.
AS, LIKE, "THANKS FOR EVERYTHING!"
HUH...
THAT, MAYBE I COULD DO.
THEN HOW ABOUT WE GO OUT FOR DESSERTS, FOR RESEARCH?
OH, I LOVE THAT IDEA!
LET'S GO, LET'S GO!!
IKEO
入口 entrance

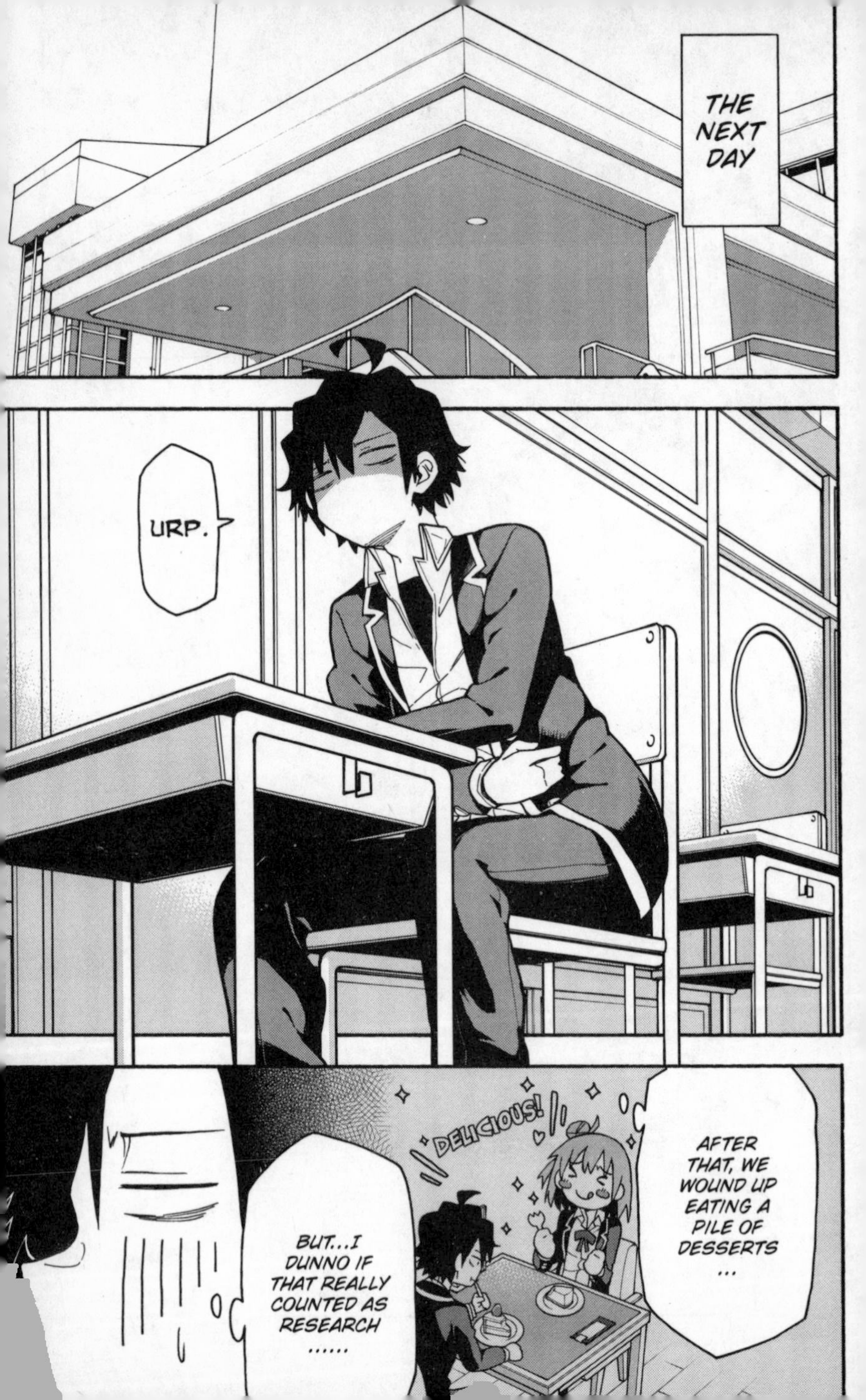
THE NEXT DAY
URP.
AFTER THAT, WE WOUND UP EATING A PILE OF DESSERTS ...
DELICIOUS!
BUT...I DUNNO IF THAT REALLY COUNTED AS RESEARCH ......

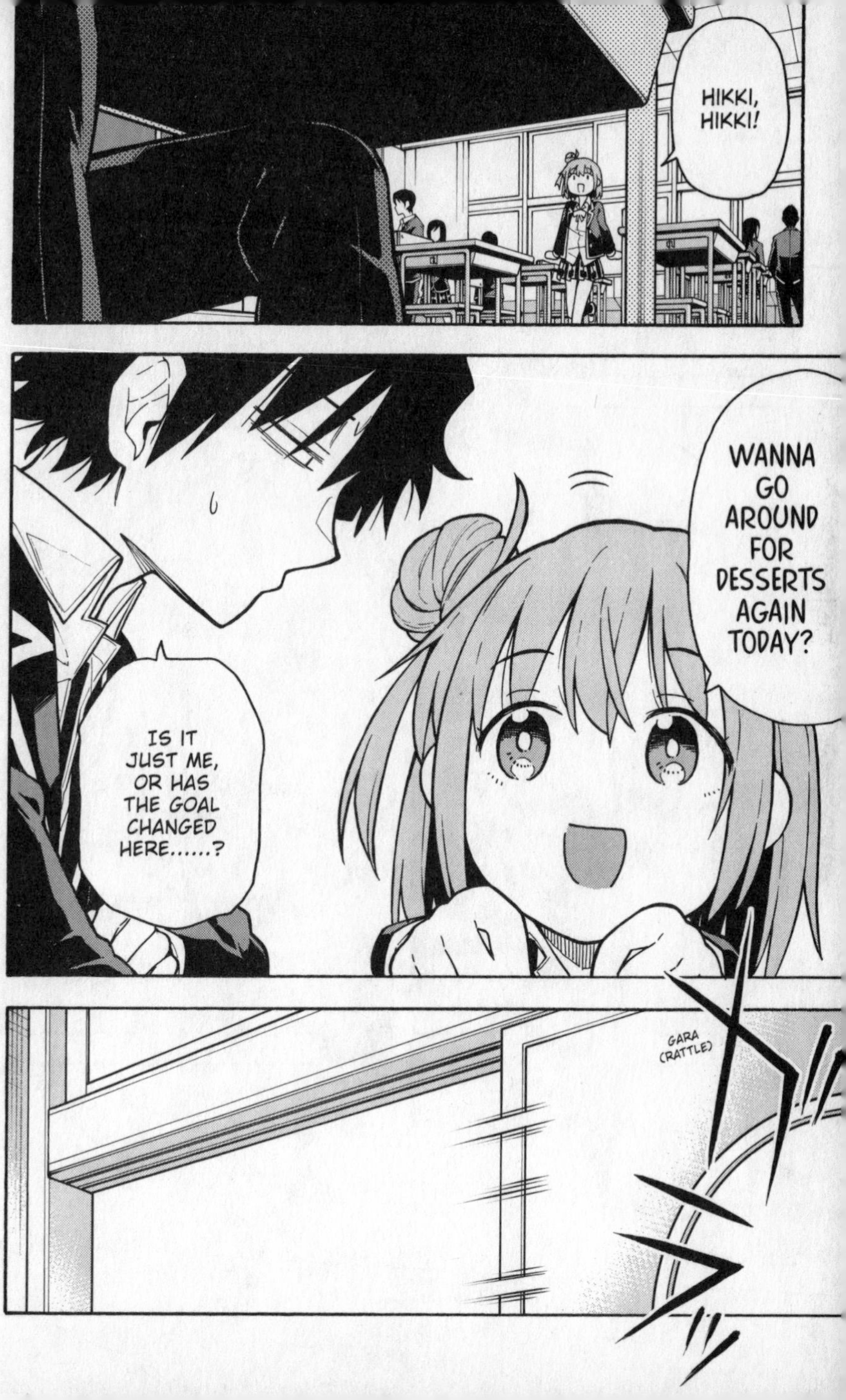
HIKKI, HIKKI!
WANNA GO AROUND FOR DESSERTS AGAIN TODAY?
IS IT JUST ME, OR HAS THE GOAL CHANGED HERE......?
GARA (RATTLE)

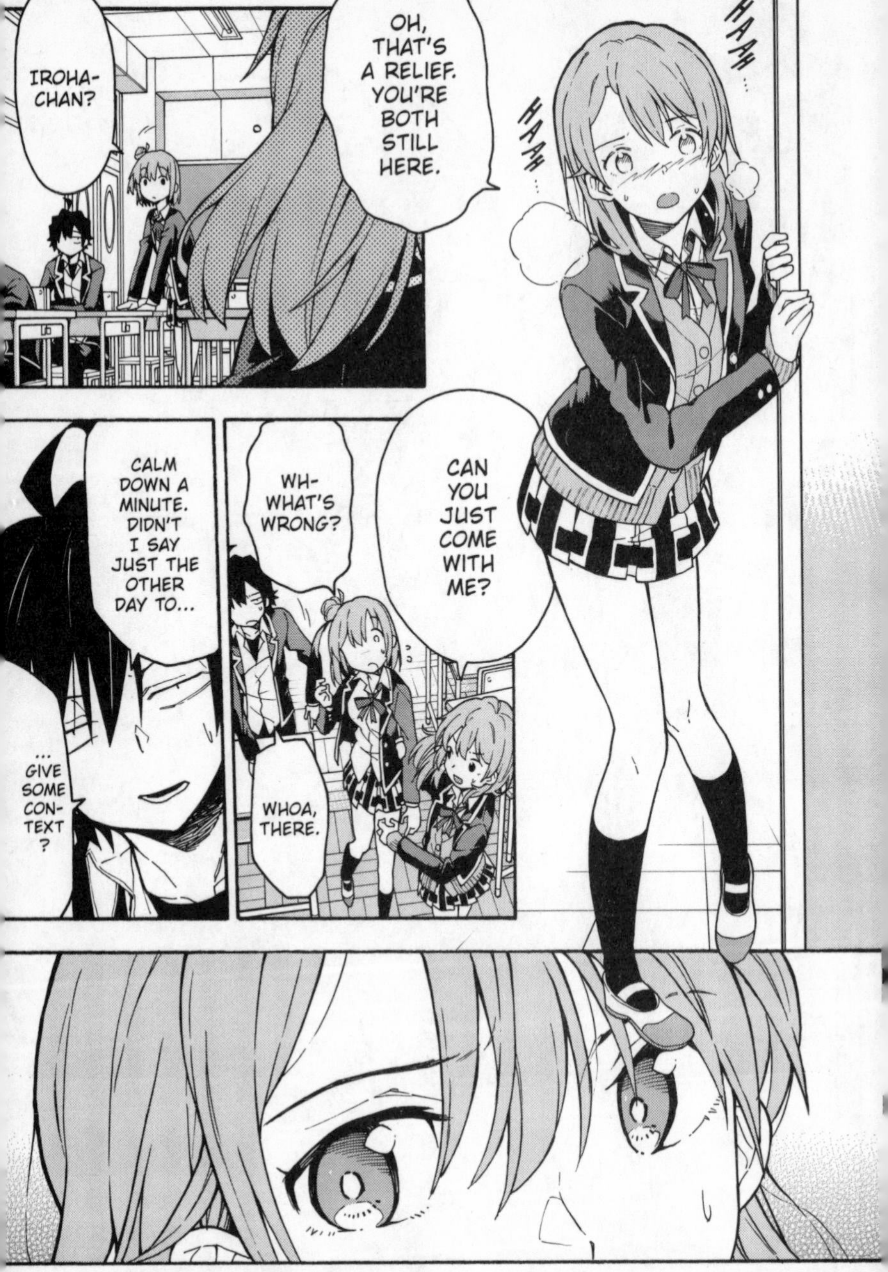
HAAH...
HAAH...
OH, THAT'S A RELIEF. YOU'RE BOTH STILL HERE.
IROHA-CHAN?
CAN YOU JUST COME WITH ME?
WH-WHAT'S WRONG?
WHOA, THERE.
CALM DOWN A MINUTE. DIDN'T I SAY JUST THE OTHER DAY TO...
...GIVE SOME CON-TEXT?

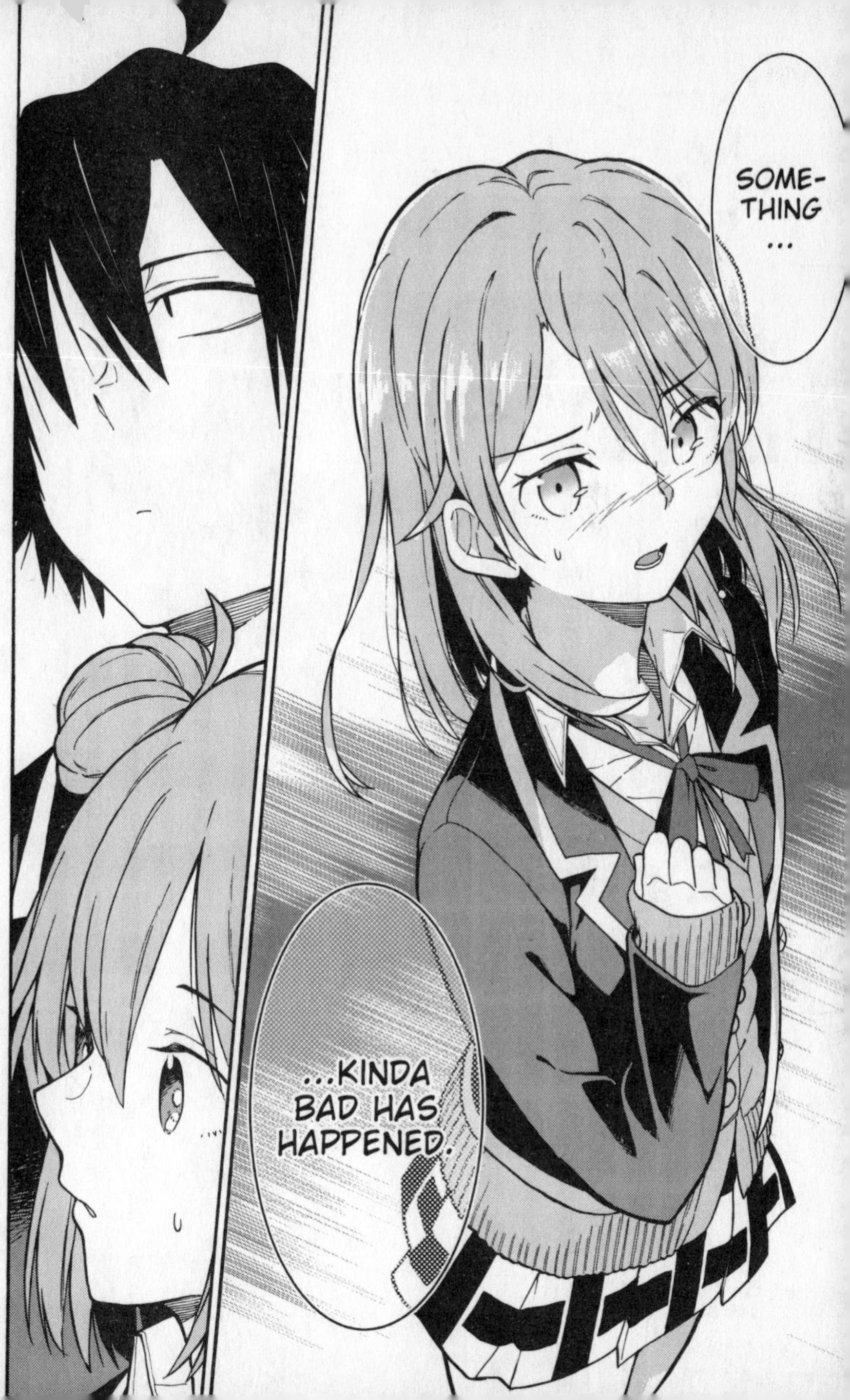
SOME-THING ...
...KINDA BAD HAS HAPPENED.

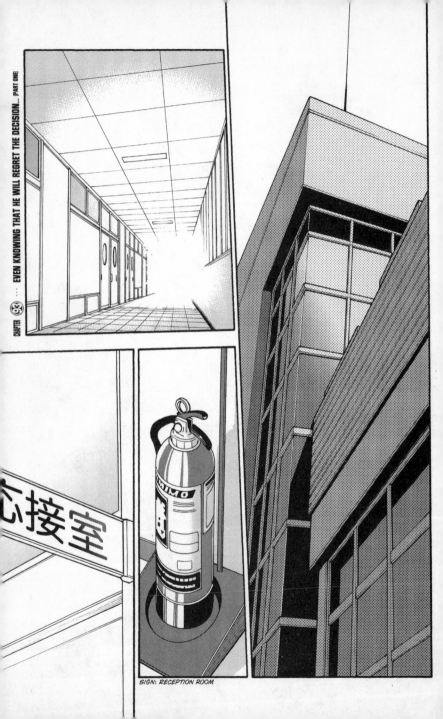

SIGN: RECEPTION ROOM

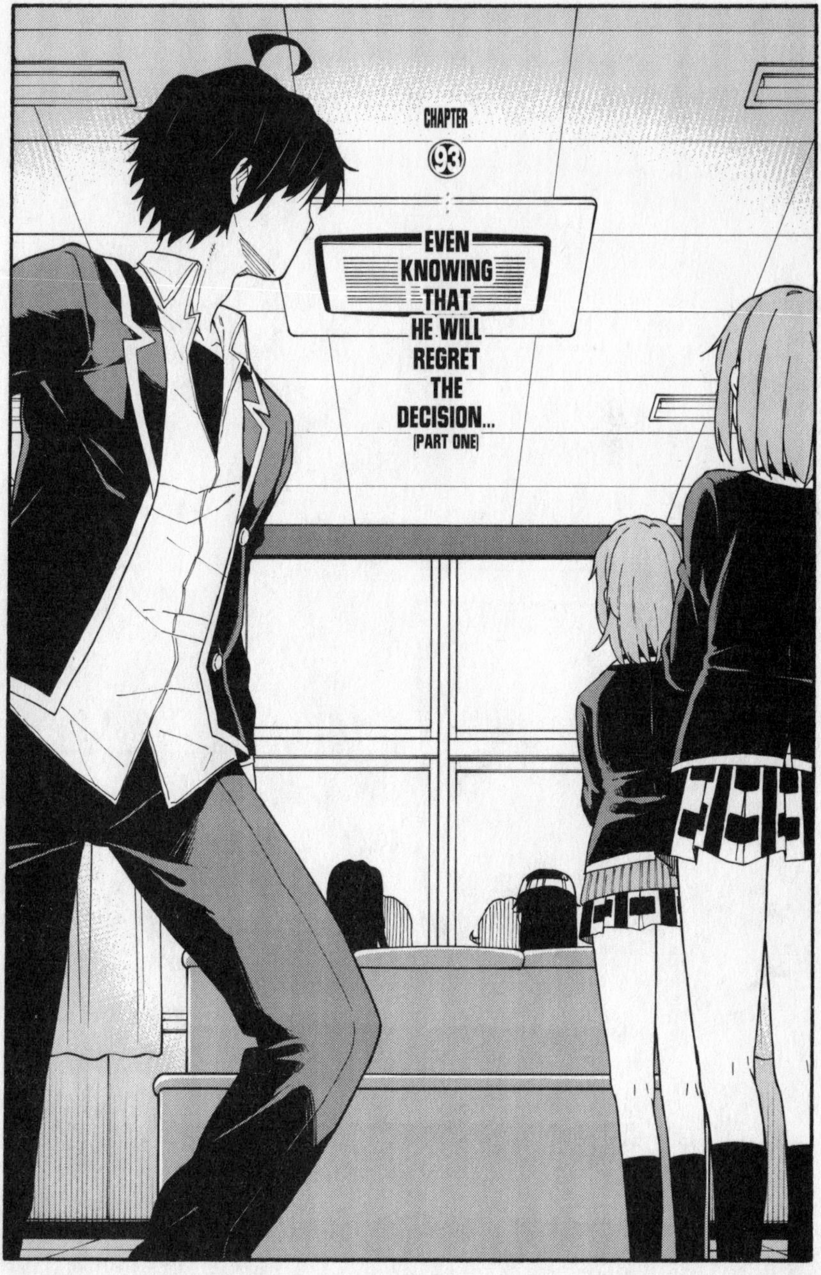
CHAPTER
93
EVEN KNOWING THAT HE WILL REGRET THE DECISION...
(PART ONE)

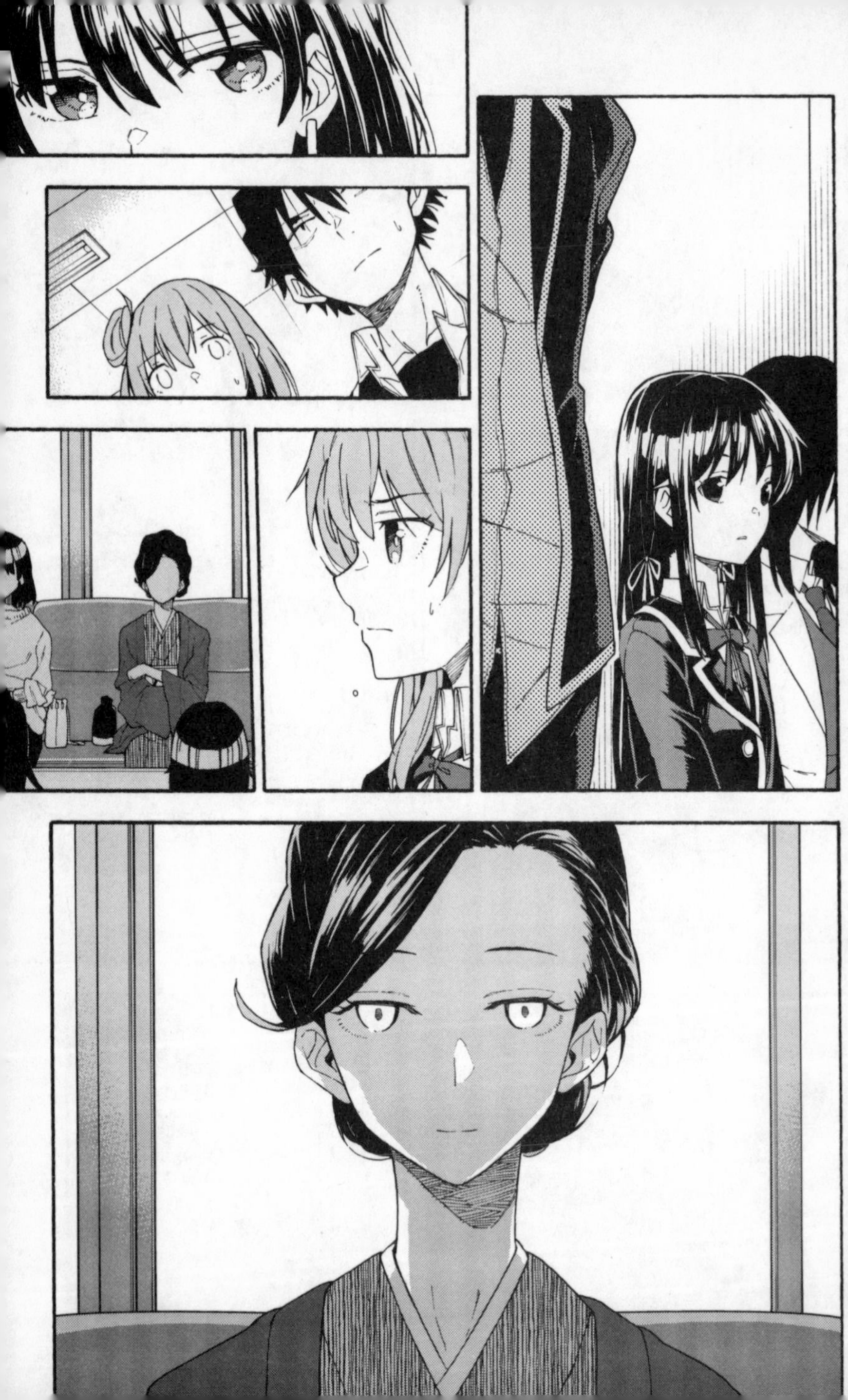

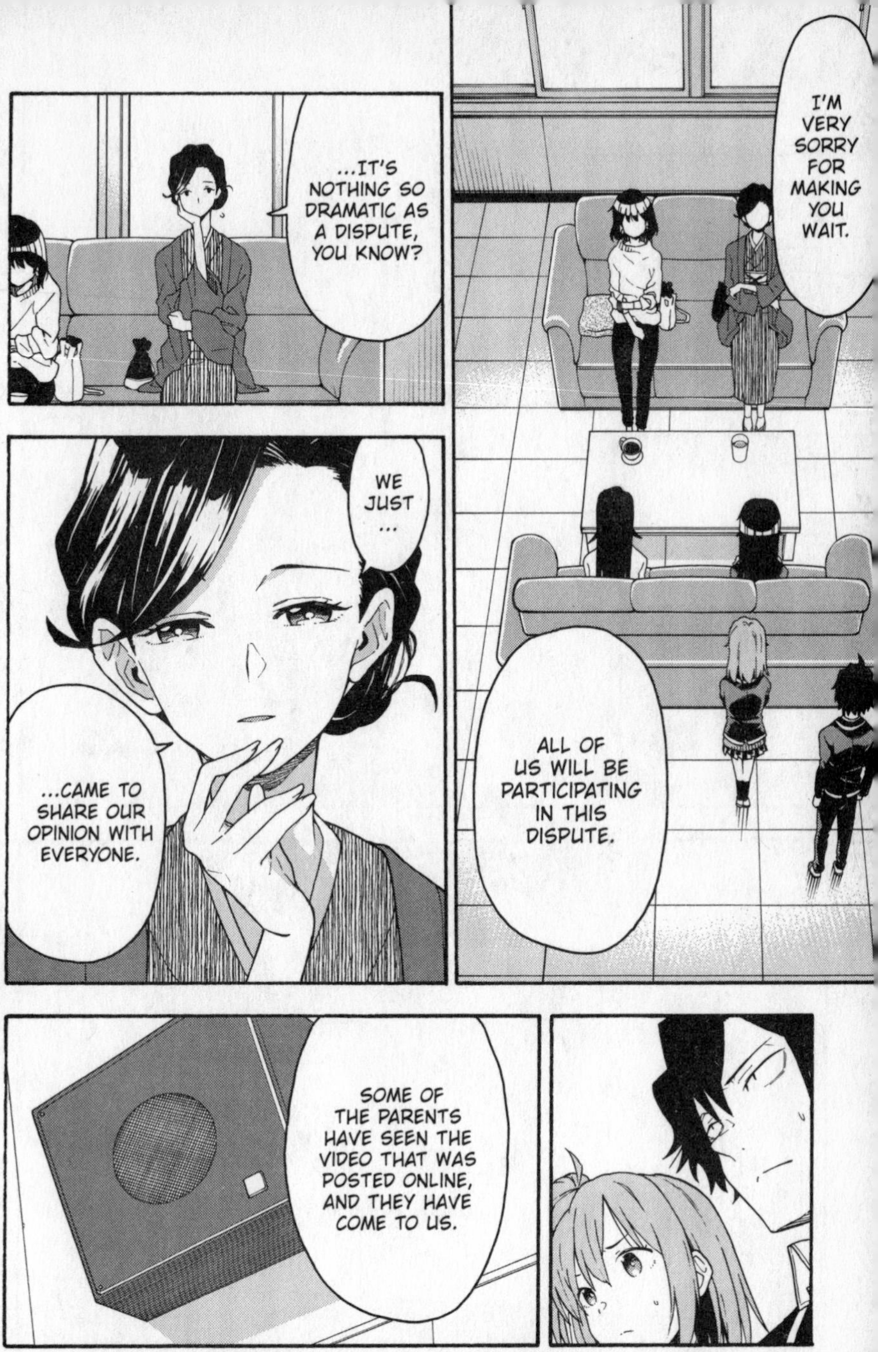
I'M VERY SORRY FOR MAKING YOU WAIT.
ALL OF US WILL BE PARTICIPATING IN THIS DISPUTE.
...IT'S NOTHING SO DRAMATIC AS A DISPUTE, YOU KNOW?
WE JUST...
...CAME TO SHARE OUR OPINION WITH EVERYONE.
SOME OF THE PARENTS HAVE SEEN THE VIDEO THAT WAS POSTED ONLINE, AND THEY HAVE COME TO US.

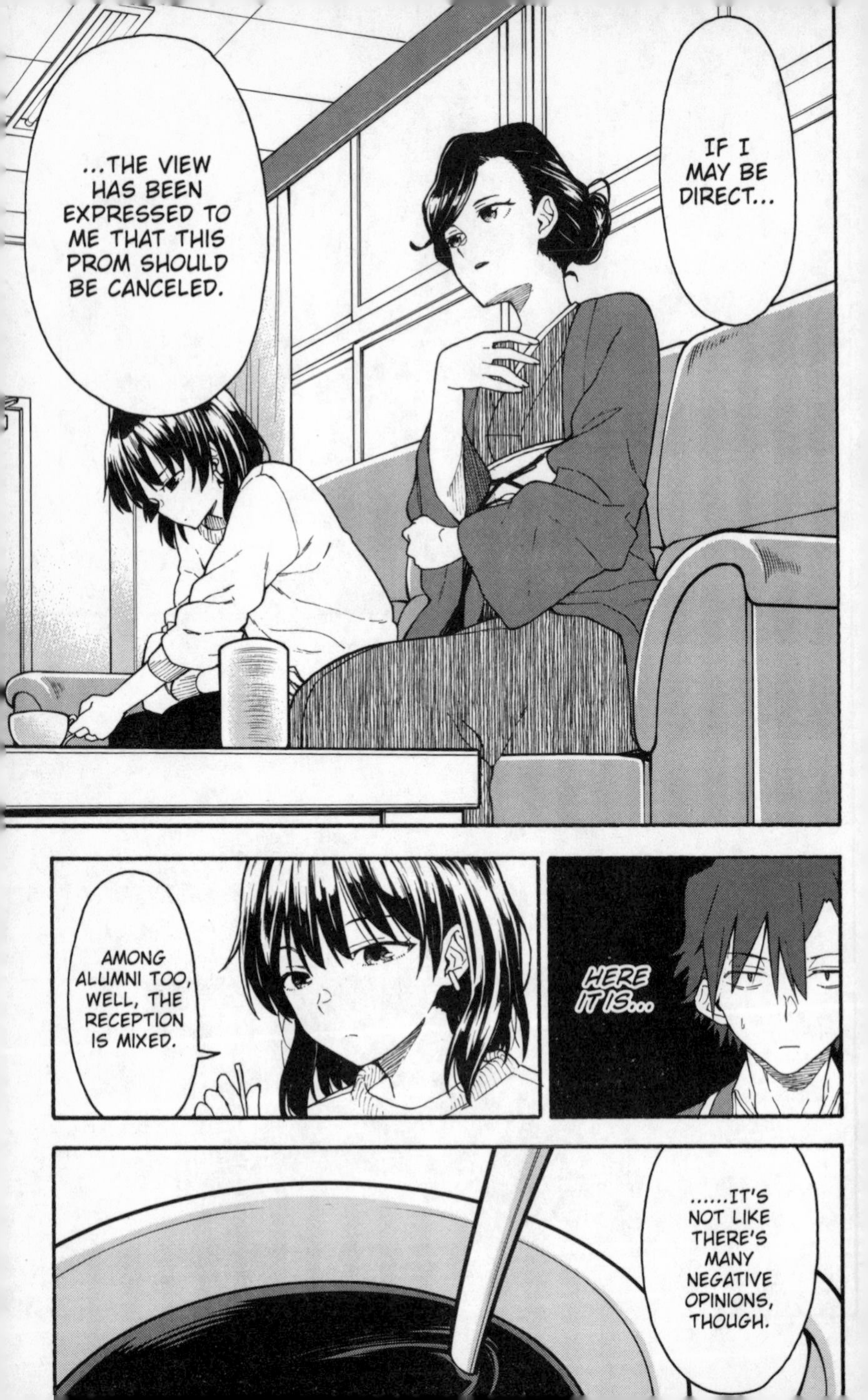
IF I MAY BE DIRECT...
...THE VIEW HAS BEEN EXPRESSED TO ME THAT THIS PROM SHOULD BE CANCELED.
HERE IT IS...
AMONG ALUMNI TOO, WELL, THE RECEPTION IS MIXED.
......IT'S NOT LIKE THERE'S MANY NEGATIVE OPINIONS, THOUGH.

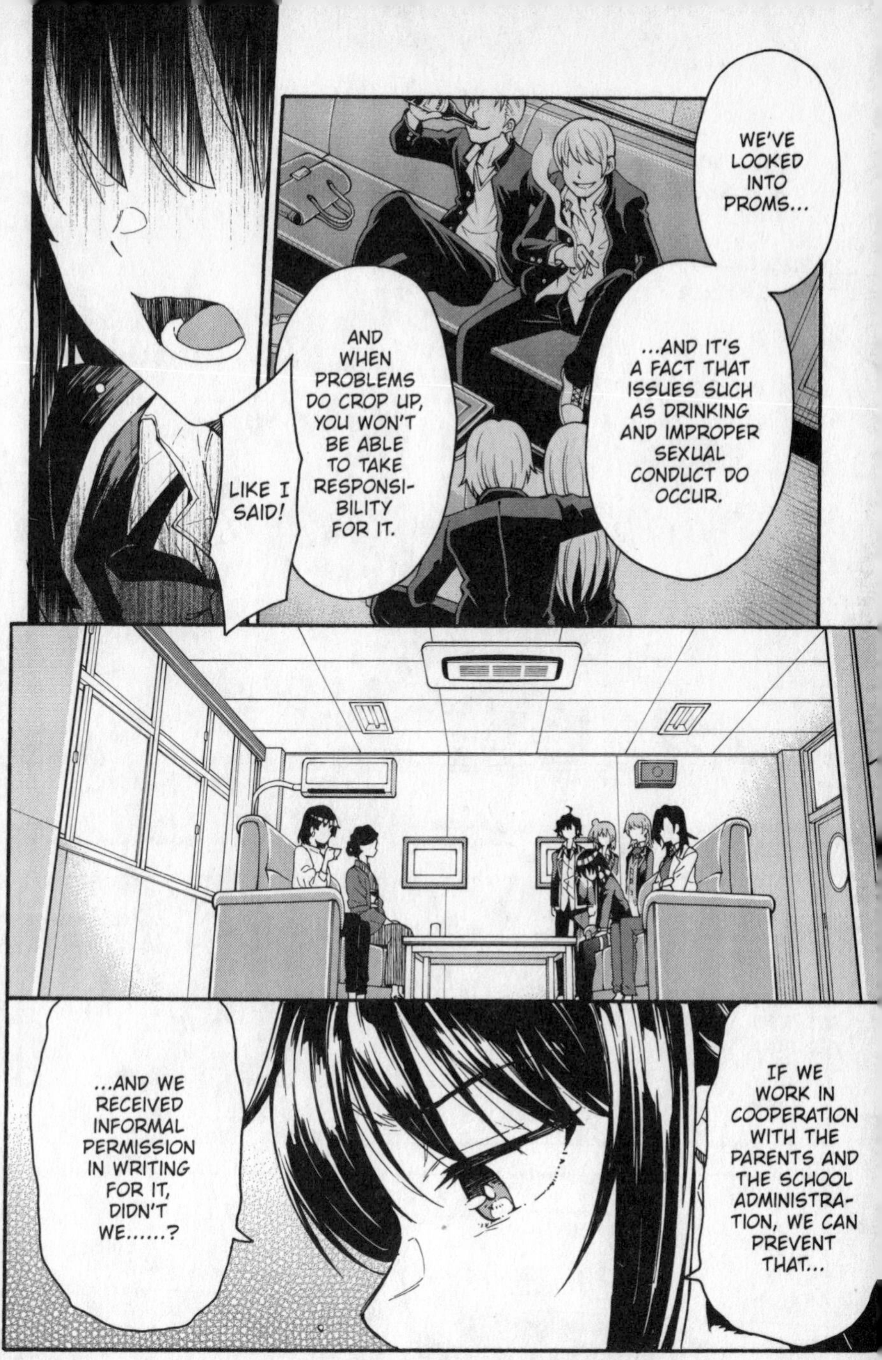
WE'VE LOOKED INTO PROMS...
...AND IT'S A FACT THAT ISSUES SUCH AS DRINKING AND IMPROPER SEXUAL CONDUCT DO OCCUR.
AND WHEN PROBLEMS DO CROP UP, YOU WON'T BE ABLE TO TAKE RESPONSIBILITY FOR IT.
LIKE I SAID!
IF WE WORK IN COOPERATION WITH THE PARENTS AND THE SCHOOL ADMINISTRATION, WE CAN PREVENT THAT...
...AND WE RECEIVED INFORMAL PERMISSION IN WRITING FOR IT, DIDN'T WE......?

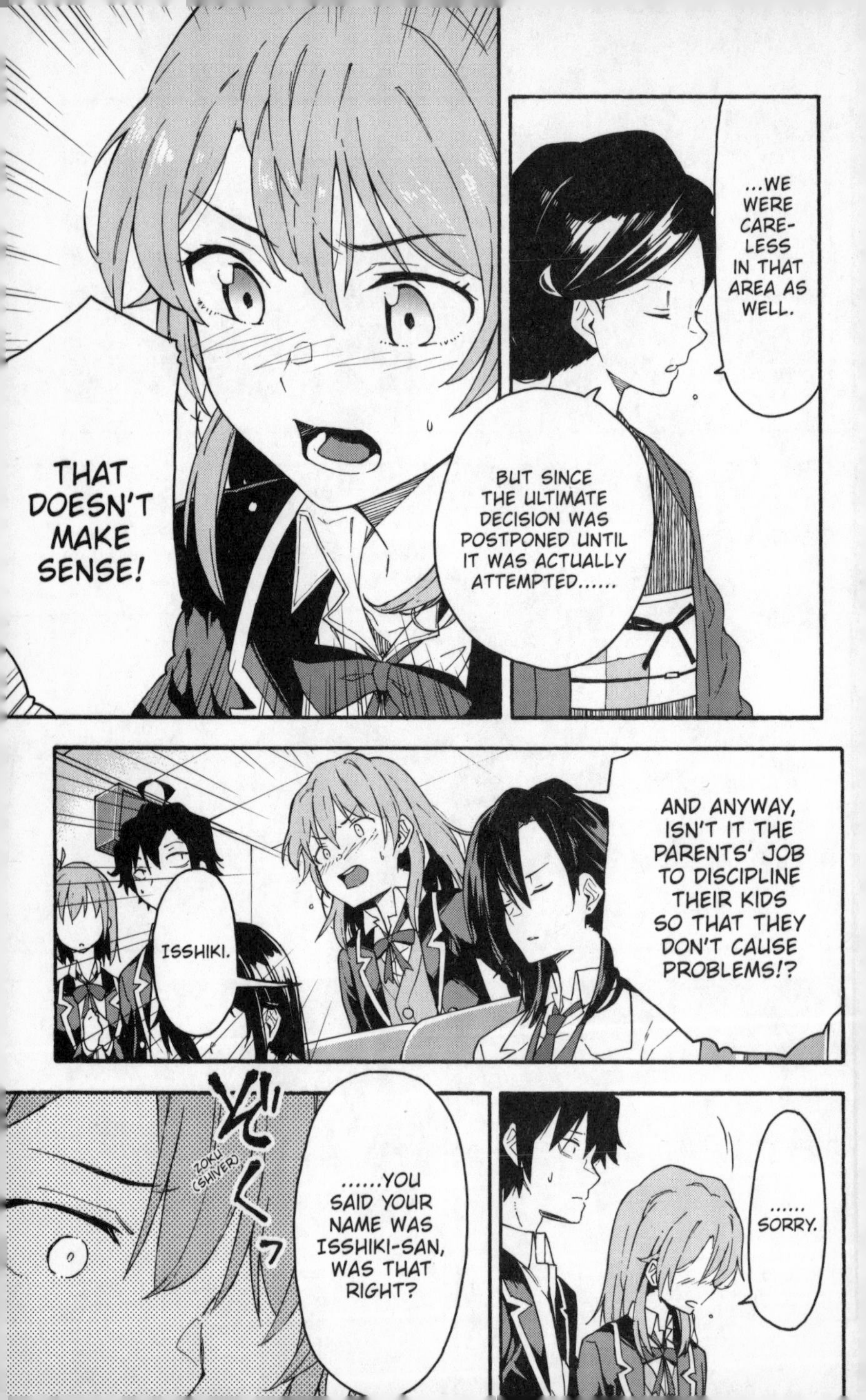
...WE WERE CARE-LESS IN THAT AREA AS WELL.
BUT SINCE THE ULTIMATE DECISION WAS POSTPONED UNTIL IT WAS ACTUALLY ATTEMPTED......
THAT DOESN'T MAKE SENSE!
AND ANYWAY, ISN'T IT THE PARENTS' JOB TO DISCIPLINE THEIR KIDS SO THAT THEY DON'T CAUSE PROBLEMS!?
ISSHIKI.
......SORRY.
......YOU SAID YOUR NAME WAS ISSHIKI-SAN, WAS THAT RIGHT?
ZOKU (SHIVER)

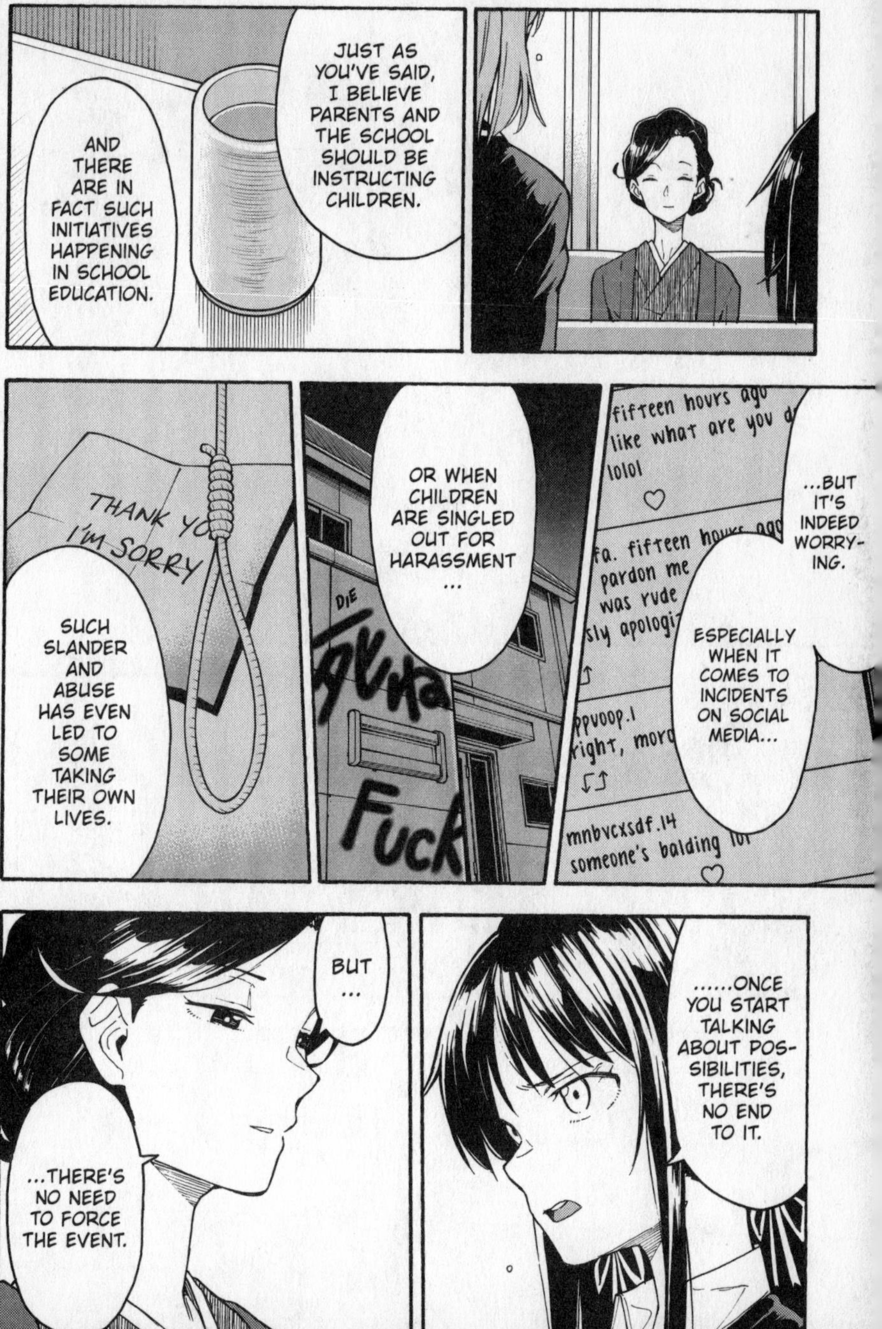
JUST AS YOU'VE SAID, I BELIEVE PARENTS AND THE SCHOOL SHOULD BE INSTRUCTING CHILDREN.
AND THERE ARE IN FACT SUCH INITIATIVES HAPPENING IN SCHOOL EDUCATION.
fifteen hours ago
like what are you d
lolol
fa. fifteen hours ago
pardon me
was rude
sly apologi
ppvoop.1
right, mora
mnbvcxsdf.14
someone's balding lol
...BUT IT'S INDEED WORRYING.
ESPECIALLY WHEN IT COMES TO INCIDENTS ON SOCIAL MEDIA...
OR WHEN CHILDREN ARE SINGLED OUT FOR HARASSMENT ...
DIE
Fuck
THANK YO
I'M SORRY
SUCH SLANDER AND ABUSE HAS EVEN LED TO SOME TAKING THEIR OWN LIVES.
......ONCE YOU START TALKING ABOUT POSSIBILITIES, THERE'S NO END TO IT.
BUT ...
...THERE'S NO NEED TO FORCE THE EVENT.

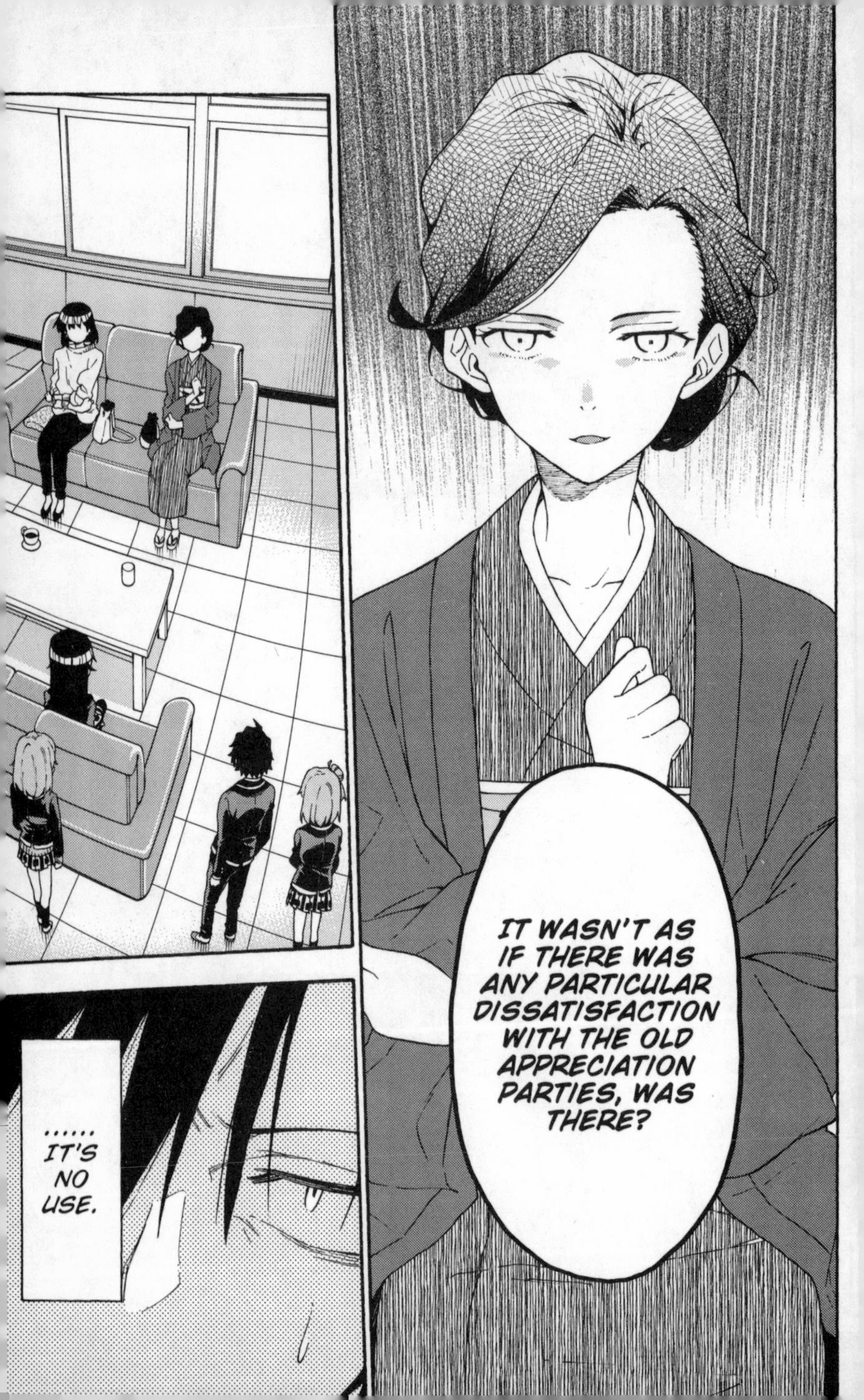
IT WASN'T AS IF THERE WAS ANY PARTICULAR DISSATISFACTION WITH THE OLD APPRECIATION PARTIES, WAS THERE?
...... IT'S NO USE.

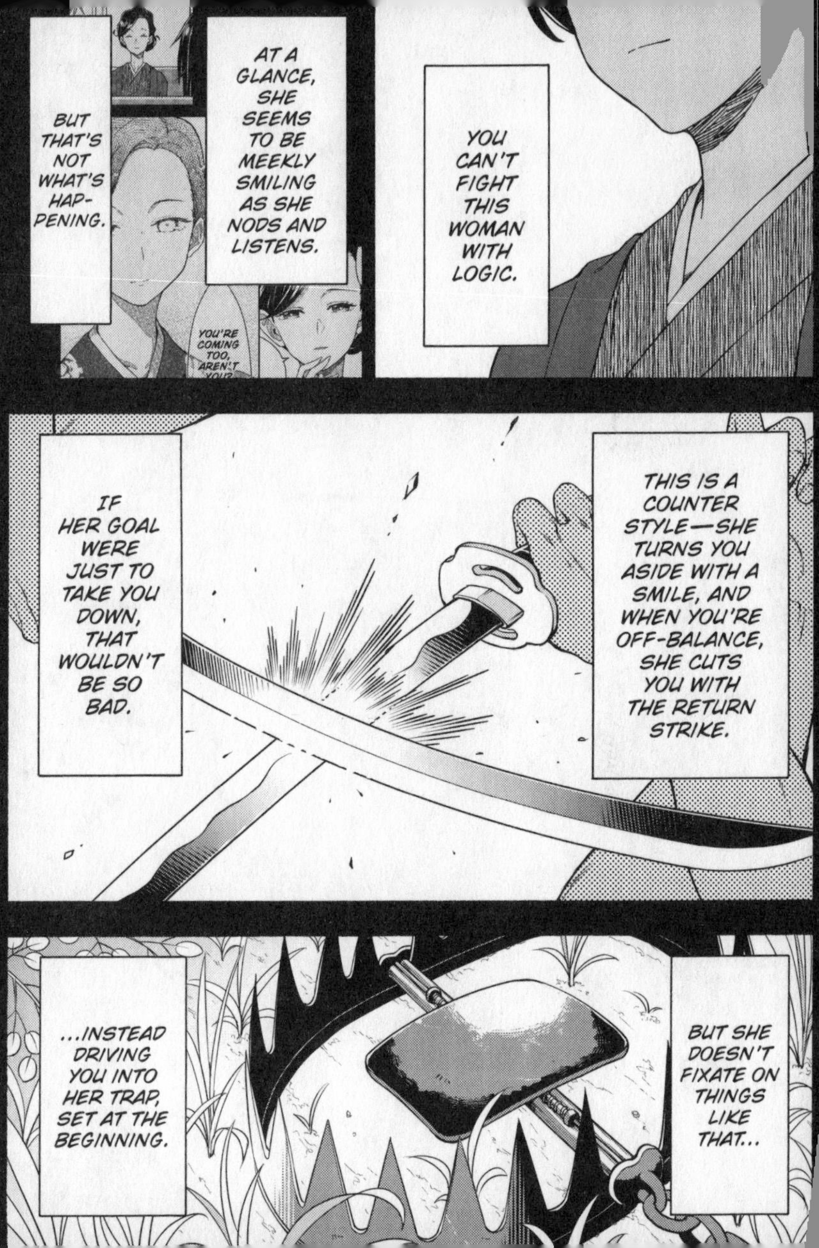
YOU CAN'T FIGHT THIS WOMAN WITH LOGIC.
AT A GLANCE, SHE SEEMS TO BE MEEKLY SMILING AS SHE NODS AND LISTENS.
BUT THAT'S NOT WHAT'S HAP-PENING.
YOU'RE COMING TOO, AREN'T YOU?
THIS IS A COUNTER STYLE—SHE TURNS YOU ASIDE WITH A SMILE, AND WHEN YOU'RE OFF-BALANCE, SHE CUTS YOU WITH THE RETURN STRIKE.
IF HER GOAL WERE JUST TO TAKE YOU DOWN, THAT WOULDN'T BE SO BAD.
BUT SHE DOESN'T FIXATE ON THINGS LIKE THAT...
...INSTEAD DRIVING YOU INTO HER TRAP, SET AT THE BEGINNING.

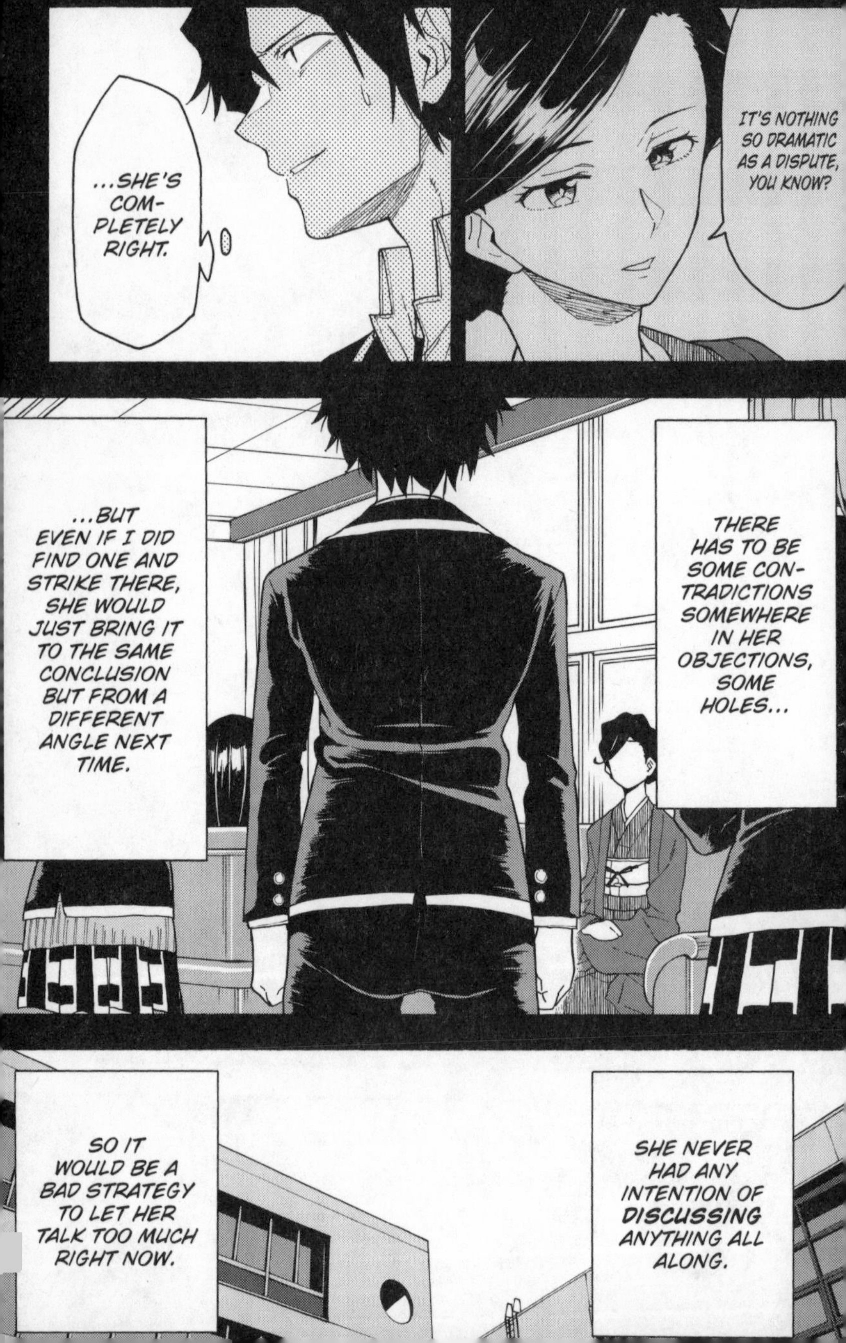
IT'S NOTHING SO DRAMATIC AS A DISPUTE, YOU KNOW?
...SHE'S COM-PLETELY RIGHT.
THERE HAS TO BE SOME CON-TRADICTIONS SOMEWHERE IN HER OBJECTIONS, SOME HOLES...
...BUT EVEN IF I DID FIND ONE AND STRIKE THERE, SHE WOULD JUST BRING IT TO THE SAME CONCLUSION BUT FROM A DIFFERENT ANGLE NEXT TIME.
SHE NEVER HAD ANY INTENTION OF DISCUSSING ANYTHING ALL ALONG.
SO IT WOULD BE A BAD STRATEGY TO LET HER TALK TOO MUCH RIGHT NOW.

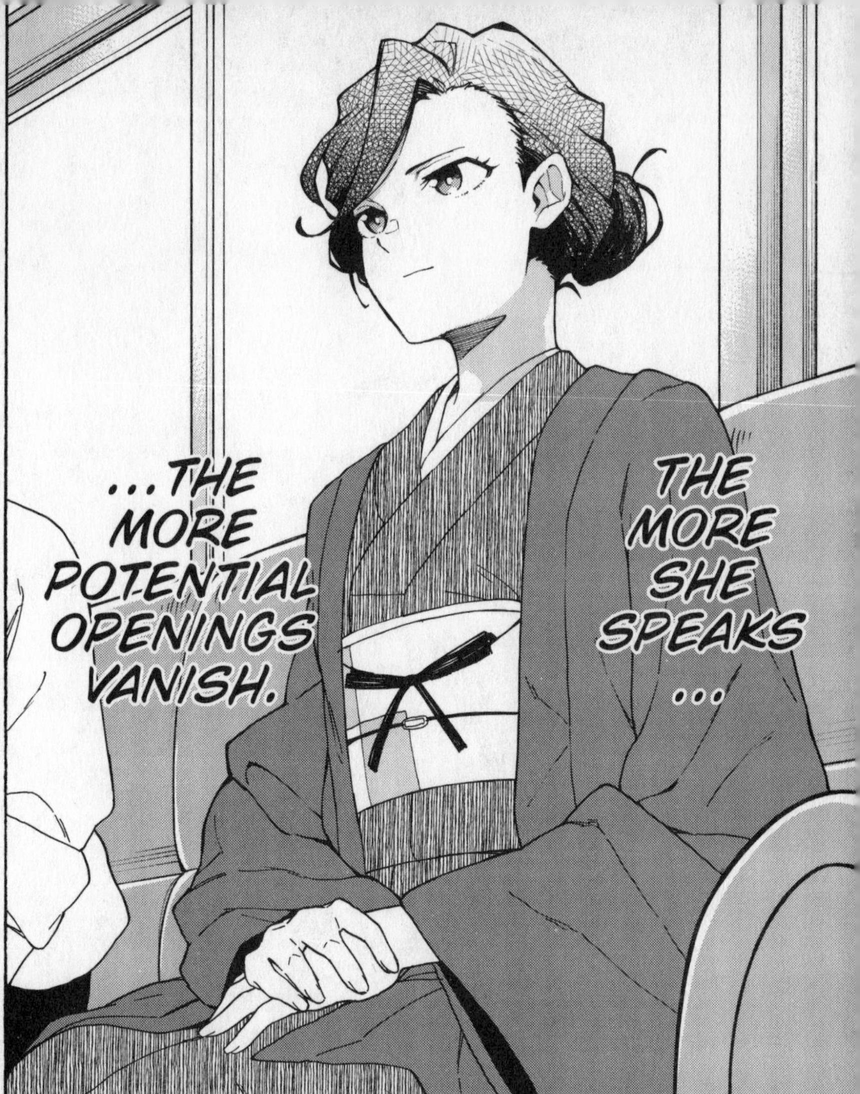
THE MORE SHE SPEAKS...
...THE MORE POTENTIAL OPENINGS VANISH.
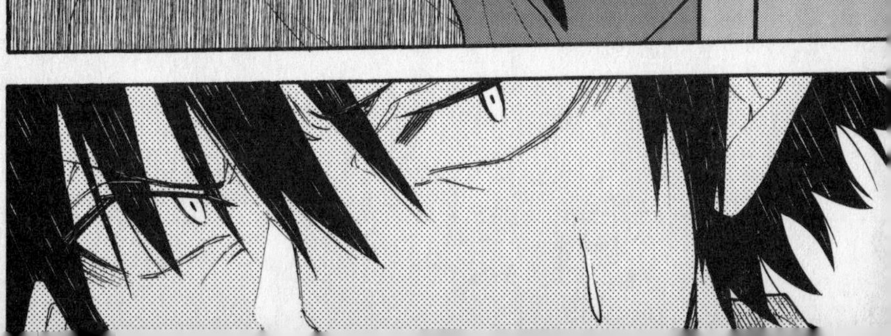

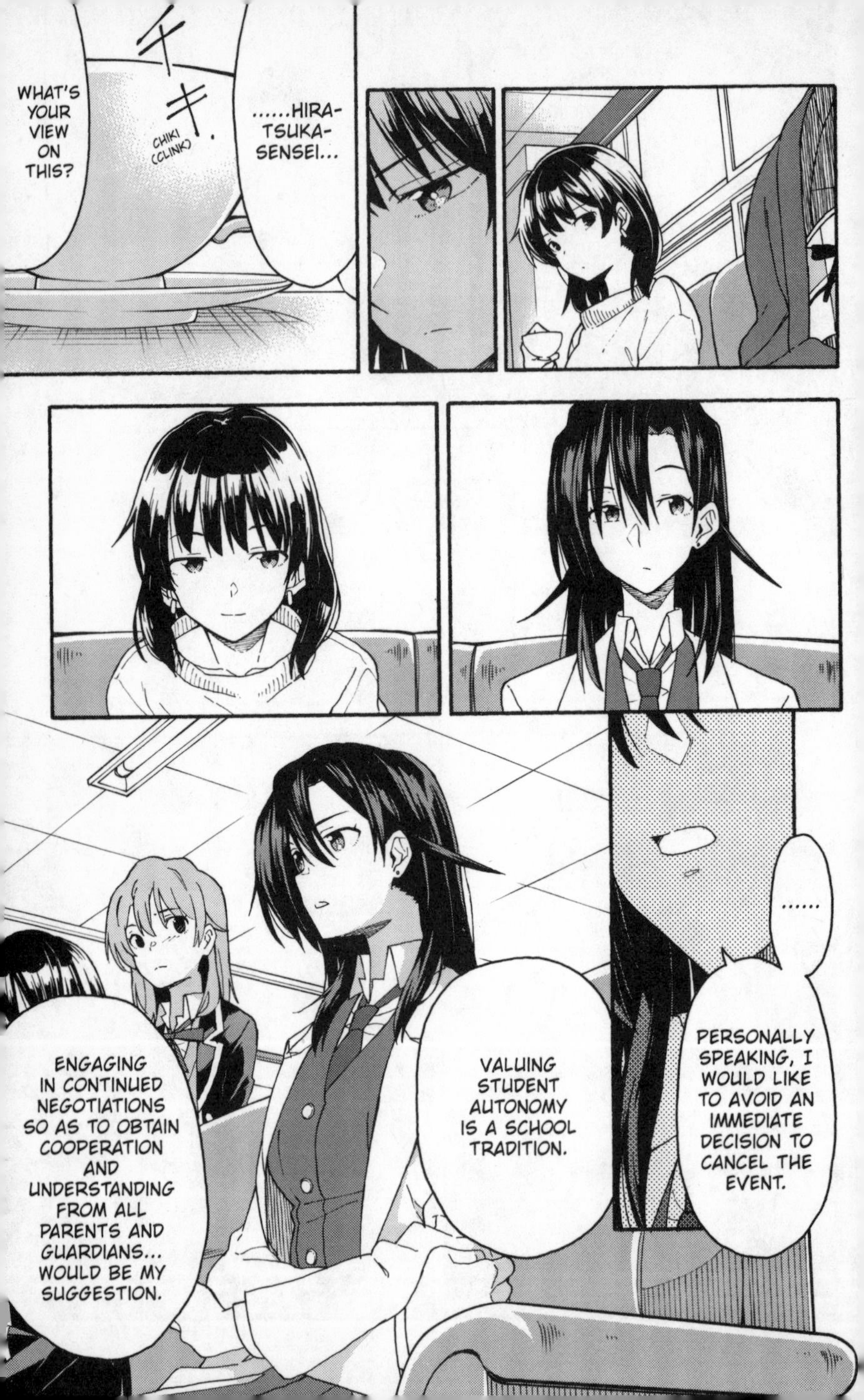

......HIRA-TSUKA-SENSEI...
CHIKI (CLINK)
WHAT'S YOUR VIEW ON THIS?
......
PERSONALLY SPEAKING, I WOULD LIKE TO AVOID AN IMMEDIATE DECISION TO CANCEL THE EVENT.
VALUING STUDENT AUTONOMY IS A SCHOOL TRADITION.
ENGAGING IN CONTINUED NEGOTIATIONS SO AS TO OBTAIN COOPERATION AND UNDERSTANDING FROM ALL PARENTS AND GUARDIANS... WOULD BE MY SUGGESTION.

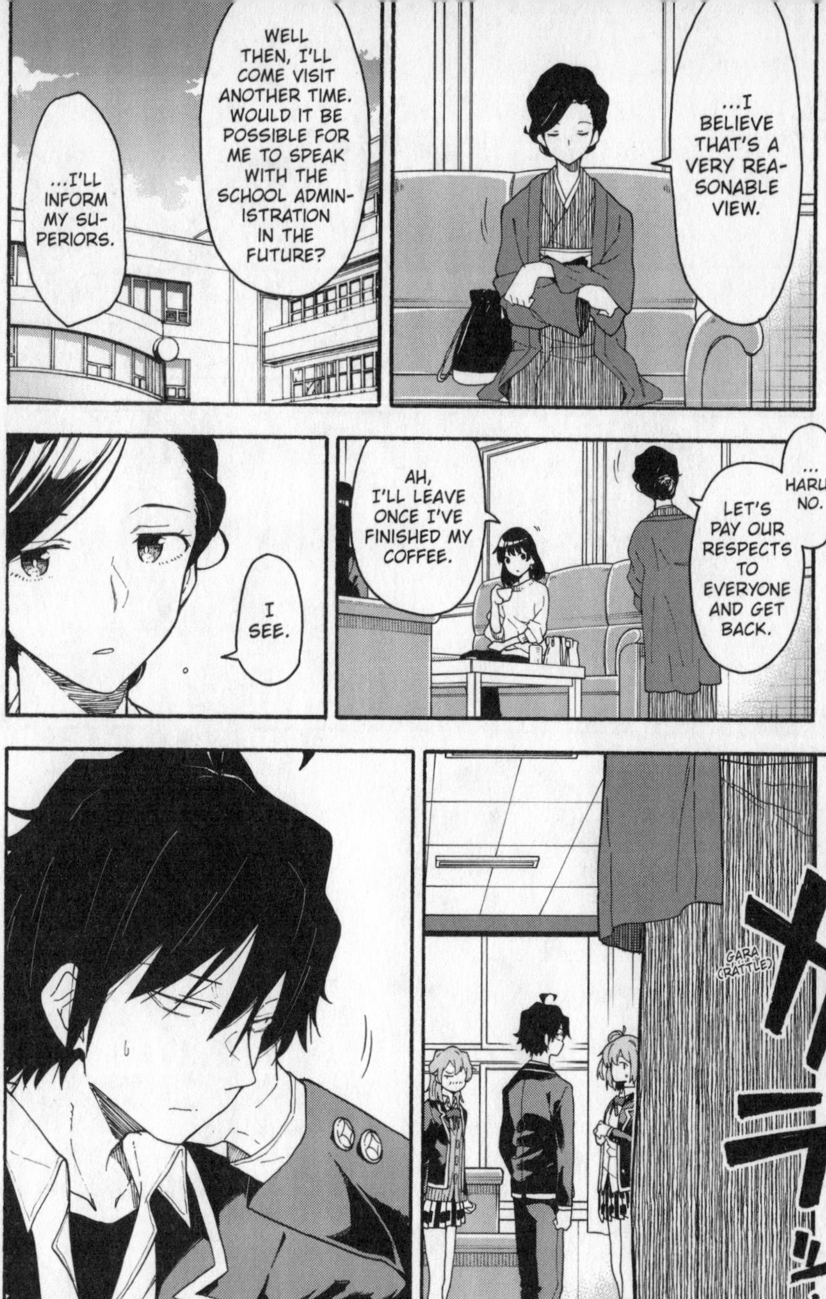
...I BELIEVE THAT'S A VERY REASONABLE VIEW.
WELL THEN, I'LL COME VISIT ANOTHER TIME. WOULD IT BE POSSIBLE FOR ME TO SPEAK WITH THE SCHOOL ADMINISTRATION IN THE FUTURE?
...I'LL INFORM MY SUPERIORS.
...HARUNO.
LET'S PAY OUR RESPECTS TO EVERYONE AND GET BACK.
AH, I'LL LEAVE ONCE I'VE FINISHED MY COFFEE.
I SEE.
GARA (RATTLE)

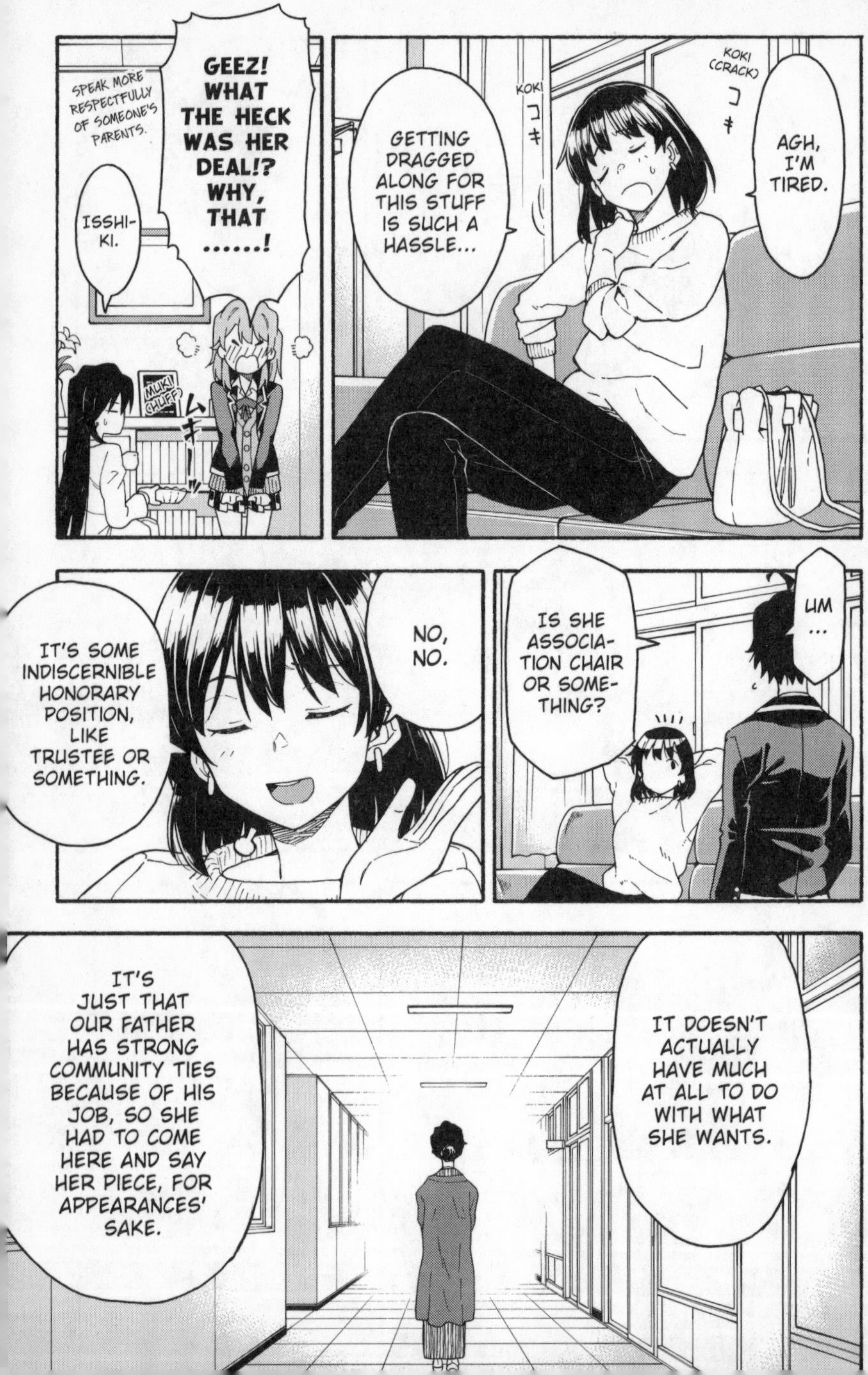
KOKI (CRACK)
コキ
AGH, I'M TIRED.
KOKI
コキ
GETTING DRAGGED ALONG FOR THIS STUFF IS SUCH A HASSLE...
GEEZ! WHAT THE HECK WAS HER DEAL!? WHY, THAT ......!
SPEAK MORE RESPECTFULLY OF SOMEONE'S PARENTS.
ISSHIKI.
MUKI (CHUFF)
ムキー!!
UM ...
IS SHE ASSOCIATION CHAIR OR SOMETHING?
NO, NO.
IT'S SOME INDISCERNIBLE HONORARY POSITION, LIKE TRUSTEE OR SOMETHING.
IT DOESN'T ACTUALLY HAVE MUCH AT ALL TO DO WITH WHAT SHE WANTS.
IT'S JUST THAT OUR FATHER HAS STRONG COMMUNITY TIES BECAUSE OF HIS JOB, SO SHE HAD TO COME HERE AND SAY HER PIECE, FOR APPEARANCES' SAKE.

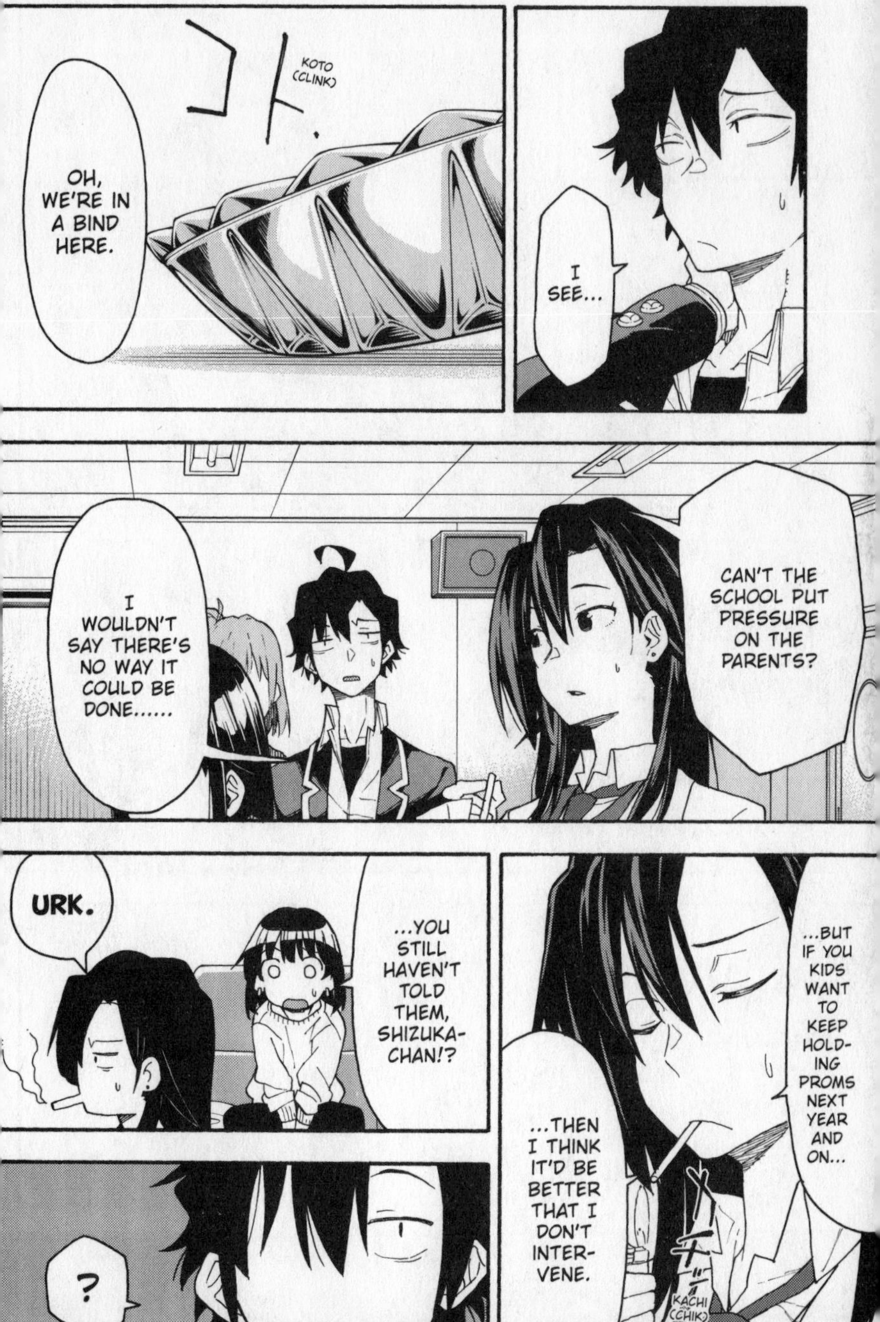
I SEE...
KOTO (CLINK)
OH, WE'RE IN A BIND HERE.
CAN'T THE SCHOOL PUT PRESSURE ON THE PARENTS?
I WOULDN'T SAY THERE'S NO WAY IT COULD BE DONE......
...BUT IF YOU KIDS WANT TO KEEP HOLD-ING PROMS NEXT YEAR AND ON...
...THEN I THINK IT'D BE BETTER THAT I DON'T INTER-VENE.
KACHI (CHIK)
...YOU STILL HAVEN'T TOLD THEM, SHIZUKA-CHAN!?
URK.
?

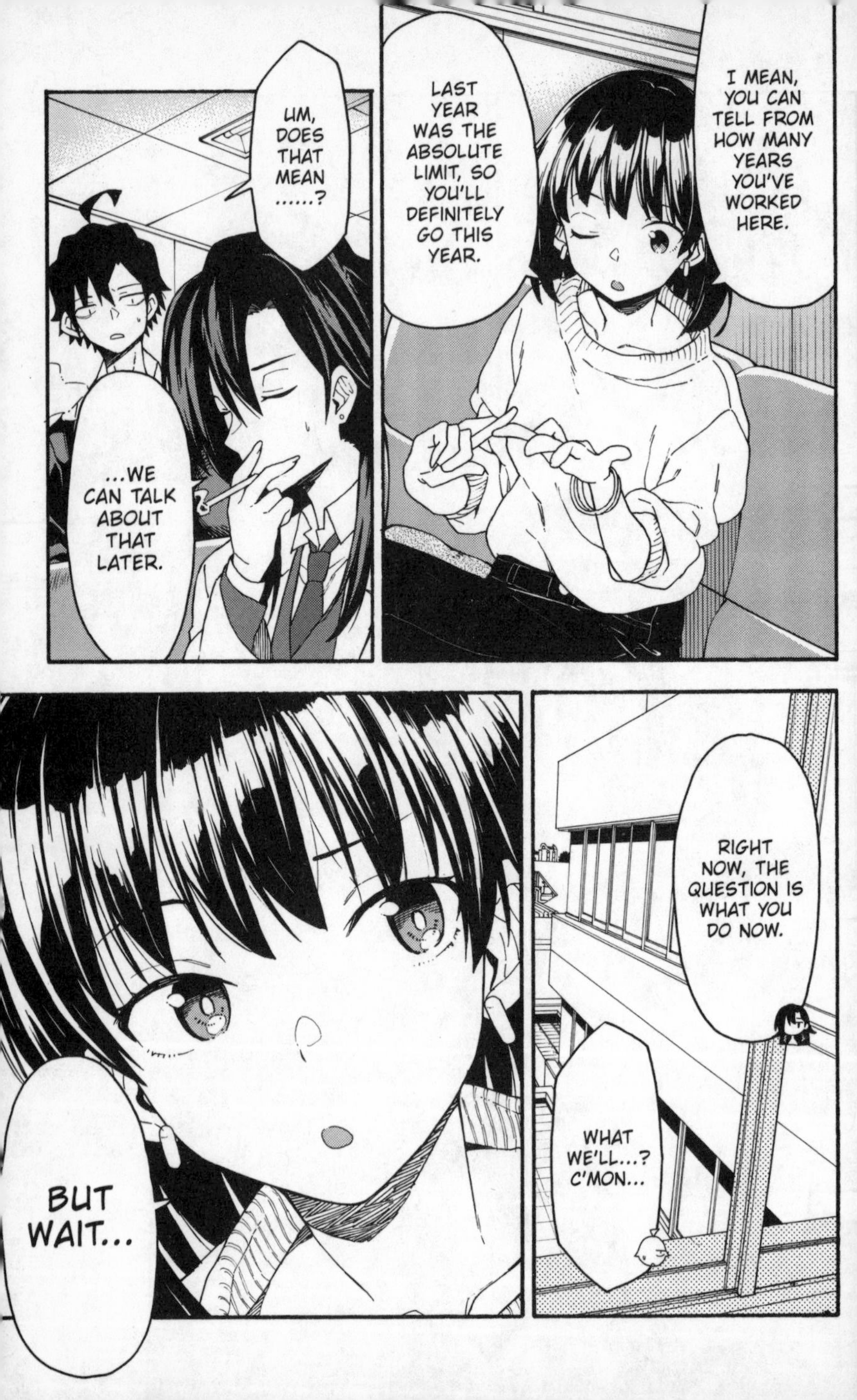
I MEAN, YOU CAN TELL FROM HOW MANY YEARS YOU'VE WORKED HERE.
LAST YEAR WAS THE ABSOLUTE LIMIT, SO YOU'LL DEFINITELY GO THIS YEAR.
UM, DOES THAT MEAN ......?
...WE CAN TALK ABOUT THAT LATER.
RIGHT NOW, THE QUESTION IS WHAT YOU DO NOW.
WHAT WE'LL...? C'MON...
BUT WAIT...

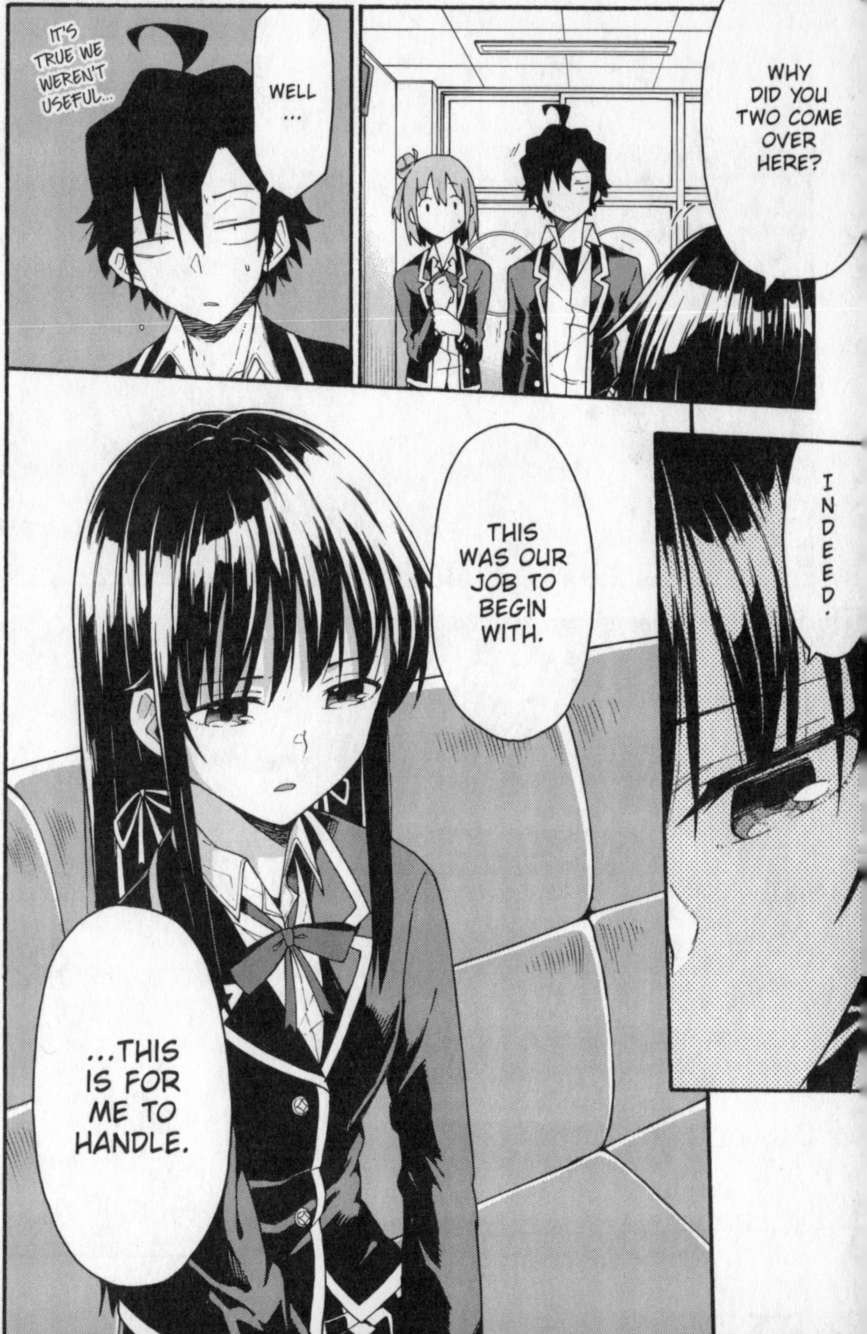
WHY DID YOU TWO COME OVER HERE?
WELL ...
IT'S TRUE WE WEREN'T USEFUL...
INDEED.
THIS WAS OUR JOB TO BEGIN WITH.
...THIS IS FOR ME TO HANDLE.

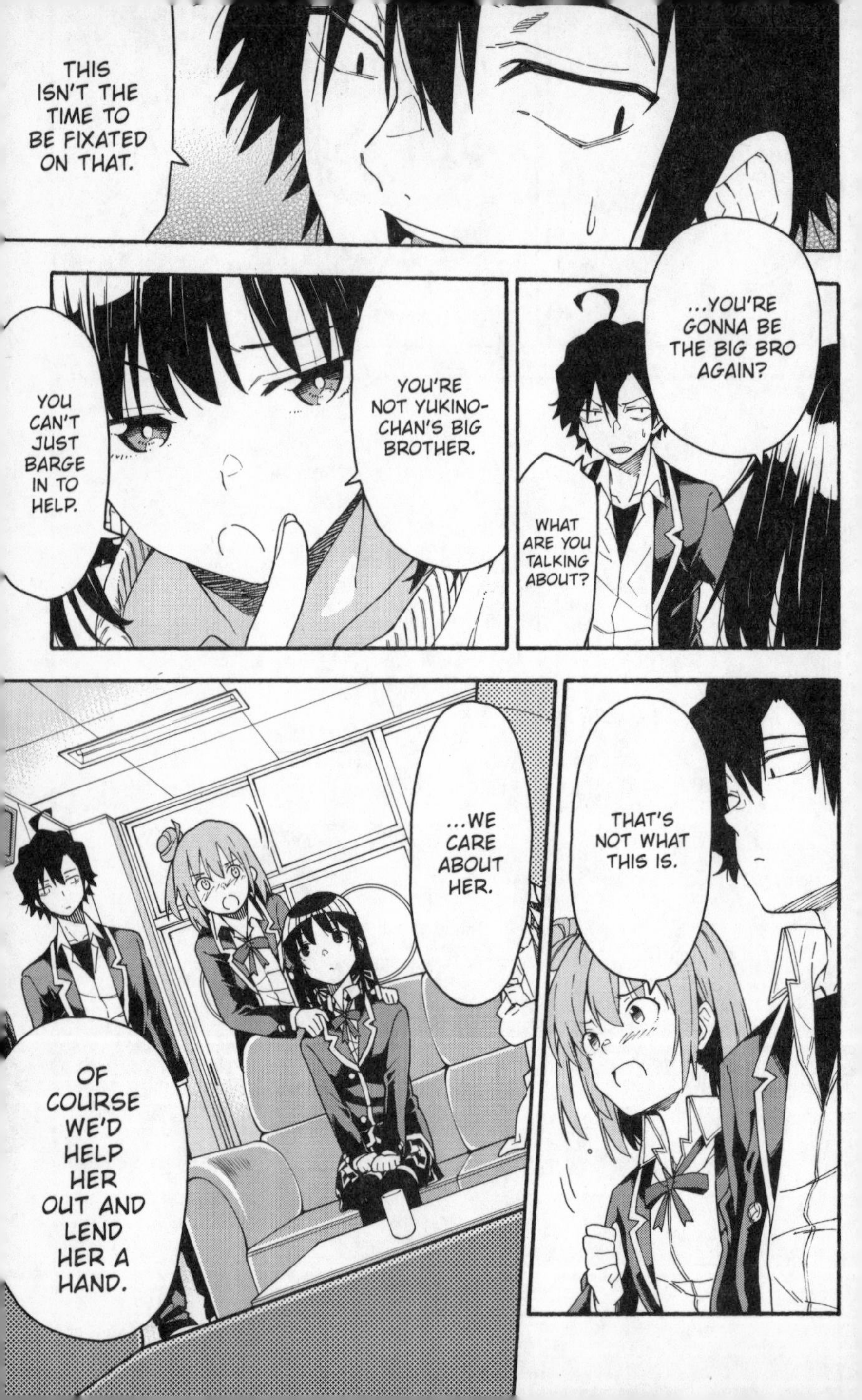
THIS ISN'T THE TIME TO BE FIXATED ON THAT.
...YOU'RE GONNA BE THE BIG BRO AGAIN?
WHAT ARE YOU TALKING ABOUT?
YOU'RE NOT YUKINO-CHAN'S BIG BROTHER.
YOU CAN'T JUST BARGE IN TO HELP.
THAT'S NOT WHAT THIS IS.
...WE CARE ABOUT HER.
OF COURSE WE'D HELP HER OUT AND LEND HER A HAND.

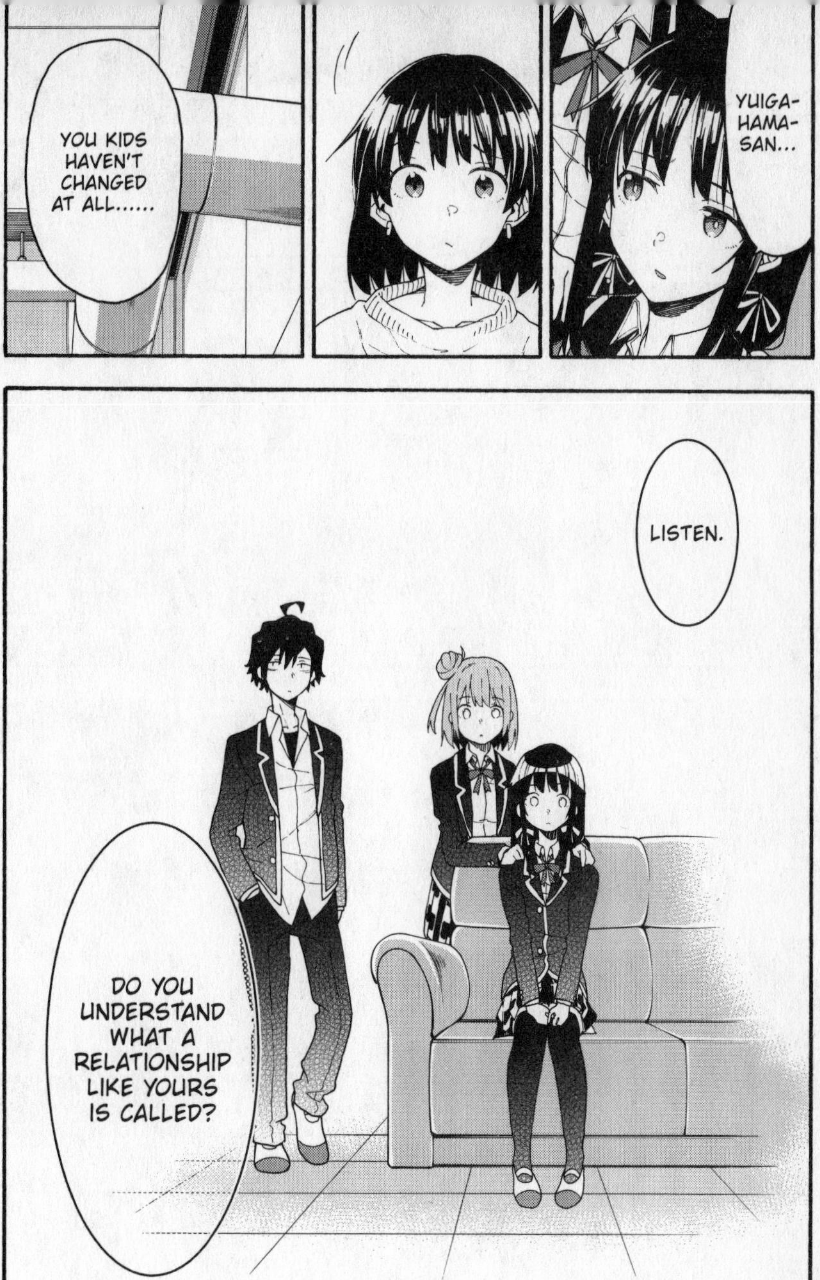
YUIGA-HAMA-SAN...
YOU KIDS HAVEN'T CHANGED AT ALL......
LISTEN.
DO YOU UNDERSTAND WHAT A RELATIONSHIP LIKE YOURS IS CALLED?

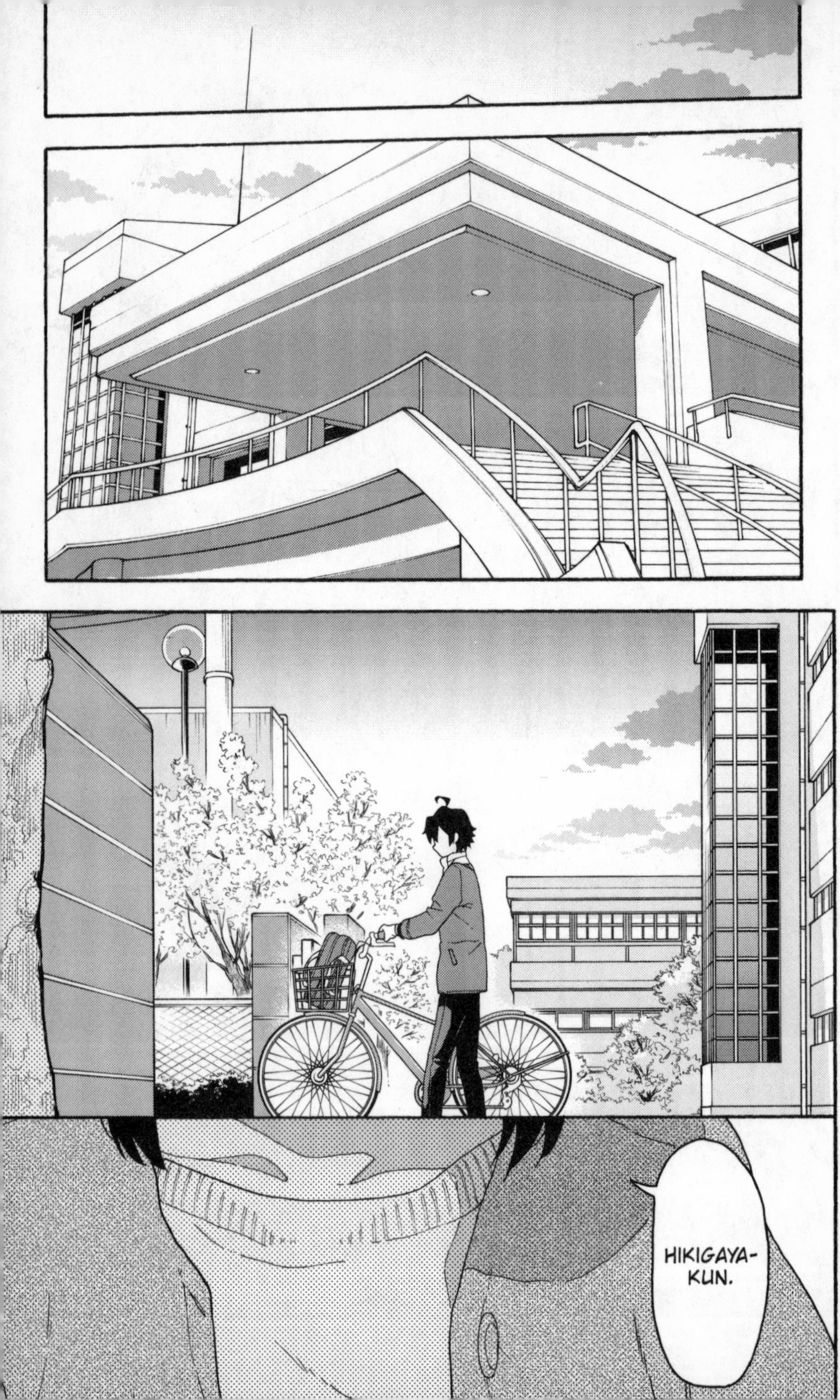
HIKIGAYA-KUN.

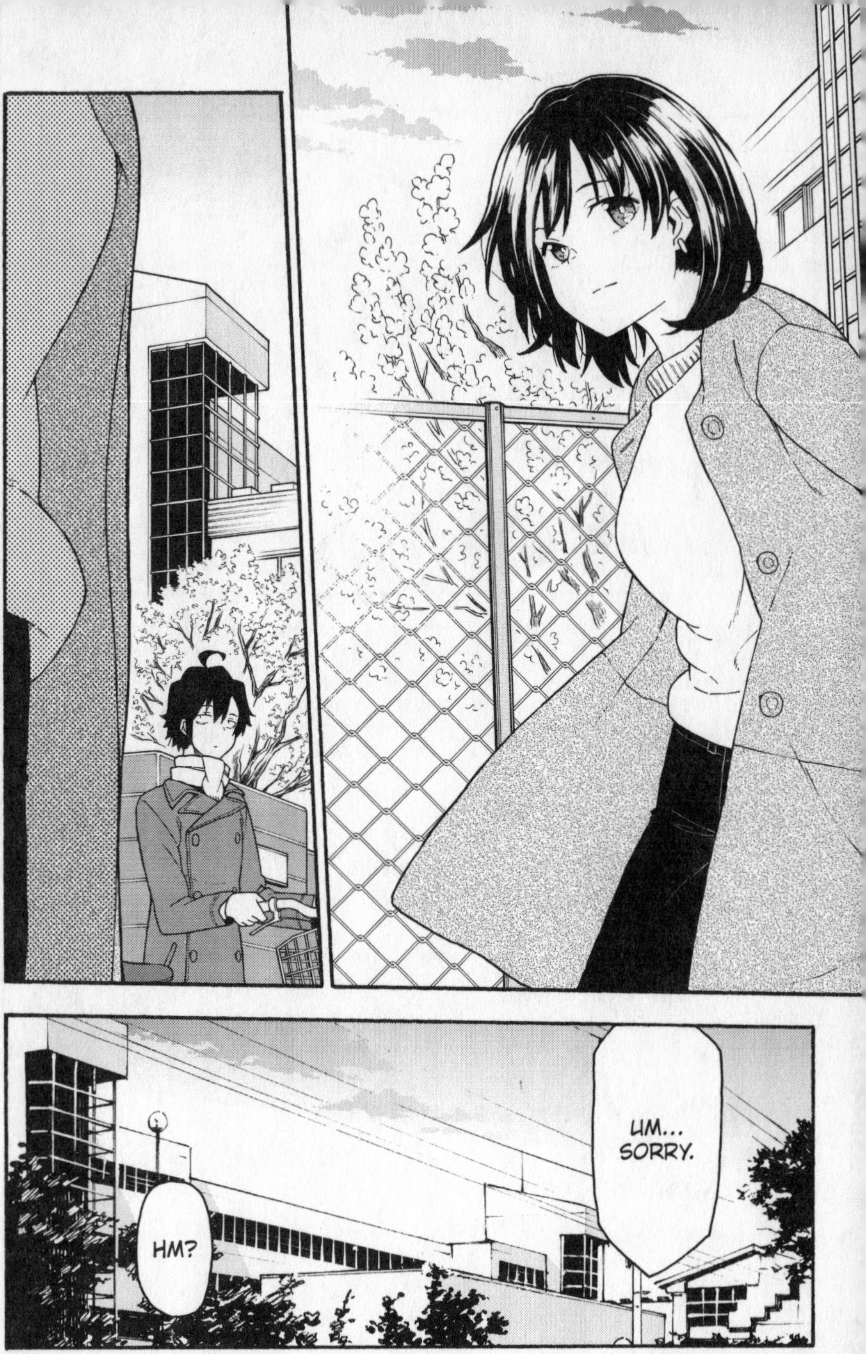
UM... SORRY.
HM?

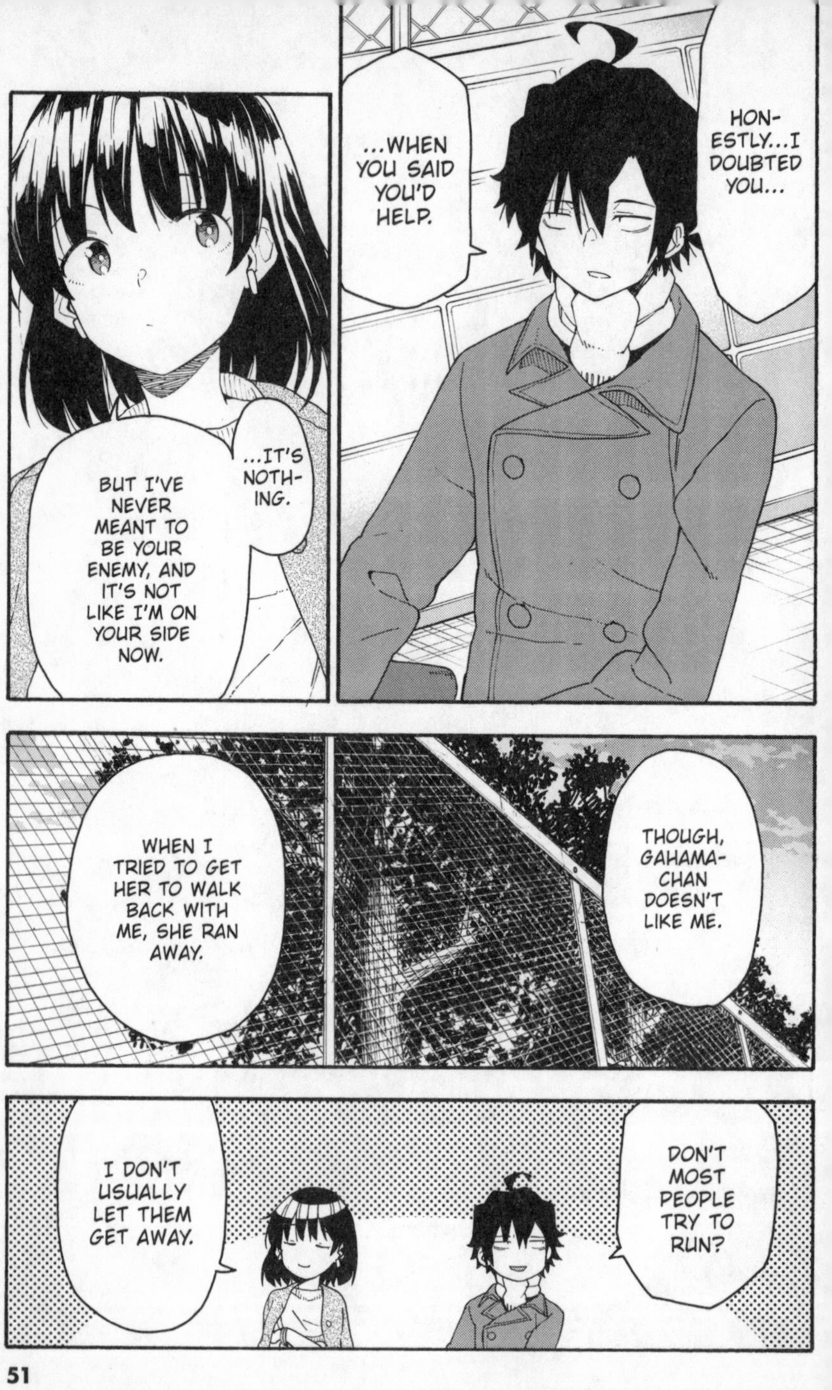
HON-ESTLY...I DOUBTED YOU...
...WHEN YOU SAID YOU'D HELP.
...IT'S NOTH-ING.
BUT I'VE NEVER MEANT TO BE YOUR ENEMY, AND IT'S NOT LIKE I'M ON YOUR SIDE NOW.
THOUGH, GAHAMA-CHAN DOESN'T LIKE ME.
WHEN I TRIED TO GET HER TO WALK BACK WITH ME, SHE RAN AWAY.
DON'T MOST PEOPLE TRY TO RUN?
I DON'T USUALLY LET THEM GET AWAY.

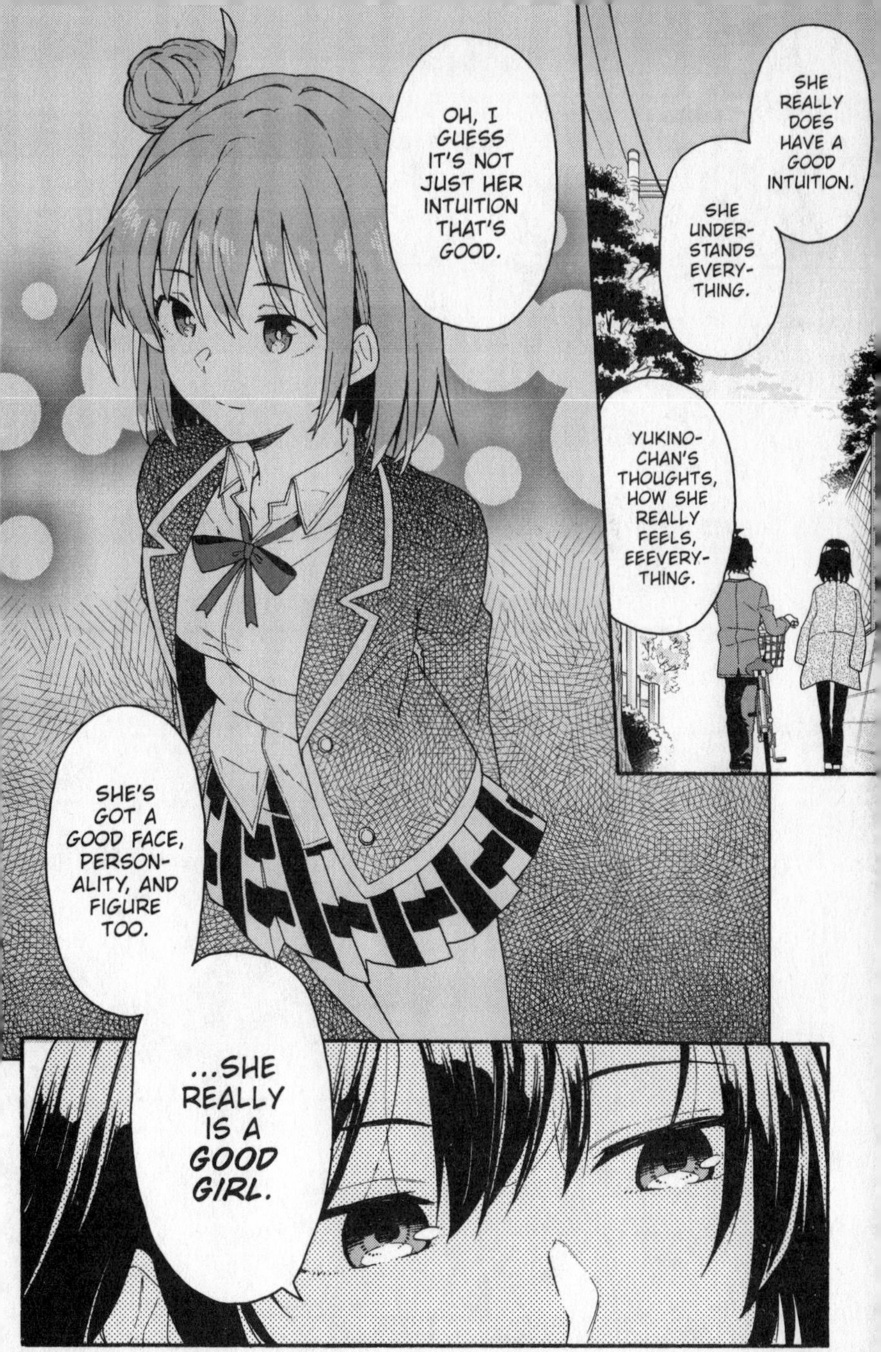
SHE REALLY DOES HAVE A GOOD INTUITION.
SHE UNDERSTANDS EVERYTHING.
YUKINO-CHAN'S THOUGHTS, HOW SHE REALLY FEELS, EEEVERYTHING.
OH, I GUESS IT'S NOT JUST HER INTUITION THAT'S GOOD.
SHE'S GOT A GOOD FACE, PERSONALITY, AND FIGURE TOO.
...SHE REALLY IS A *GOOD GIRL*.

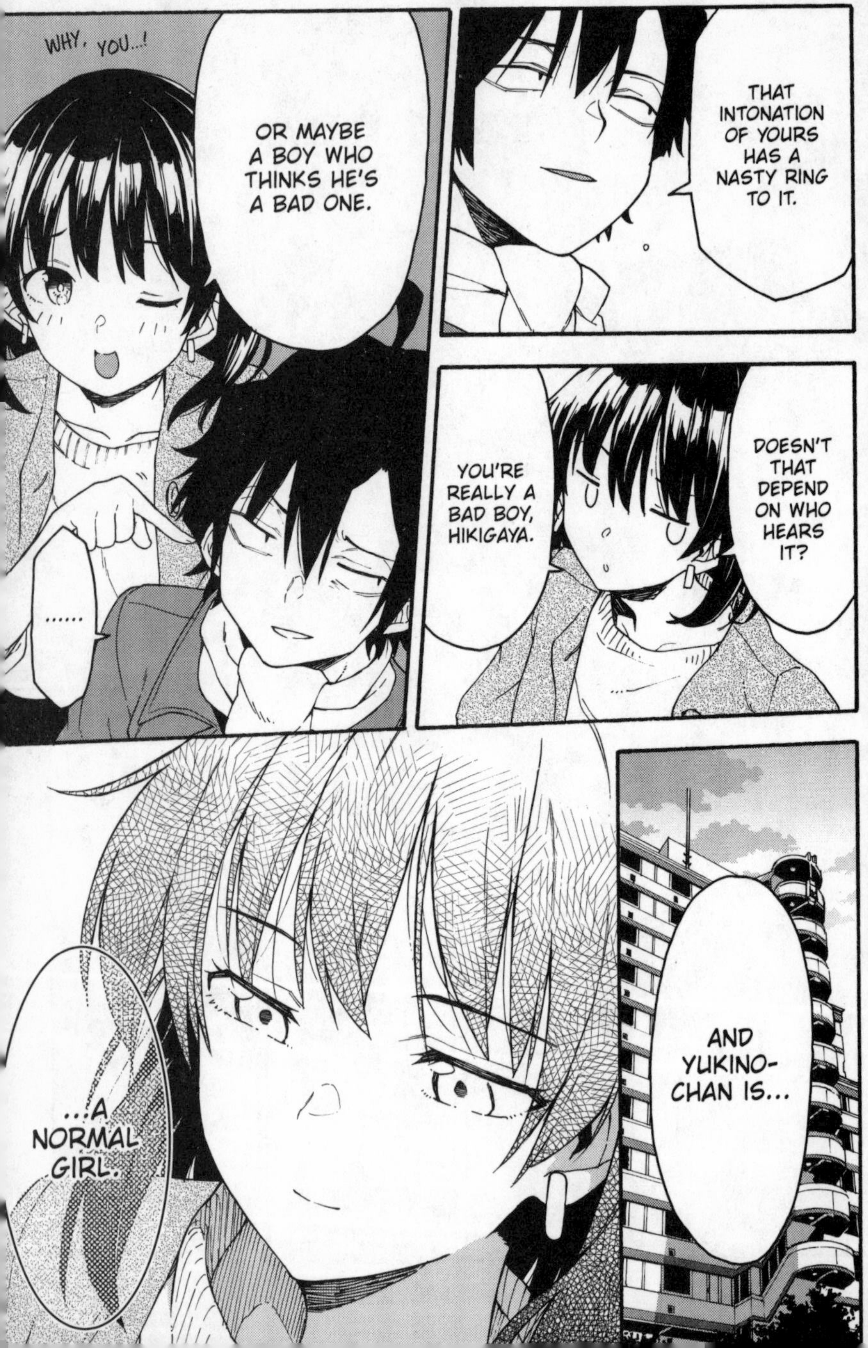
THAT INTONATION OF YOURS HAS A NASTY RING TO IT.
DOESN'T THAT DEPEND ON WHO HEARS IT?
YOU'RE REALLY A BAD BOY, HIKIGAYA.
WHY, YOU...!
OR MAYBE A BOY WHO THINKS HE'S A BAD ONE.
......
AND YUKINO-CHAN IS...
...A NORMAL GIRL.

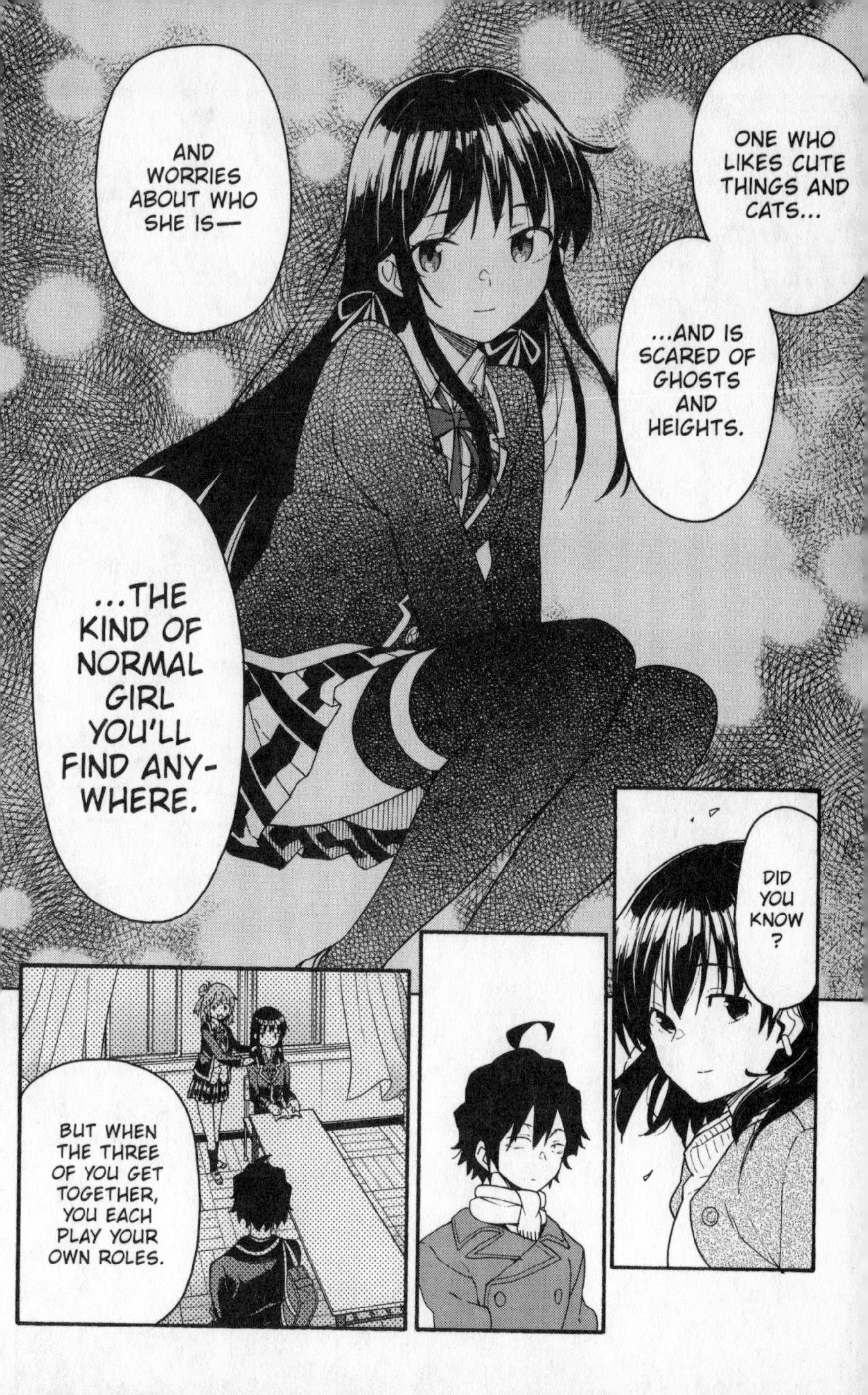

ONE WHO LIKES CUTE THINGS AND CATS...
...AND IS SCARED OF GHOSTS AND HEIGHTS.
AND WORRIES ABOUT WHO SHE IS—
...THE KIND OF NORMAL GIRL YOU'LL FIND ANY-WHERE.
DID YOU KNOW?
BUT WHEN THE THREE OF YOU GET TOGETHER, YOU EACH PLAY YOUR OWN ROLES.

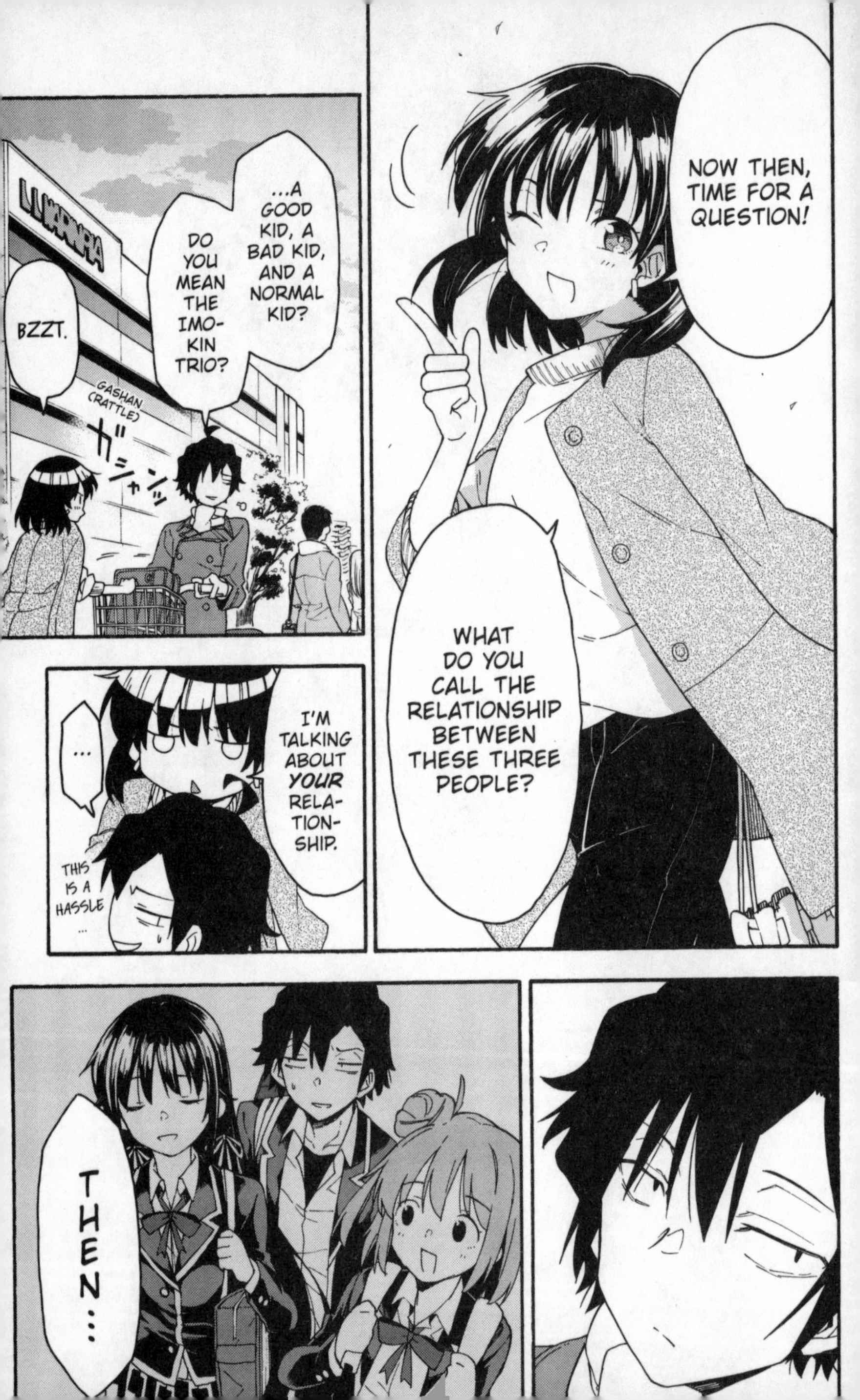
NOW THEN, TIME FOR A QUESTION!
WHAT DO YOU CALL THE RELATIONSHIP BETWEEN THESE THREE PEOPLE?
...A GOOD KID, A BAD KID, AND A NORMAL KID?
DO YOU MEAN THE IMO-KIN TRIO?
GASHAN (RATTLE)
BZZT.
I'M TALKING ABOUT *YOUR* RELA-TION-SHIP.
...
THIS IS A HASSLE ...
THEN...

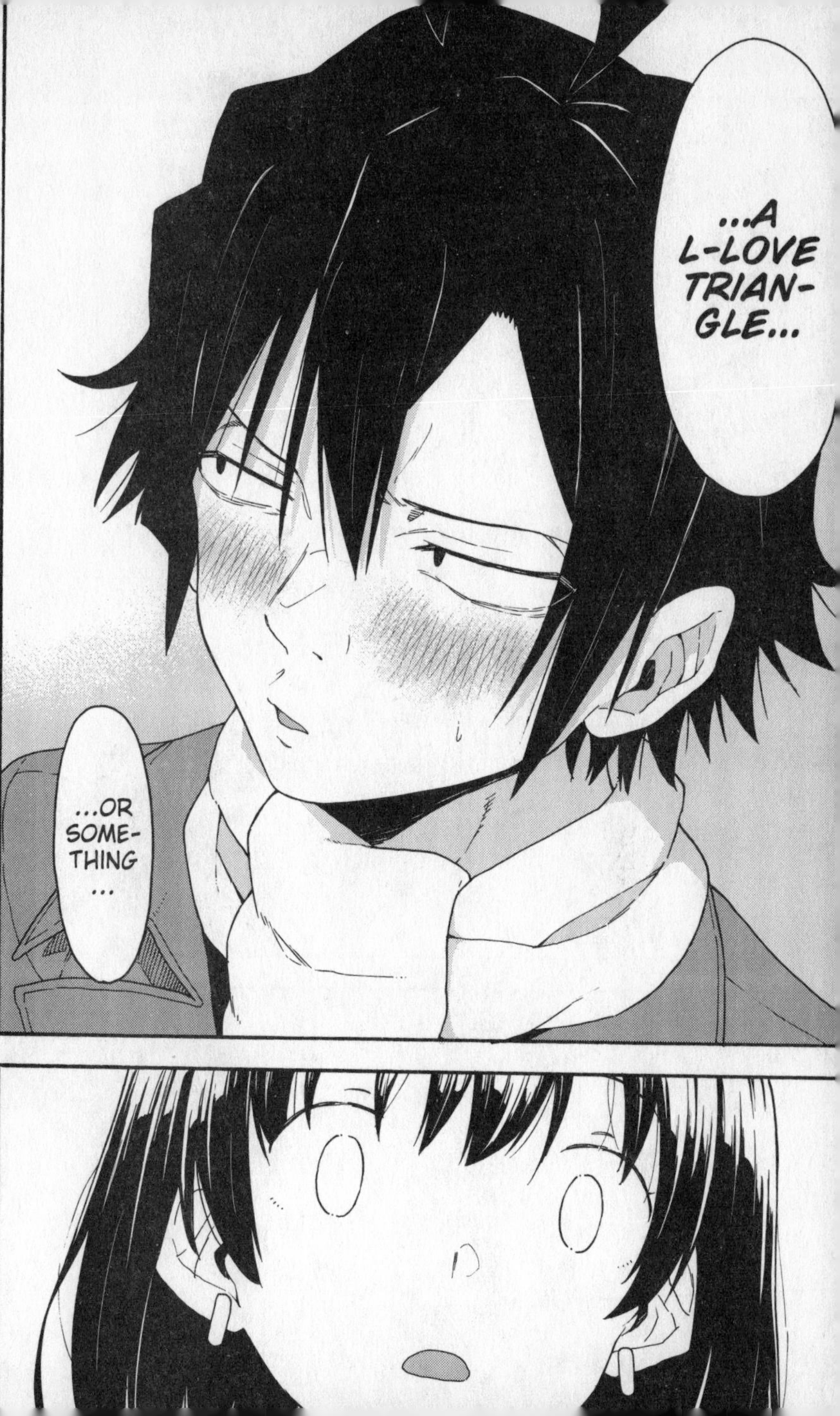
...A L-LOVE TRIAN-GLE...
...OR SOME-THING ...

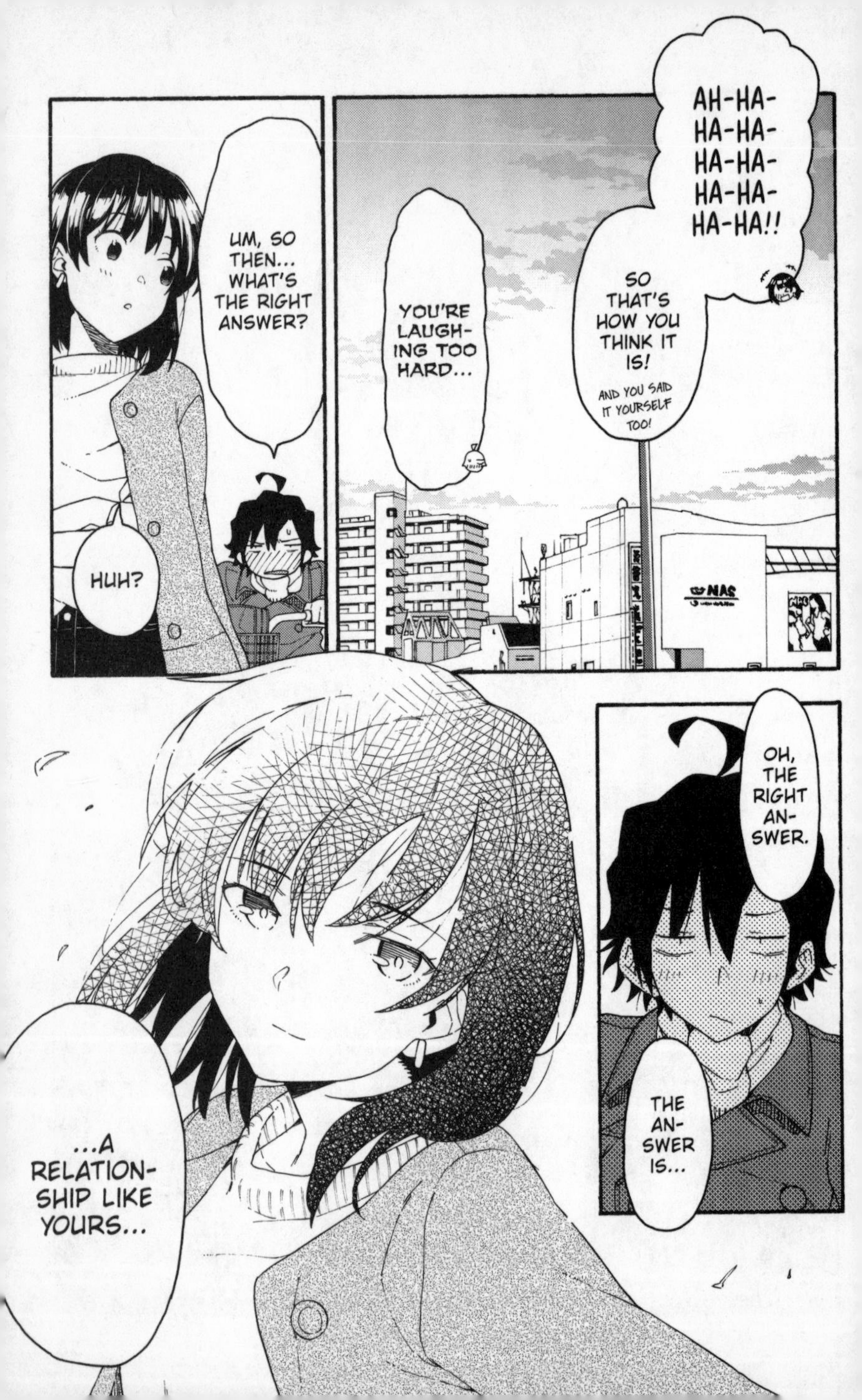
AH-HA-HA-HA-HA-HA-HA-HA-HA-HA!!
SO THAT'S HOW YOU THINK IT IS!
AND YOU SAID IT YOURSELF TOO!
YOU'RE LAUGHING TOO HARD...
UM, SO THEN... WHAT'S THE RIGHT ANSWER?
HUH?
OH, THE RIGHT ANSWER.
THE ANSWER IS...
...A RELATIONSHIP LIKE YOURS...

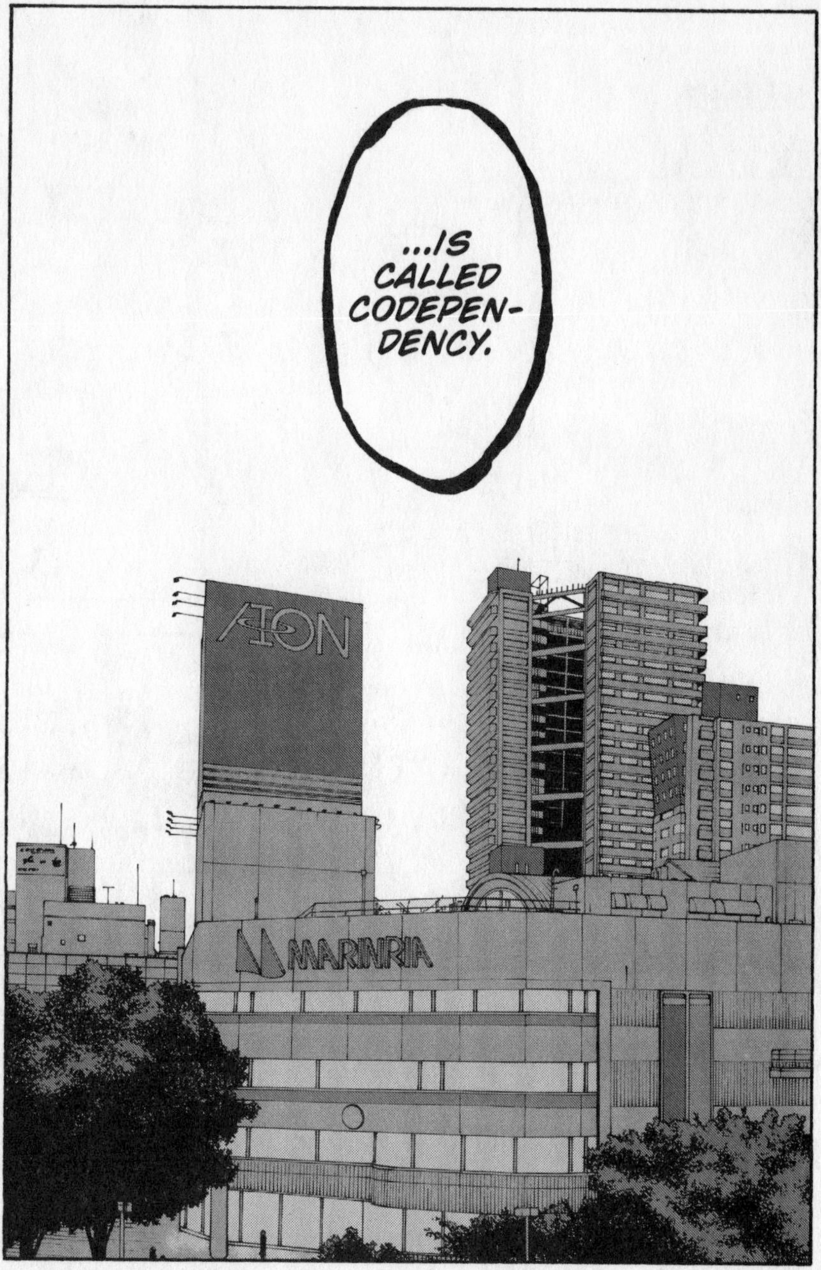
...IS CALLED CODEPEN-DENCY.
AEON
MARINRIA

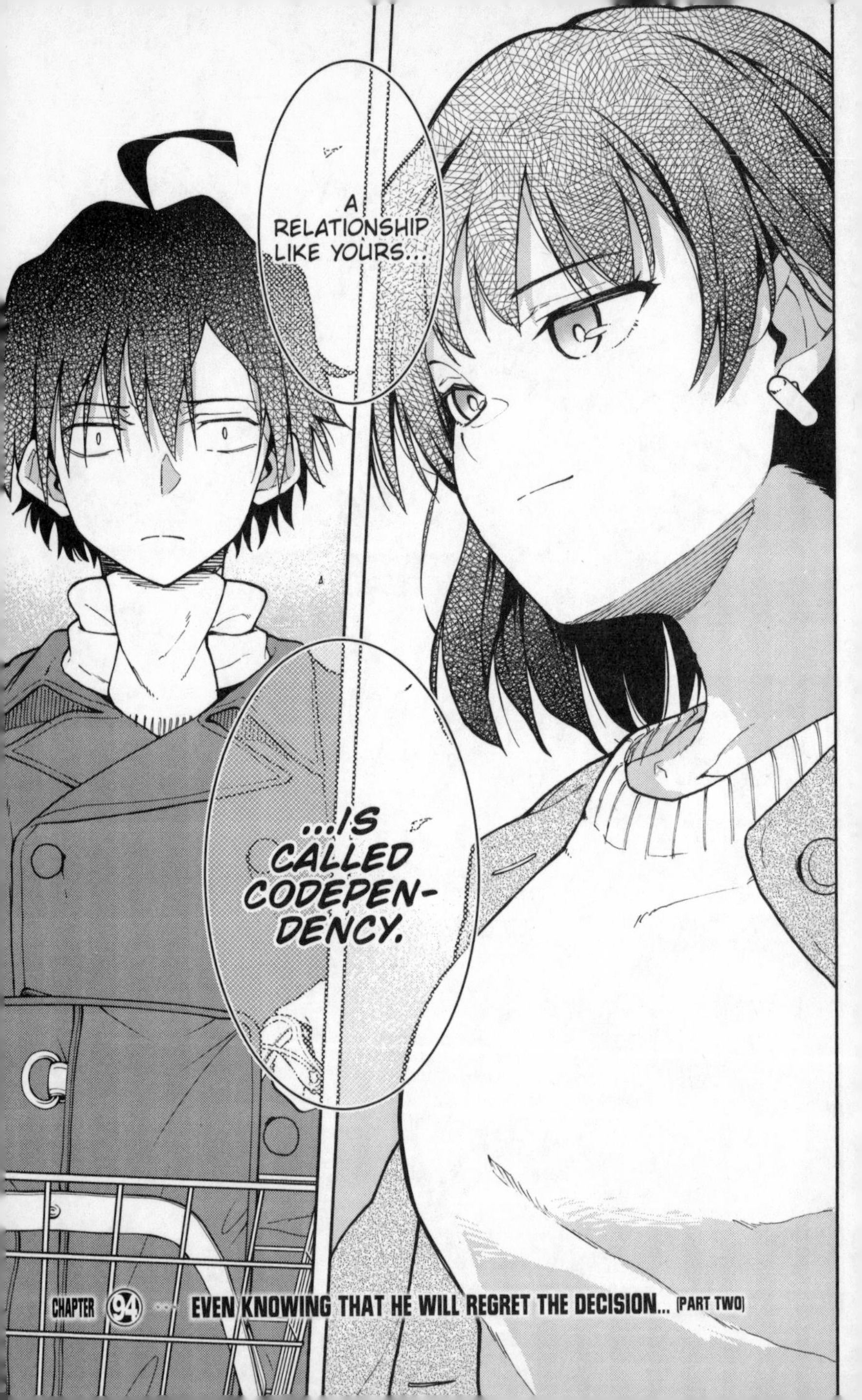
A RELATIONSHIP LIKE YOURS...
...IS CALLED CODEPEN-DENCY.
CHAPTER 94 EVEN KNOWING THAT HE WILL REGRET THE DECISION... (PART TWO)

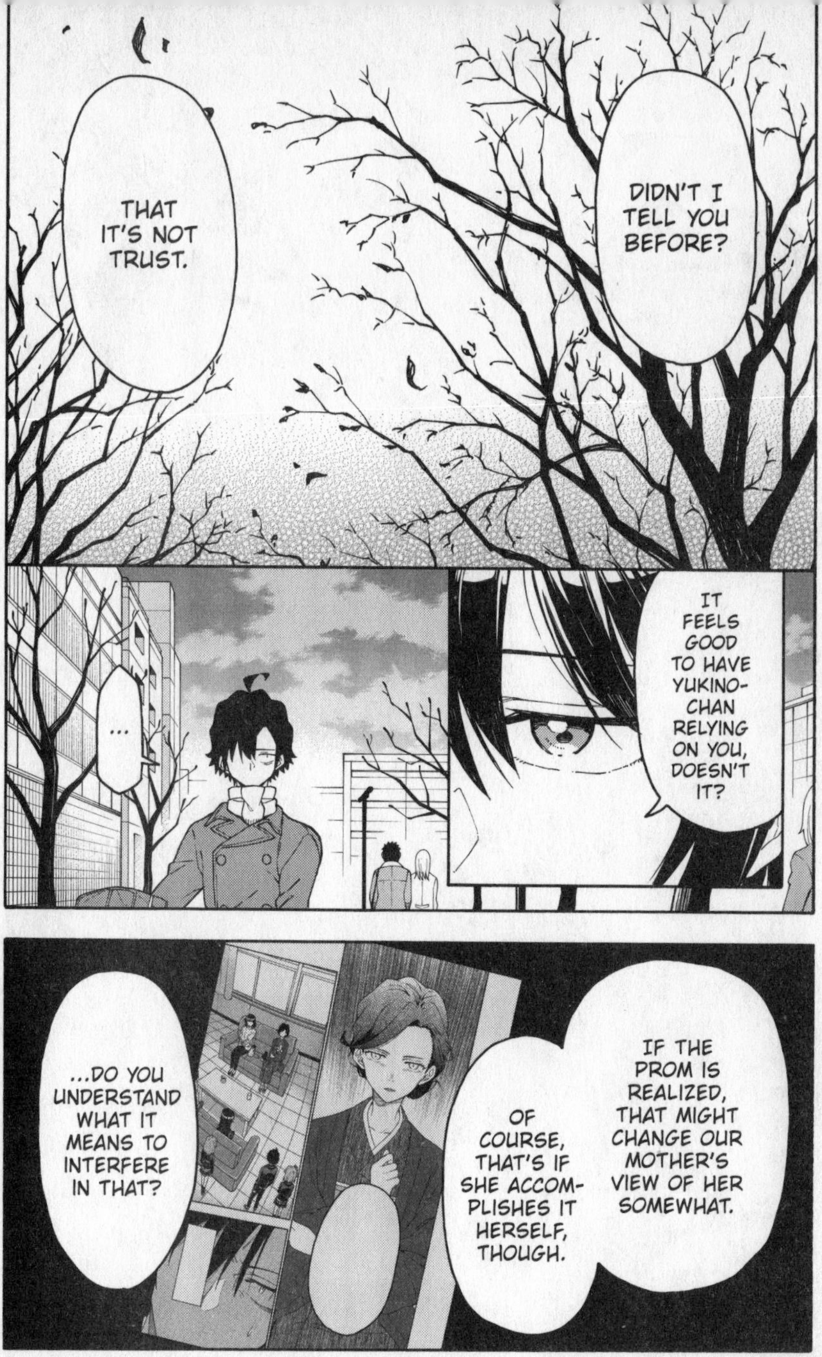
DIDN'T I TELL YOU BEFORE?
THAT IT'S NOT TRUST.
IT FEELS GOOD TO HAVE YUKINO-CHAN RELYING ON YOU, DOESN'T IT?
...
IF THE PROM IS REALIZED, THAT MIGHT CHANGE OUR MOTHER'S VIEW OF HER SOMEWHAT.
OF COURSE, THAT'S IF SHE ACCOMPLISHES IT HERSELF, THOUGH.
...DO YOU UNDERSTAND WHAT IT MEANS TO INTERFERE IN THAT?

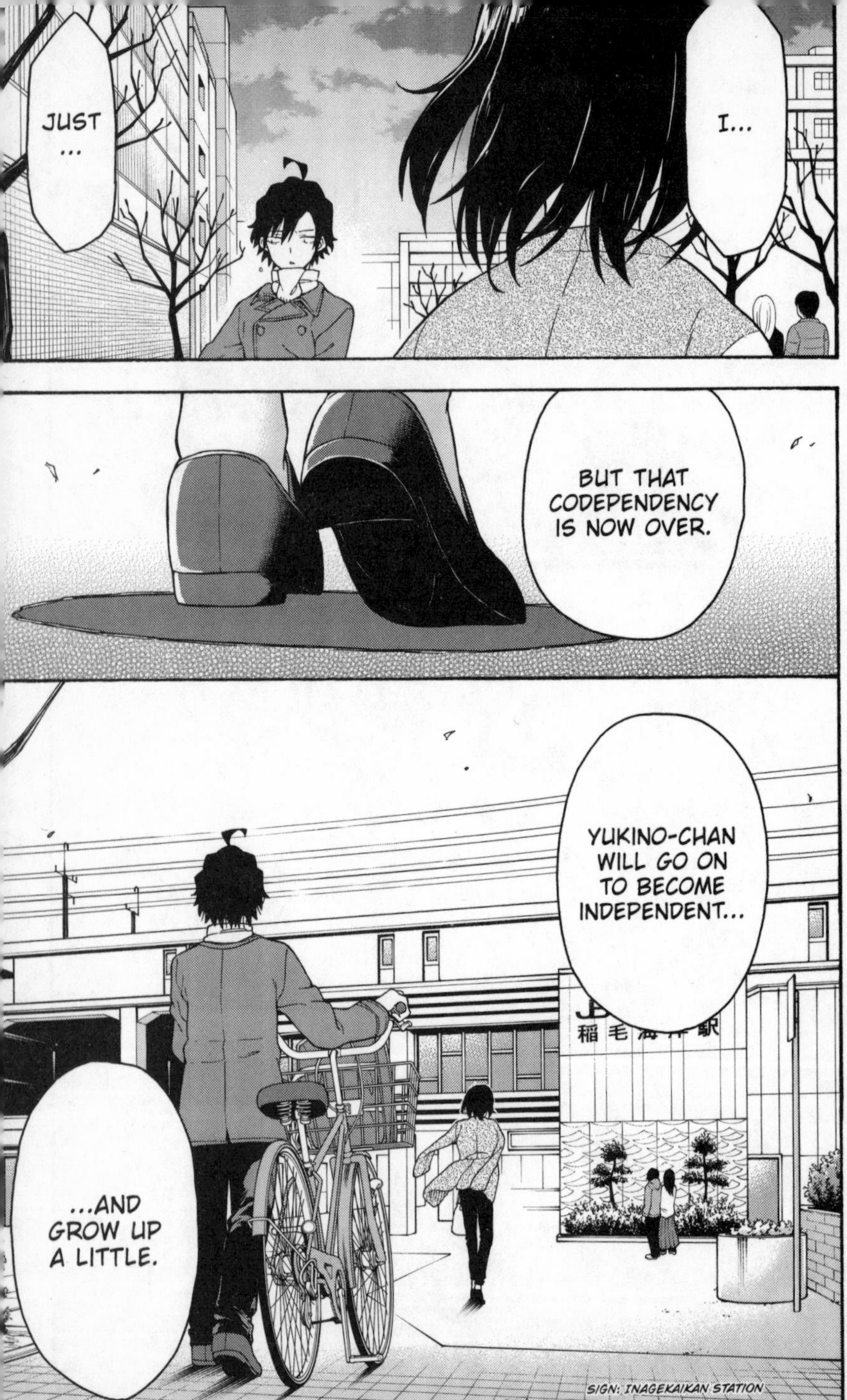
I...
JUST ...
BUT THAT CODEPENDENCY IS NOW OVER.
YUKINO-CHAN WILL GO ON TO BECOME INDEPENDENT...
...AND GROW UP A LITTLE.
SIGN: INAGEKAIKAN STATION

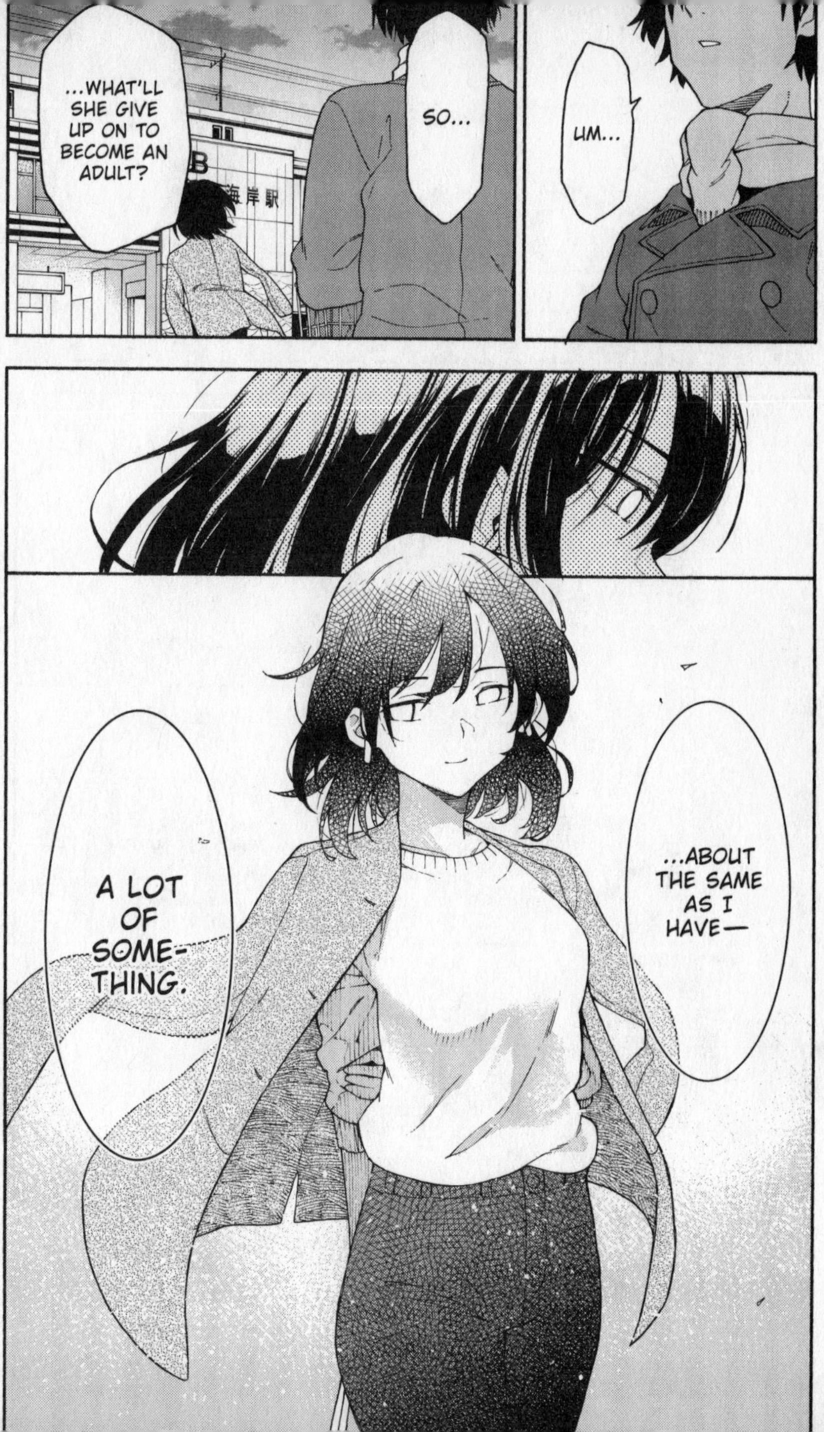
UM...
SO...
...WHAT'LL SHE GIVE UP ON TO BECOME AN ADULT?
海岸駅
...ABOUT THE SAME AS I HAVE—
A LOT OF SOME-THING.

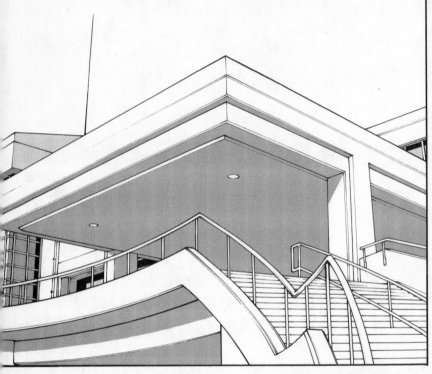

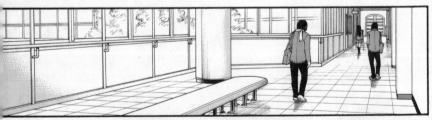

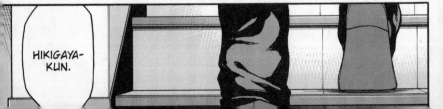

HIKIGAYA-KUN.

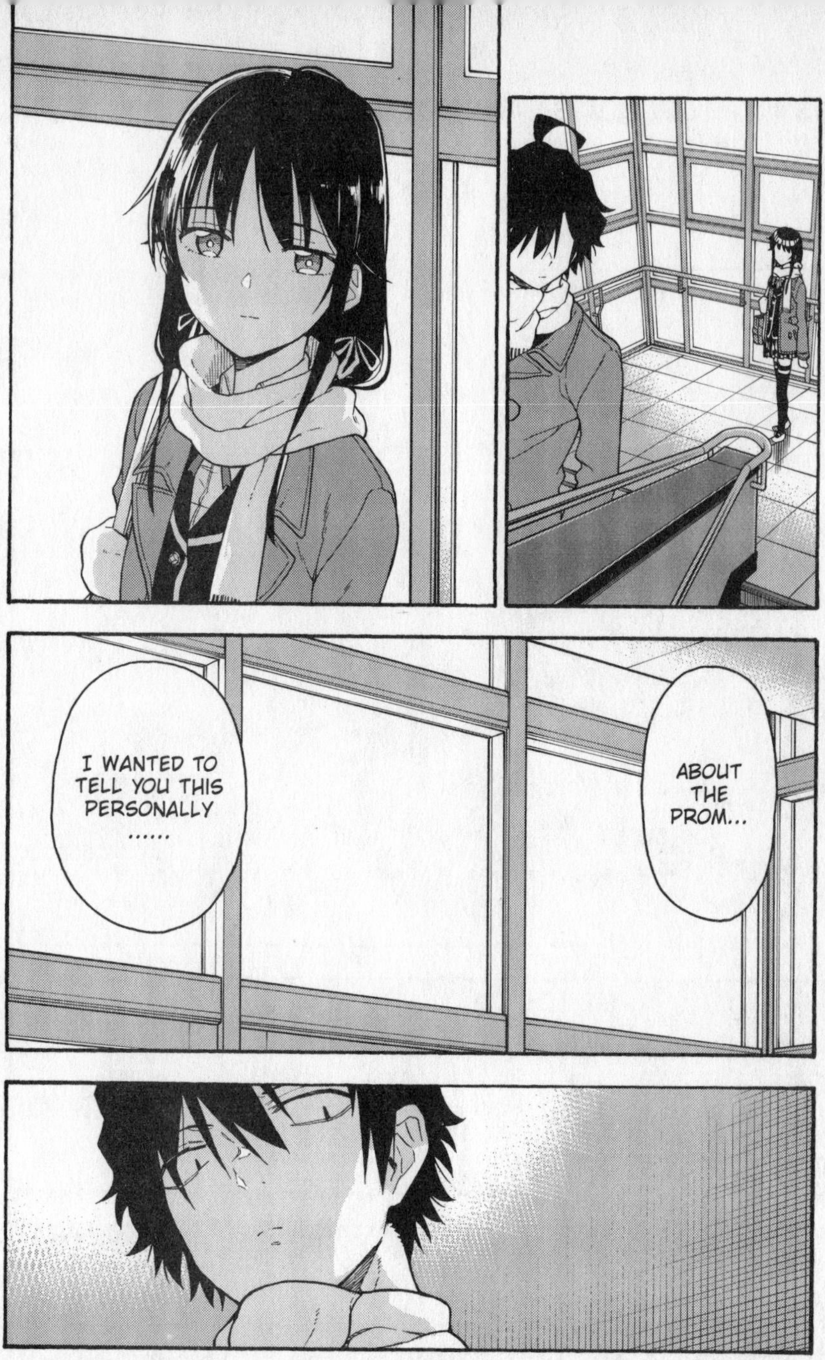
ABOUT THE PROM...
I WANTED TO TELL YOU THIS PERSONALLY ......

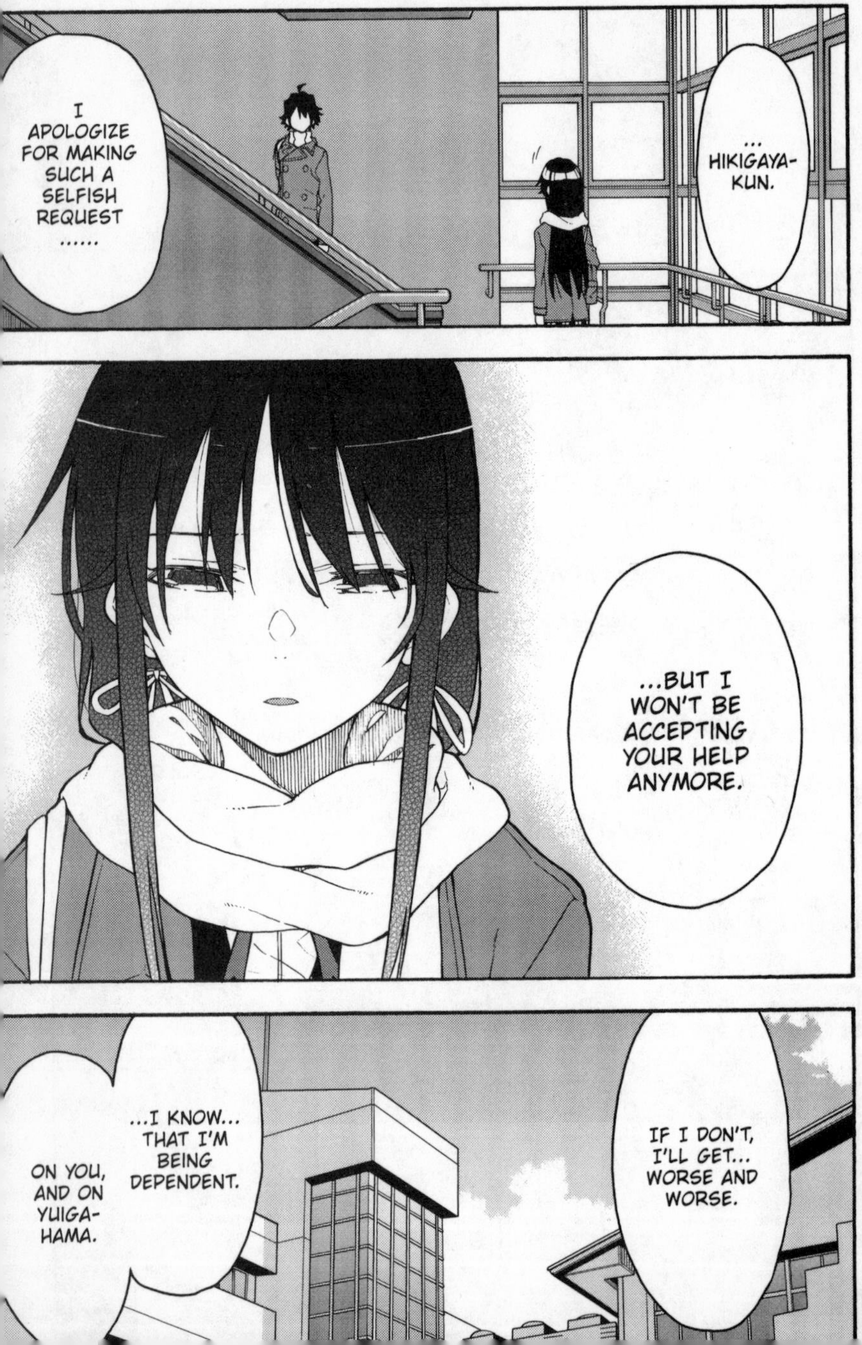
...HIKIGAYA-KUN.
I APOLOGIZE FOR MAKING SUCH A SELFISH REQUEST......
...BUT I WON'T BE ACCEPTING YOUR HELP ANYMORE.
IF I DON'T, I'LL GET... WORSE AND WORSE.
...I KNOW... THAT I'M BEING DEPENDENT.
ON YOU, AND ON YUIGA-HAMA.

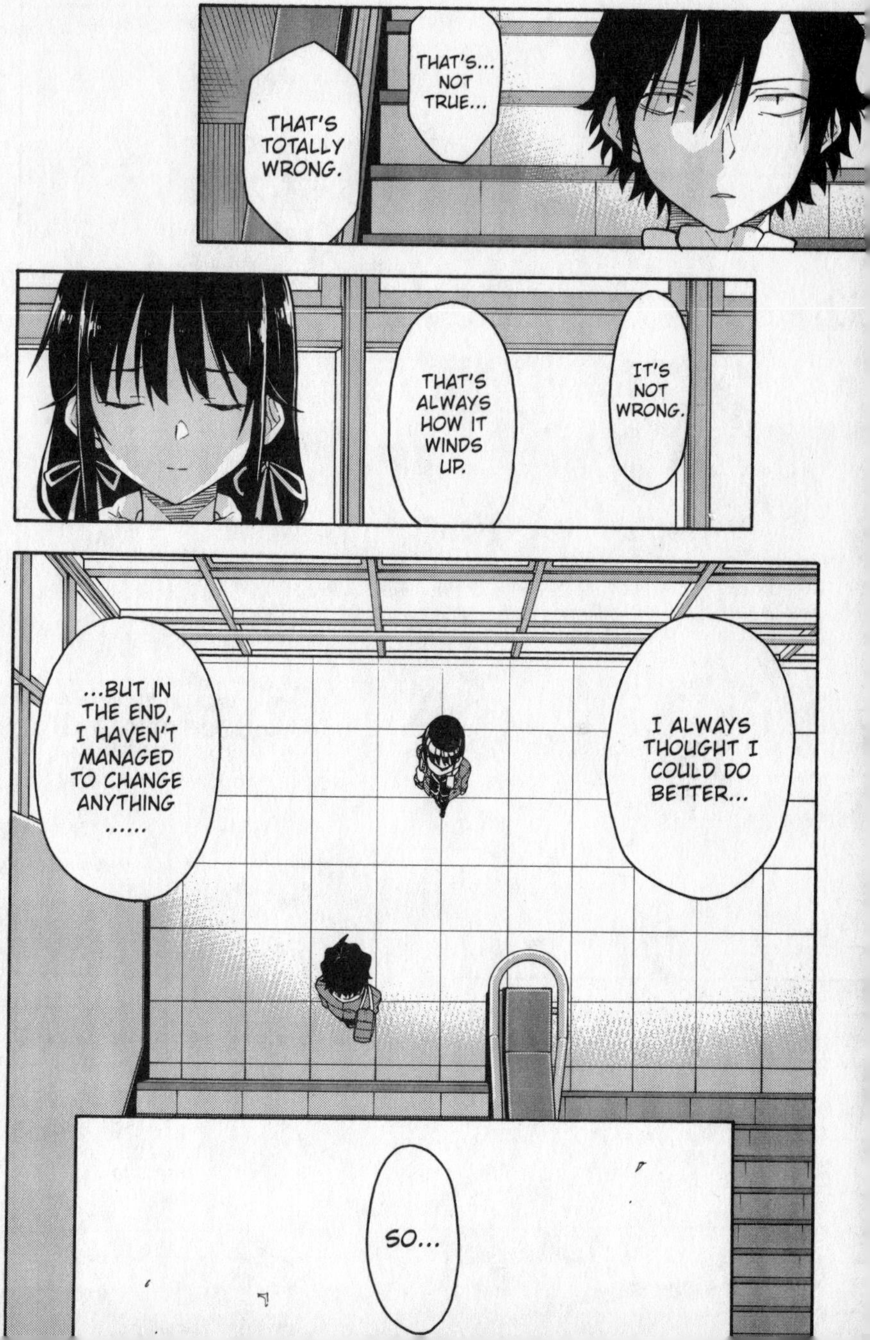
THAT'S... NOT TRUE...
THAT'S TOTALLY WRONG.
IT'S NOT WRONG.
THAT'S ALWAYS HOW IT WINDS UP.
I ALWAYS THOUGHT I COULD DO BETTER...
...BUT IN THE END, I HAVEN'T MANAGED TO CHANGE ANYTHING ......
SO...

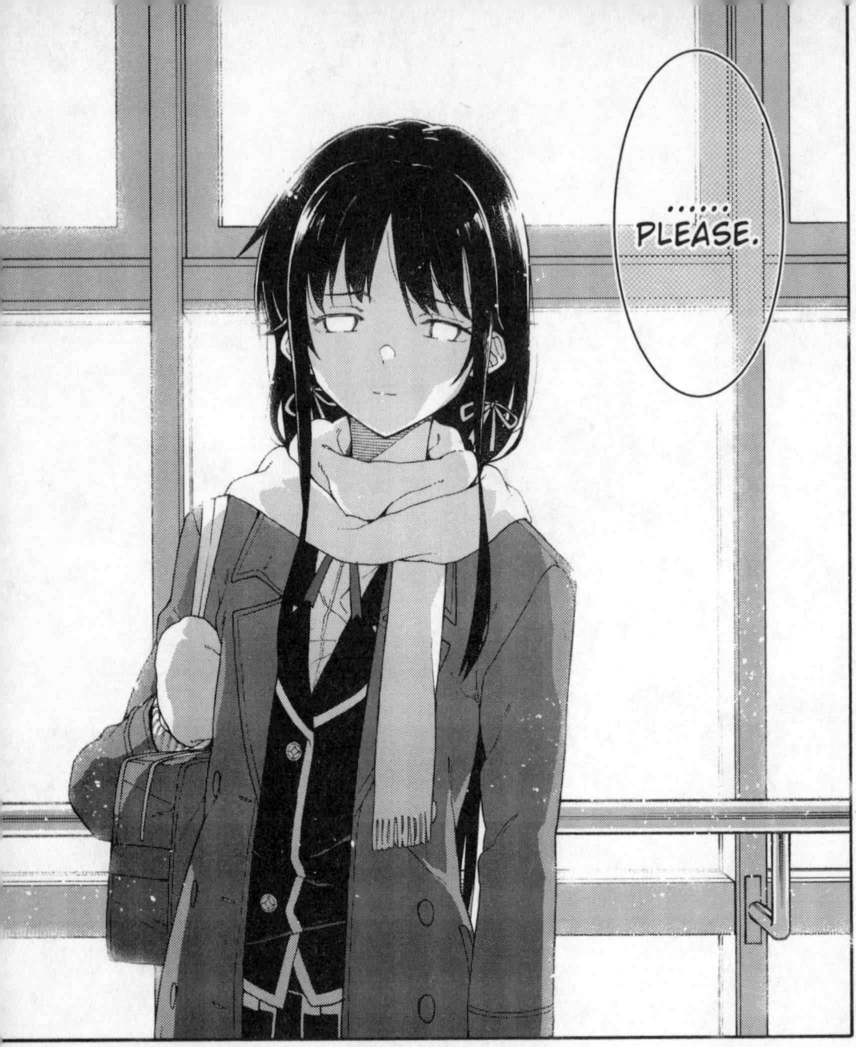
......
PLEASE.
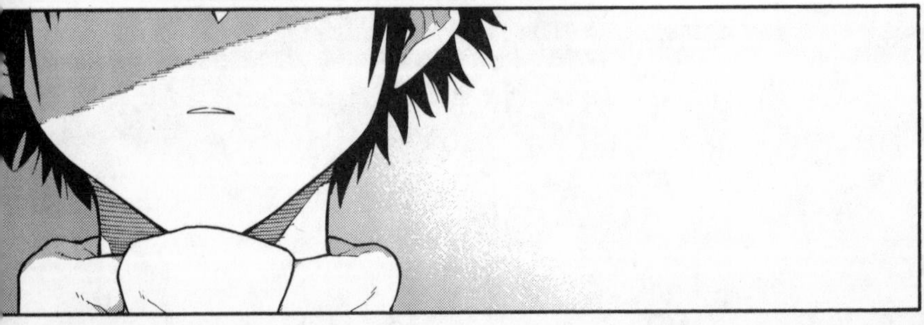

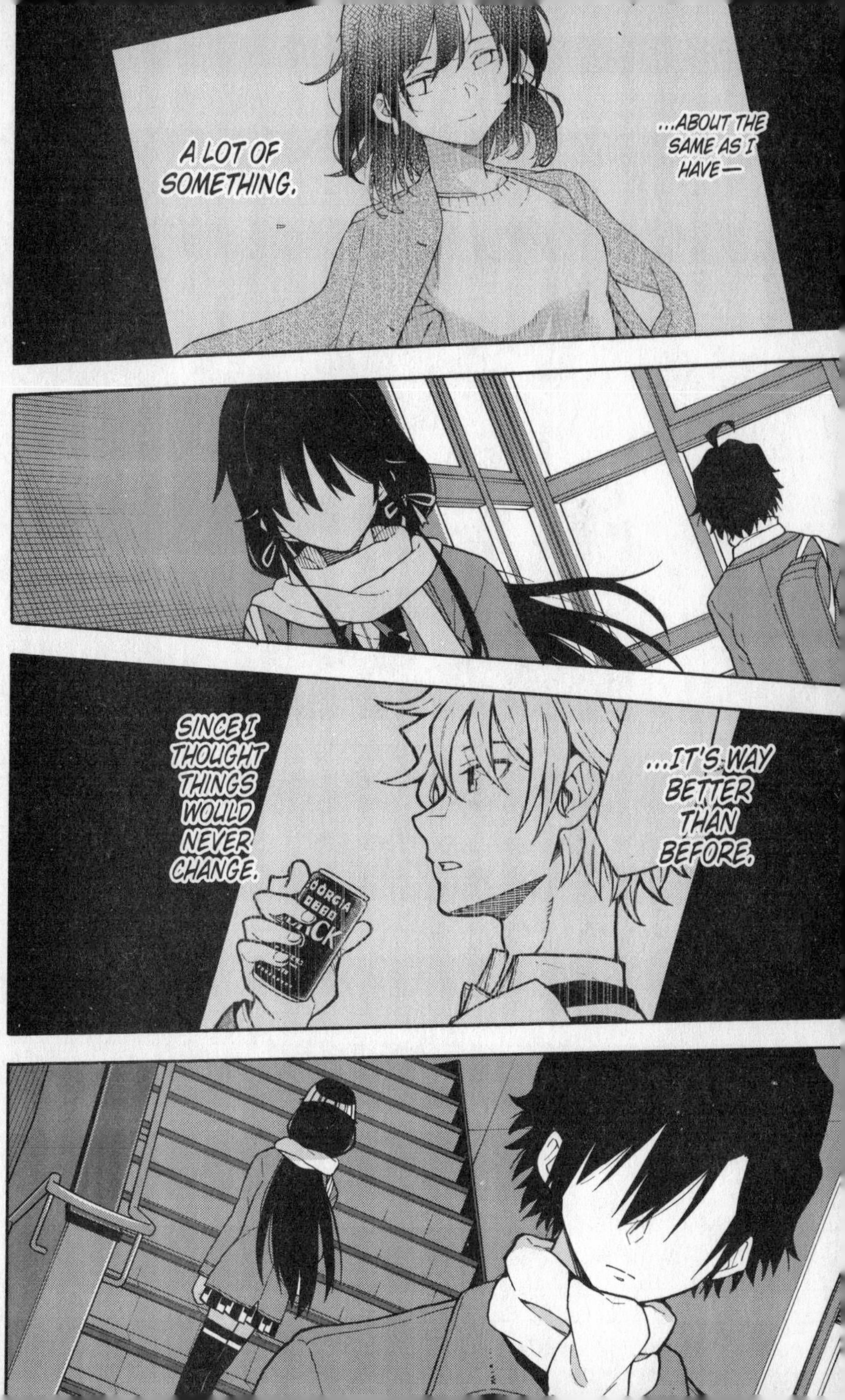
...ABOUT THE SAME AS I HAVE—
A LOT OF SOMETHING.
...IT'S WAY BETTER THAN BEFORE.
SINCE I THOUGHT THINGS WOULD NEVER CHANGE.

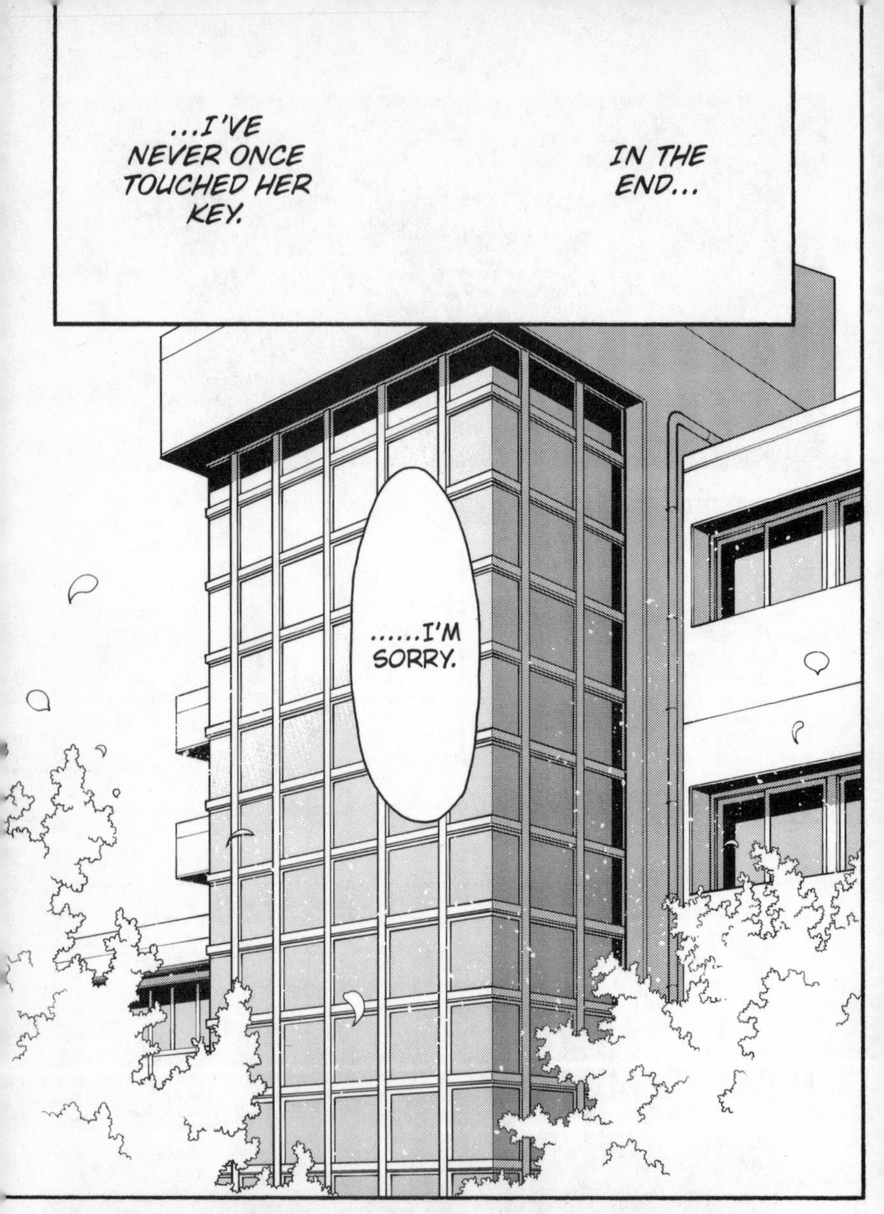
IN THE END...
...I'VE NEVER ONCE TOUCHED HER KEY.
......I'M SORRY.

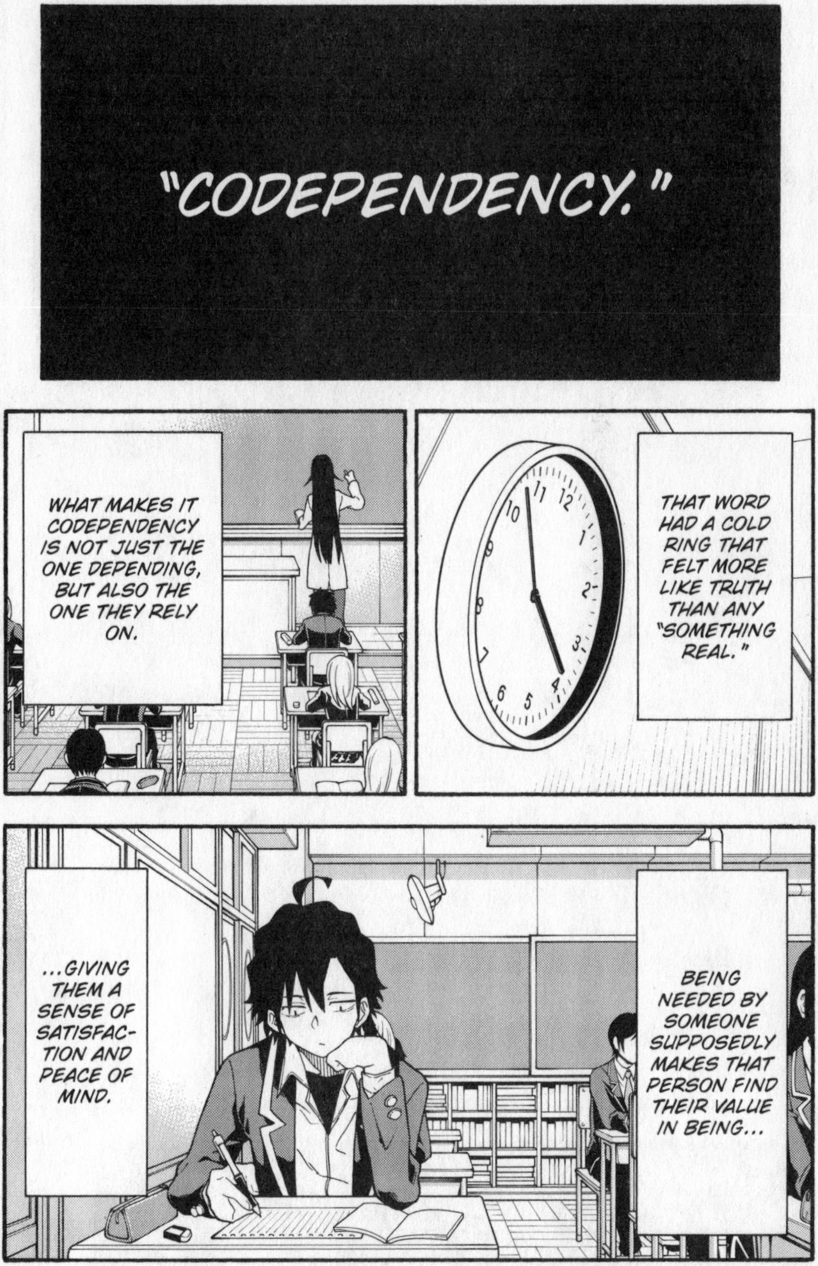
"CODEPENDENCY."
THAT WORD HAD A COLD RING THAT FELT MORE LIKE TRUTH THAN ANY "SOMETHING REAL."
WHAT MAKES IT CODEPENDENCY IS NOT JUST THE ONE DEPENDING, BUT ALSO THE ONE THEY RELY ON.
BEING NEEDED BY SOMEONE SUPPOSEDLY MAKES THAT PERSON FIND THEIR VALUE IN BEING...
...GIVING THEM A SENSE OF SATISFAC-TION AND PEACE OF MIND.

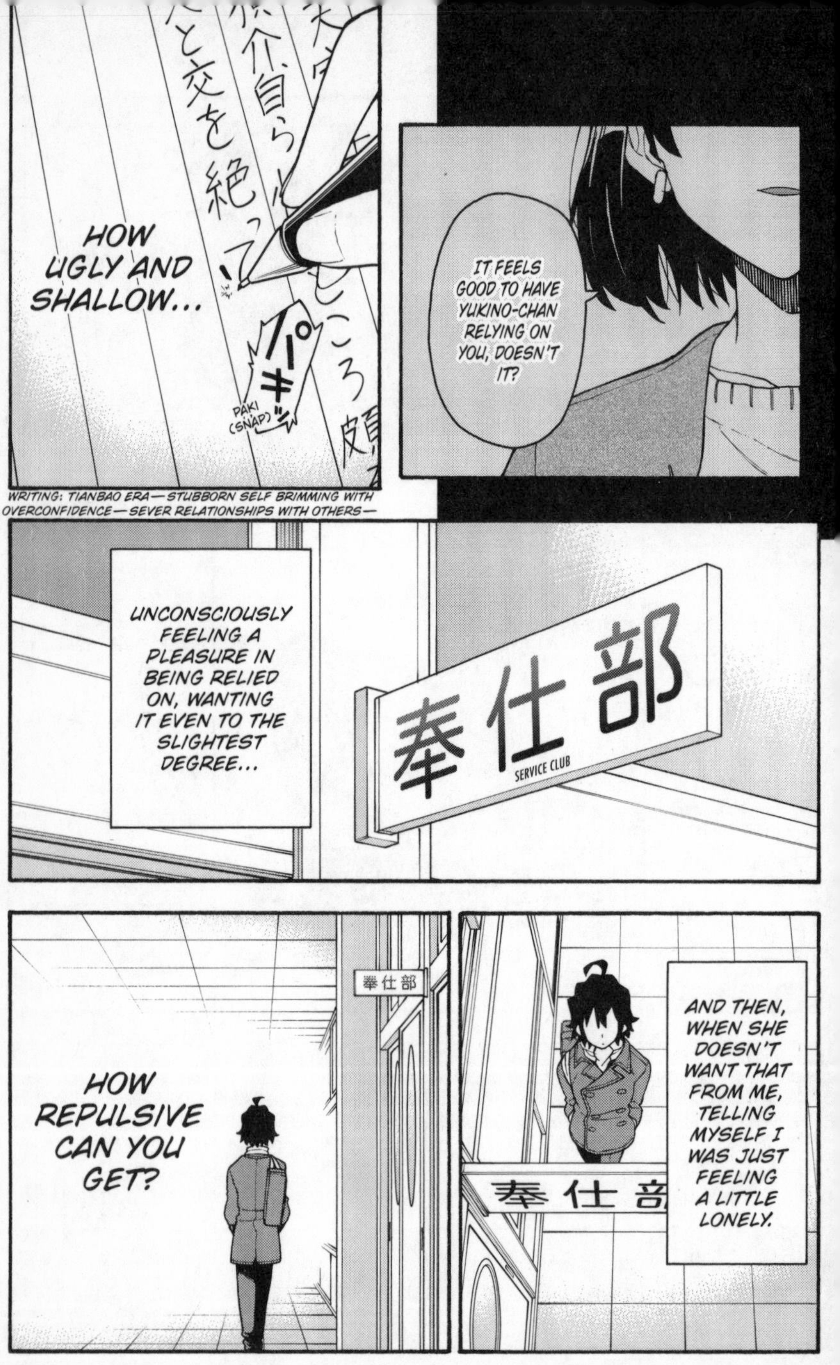
IT FEELS GOOD TO HAVE YUKINO-CHAN RELYING ON YOU, DOESN'T IT?
HOW UGLY AND SHALLOW...
パキッ
PAKI (SNAP)
WRITING: TIANBAO ERA—STUBBORN SELF BRIMMING WITH OVERCONFIDENCE—SEVER RELATIONSHIPS WITH OTHERS—
UNCONSCIOUSLY FEELING A PLEASURE IN BEING RELIED ON, WANTING IT EVEN TO THE SLIGHTEST DEGREE...
奉仕部
SERVICE CLUB
AND THEN, WHEN SHE DOESN'T WANT THAT FROM ME, TELLING MYSELF I WAS JUST FEELING A LITTLE LONELY.
奉仕部
HOW REPULSIVE CAN YOU GET?

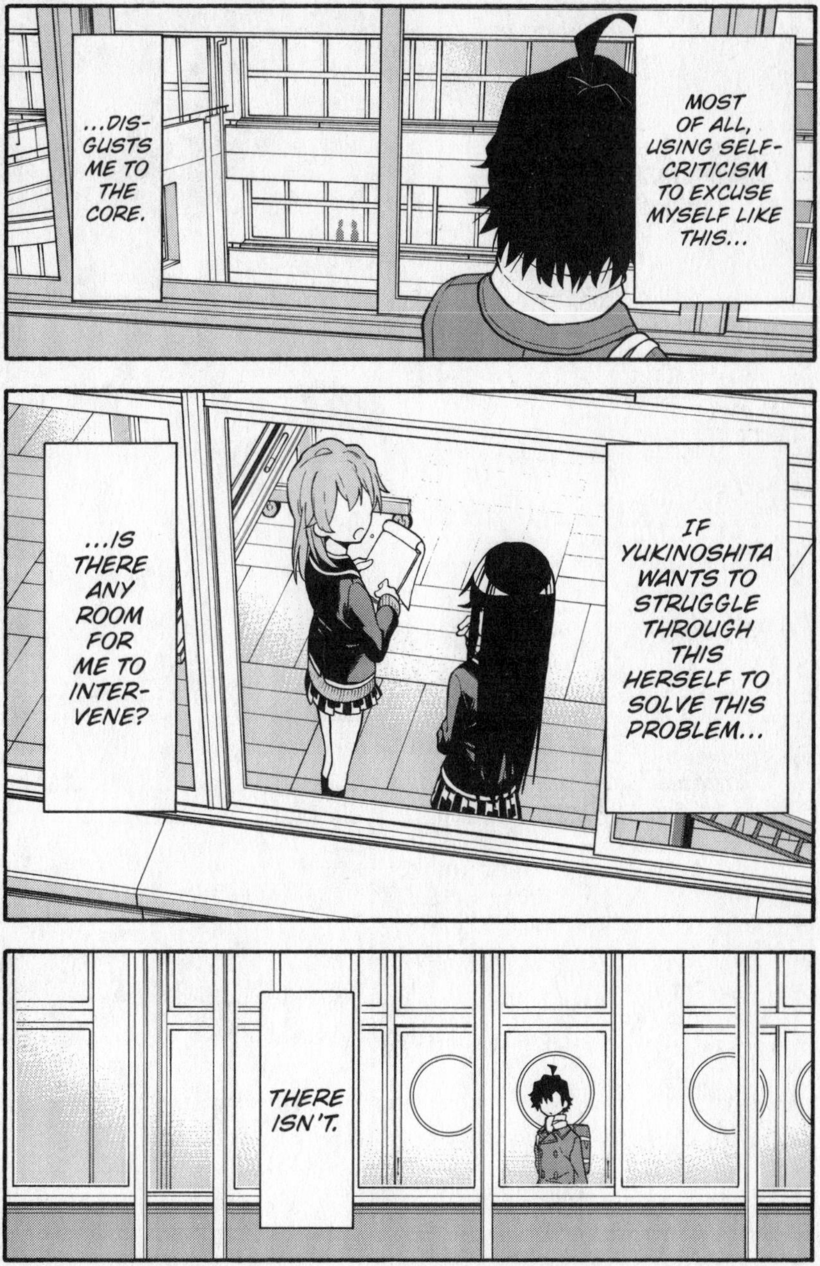
MOST OF ALL, USING SELF-CRITICISM TO EXCUSE MYSELF LIKE THIS...
...DIS-GUSTS ME TO THE CORE.
IF YUKINOSHITA WANTS TO STRUGGLE THROUGH THIS HERSELF TO SOLVE THIS PROBLEM...
...IS THERE ANY ROOM FOR ME TO INTER-VENE?
THERE ISN'T.

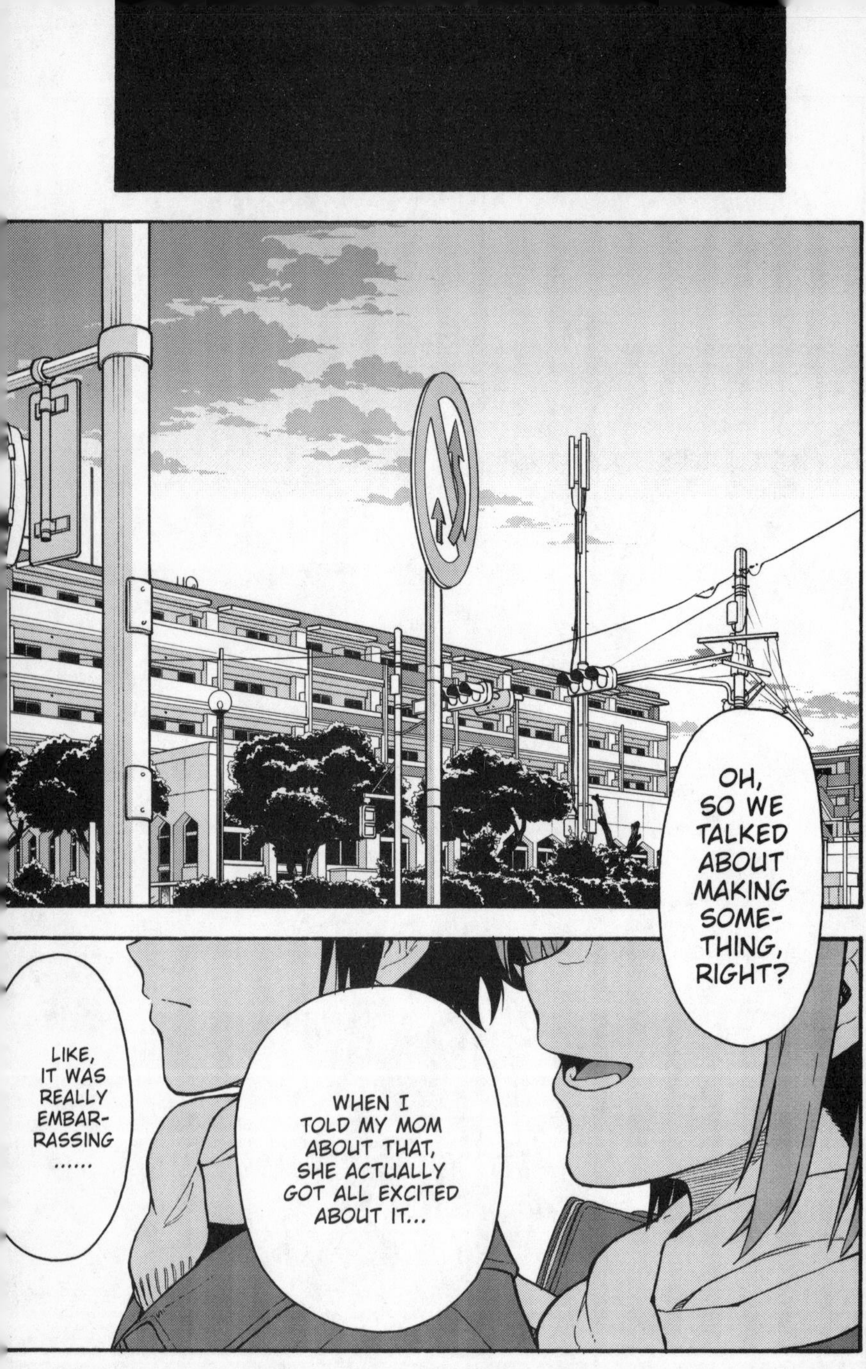
OH, SO WE TALKED ABOUT MAKING SOME-THING, RIGHT?
WHEN I TOLD MY MOM ABOUT THAT, SHE ACTUALLY GOT ALL EXCITED ABOUT IT...
LIKE, IT WAS REALLY EMBAR-RASSING ......

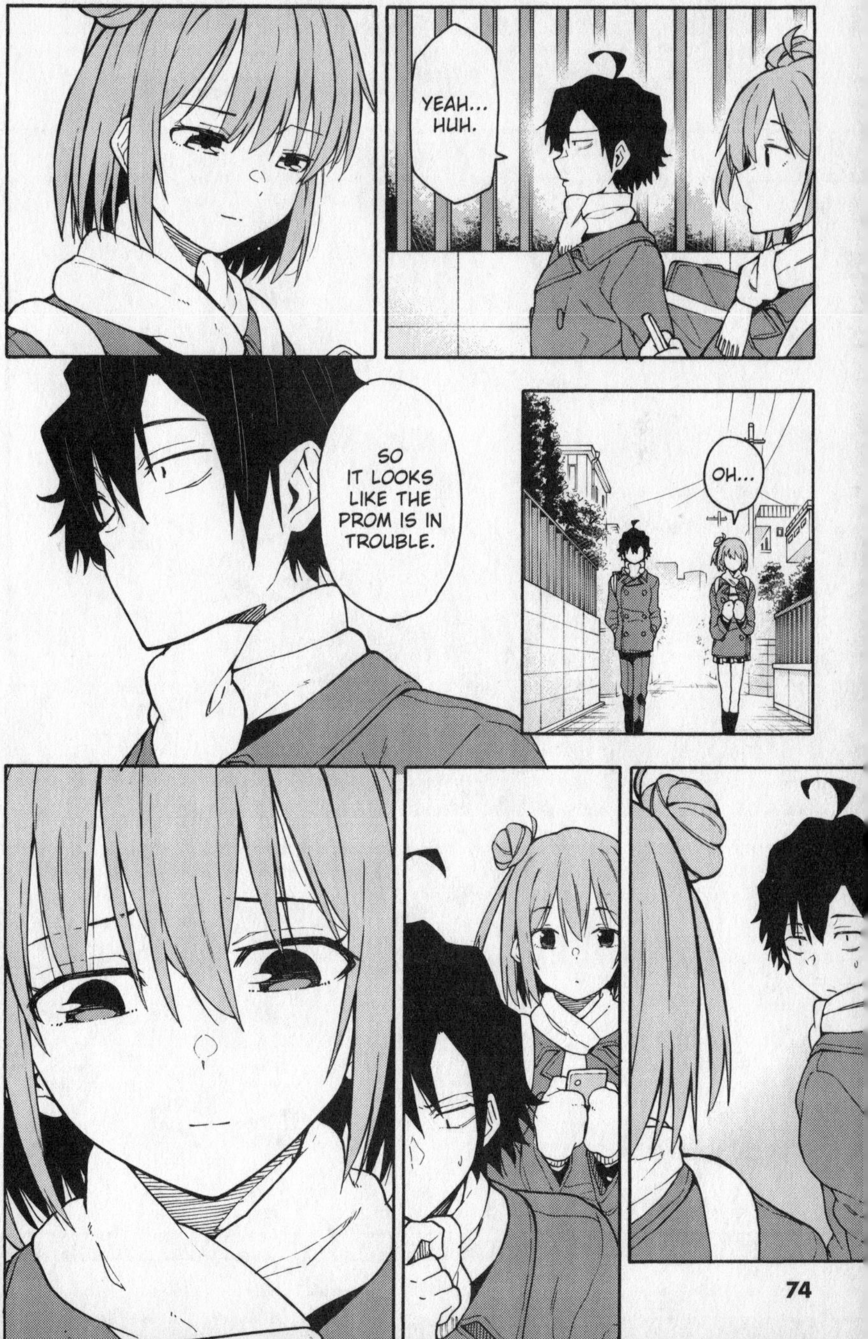
YEAH... HUH.
OH...
SO IT LOOKS LIKE THE PROM IS IN TROUBLE.

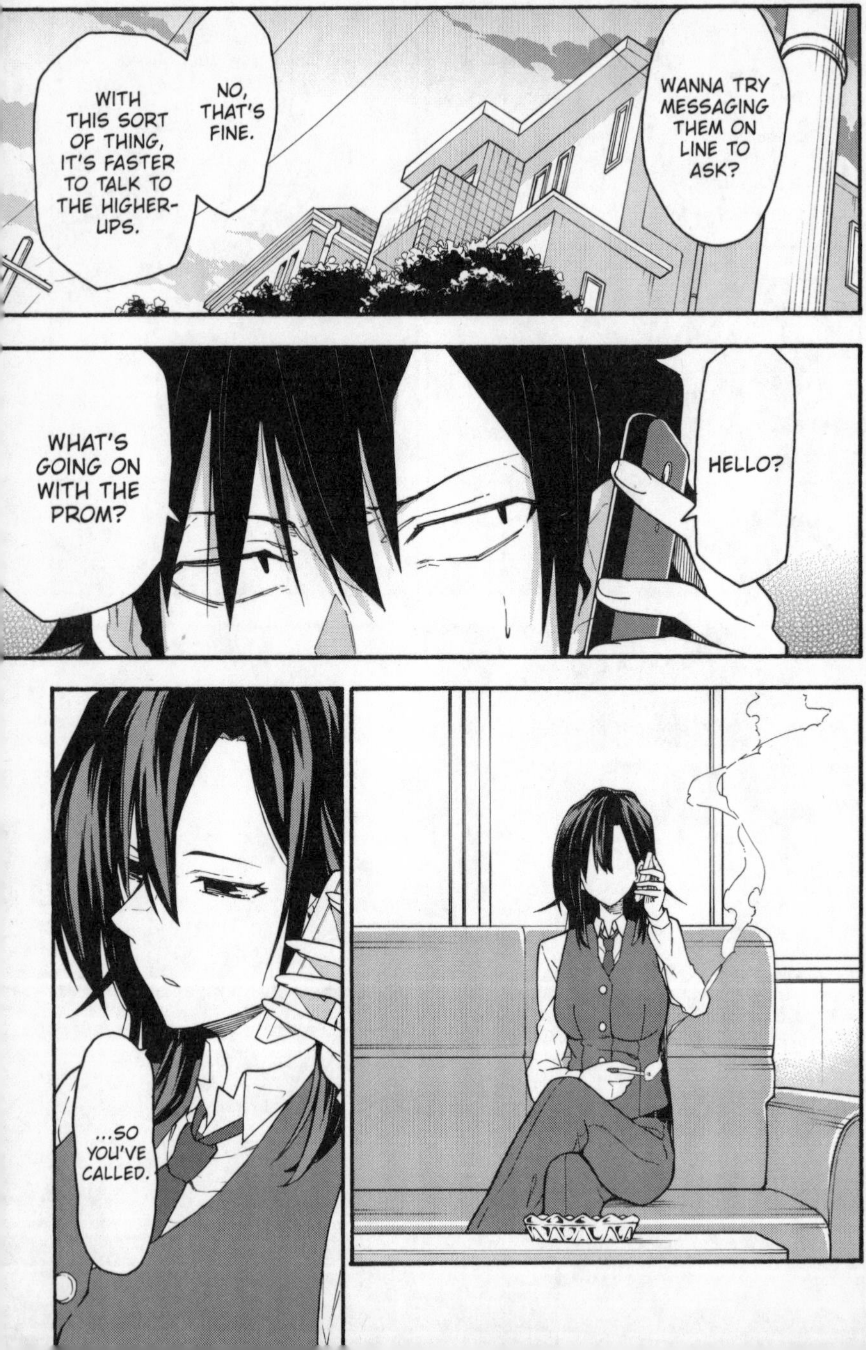
WANNA TRY MESSAGING THEM ON LINE TO ASK?
NO, THAT'S FINE.
WITH THIS SORT OF THING, IT'S FASTER TO TALK TO THE HIGHER-UPS.
HELLO?
WHAT'S GOING ON WITH THE PROM?
...SO YOU'VE CALLED.

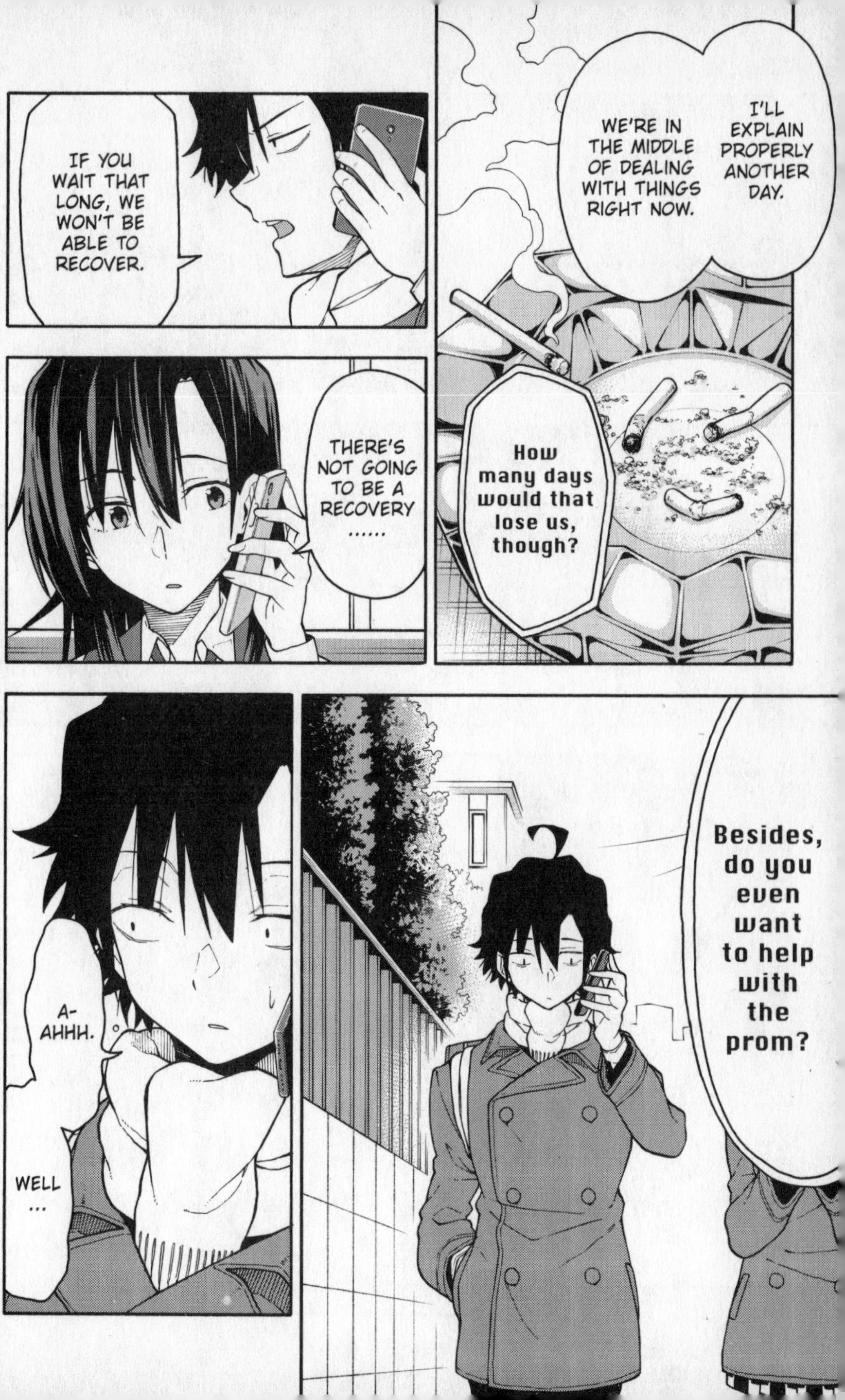
I'LL EXPLAIN PROPERLY ANOTHER DAY.
WE'RE IN THE MIDDLE OF DEALING WITH THINGS RIGHT NOW.
How many days would that lose us, though?
IF YOU WAIT THAT LONG, WE WON'T BE ABLE TO RECOVER.
THERE'S NOT GOING TO BE A RECOVERY ......
Besides, do you even want to help with the prom?
A-AHHH.
WELL ...

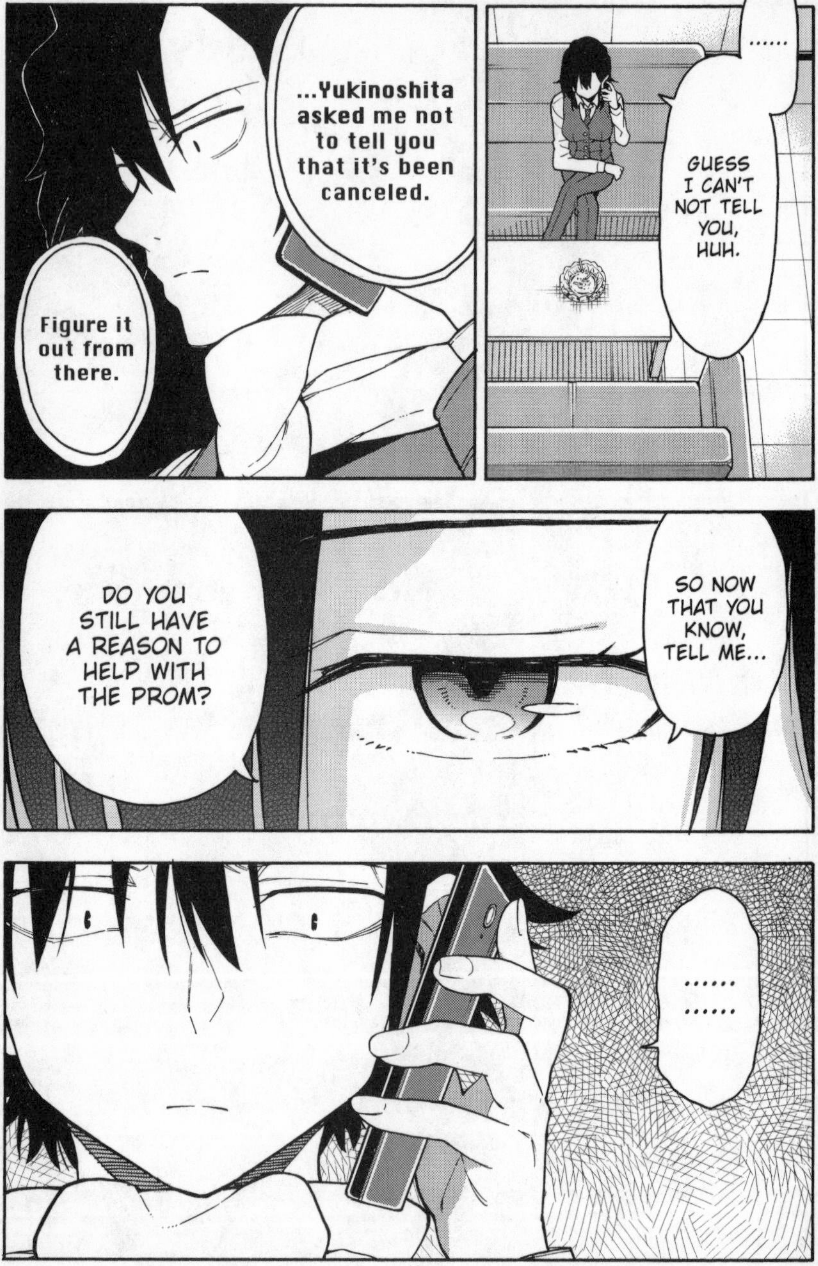
......
GUESS I CAN'T NOT TELL YOU, HUH.
...Yukinoshita asked me not to tell you that it's been canceled.
Figure it out from there.
SO NOW THAT YOU KNOW, TELL ME...
DO YOU STILL HAVE A REASON TO HELP WITH THE PROM?
......
......

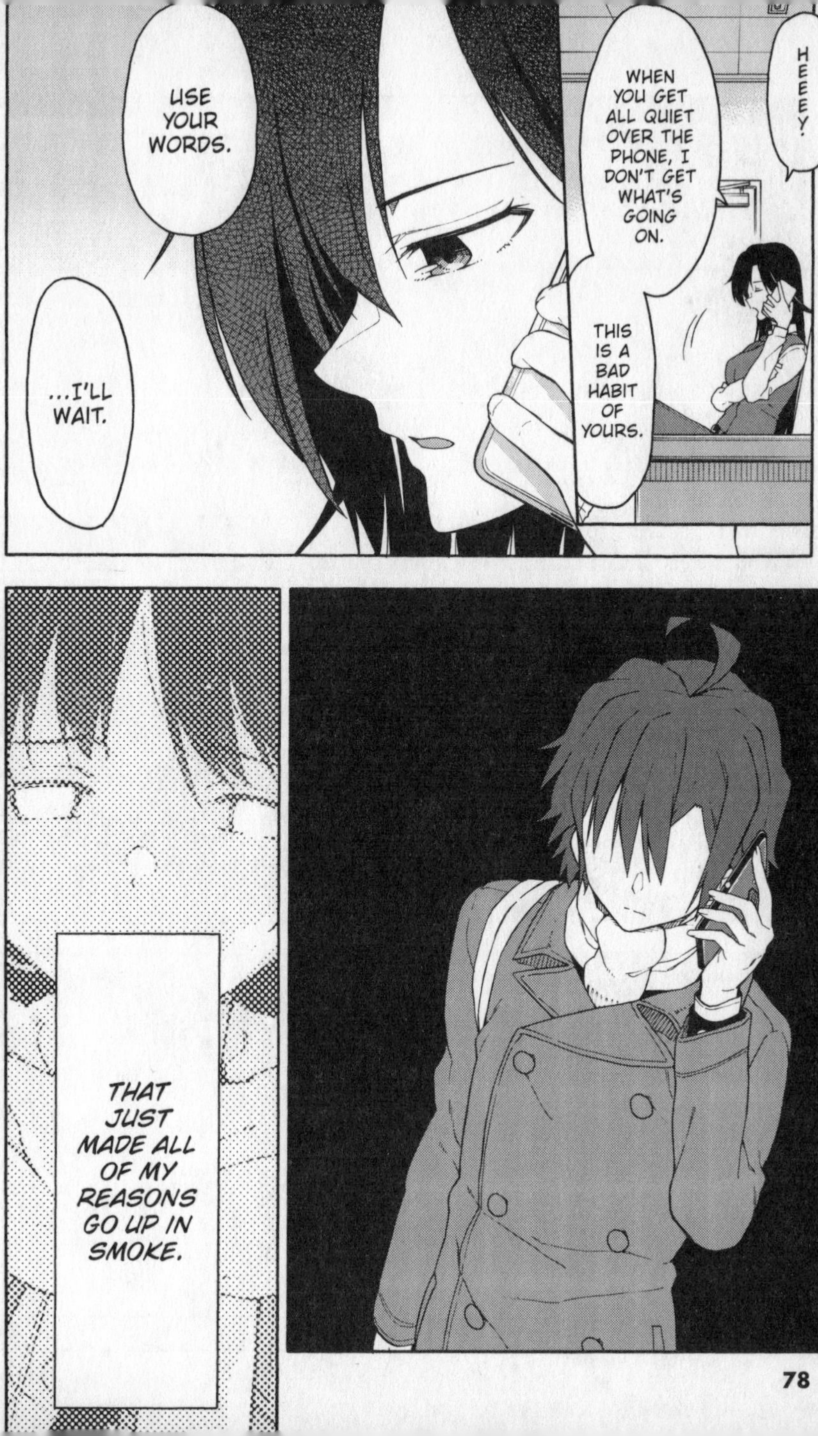
HEEEY.
WHEN YOU GET ALL QUIET OVER THE PHONE, I DON'T GET WHAT'S GOING ON.
THIS IS A BAD HABIT OF YOURS.
USE YOUR WORDS.
...I'LL WAIT.
THAT JUST MADE ALL OF MY REASONS GO UP IN SMOKE.

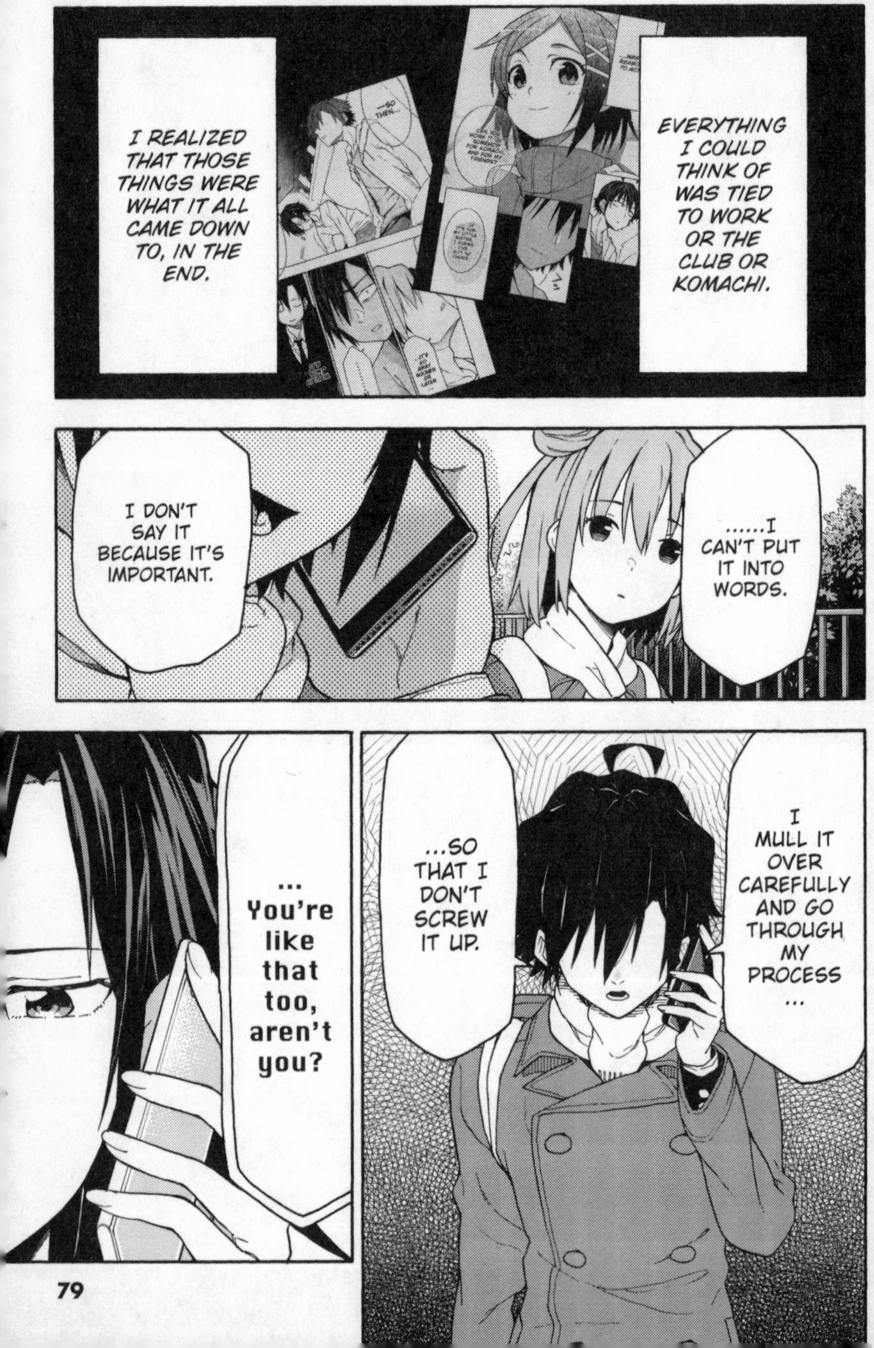
EVERYTHING I COULD THINK OF WAS TIED TO WORK OR THE CLUB OR KOMACHI.
I REALIZED THAT THOSE THINGS WERE WHAT IT ALL CAME DOWN TO, IN THE END.
......I CAN'T PUT IT INTO WORDS.
I DON'T SAY IT BECAUSE IT'S IMPORTANT.
I MULL IT OVER CAREFULLY AND GO THROUGH MY PROCESS ...
...SO THAT I DON'T SCREW IT UP.
... You're like that too, aren't you?

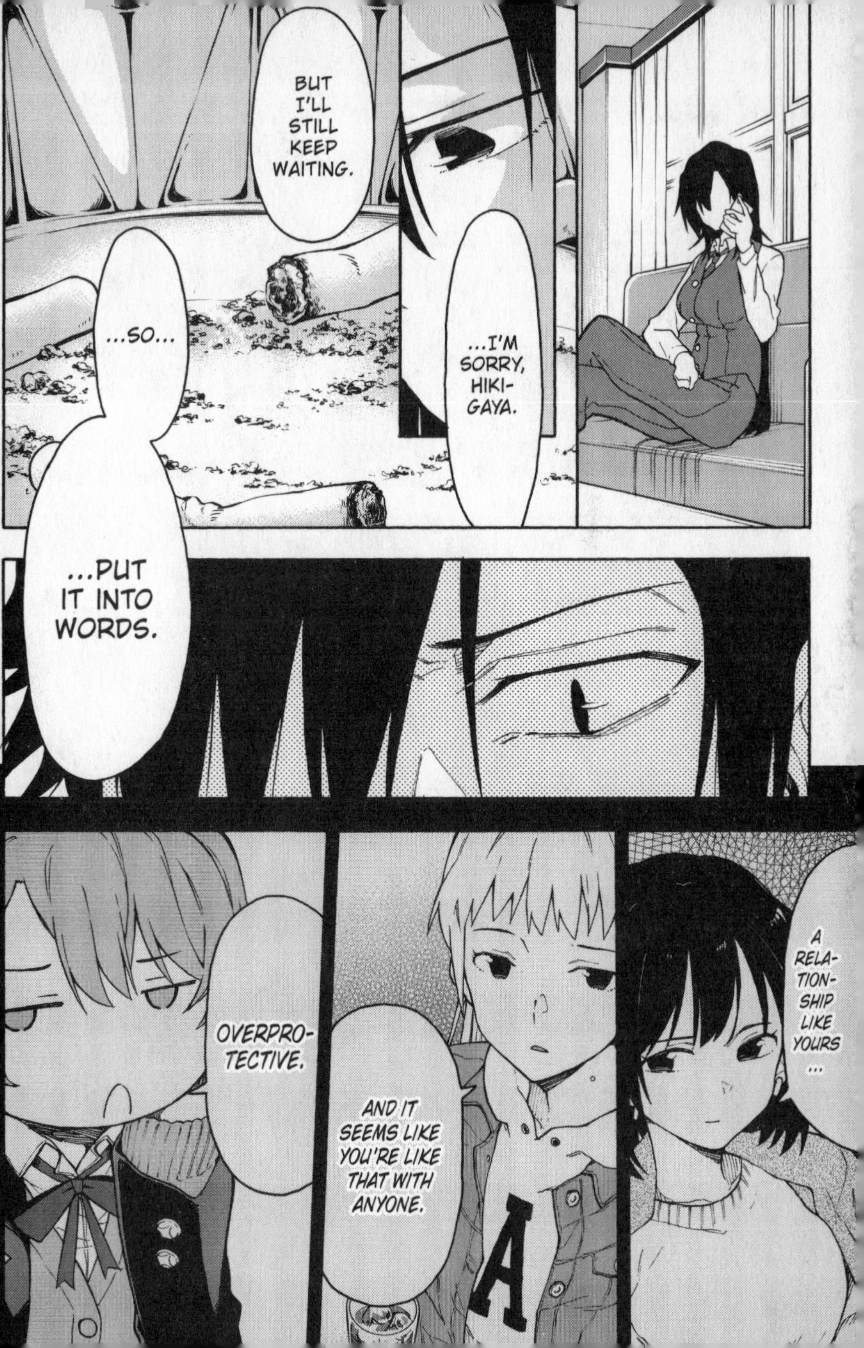

...I'M SORRY, HIKIGAYA.
BUT I'LL STILL KEEP WAITING.
...SO...
...PUT IT INTO WORDS.
A RELATIONSHIP LIKE YOURS...
OVERPROTECTIVE.
AND IT SEEMS LIKE YOU'RE LIKE THAT WITH ANYONE.

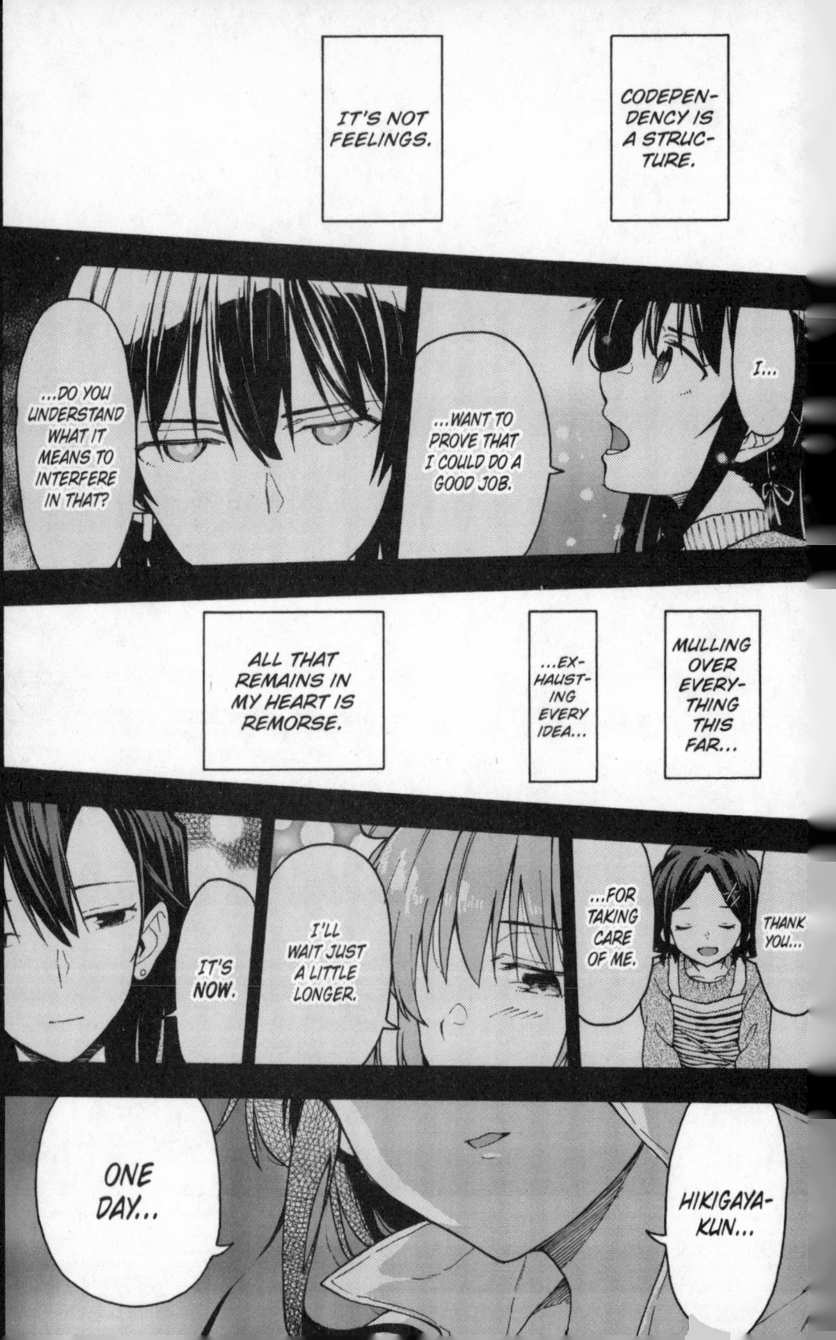
CODEPENDENCY IS A STRUCTURE.
IT'S NOT FEELINGS.
I...
...WANT TO PROVE THAT I COULD DO A GOOD JOB.
...DO YOU UNDERSTAND WHAT IT MEANS TO INTERFERE IN THAT?
MULLING OVER EVERYTHING THIS FAR...
...EXHAUSTING EVERY IDEA...
ALL THAT REMAINS IN MY HEART IS REMORSE.
THANK YOU...
...FOR TAKING CARE OF ME.
I'LL WAIT JUST A LITTLE LONGER.
IT'S NOW.
HIKIGAYA-KUN...
ONE DAY...

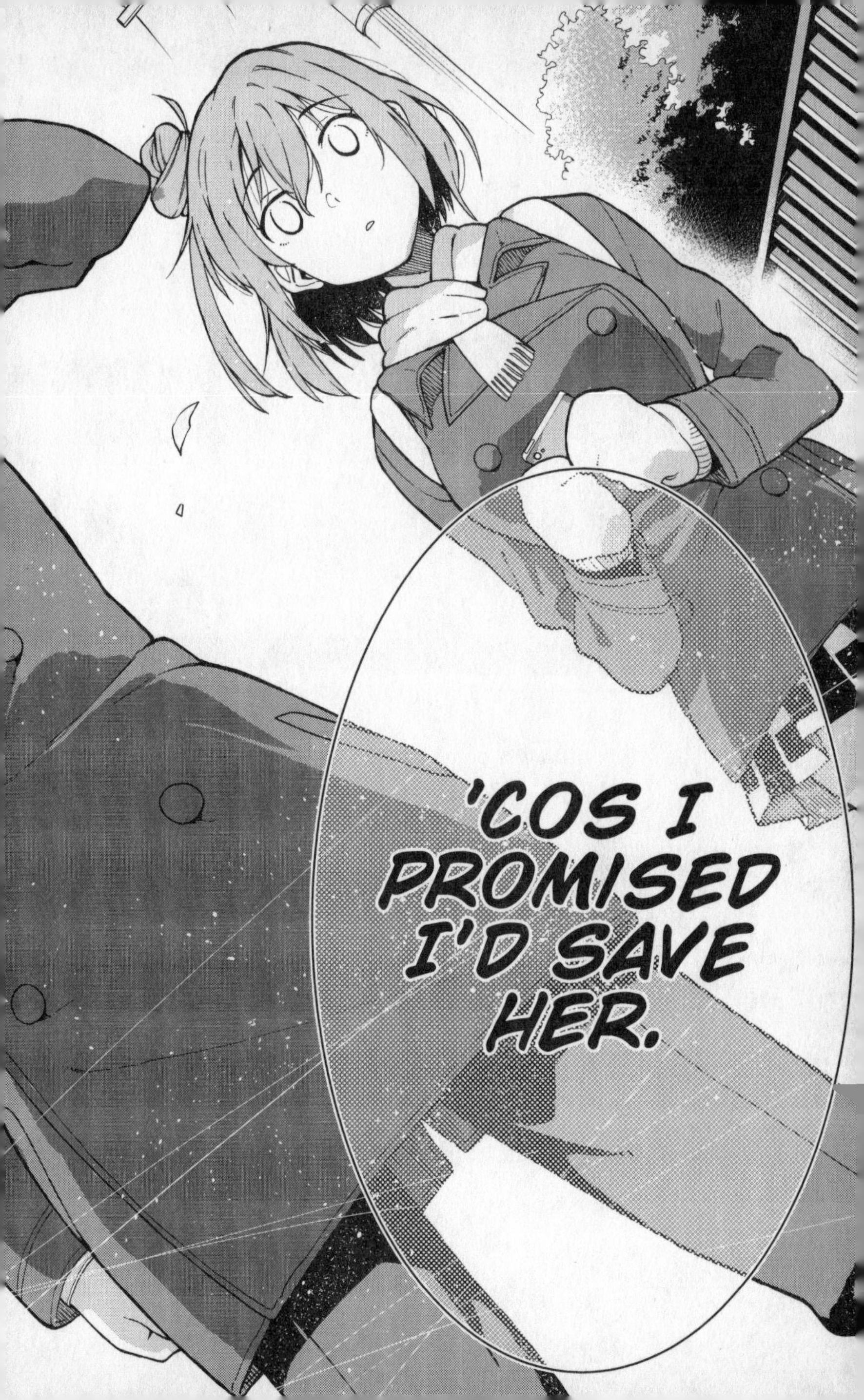
'COS I PROMISED I'D SAVE HER.

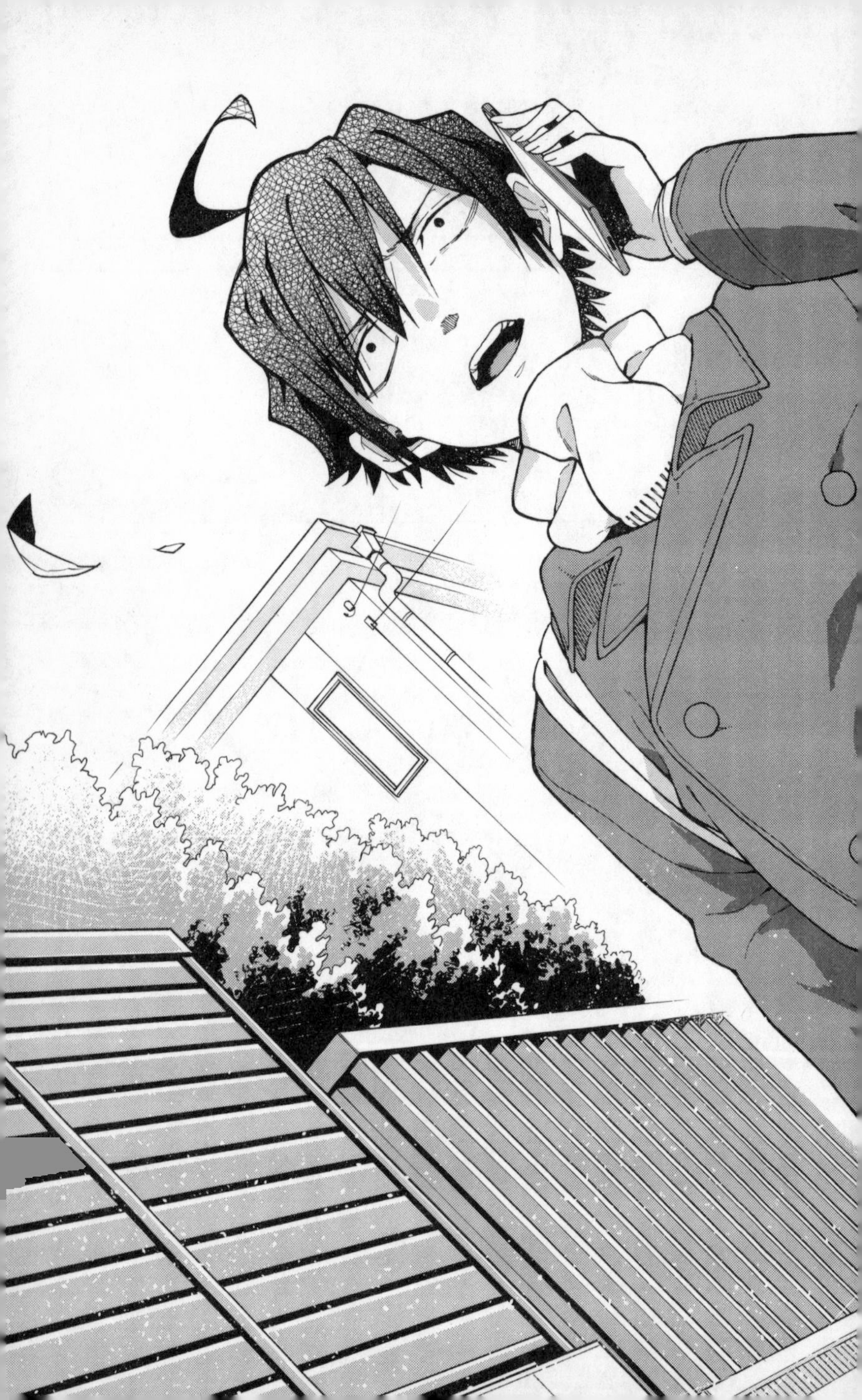

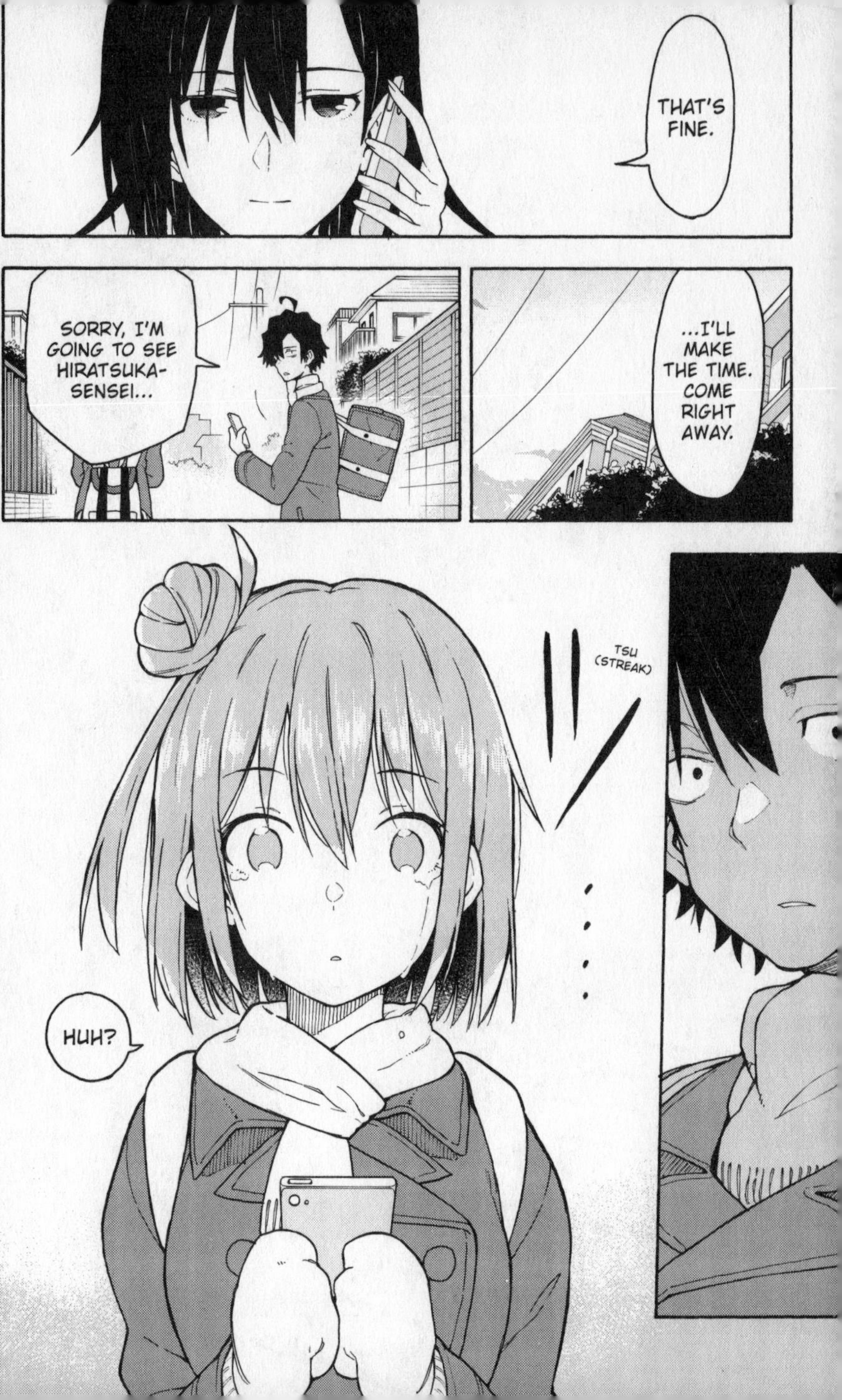
THAT'S FINE.
...I'LL MAKE THE TIME. COME RIGHT AWAY.
SORRY, I'M GOING TO SEE HIRATSUKA-SENSEI...
TSU (STREAK)
....
HUH?

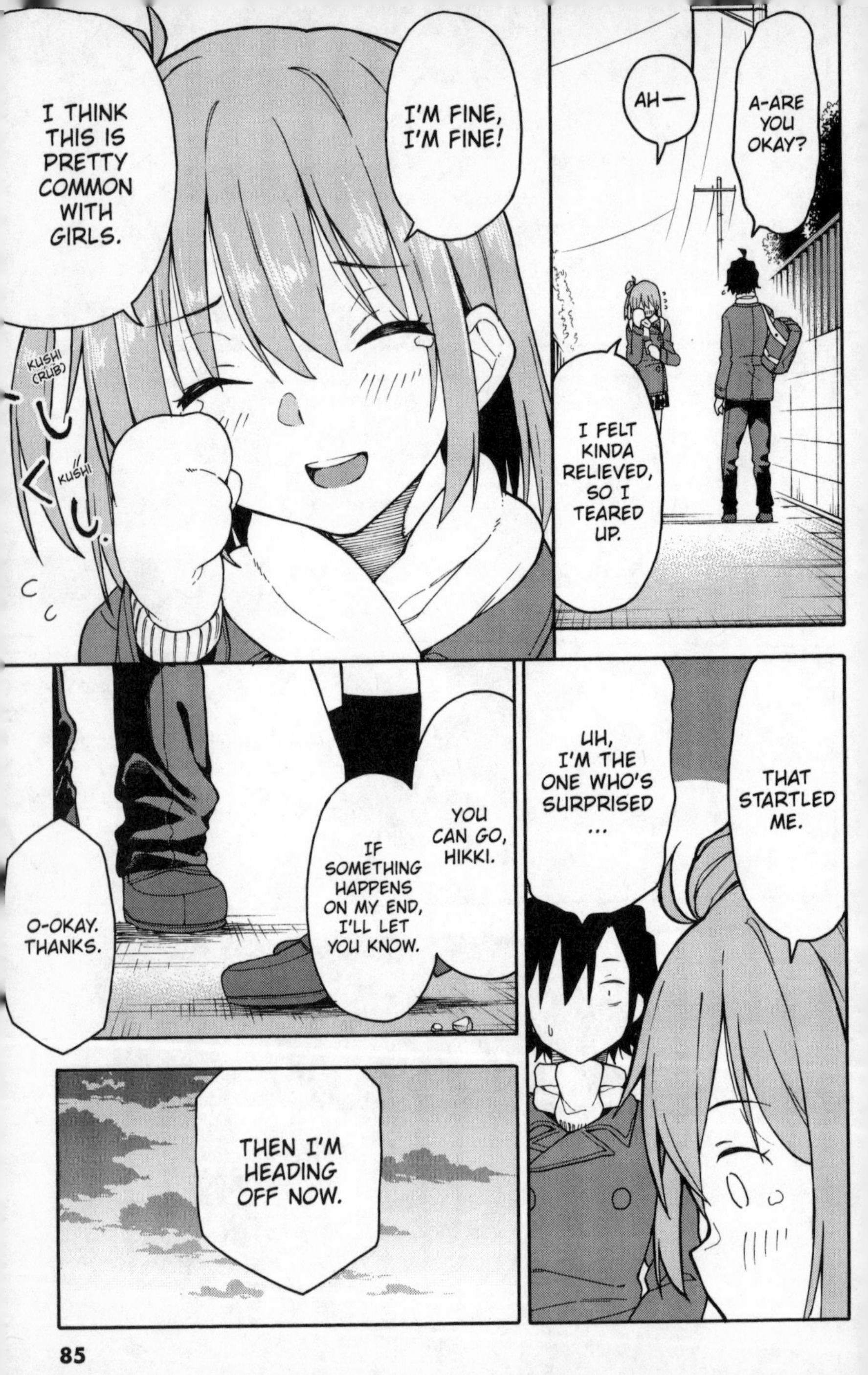
A-ARE YOU OKAY?
AH—
I FELT KINDA RELIEVED, SO I TEARED UP.
I'M FINE, I'M FINE!
I THINK THIS IS PRETTY COMMON WITH GIRLS.
KUSHI (RUB)
KUSHI
THAT STARTLED ME.
UH, I'M THE ONE WHO'S SURPRISED ...
YOU CAN GO, HIKKI.
IF SOMETHING HAPPENS ON MY END, I'LL LET YOU KNOW.
O-OKAY. THANKS.
THEN I'M HEADING OFF NOW.

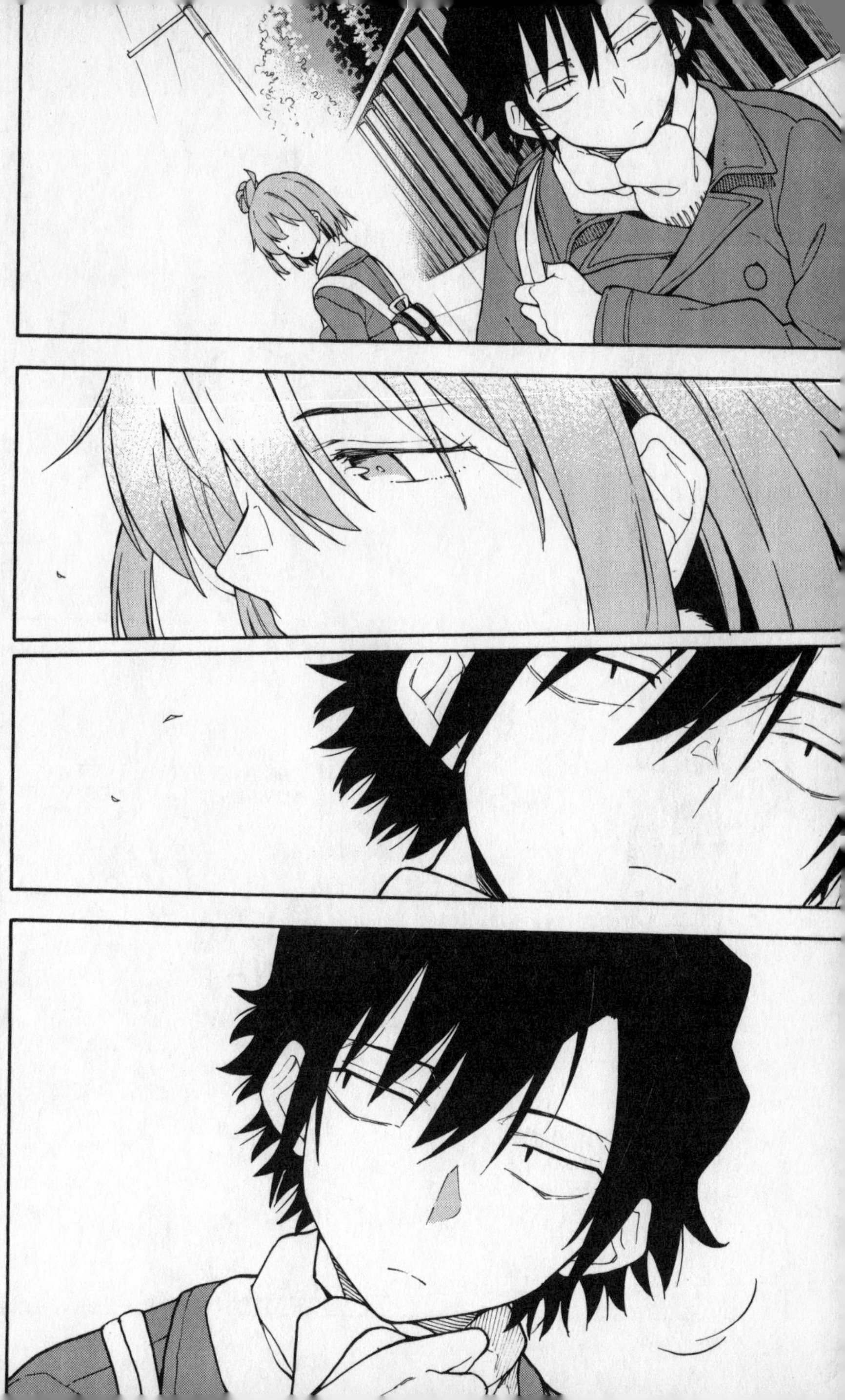

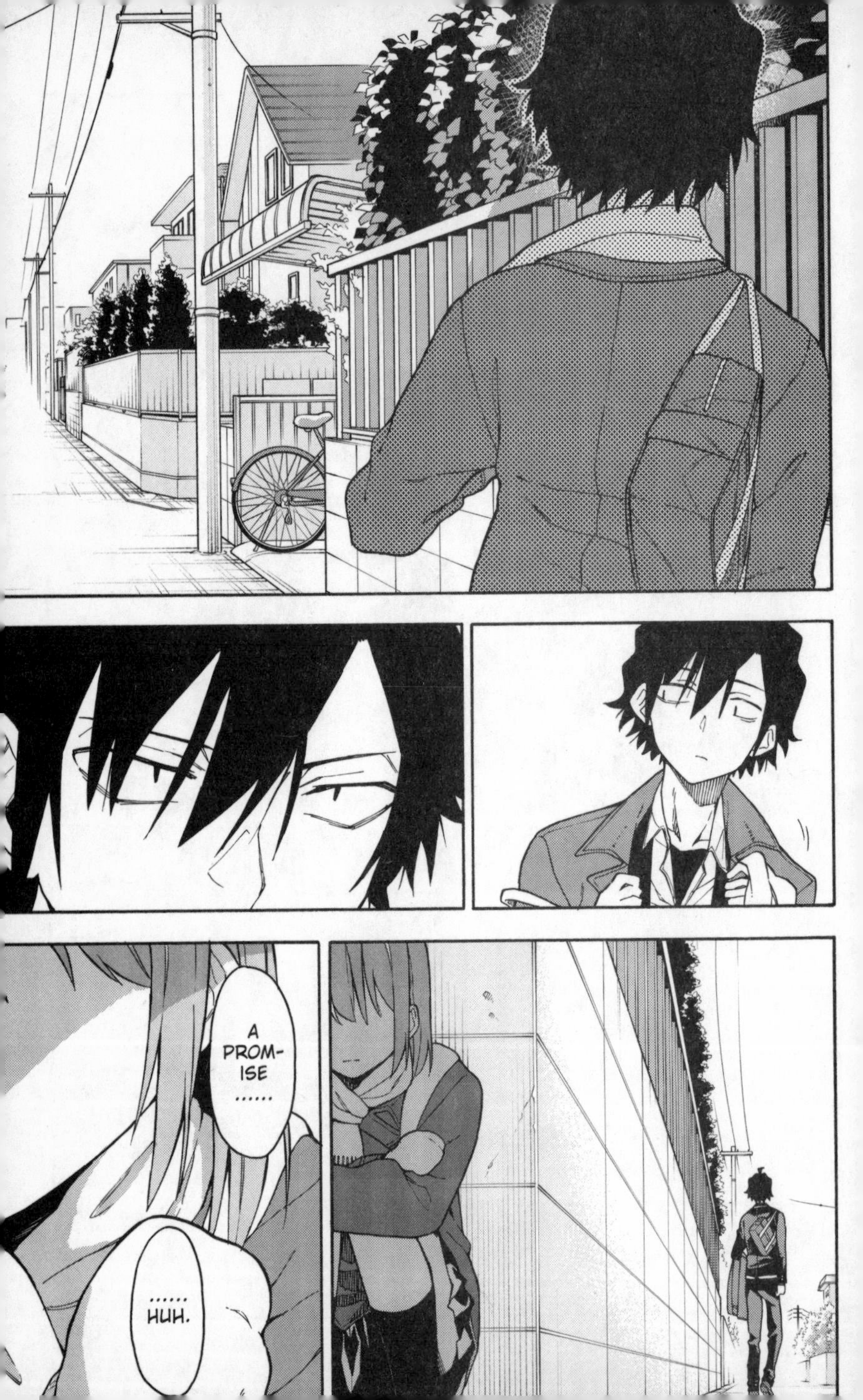
A PROMISE......
......HUH.

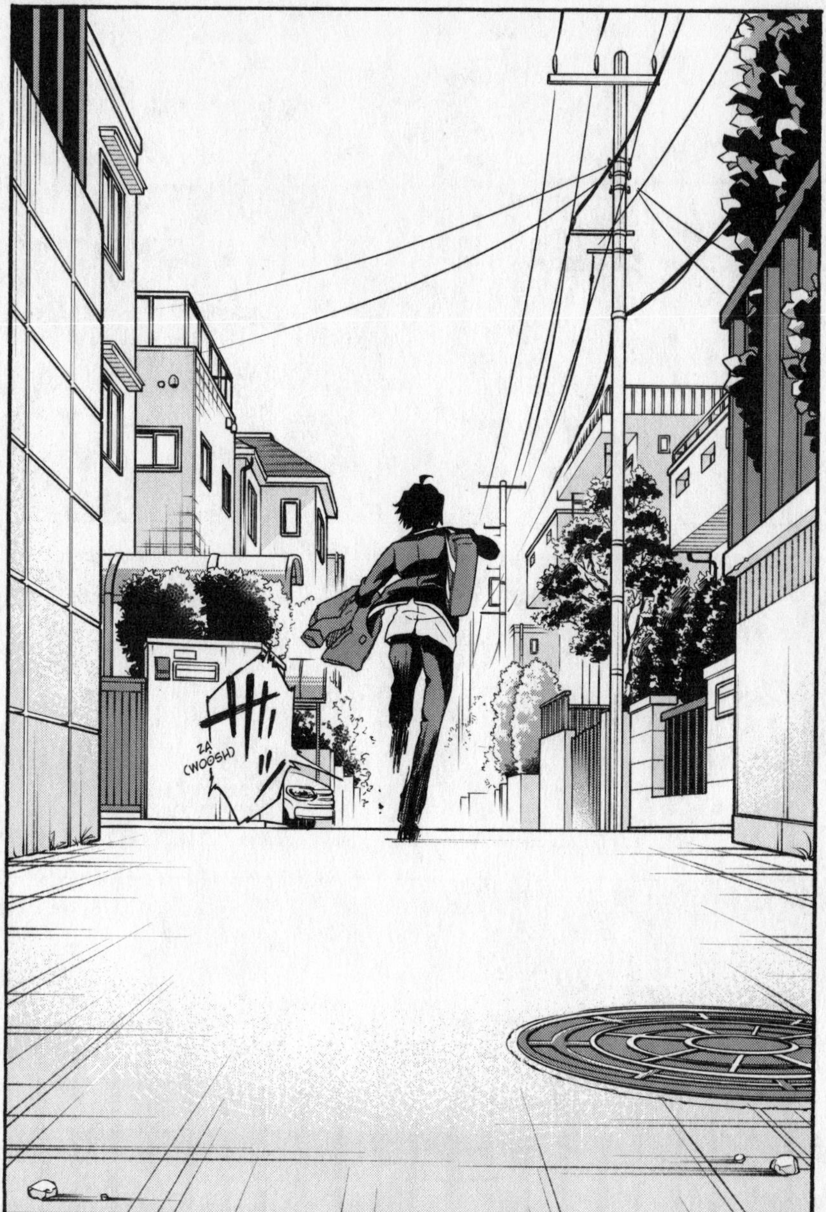
ZA
(WOOSH)

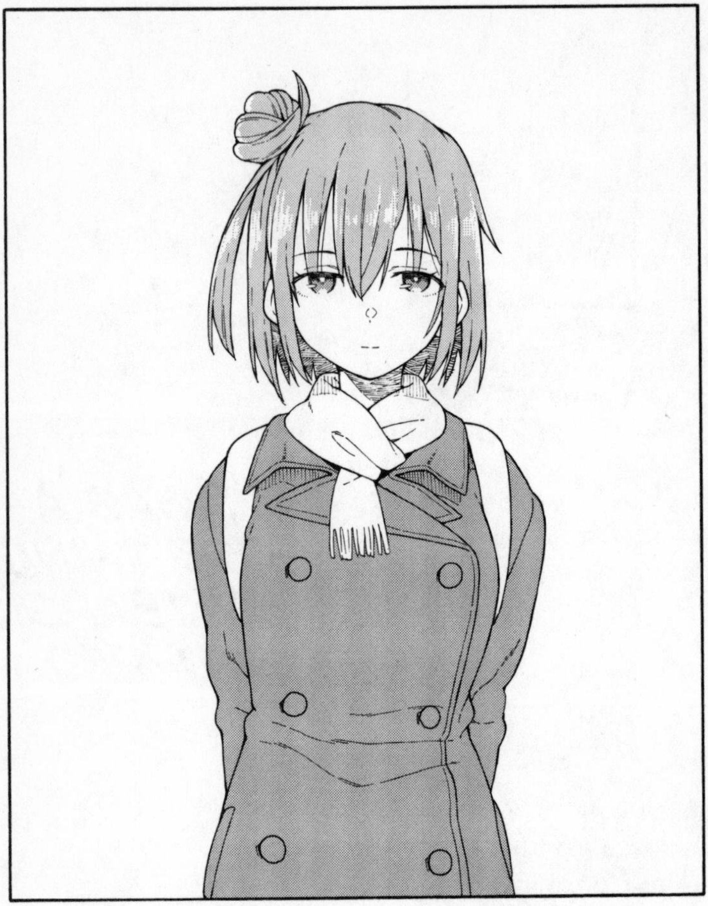

CHAPTER 94.5 ··· INTERLUDE YUI YUIGAHAMA.

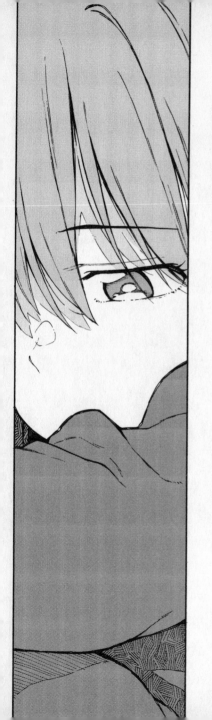

IT WAS A
GOOD THING
MY TEARS
STOPPED.

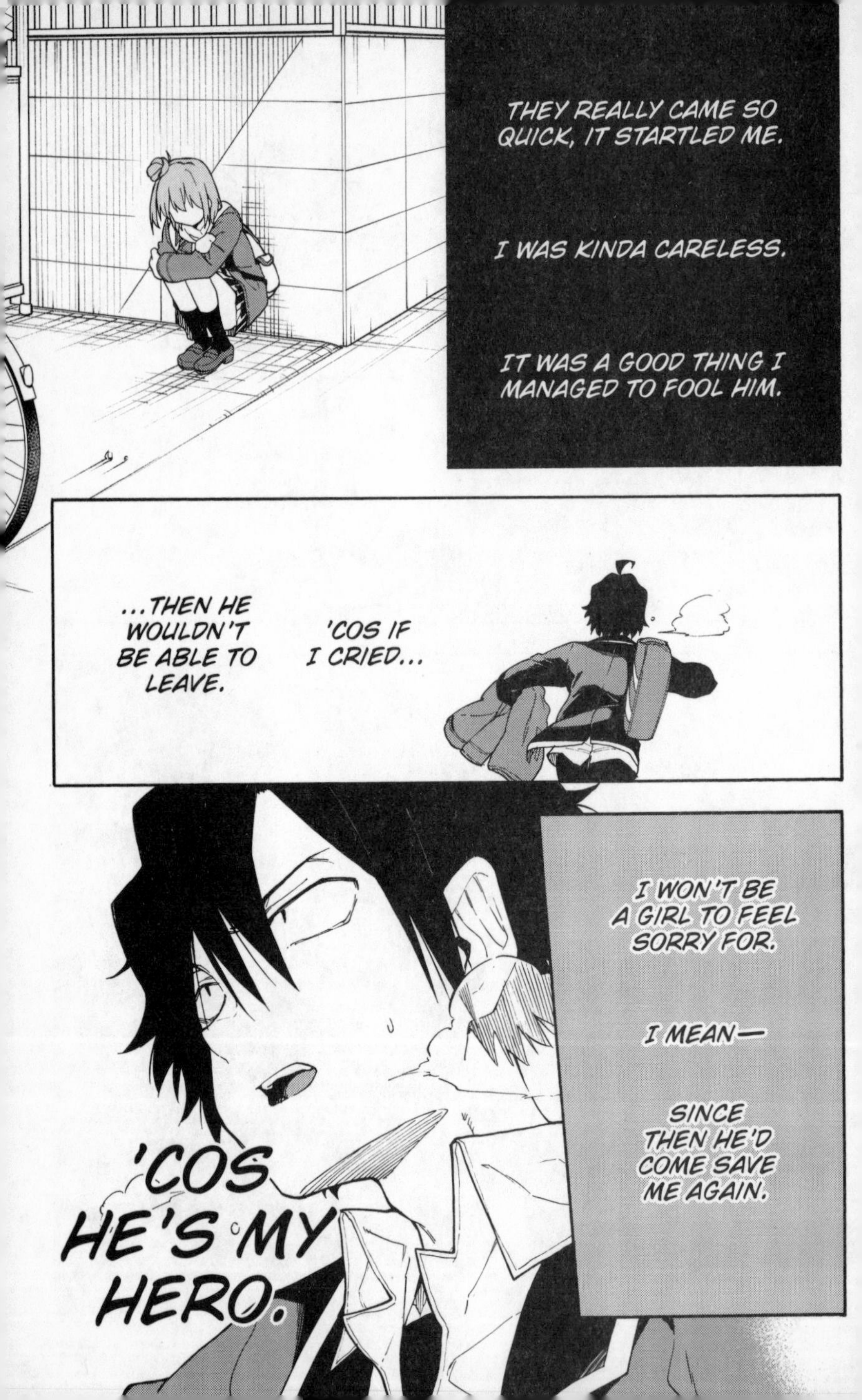
THEY REALLY CAME SO QUICK, IT STARTLED ME.
I WAS KINDA CARELESS.
IT WAS A GOOD THING I MANAGED TO FOOL HIM.
'COS IF I CRIED...
...THEN HE WOULDN'T BE ABLE TO LEAVE.
I WON'T BE A GIRL TO FEEL SORRY FOR.
I MEAN—
SINCE THEN HE'D COME SAVE ME AGAIN.
'COS HE'S MY HERO.

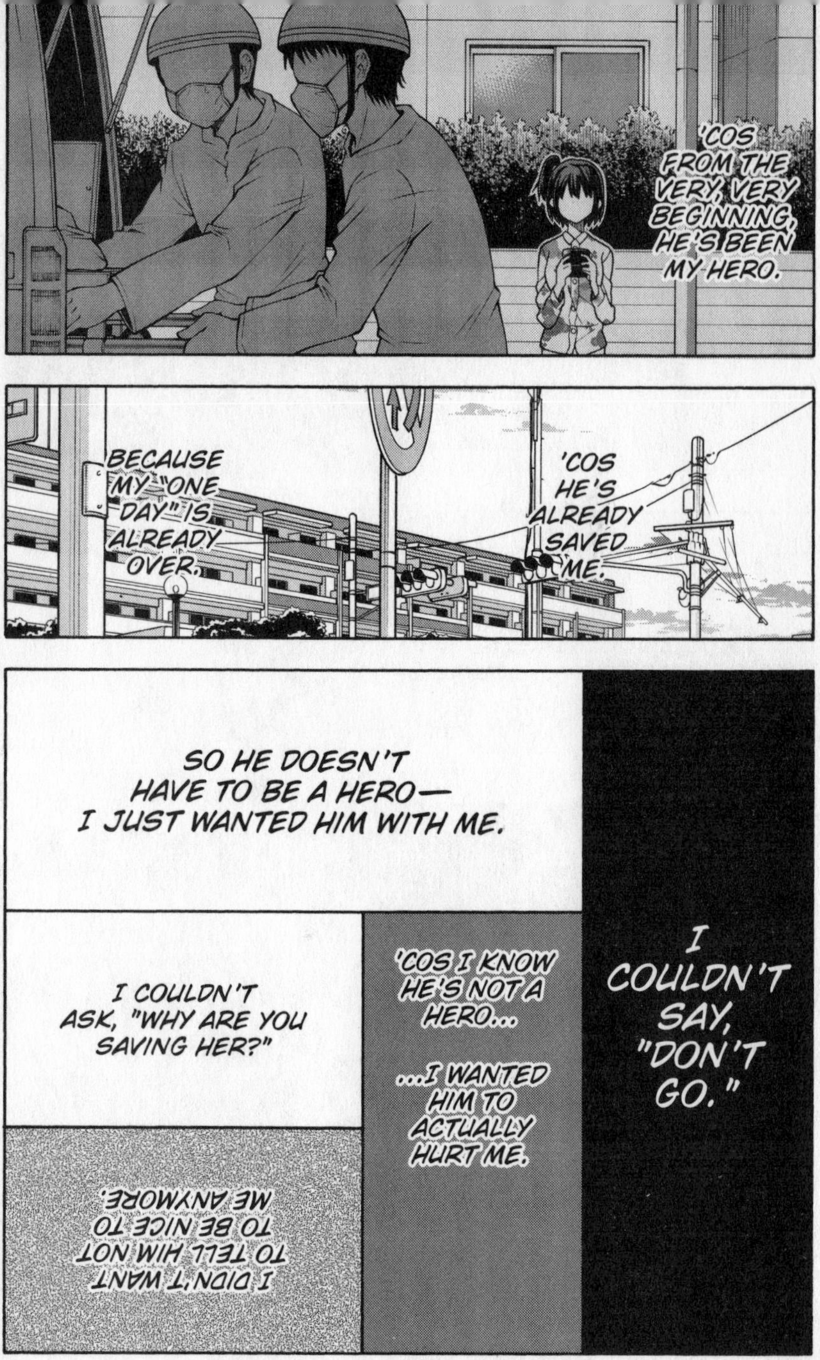
'COS FROM THE VERY, VERY BEGINNING, HE'S BEEN MY HERO.
'COS HE'S ALREADY SAVED ME.
BECAUSE MY "ONE DAY" IS ALREADY OVER.
I COULDN'T SAY, "DON'T GO."
SO HE DOESN'T HAVE TO BE A HERO— I JUST WANTED HIM WITH ME.
'COS I KNOW HE'S NOT A HERO...
...I WANTED HIM TO ACTUALLY HURT ME.
I COULDN'T ASK, "WHY ARE YOU SAVING HER?"
I DIDN'T WANT TO TELL HIM NOT TO BE NICE TO ME ANYMORE.

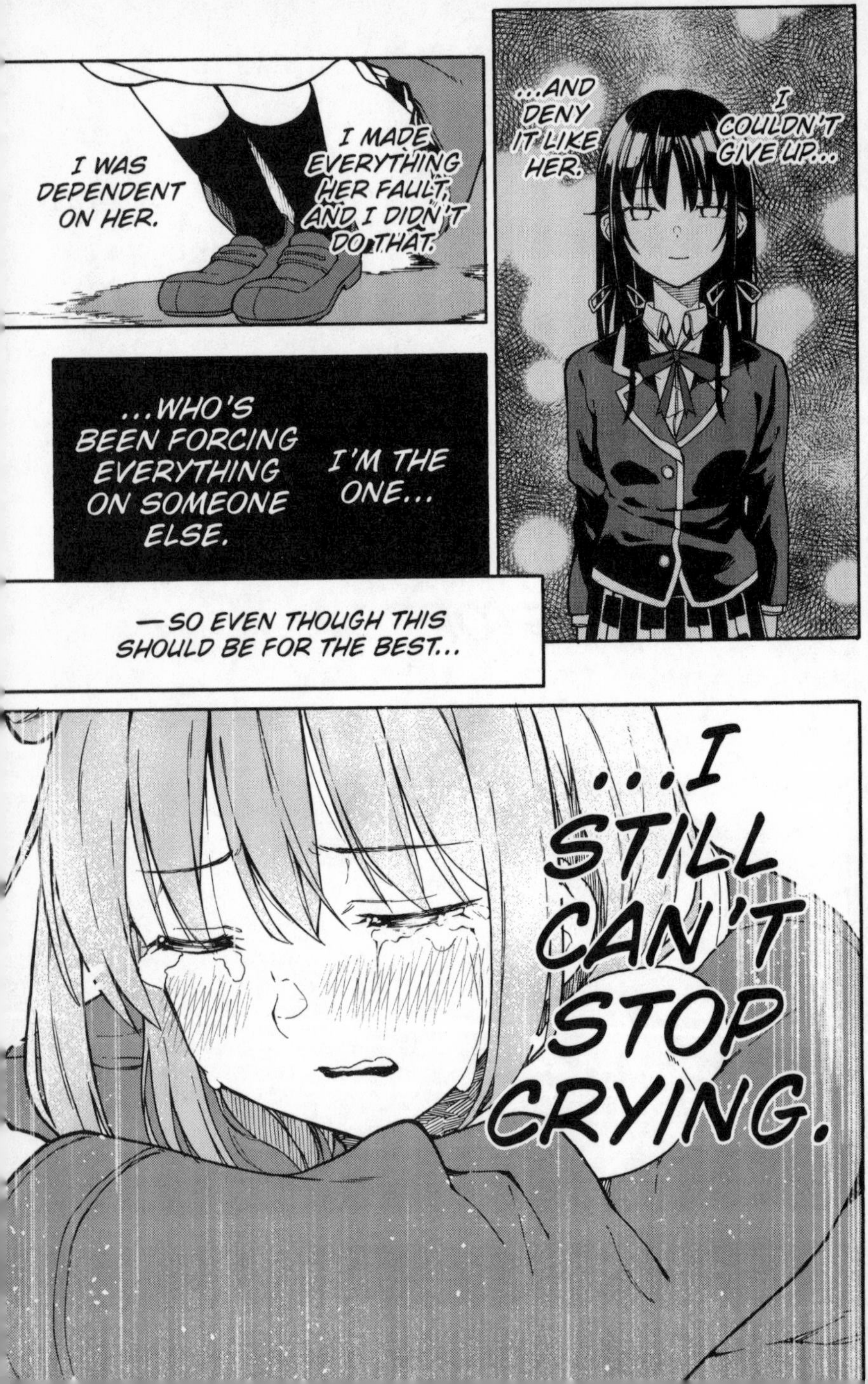
I COULDN'T GIVE UP...
...AND DENY IT LIKE HER.
I MADE EVERYTHING HER FAULT, AND I DIDN'T DO THAT.
I WAS DEPENDENT ON HER.
I'M THE ONE...
...WHO'S BEEN FORCING EVERYTHING ON SOMEONE ELSE.
—SO EVEN THOUGH THIS SHOULD BE FOR THE BEST...
...I STILL CAN'T STOP CRYING.

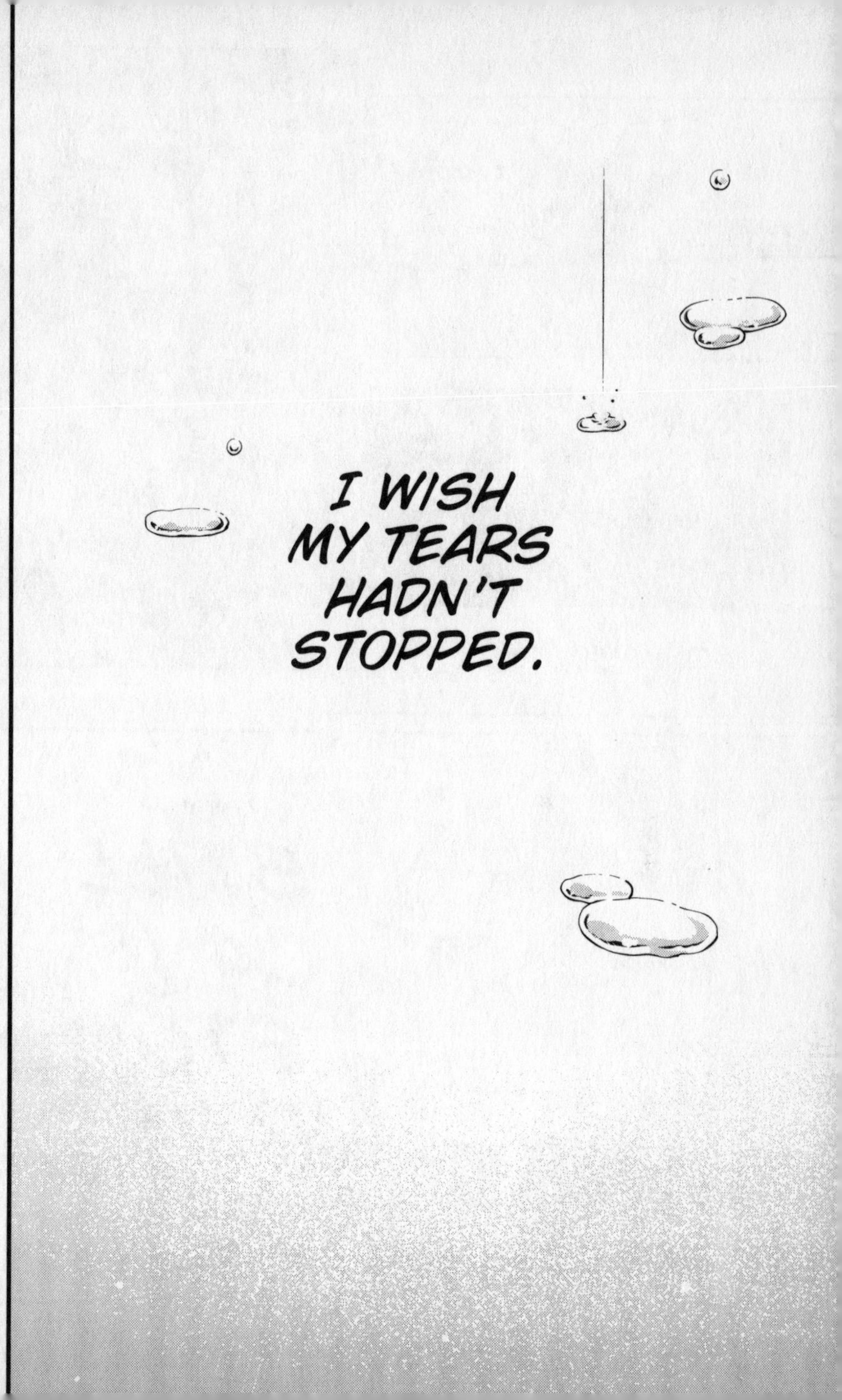
I WISH MY TEARS HADN'T STOPPED.

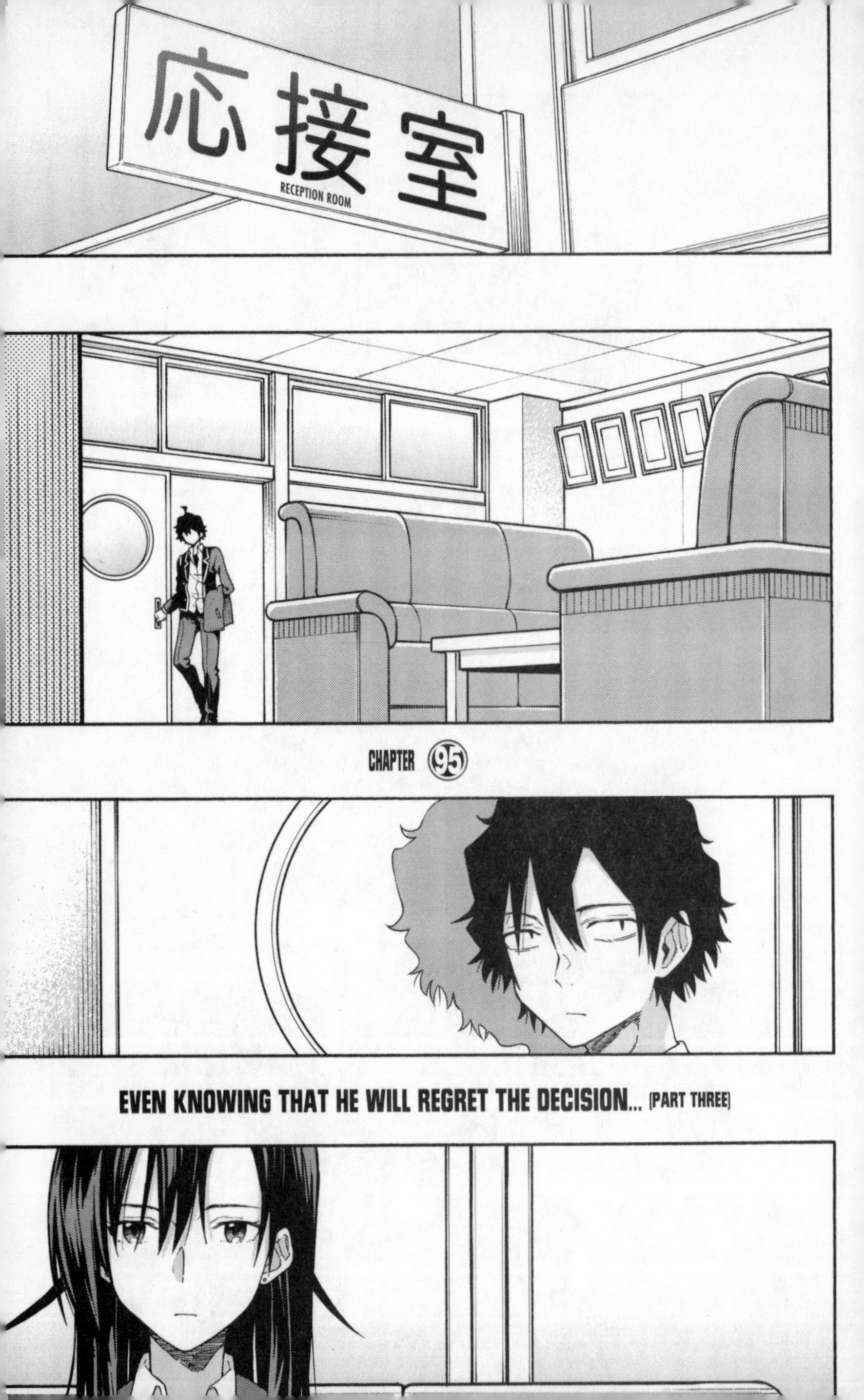
応接室
RECEPTION ROOM
CHAPTER 95
EVEN KNOWING THAT HE WILL REGRET THE DECISION... (PART THREE)

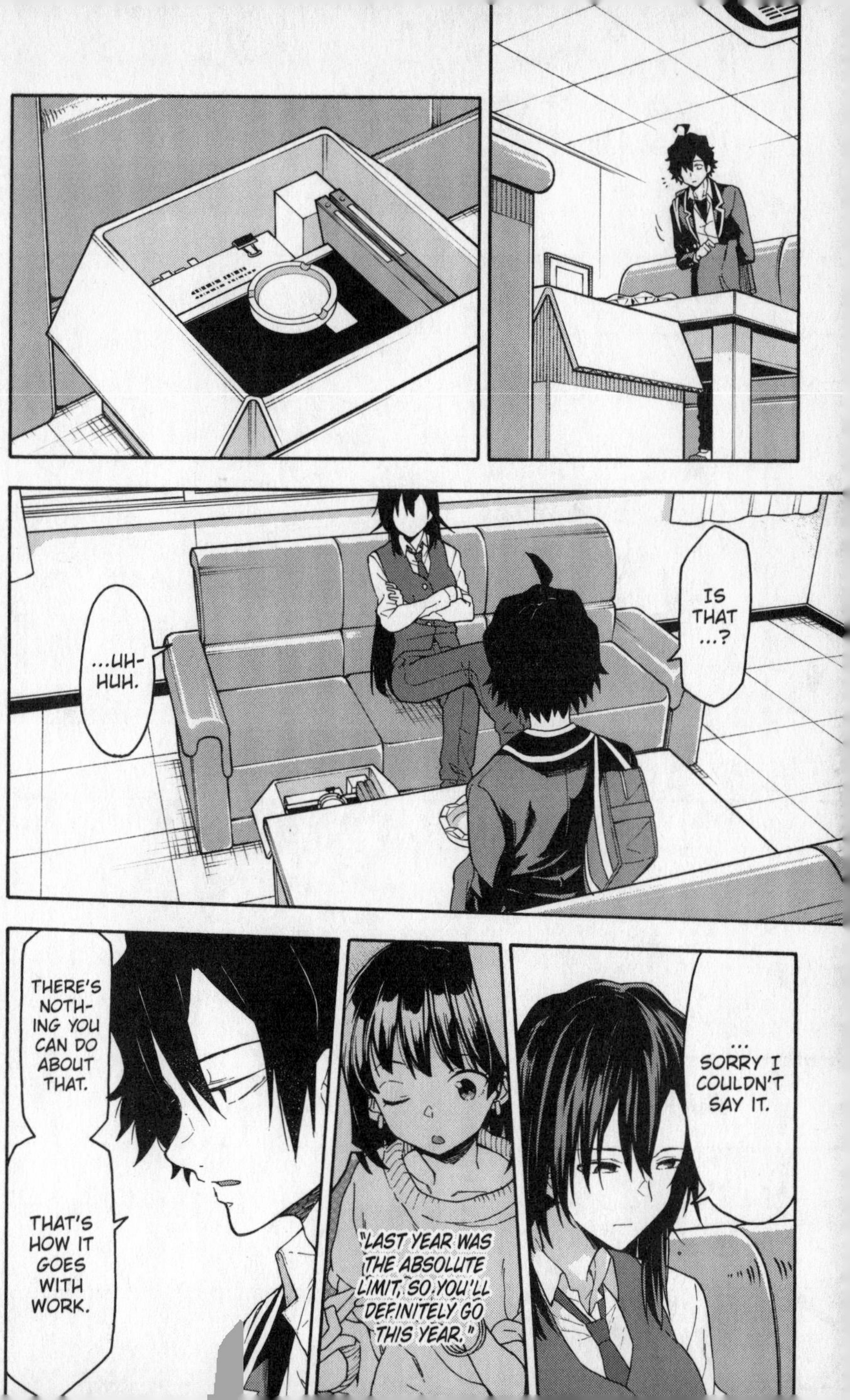
IS THAT ...?
...UH-HUH.
... SORRY I COULDN'T SAY IT.
"LAST YEAR WAS THE ABSOLUTE LIMIT, SO YOU'LL DEFINITELY GO THIS YEAR."
THERE'S NOTHING YOU CAN DO ABOUT THAT.
THAT'S HOW IT GOES WITH WORK.

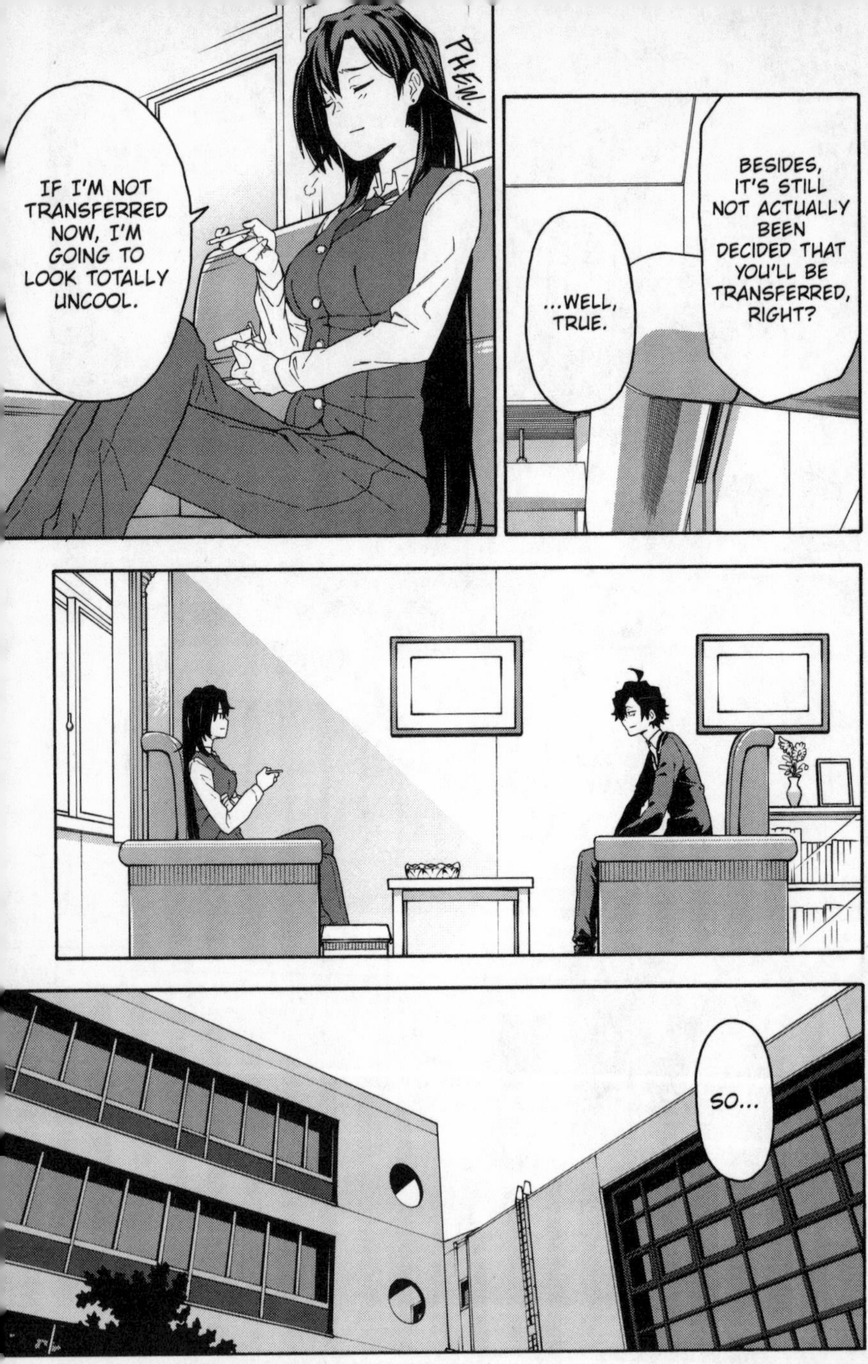
BESIDES, IT'S STILL NOT ACTUALLY BEEN DECIDED THAT YOU'LL BE TRANSFERRED, RIGHT?
...WELL, TRUE.
PHEW.
IF I'M NOT TRANSFERRED NOW, I'M GOING TO LOOK TOTALLY UNCOOL.
SO...

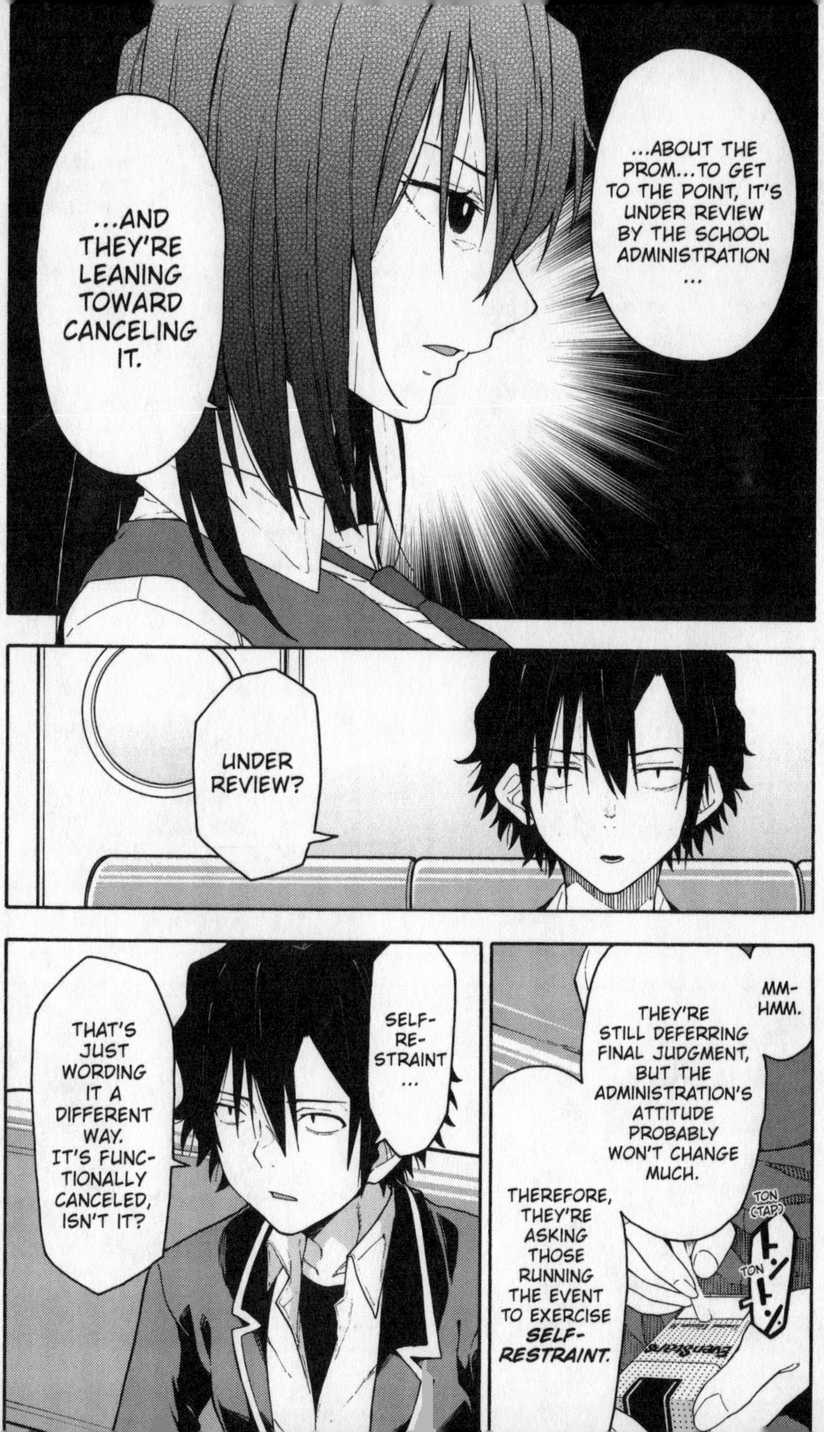
...ABOUT THE PROM...TO GET TO THE POINT, IT'S UNDER REVIEW BY THE SCHOOL ADMINISTRATION ...
...AND THEY'RE LEANING TOWARD CANCELING IT.
UNDER REVIEW?
MM-HMM.
THEY'RE STILL DEFERRING FINAL JUDGMENT, BUT THE ADMINISTRATION'S ATTITUDE PROBABLY WON'T CHANGE MUCH.
THEREFORE, THEY'RE ASKING THOSE RUNNING THE EVENT TO EXERCISE ***SELF-RESTRAINT.***
TON (TAP)
TON
SELF-RESTRAINT ...
THAT'S JUST WORDING IT A DIFFERENT WAY. IT'S FUNCTIONALLY CANCELED, ISN'T IT?

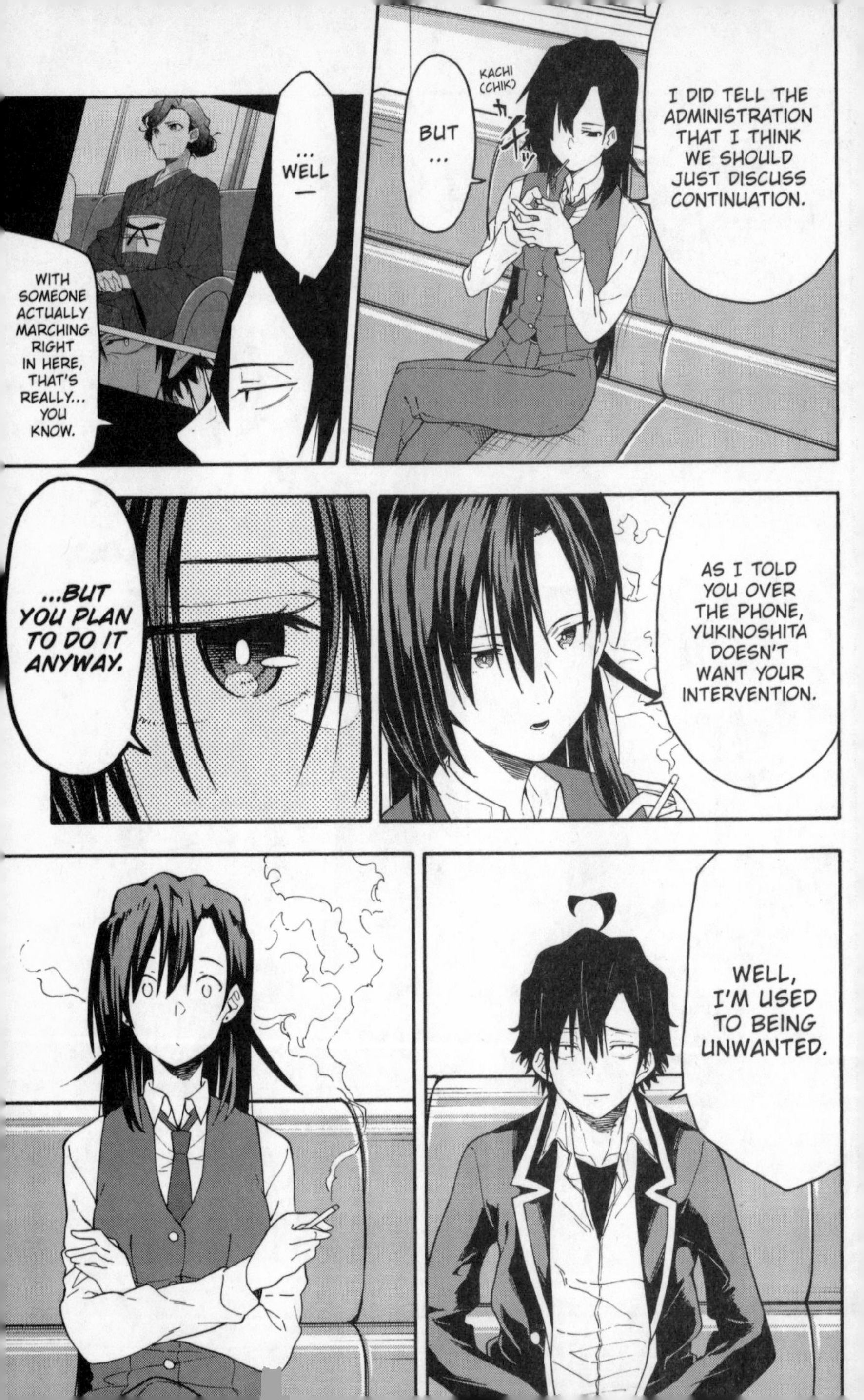
I DID TELL THE ADMINISTRATION THAT I THINK WE SHOULD JUST DISCUSS CONTINUATION.
KACHI (CHIK)
BUT ...
... WELL —
WITH SOMEONE ACTUALLY MARCHING RIGHT IN HERE, THAT'S REALLY... YOU KNOW.
AS I TOLD YOU OVER THE PHONE, YUKINOSHITA DOESN'T WANT YOUR INTERVENTION.
...BUT YOU PLAN TO DO IT ANYWAY.
WELL, I'M USED TO BEING UNWANTED.

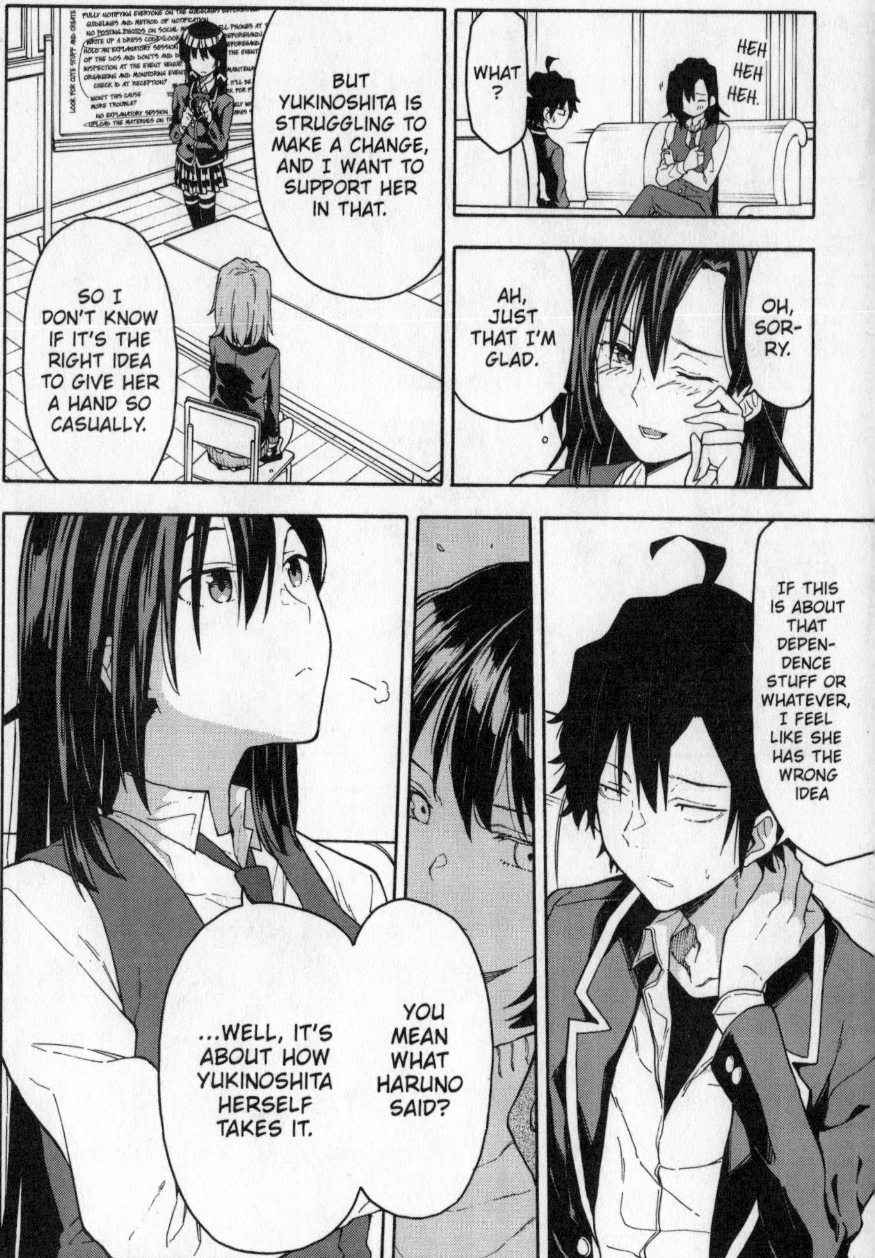
HEH HEH HEH.
WHAT?
OH, SORRY.
AH, JUST THAT I'M GLAD.
BUT YUKINOSHITA IS STRUGGLING TO MAKE A CHANGE, AND I WANT TO SUPPORT HER IN THAT.
SO I DON'T KNOW IF IT'S THE RIGHT IDEA TO GIVE HER A HAND SO CASUALLY.
IF THIS IS ABOUT THAT DEPENDENCE STUFF OR WHATEVER, I FEEL LIKE SHE HAS THE WRONG IDEA
YOU MEAN WHAT HARUNO SAID?
...WELL, IT'S ABOUT HOW YUKINOSHITA HERSELF TAKES IT.

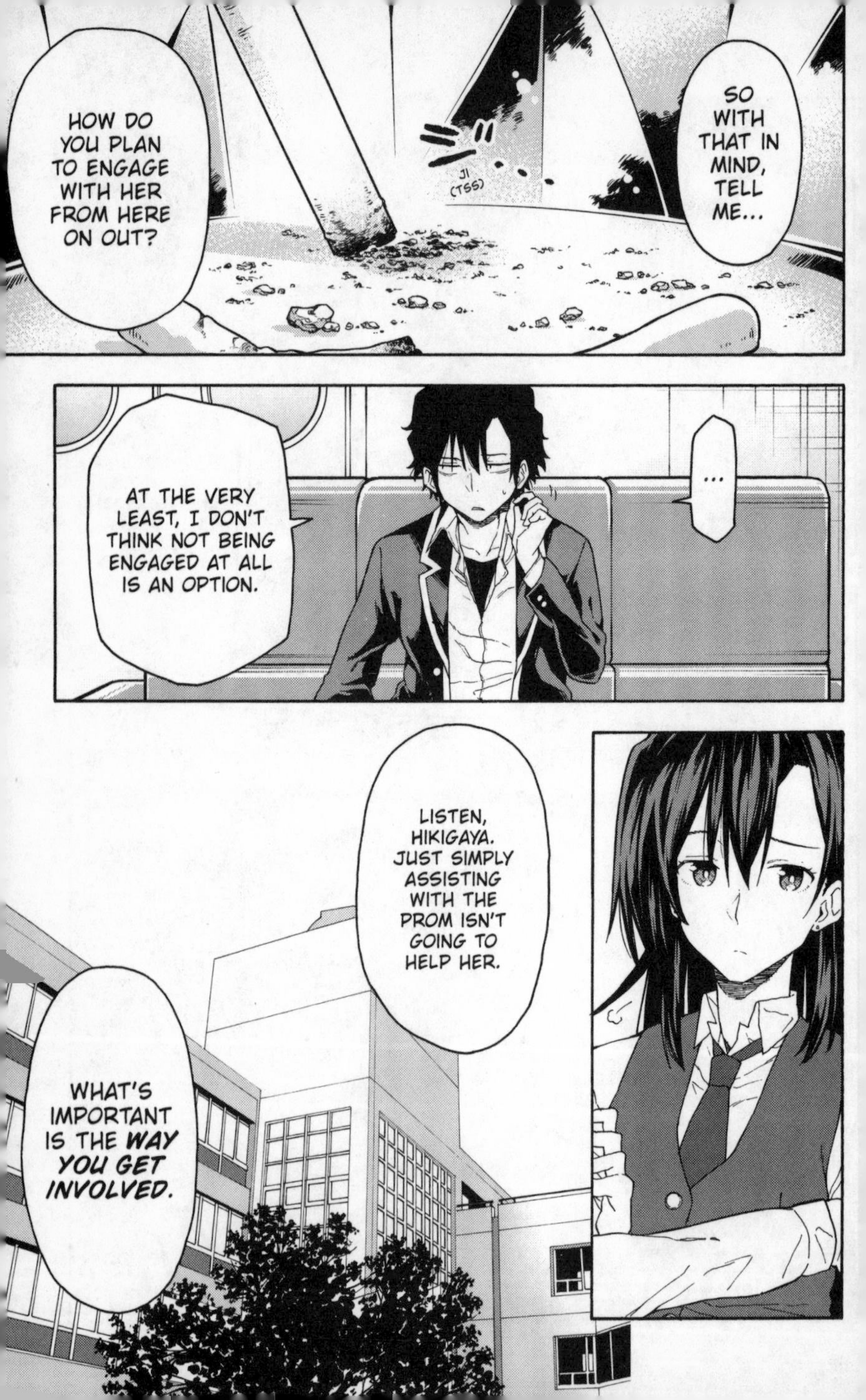
SO WITH THAT IN MIND, TELL ME...
JI (TSS)
HOW DO YOU PLAN TO ENGAGE WITH HER FROM HERE ON OUT?
...
AT THE VERY LEAST, I DON'T THINK NOT BEING ENGAGED AT ALL IS AN OPTION.
LISTEN, HIKIGAYA. JUST SIMPLY ASSISTING WITH THE PROM ISN'T GOING TO HELP HER.
WHAT'S IMPORTANT IS THE WAY YOU GET INVOLVED.

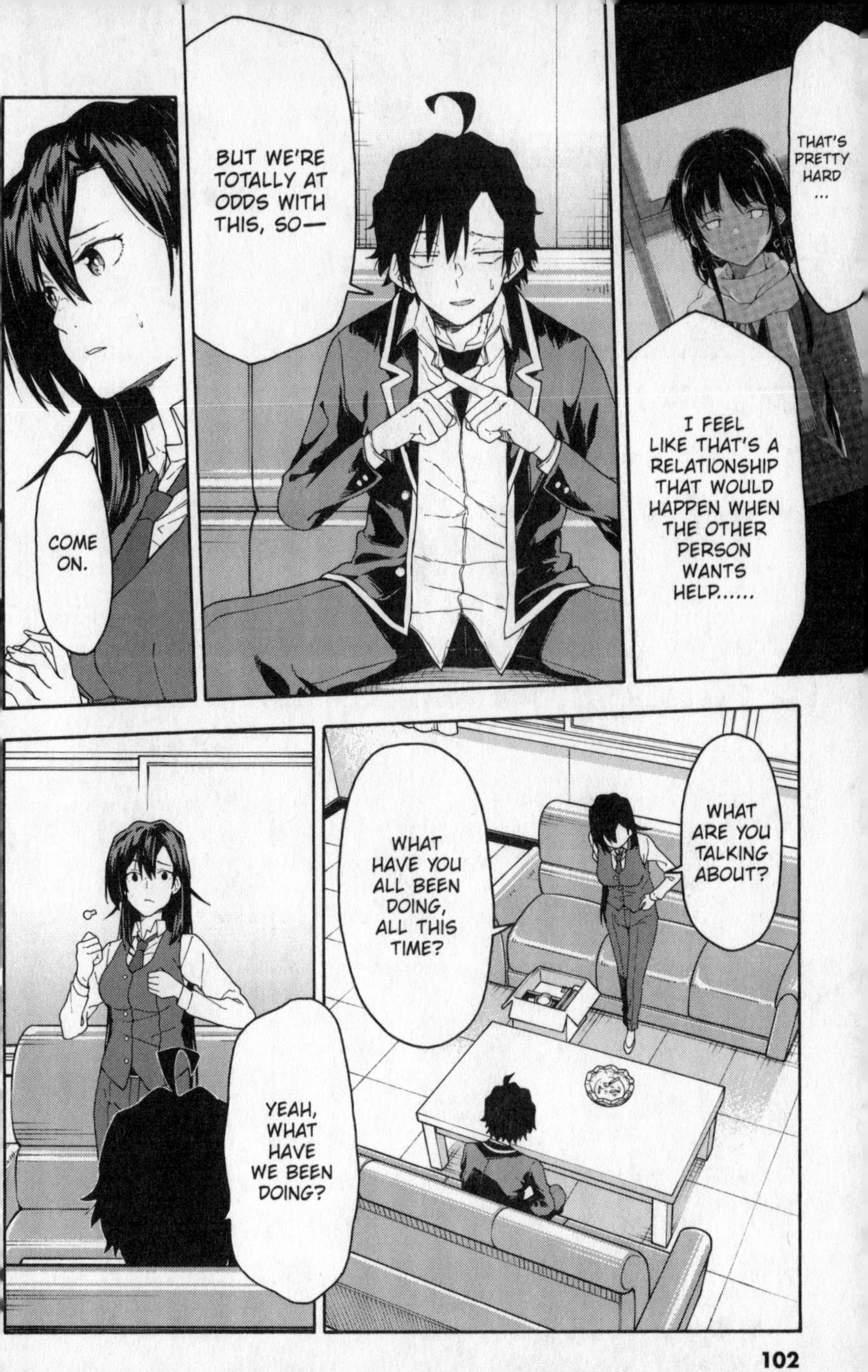
THAT'S PRETTY HARD ...
I FEEL LIKE THAT'S A RELATIONSHIP THAT WOULD HAPPEN WHEN THE OTHER PERSON WANTS HELP......
BUT WE'RE TOTALLY AT ODDS WITH THIS, SO—
COME ON.
WHAT ARE YOU TALKING ABOUT?
WHAT HAVE YOU ALL BEEN DOING, ALL THIS TIME?
YEAH, WHAT HAVE WE BEEN DOING?

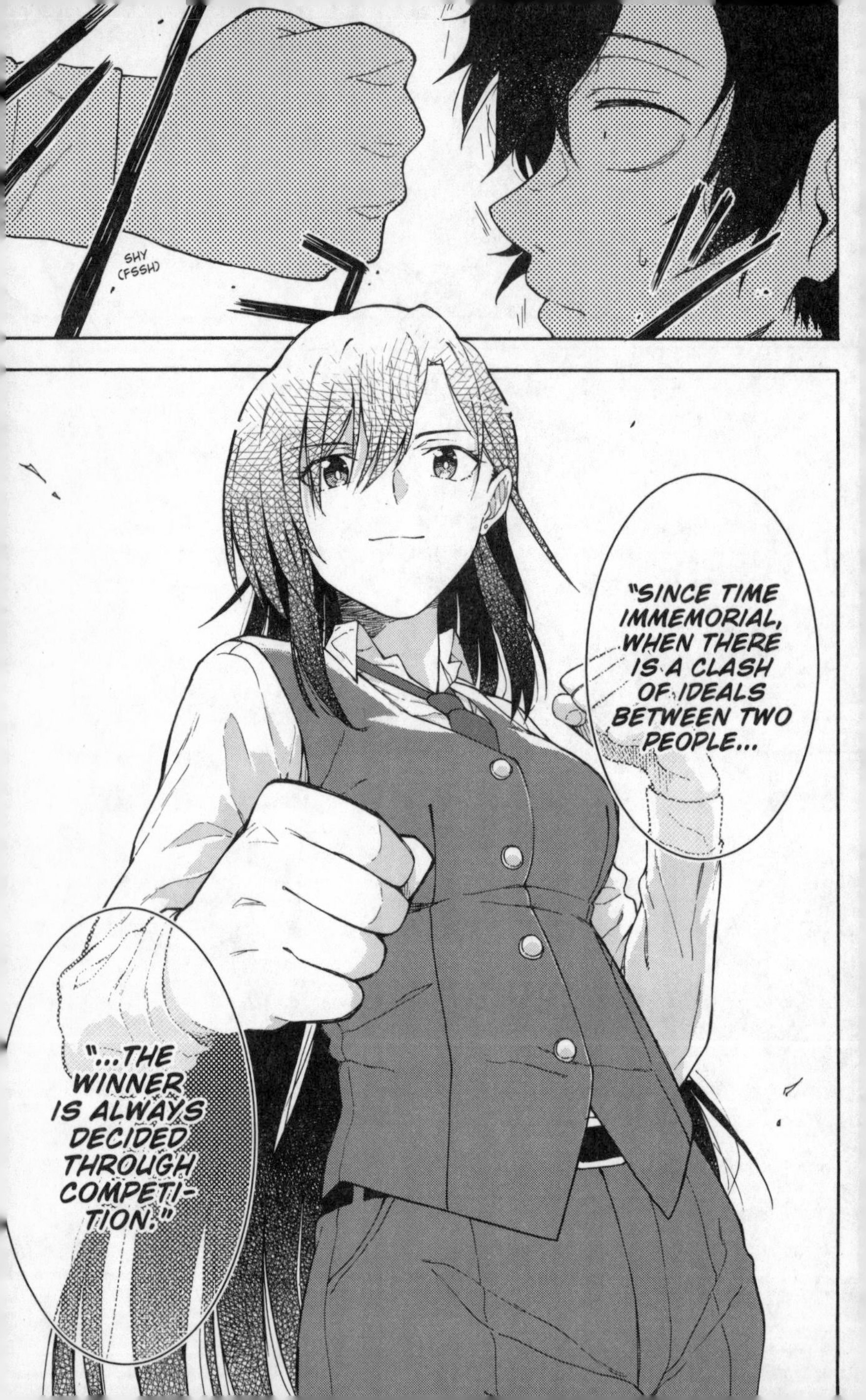
SHY (FSSH)
"SINCE TIME IMMEMORIAL, WHEN THERE IS A CLASH OF IDEALS BETWEEN TWO PEOPLE...
"...THE WINNER IS ALWAYS DECIDED THROUGH COMPETI-TION."

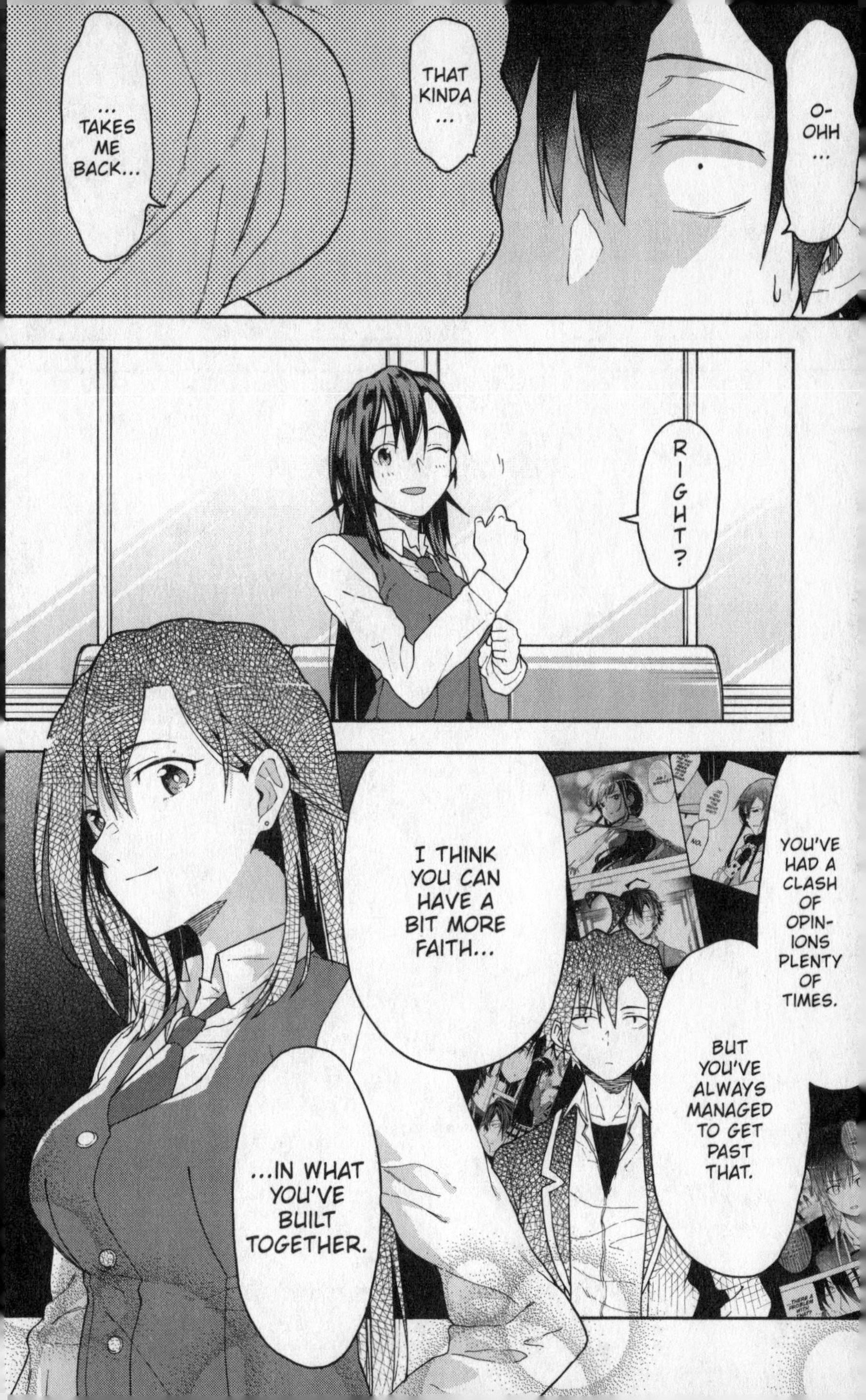
O-OHH...
THAT KINDA...
...TAKES ME BACK...
RIGHT?
YOU'VE HAD A CLASH OF OPINIONS PLENTY OF TIMES.
BUT YOU'VE ALWAYS MANAGED TO GET PAST THAT.
I THINK YOU CAN HAVE A BIT MORE FAITH...
...IN WHAT YOU'VE BUILT TOGETHER.

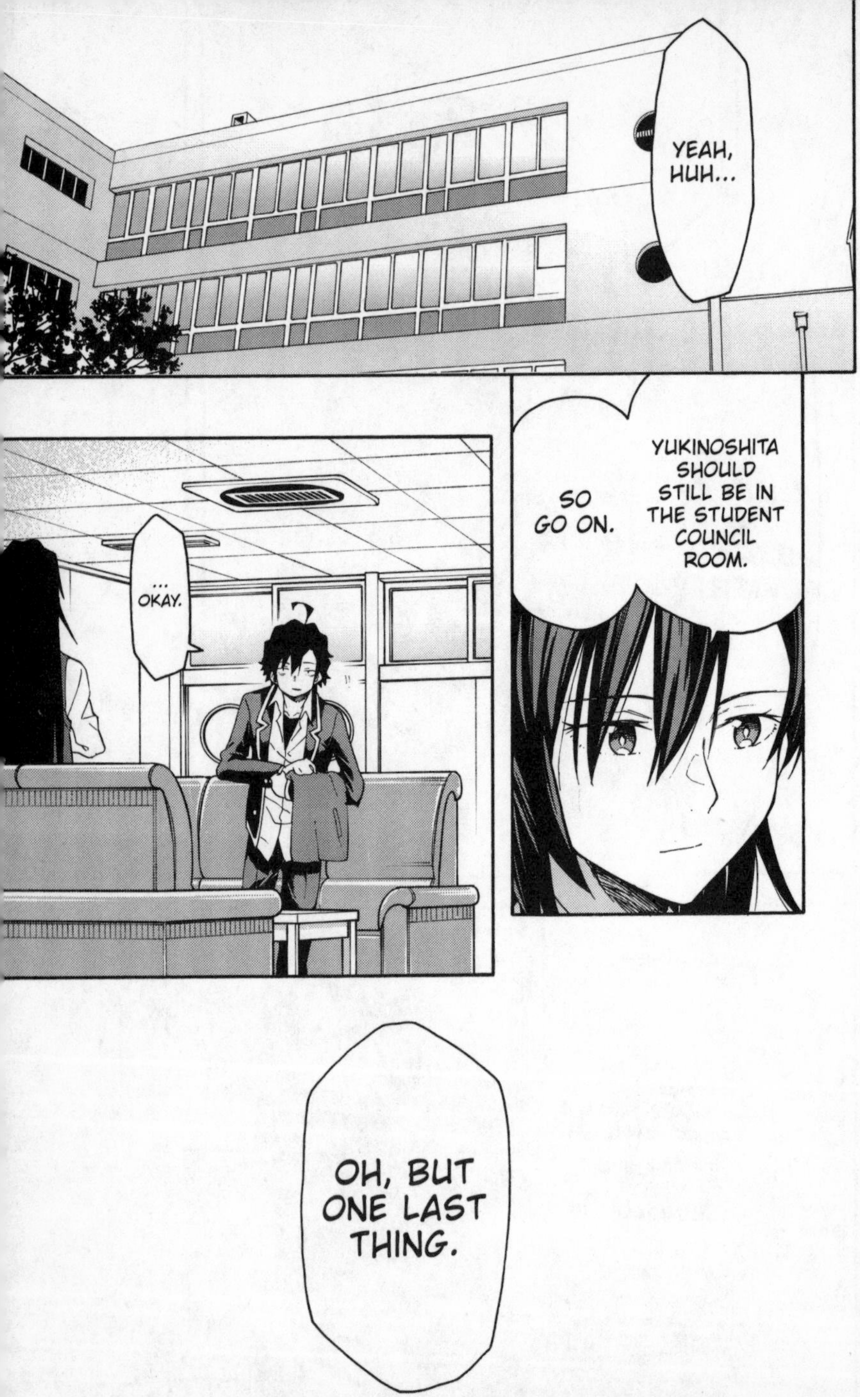
YEAH, HUH...
YUKINOSHITA SHOULD STILL BE IN THE STUDENT COUNCIL ROOM.
SO GO ON.
...OKAY.
OH, BUT ONE LAST THING.

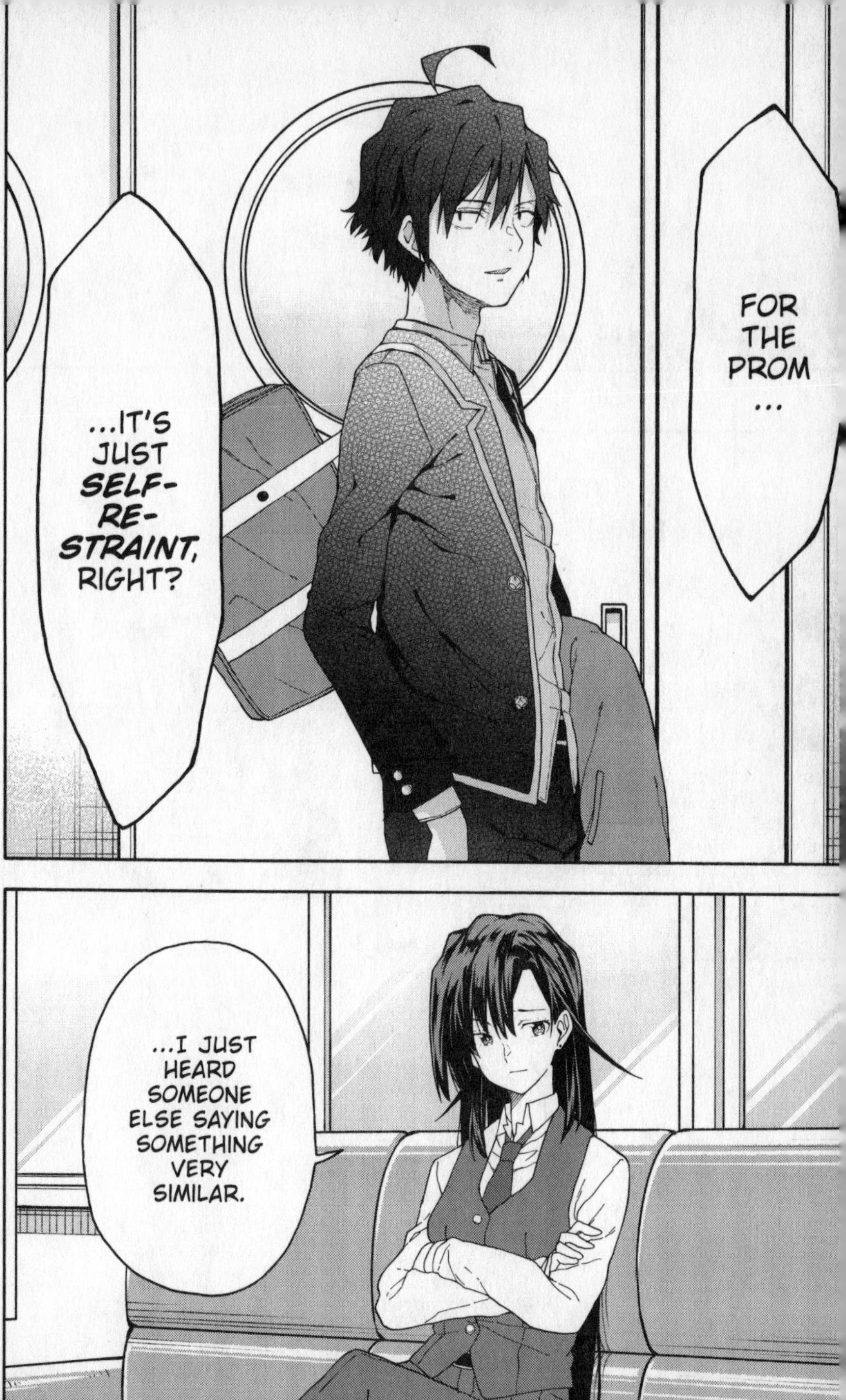
FOR THE PROM...
...IT'S JUST *SELF-RESTRAINT*, RIGHT?
...I JUST HEARD SOMEONE ELSE SAYING SOMETHING VERY SIMILAR.

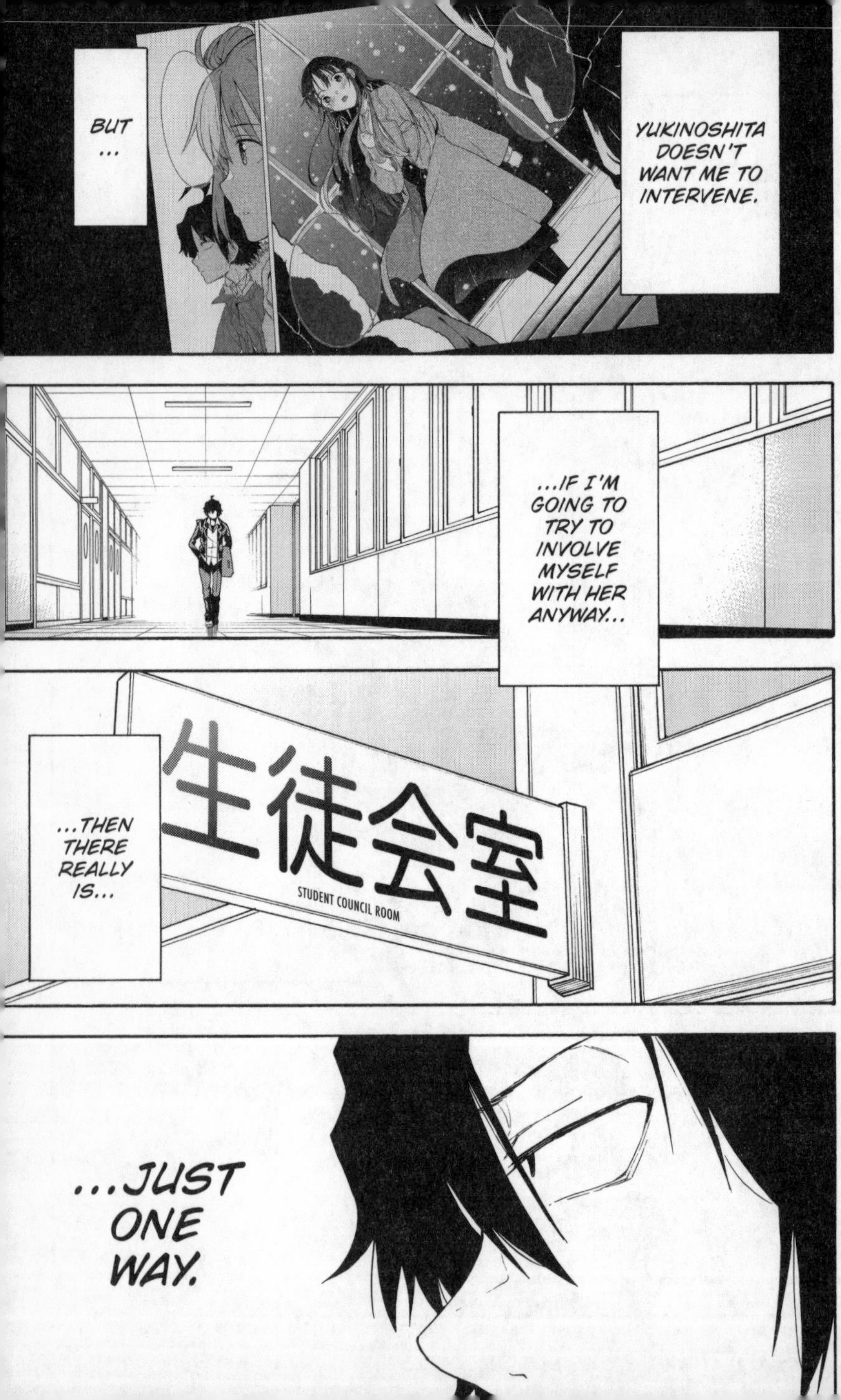
YUKINOSHITA DOESN'T WANT ME TO INTERVENE.
BUT ...
...IF I'M GOING TO TRY TO INVOLVE MYSELF WITH HER ANYWAY...
生徒会室
STUDENT COUNCIL ROOM
...THEN THERE REALLY IS...
...JUST ONE WAY.

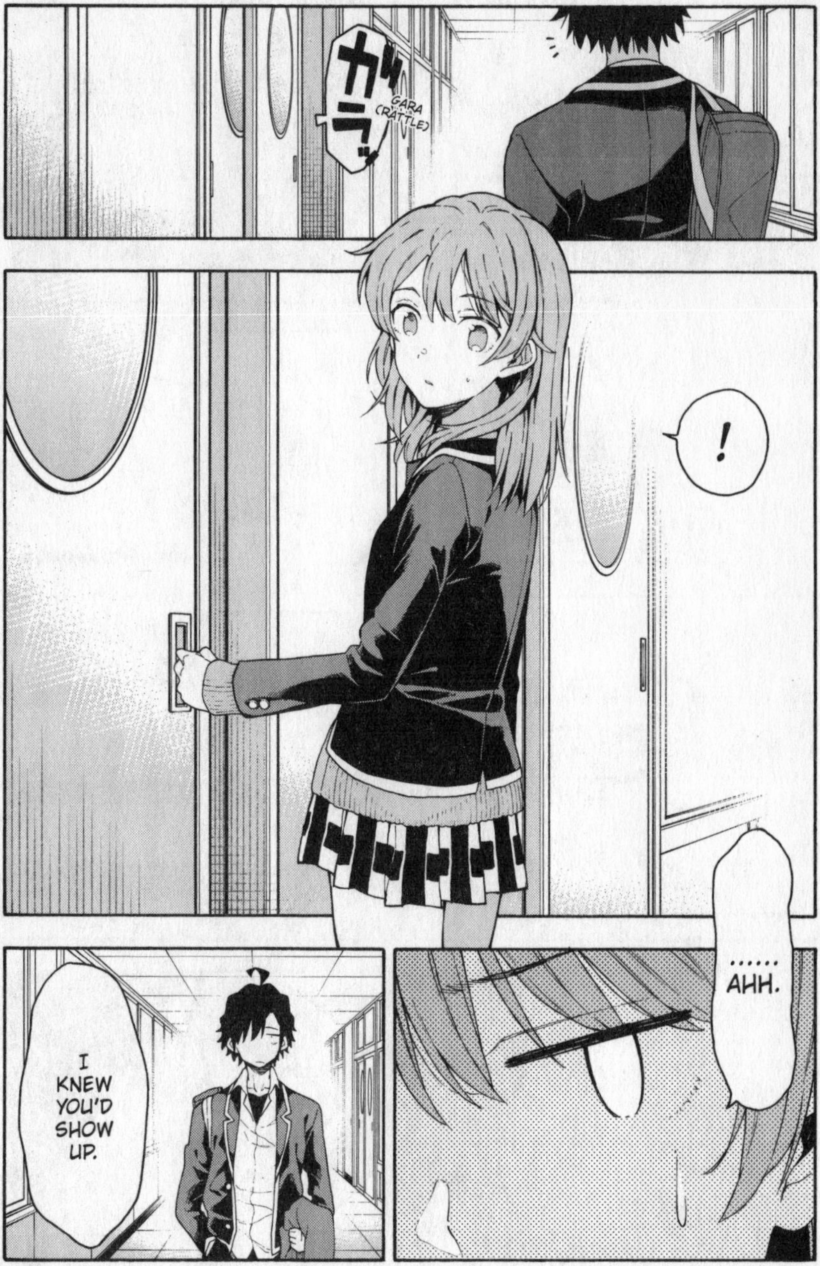
ガラッ
GARA (RATTLE)
!
...... AHH.
I KNEW YOU'D SHOW UP.

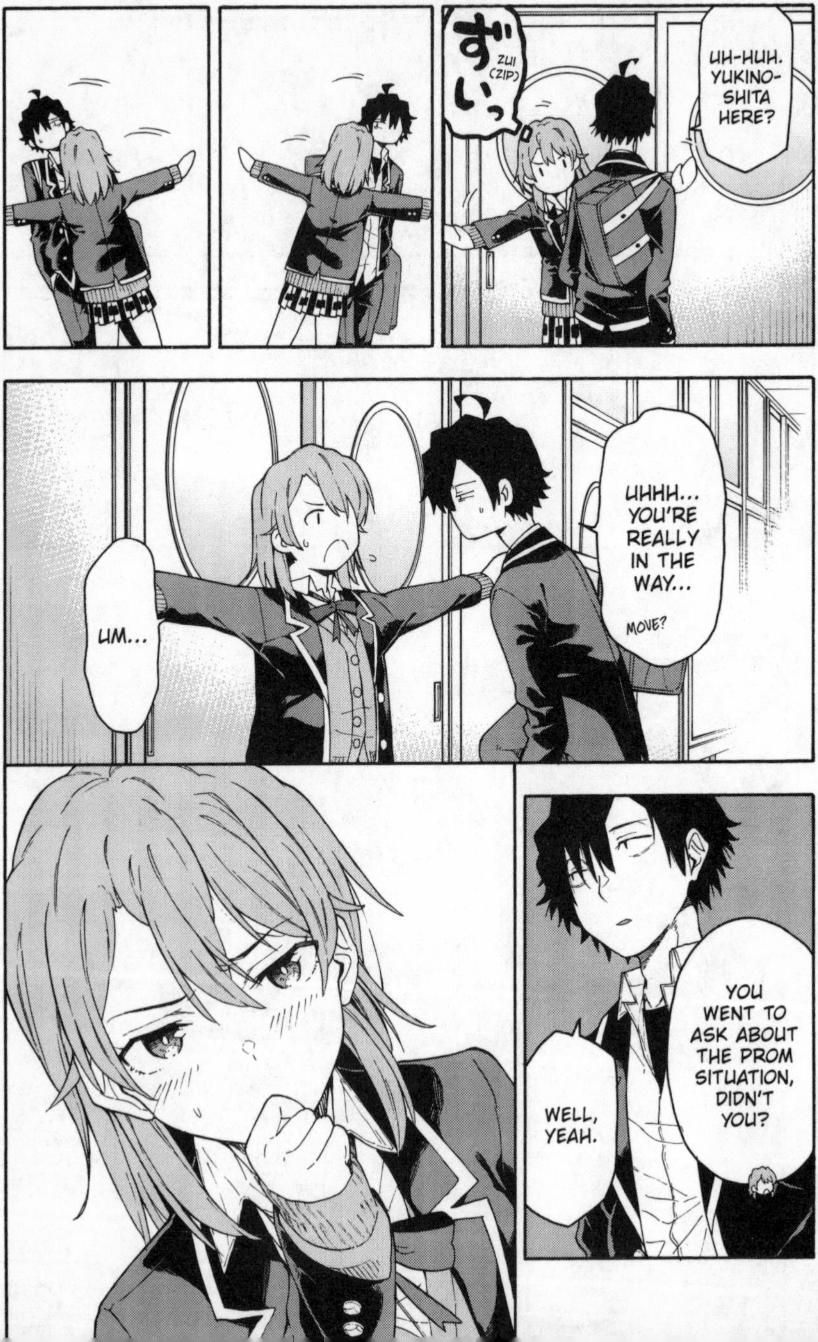
UH-HUH. YUKINO-SHITA HERE?
ずいっ
ZUI (ZIP)
UHHH... YOU'RE REALLY IN THE WAY...
MOVE?
UM...
YOU WENT TO ASK ABOUT THE PROM SITUATION, DIDN'T YOU?
WELL, YEAH.

HEY?

HUH
?

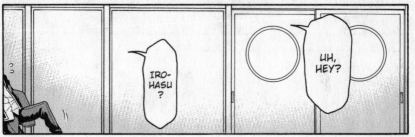

IRO-
HASU
?

UH,
HEY?

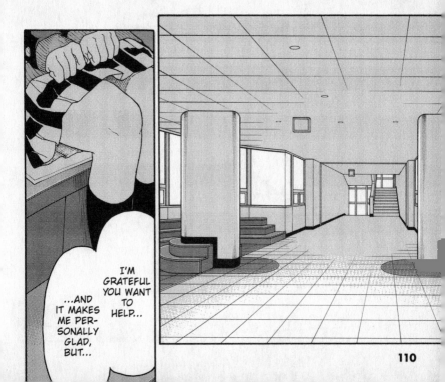

I'M
GRATEFUL
YOU WANT
TO
HELP...

...AND
IT MAKES
ME PER-
SONALLY
GLAD,
BUT...

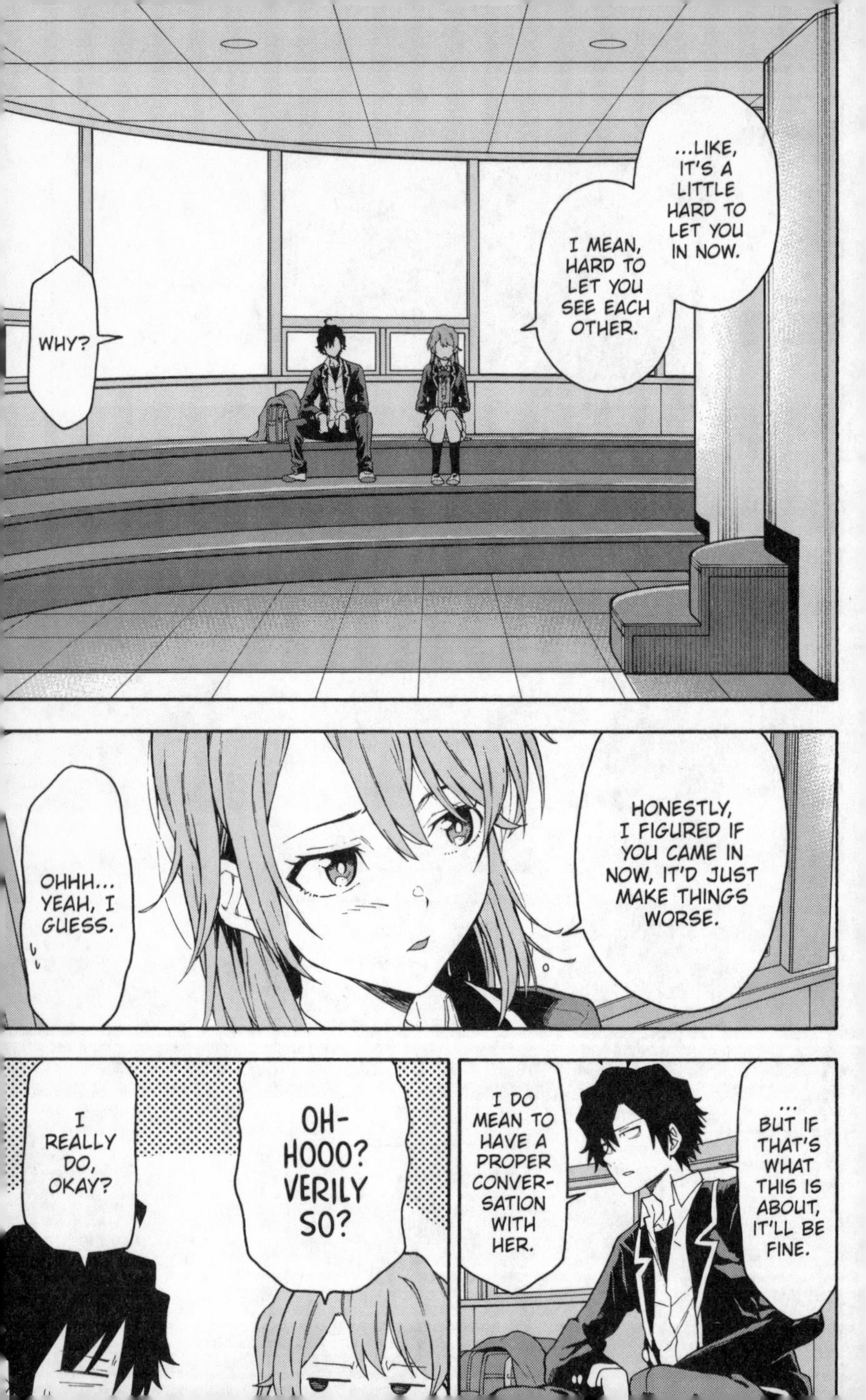

...LIKE, IT'S A LITTLE HARD TO LET YOU IN NOW.
I MEAN, HARD TO LET YOU SEE EACH OTHER.
WHY?
HONESTLY, I FIGURED IF YOU CAME IN NOW, IT'D JUST MAKE THINGS WORSE.
OHHH... YEAH, I GUESS.
... BUT IF THAT'S WHAT THIS IS ABOUT, IT'LL BE FINE.
I DO MEAN TO HAVE A PROPER CONVER-SATION WITH HER.
OH-HOOO? VERILY SO?
I REALLY DO, OKAY?

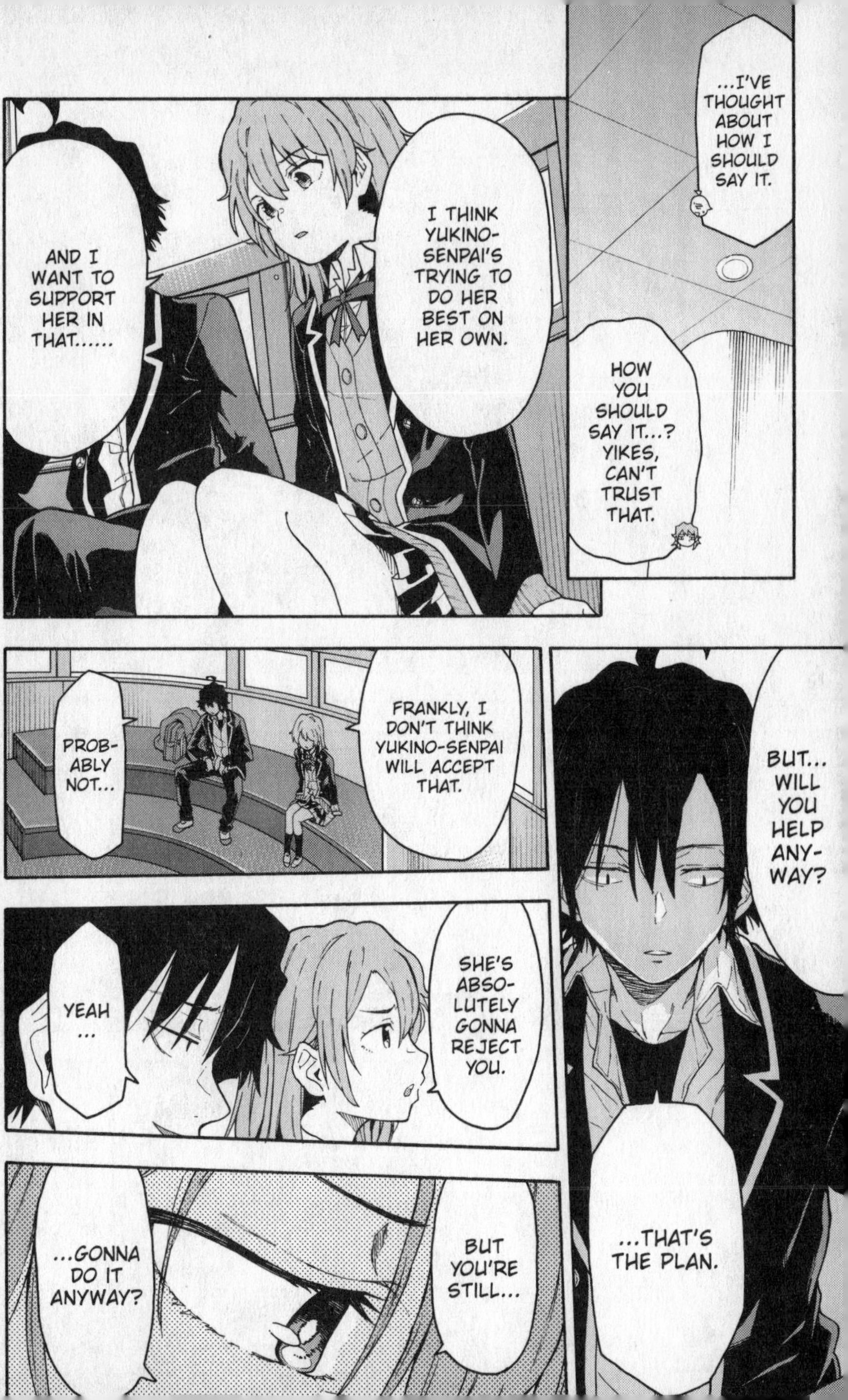
...I'VE THOUGHT ABOUT HOW I SHOULD SAY IT.
HOW YOU SHOULD SAY IT...? YIKES, CAN'T TRUST THAT.
I THINK YUKINO-SENPAI'S TRYING TO DO HER BEST ON HER OWN.
AND I WANT TO SUPPORT HER IN THAT......
BUT... WILL YOU HELP ANYWAY?
...THAT'S THE PLAN.
FRANKLY, I DON'T THINK YUKINO-SENPAI WILL ACCEPT THAT.
PROBABLY NOT...
SHE'S ABSOLUTELY GONNA REJECT YOU.
YEAH ...
BUT YOU'RE STILL...
...GONNA DO IT ANYWAY?

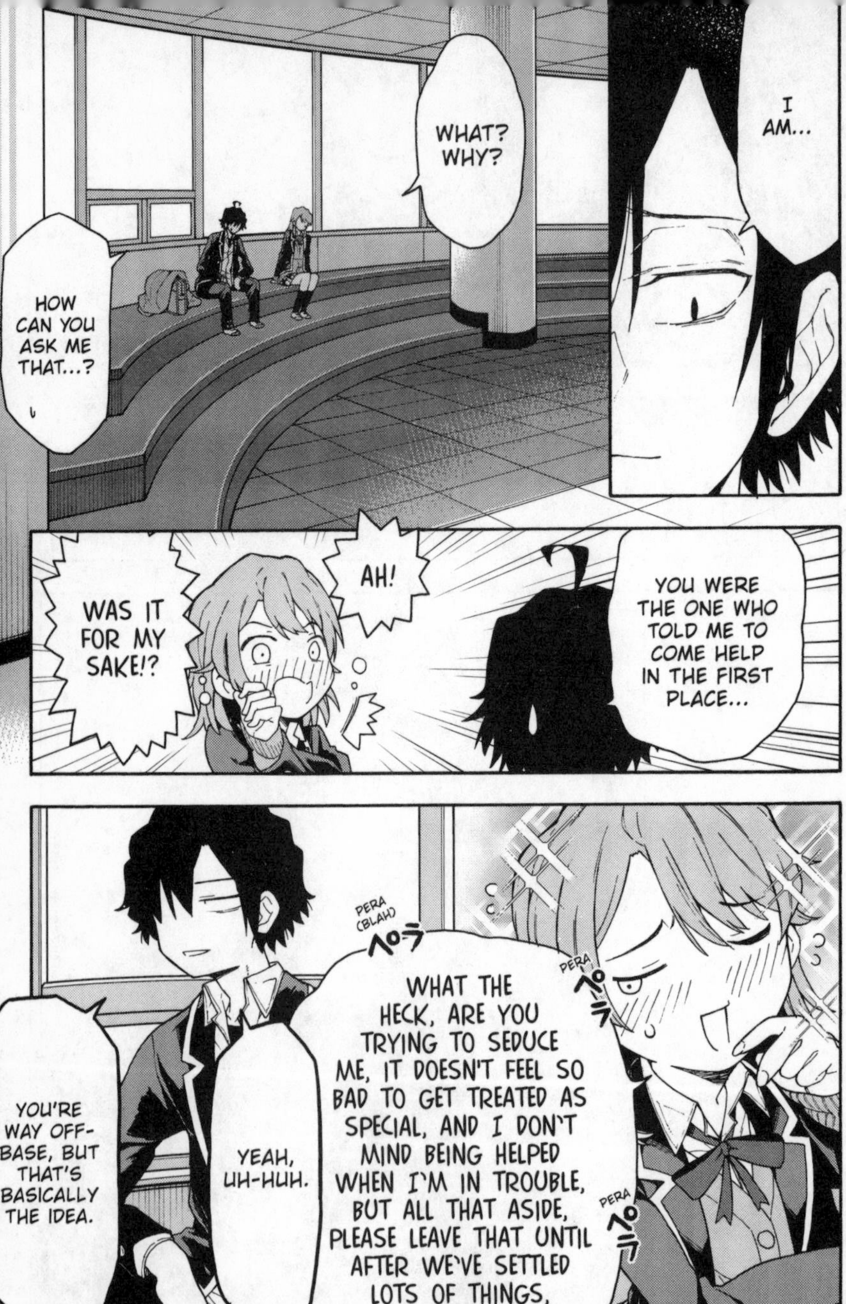
I AM...
WHAT? WHY?
HOW CAN YOU ASK ME THAT...?
YOU WERE THE ONE WHO TOLD ME TO COME HELP IN THE FIRST PLACE...
AH!
WAS IT FOR MY SAKE!?
PERA (BLAH)
ペラ
PERA
ペラ
WHAT THE HECK, ARE YOU TRYING TO SEDUCE ME, IT DOESN'T FEEL SO BAD TO GET TREATED AS SPECIAL, AND I DON'T MIND BEING HELPED WHEN I'M IN TROUBLE, BUT ALL THAT ASIDE, PLEASE LEAVE THAT UNTIL AFTER WE'VE SETTLED LOTS OF THINGS, I'M SORRY.
PERA
ペラ
YEAH, UH-HUH.
YOU'RE WAY OFF-BASE, BUT THAT'S BASICALLY THE IDEA.

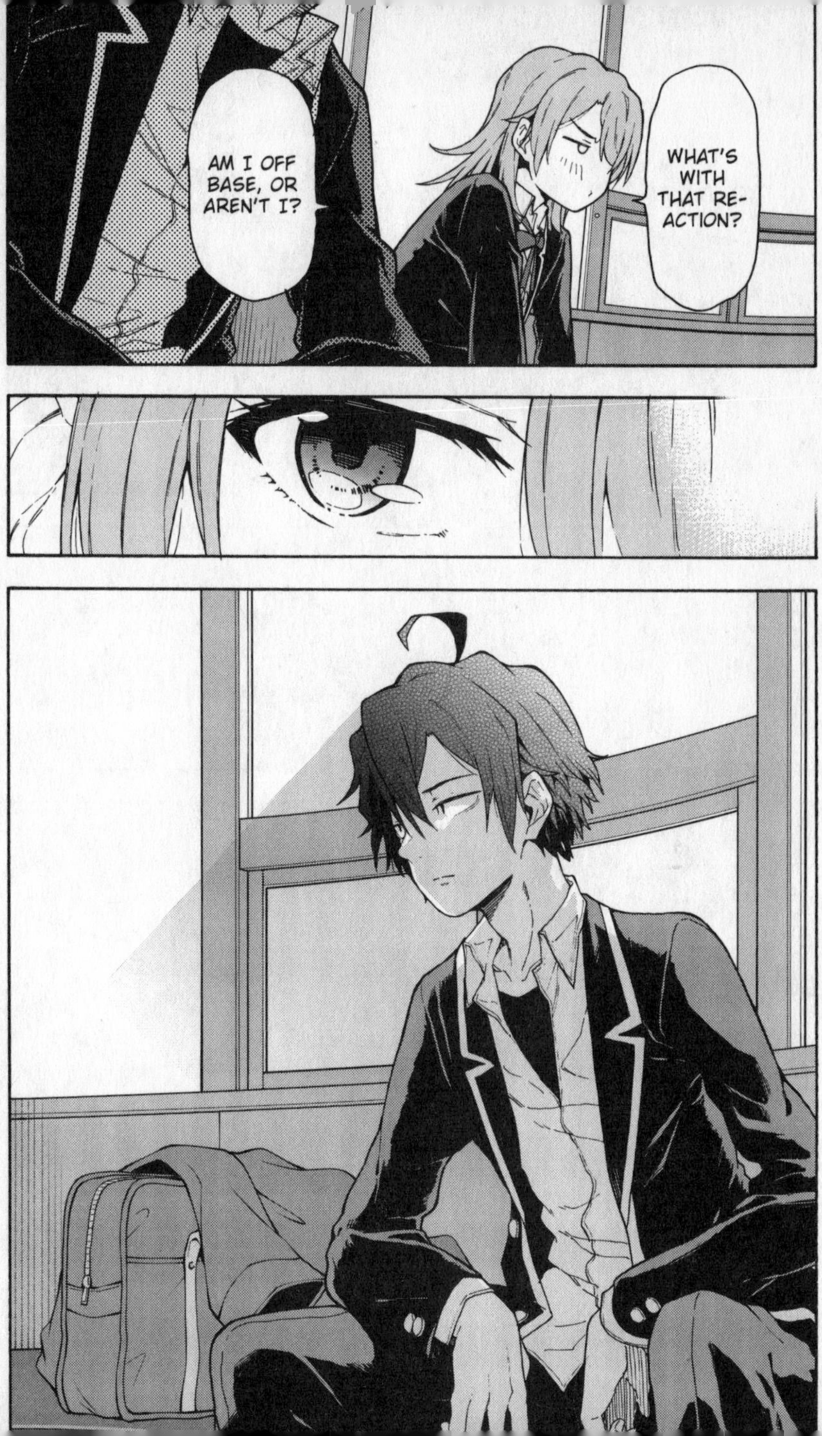
WHAT'S WITH THAT RE-ACTION?
AM I OFF BASE, OR AREN'T I?

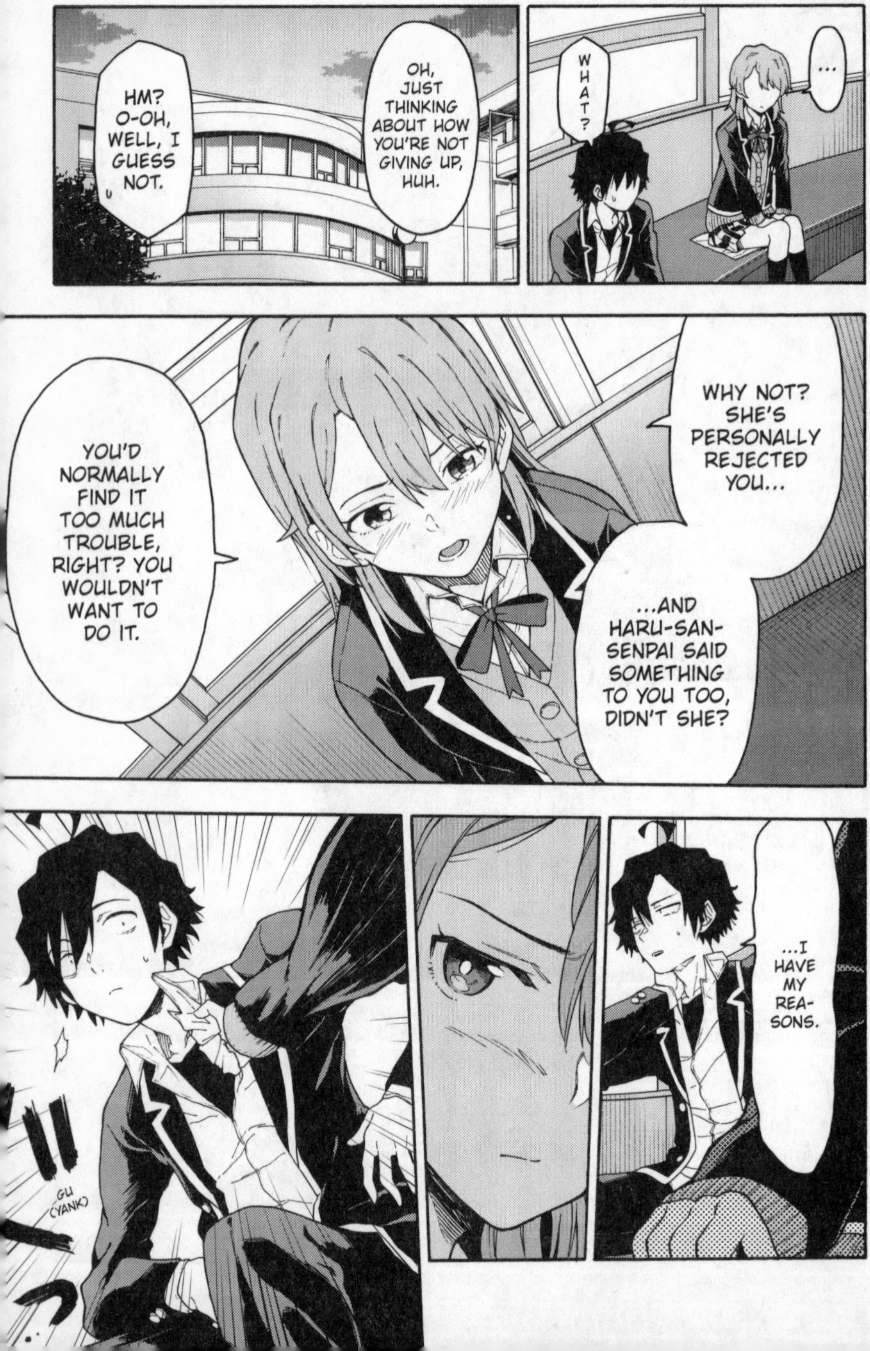
...
WHAT?
OH, JUST THINKING ABOUT HOW YOU'RE NOT GIVING UP, HUH.
HM? O-OH, WELL, I GUESS NOT.
WHY NOT? SHE'S PERSONALLY REJECTED YOU...
...AND HARU-SAN-SENPAI SAID SOMETHING TO YOU TOO, DIDN'T SHE?
YOU'D NORMALLY FIND IT TOO MUCH TROUBLE, RIGHT? YOU WOULDN'T WANT TO DO IT.
...I HAVE MY REA-SONS.
GU (YANK)

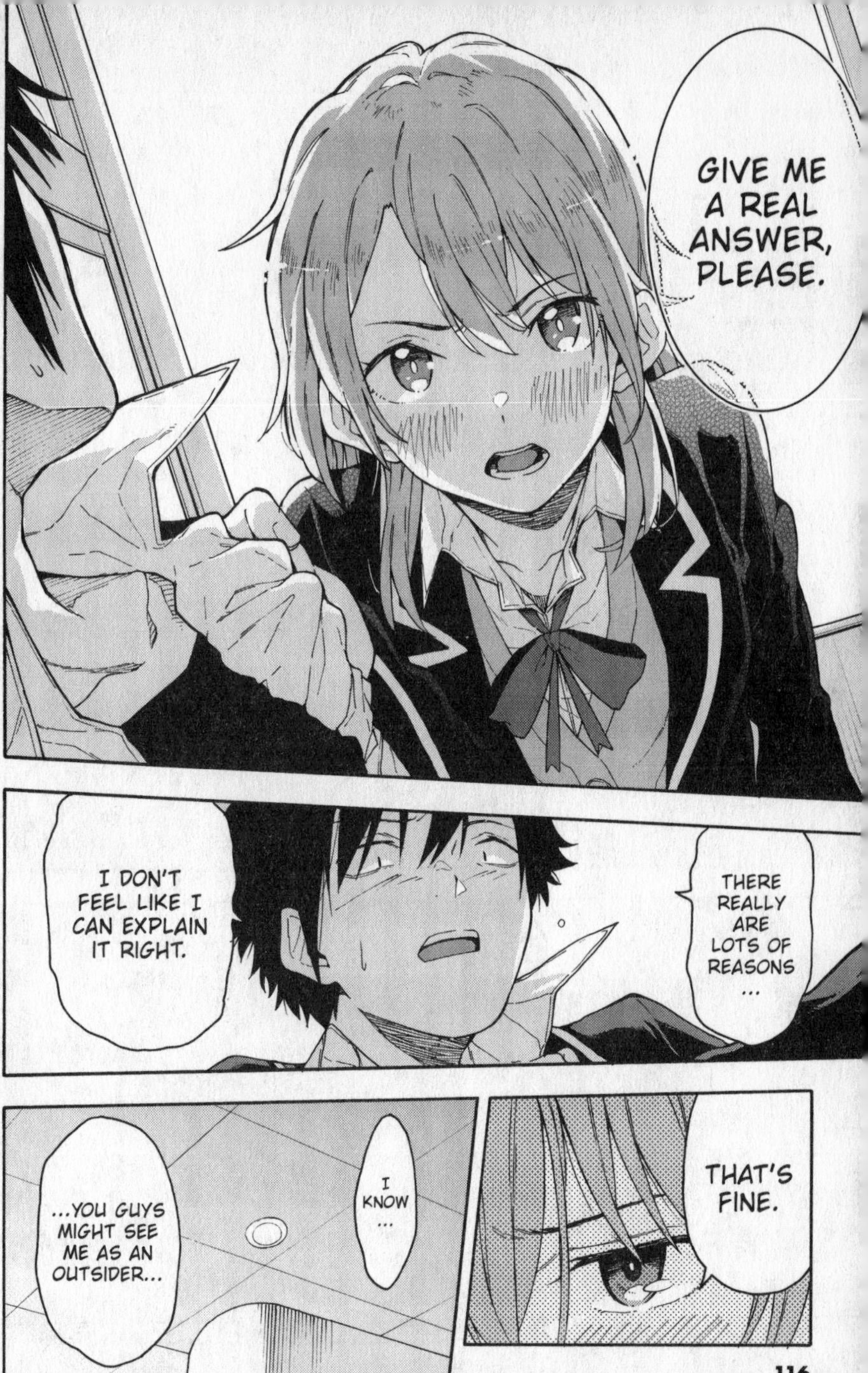
GIVE ME A REAL ANSWER, PLEASE.
THERE REALLY ARE LOTS OF REASONS ...
I DON'T FEEL LIKE I CAN EXPLAIN IT RIGHT.
THAT'S FINE.
I KNOW ...
...YOU GUYS MIGHT SEE ME AS AN OUTSIDER...

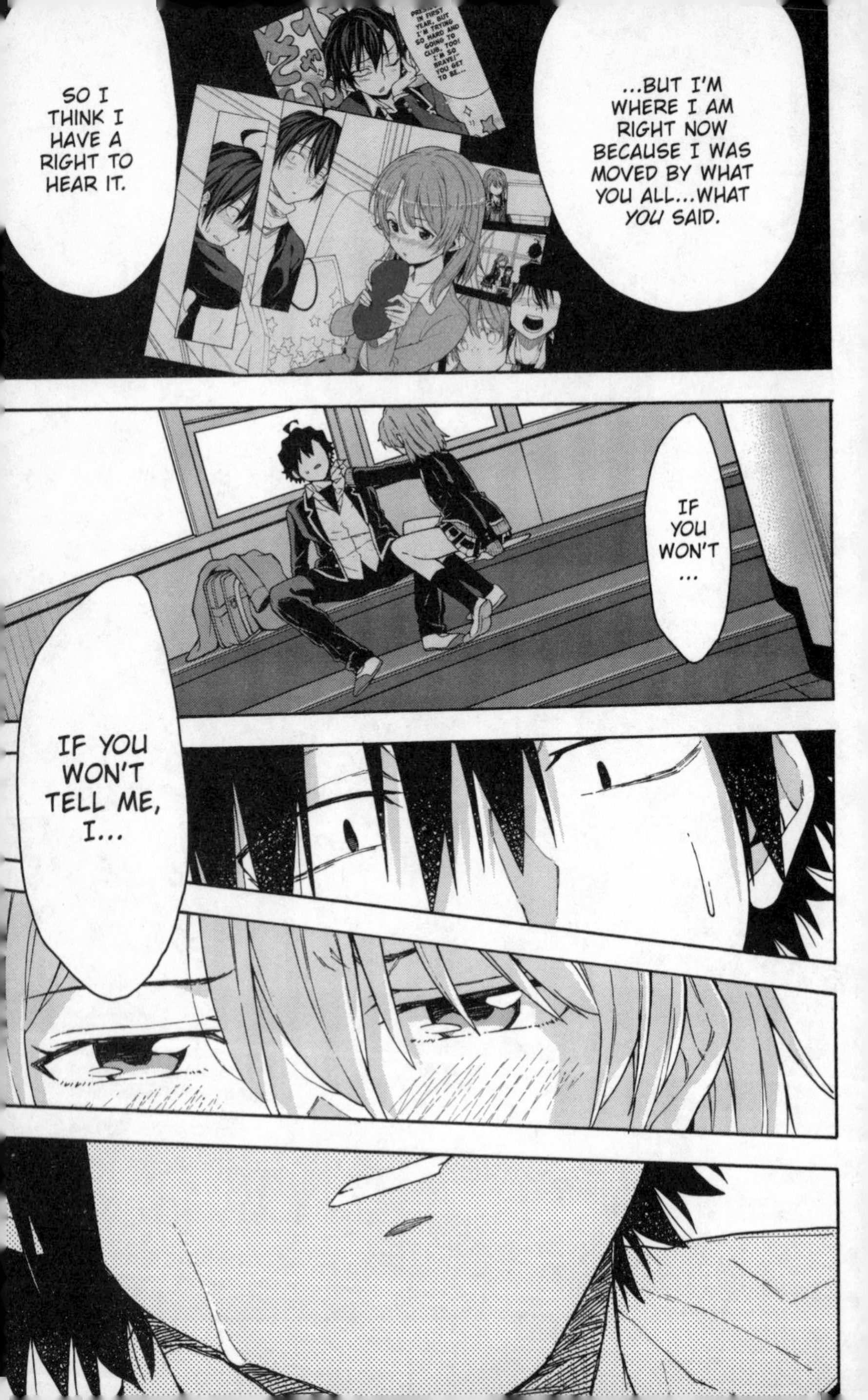
...BUT I'M WHERE I AM RIGHT NOW BECAUSE I WAS MOVED BY WHAT YOU ALL...WHAT *YOU* SAID.
IN FIRST YEAR, BUT I'M TRYING SO HARD AND GOING TO CLUB, TOO! I'M SO BRAVE! YOU GET TO BE...
SO I THINK I HAVE A RIGHT TO HEAR IT.
IF YOU WON'T...
IF YOU WON'T TELL ME, I...

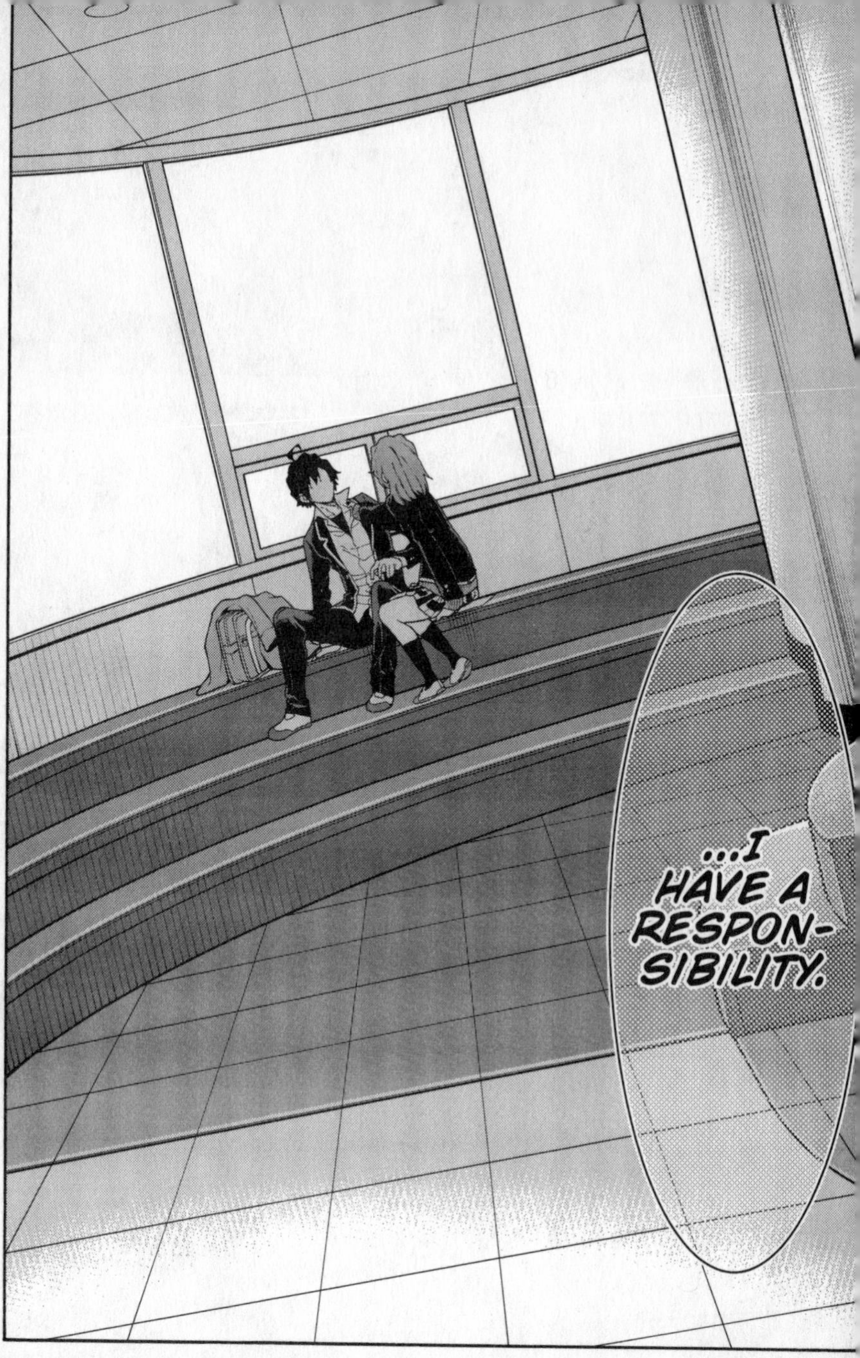
...I HAVE A RESPON-SIBILITY.

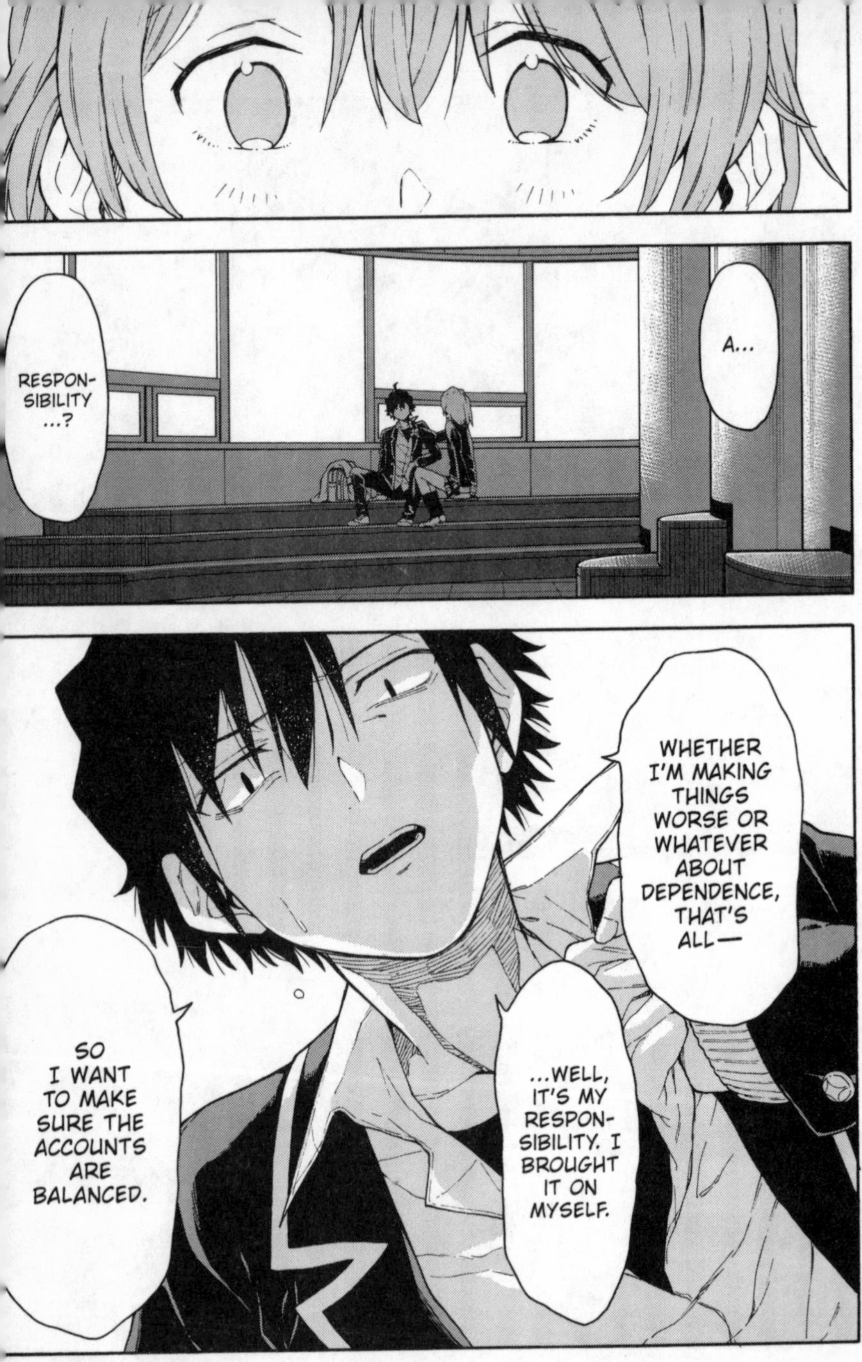
A...
RESPON-SIBILITY ...?
WHETHER I'M MAKING THINGS WORSE OR WHATEVER ABOUT DEPENDENCE, THAT'S ALL—
...WELL, IT'S MY RESPON-SIBILITY. I BROUGHT IT ON MYSELF.
SO I WANT TO MAKE SURE THE ACCOUNTS ARE BALANCED.

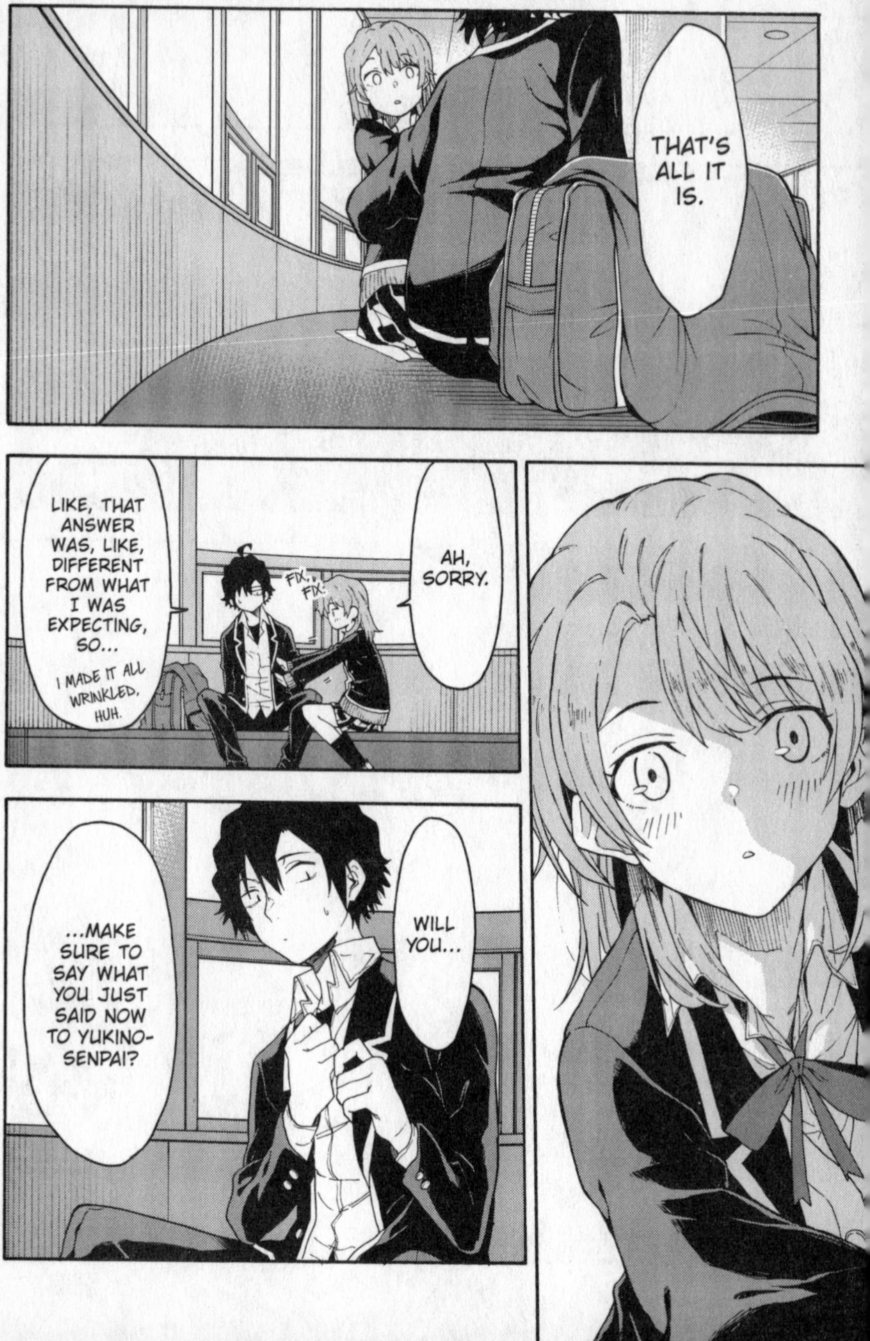
THAT'S ALL IT IS.
AH, SORRY.
FIX, FIX
LIKE, THAT ANSWER WAS, LIKE, DIFFERENT FROM WHAT I WAS EXPECTING, SO...
I MADE IT ALL WRINKLED, HUH.
WILL YOU...
...MAKE SURE TO SAY WHAT YOU JUST SAID NOW TO YUKINO-SENPAI?

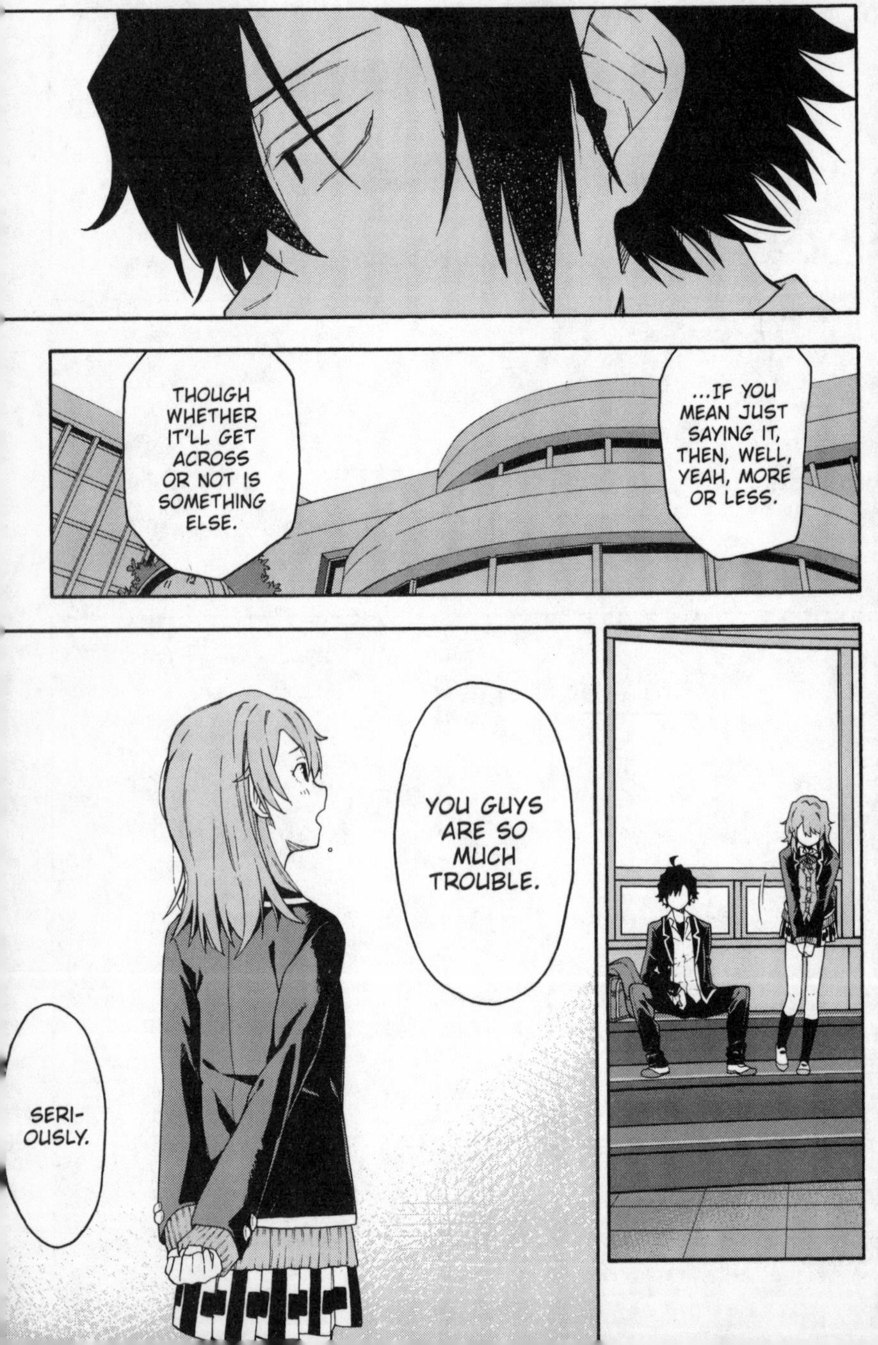
...IF YOU MEAN JUST SAYING IT, THEN, WELL, YEAH, MORE OR LESS.
THOUGH WHETHER IT'LL GET ACROSS OR NOT IS SOMETHING ELSE.
YOU GUYS ARE SO MUCH TROUBLE.
SERI-OUSLY.

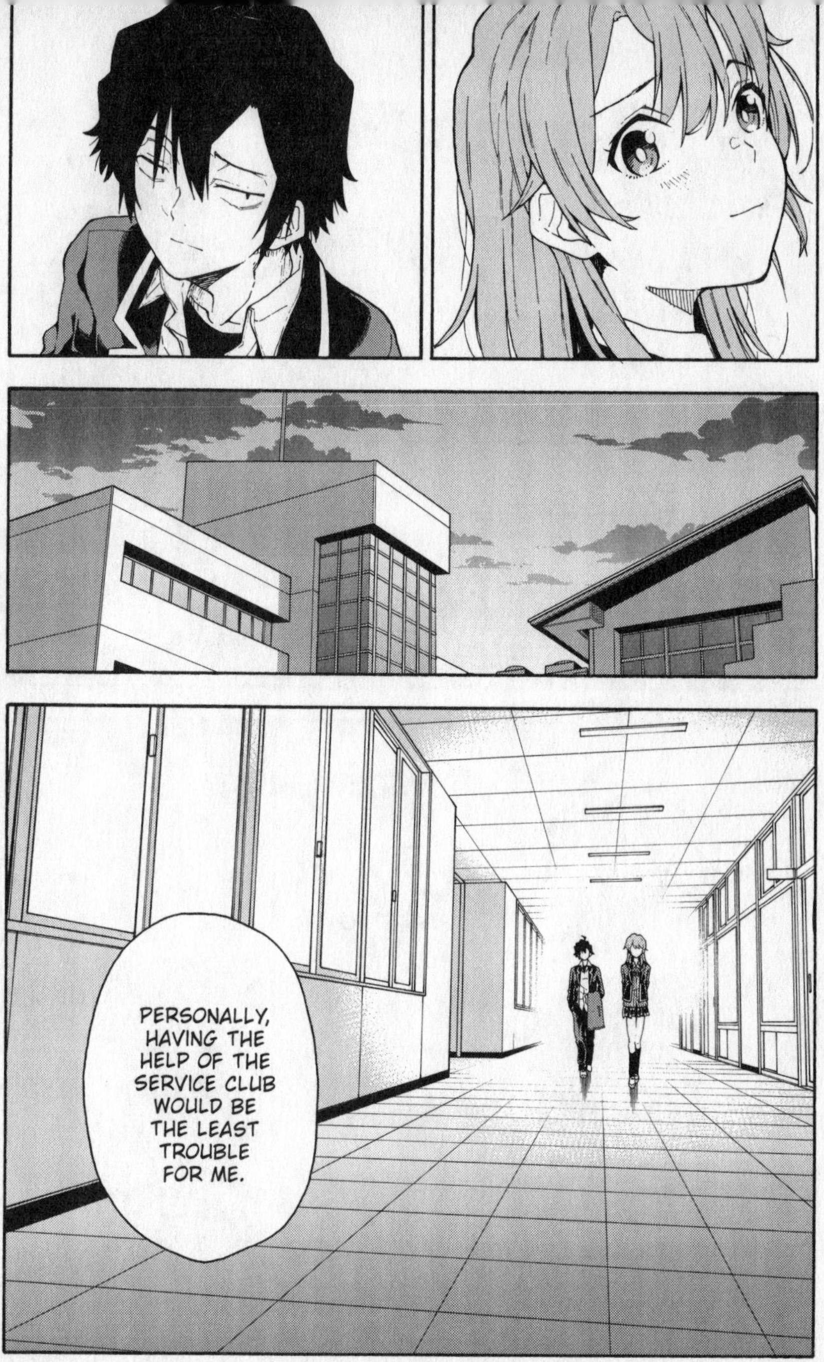
PERSONALLY, HAVING THE HELP OF THE SERVICE CLUB WOULD BE THE LEAST TROUBLE FOR ME.

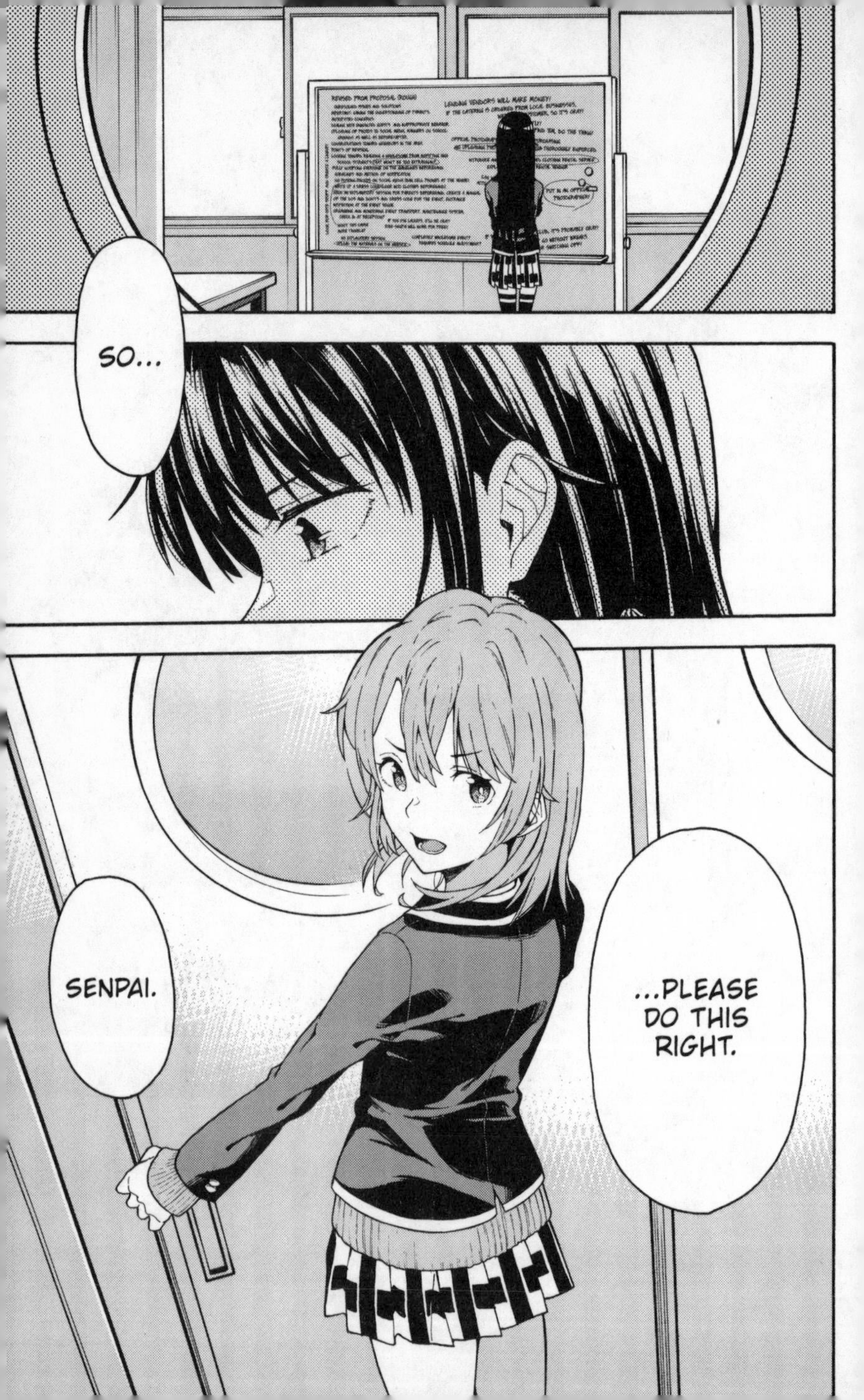
SO...
...PLEASE DO THIS RIGHT.
SENPAI.

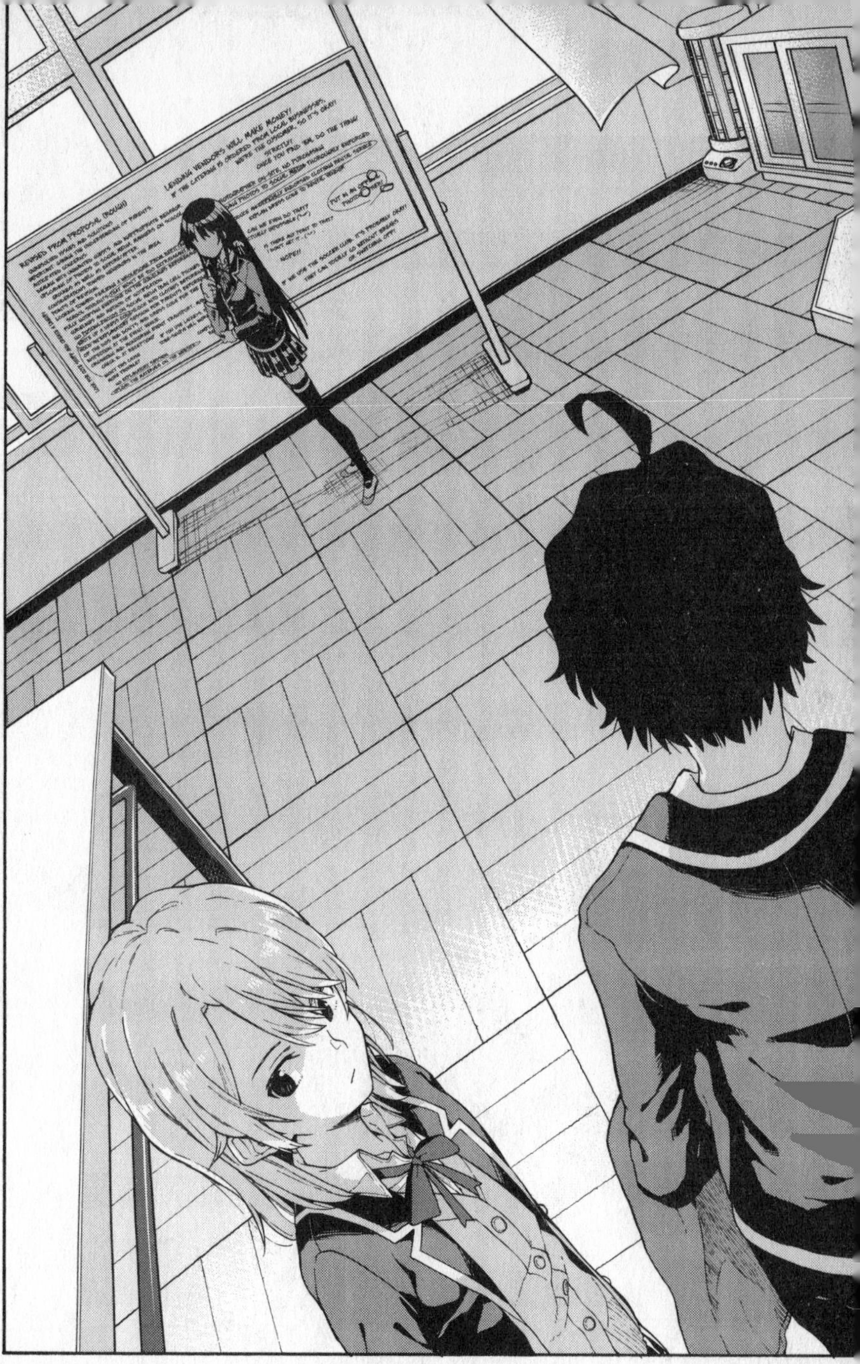
REVISED FROM PROPOSAL (ROUGH)
LEADING VENDORS WILL MAKE MONEY!
IF THE CATERING IS ORDERED FROM LOCAL BUSINESSES,
WE'RE THE CUSTOMER, SO IT'S OKAY!
STRICTLY!
NOPE!!
IF WE USE THE SOCCER CLUB, IT'S PROBABLY OKAY!
THEY CAN TOTALLY GO WITHOUT BREAKS
OR SWITCHING OFF!

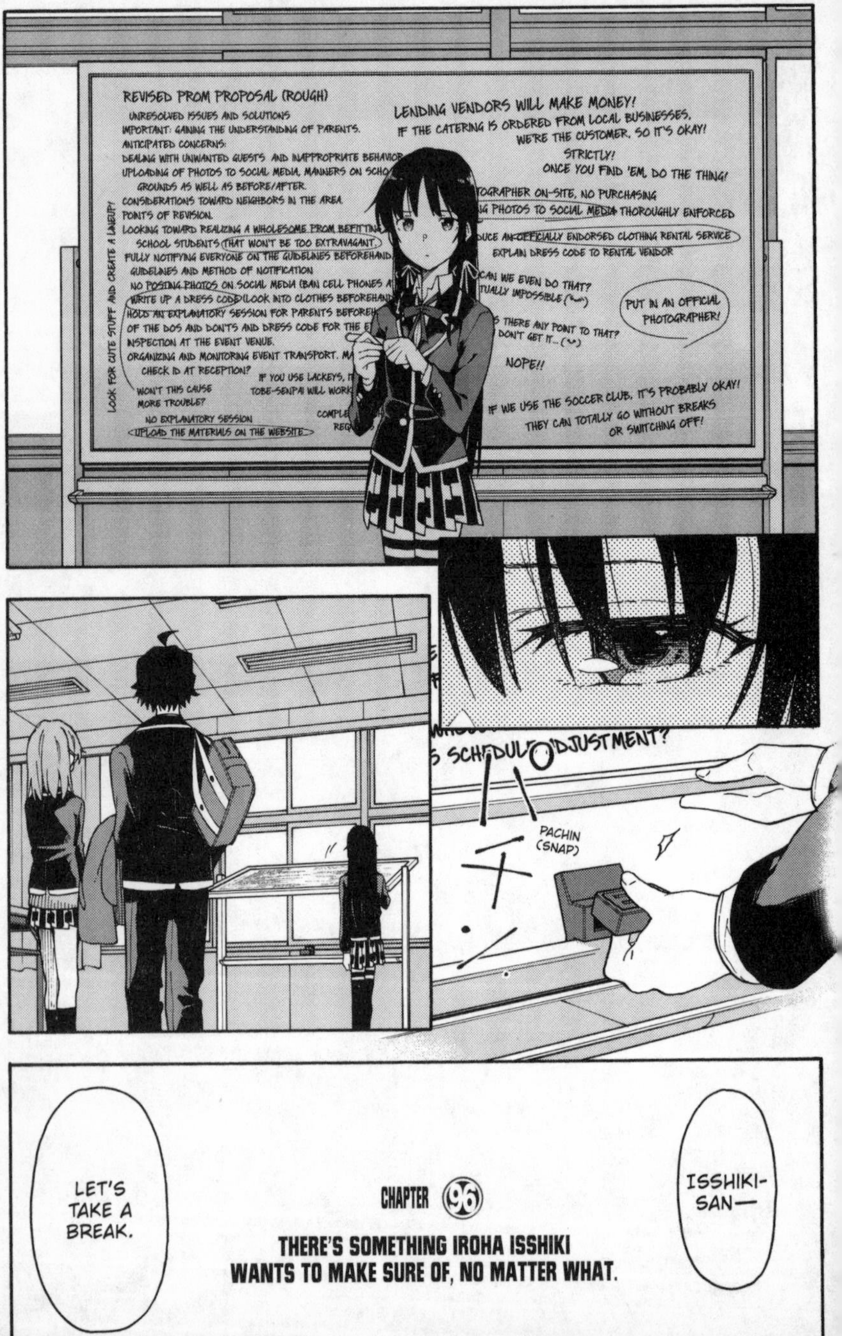

REVISED PROM PROPOSAL (ROUGH)
UNRESOLVED ISSUES AND SOLUTIONS
IMPORTANT: GAINING THE UNDERSTANDING OF PARENTS.
ANTICIPATED CONCERNS:
DEALING WITH UNWANTED GUESTS AND INAPPROPRIATE BEHAVIOR
UPLOADING OF PHOTOS TO SOCIAL MEDIA, MANNERS ON
GROUNDS AS WELL AS BEFORE/AFTER.
CONSIDERATIONS TOWARD NEIGHBORS IN THE AREA
POINTS OF REVISION.
LOOKING TOWARD REALIZING A WHOLESOME PROM
SCHOOL STUDENTS THAT WON'T BE TOO EXTRAVAGANT.
FULLY NOTIFYING EVERYONE ON THE GUIDELINES BEFOREHAND
GUIDELINES AND METHOD OF NOTIFICATION
NO POSTING PHOTOS ON SOCIAL MEDIA (BAN CELL PHONES
WRITE UP A DRESS CODE (LOOK INTO CLOTHES
HOLD AN EXPLANATORY SESSION FOR PARENTS
OF THE DOS AND DON'TS AND DRESS CODE FOR THE
INSPECTION AT THE EVENT VENUE.
ORGANIZING AND MONITORING EVENT TRANSPORT.
CHECK ID AT RECEPTION?
LOOK FOR CUTE STUFF AND CREATE A LINEUP!
WON'T THIS CAUSE MORE TROUBLE?
IF YOU USE LACKEYS,
TOBE-SENPAI WILL
NO EXPLANATORY SESSION
UPLOAD THE MATERIALS ON THE WEBSITE
LENDING VENDORS WILL MAKE MONEY!
IF THE CATERING IS ORDERED FROM LOCAL BUSINESSES, WE'RE THE CUSTOMER, SO IT'S OKAY!
STRICTLY!
ONCE YOU FIND 'EM, DO THE THING!
ON-SITE, NO PURCHASING
PHOTOS TO SOCIAL MEDIA THOROUGHLY ENFORCED
AN OFFICIALLY ENDORSED CLOTHING RENTAL SERVICE
EXPLAIN DRESS CODE TO RENTAL VENDOR
CAN WE EVEN DO THAT?
IMPOSSIBLE (ᵔ‿ᵔ)
THERE ANY POINT TO THAT?
DON'T GET IT... (ᵔ‿ᵔ)
PUT IN AN OFFICIAL PHOTOGRAPHER!
NOPE!!
IF WE USE THE SOCCER CLUB, IT'S PROBABLY OKAY! THEY CAN TOTALLY GO WITHOUT BREAKS OR SWITCHING OFF!
SCHEDULE ADJUSTMENT?
PACHIN (SNAP)
ISSHIKI-SAN—
LET'S TAKE A BREAK.

CHAPTER 96

THERE'S SOMETHING IROHA ISSHIKI WANTS TO MAKE SURE OF, NO MATTER WHAT.

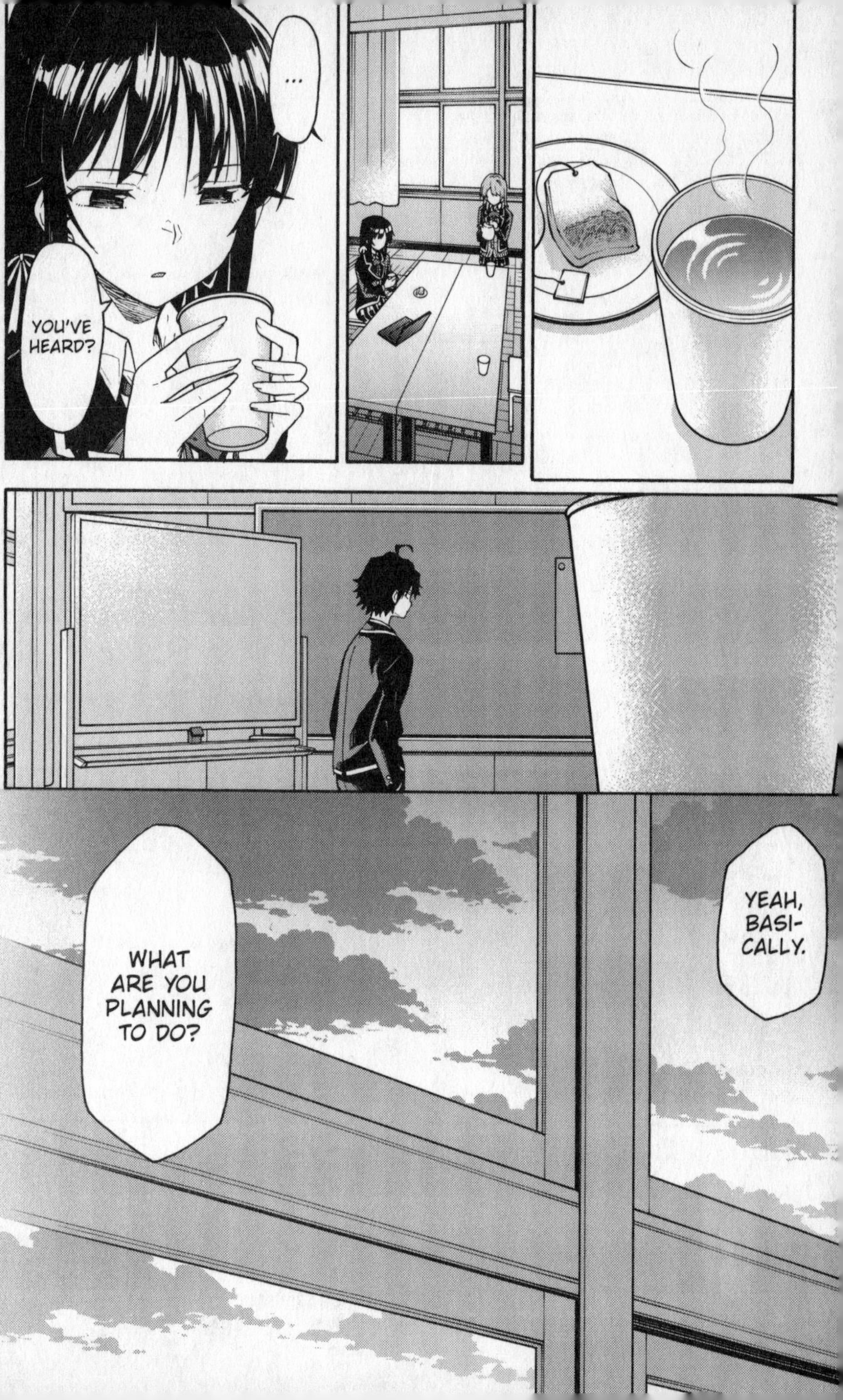
...
YOU'VE HEARD?
YEAH, BASI-CALLY.
WHAT ARE YOU PLANNING TO DO?

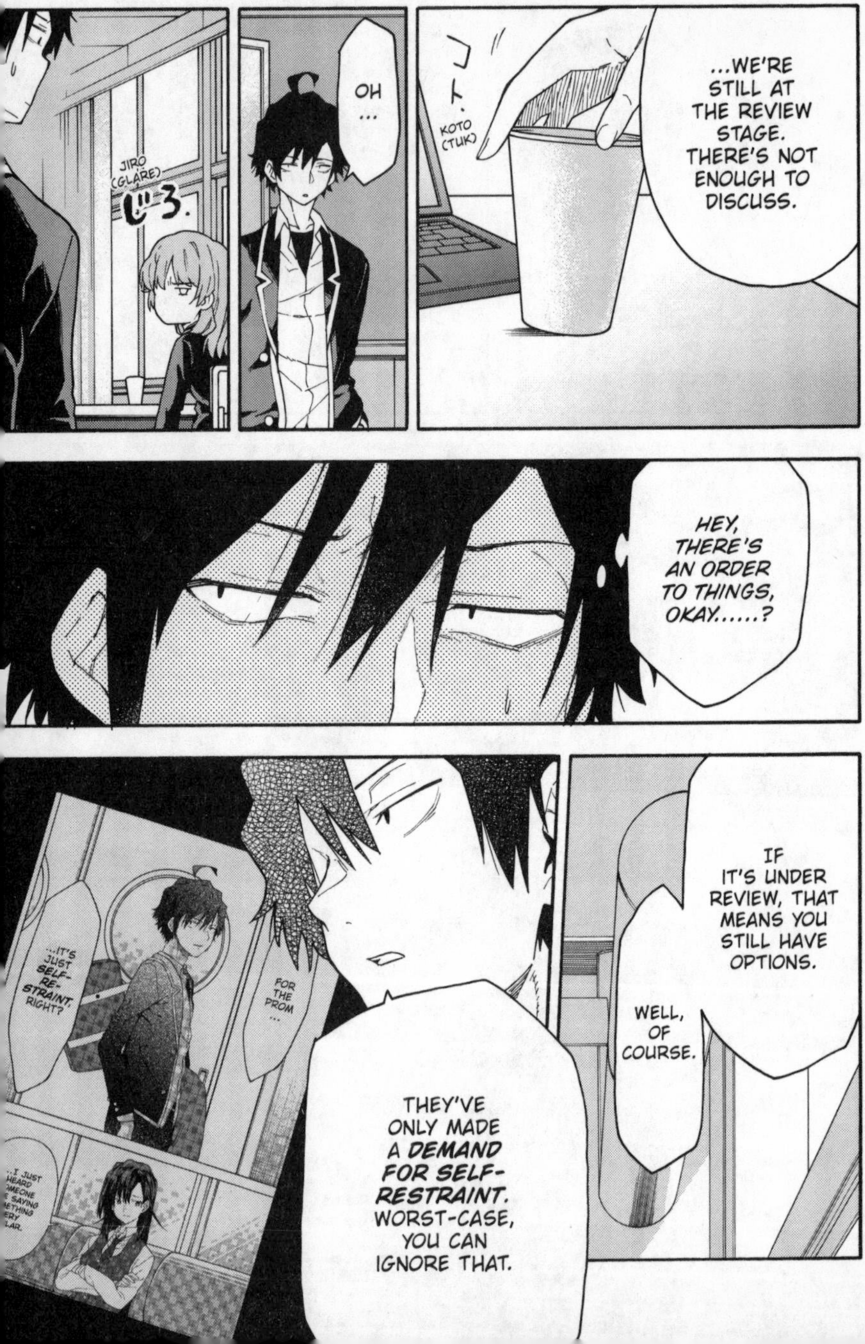
...WE'RE STILL AT THE REVIEW STAGE. THERE'S NOT ENOUGH TO DISCUSS.
KOTO (TUK)
OH ...
JIRO (GLARE)
HEY, THERE'S AN ORDER TO THINGS, OKAY......?
IF IT'S UNDER REVIEW, THAT MEANS YOU STILL HAVE OPTIONS.
WELL, OF COURSE.
THEY'VE ONLY MADE A **DEMAND FOR SELF-RESTRAINT.** WORST-CASE, YOU CAN IGNORE THAT.
FOR THE PROM ...
...IT'S JUST *SELF-RESTRAINT,* RIGHT?
...I JUST HEARD

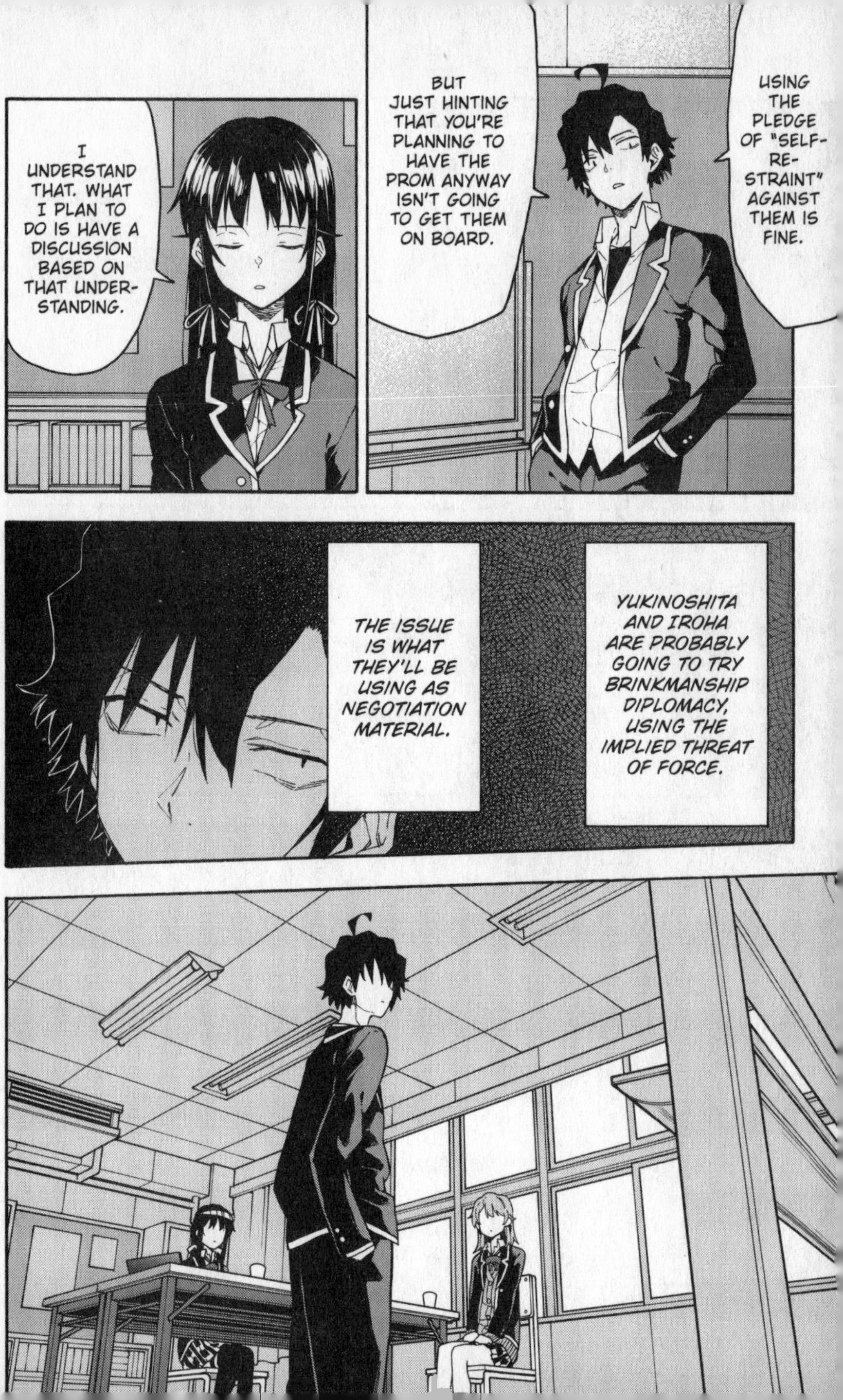
USING THE PLEDGE OF "SELF-RESTRAINT" AGAINST THEM IS FINE.
BUT JUST HINTING THAT YOU'RE PLANNING TO HAVE THE PROM ANYWAY ISN'T GOING TO GET THEM ON BOARD.
I UNDERSTAND THAT. WHAT I PLAN TO DO IS HAVE A DISCUSSION BASED ON THAT UNDER-STANDING.
YUKINOSHITA AND IROHA ARE PROBABLY GOING TO TRY BRINKMANSHIP DIPLOMACY, USING THE IMPLIED THREAT OF FORCE.
THE ISSUE IS WHAT THEY'LL BE USING AS NEGOTIATION MATERIAL.

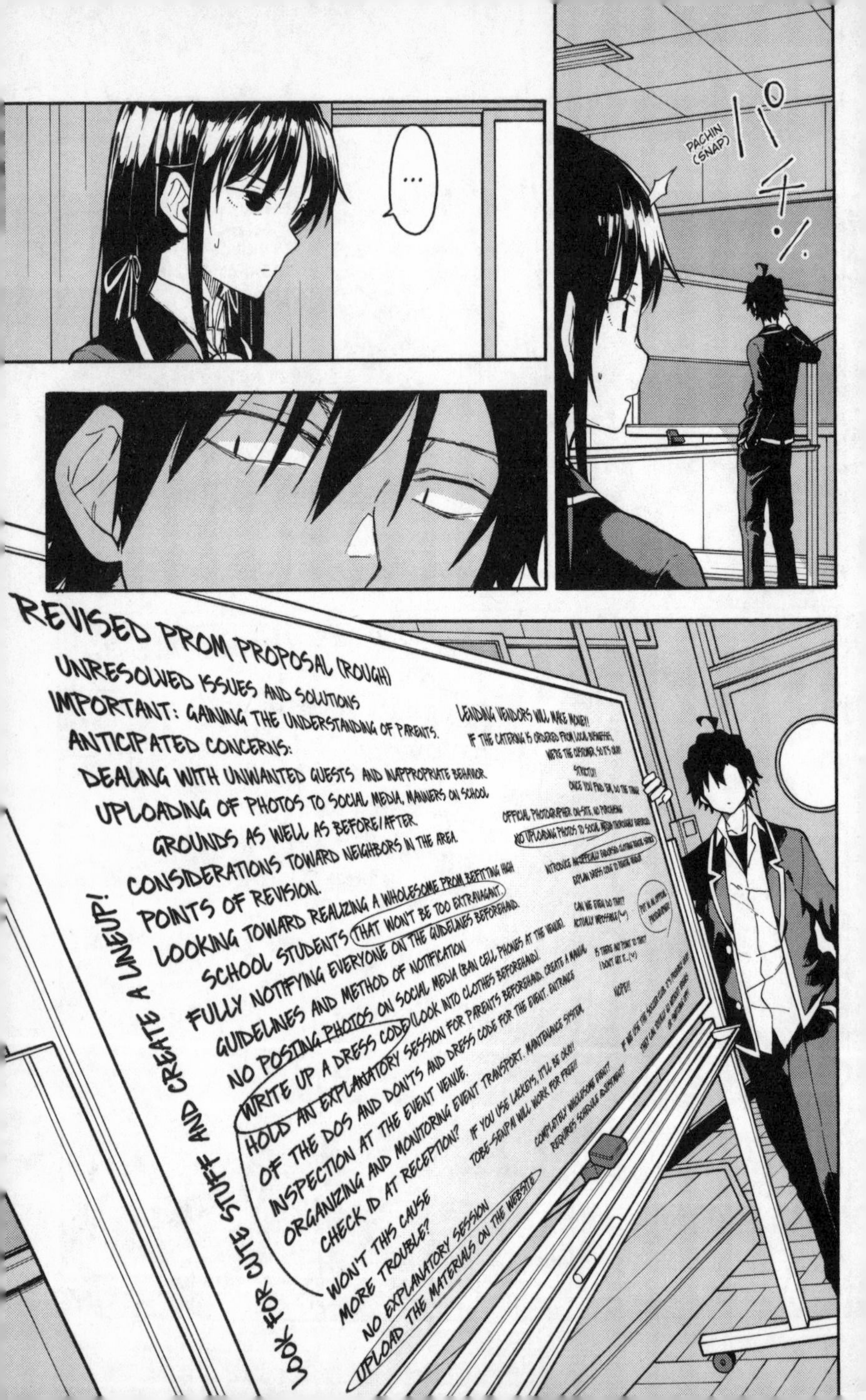
PACHIN (SNAP)
パチン
...
REVISED PROM PROPOSAL
UNRESOLVED ISSUES AND SOLUTIONS (ROUGH)
IMPORTANT: GAINING THE UNDERSTANDING OF PARENTS.
ANTICIPATED CONCERNS:
DEALING WITH UNWANTED GUESTS AND INAPPROPRIATE BEHAVIOR
UPLOADING OF PHOTOS TO SOCIAL MEDIA, MANNERS ON SCHOOL GROUNDS AS WELL AS BEFORE/AFTER.
CONSIDERATIONS TOWARD NEIGHBORS IN THE AREA.
POINTS OF REVISION.
LOOKING TOWARD REALIZING A WHOLESOME PROM BEFITTING HIGH SCHOOL STUDENTS THAT WON'T BE TOO EXTRAVAGANT.
FULLY NOTIFYING EVERYONE ON THE GUIDELINES BEFOREHAND.
GUIDELINES AND METHOD OF NOTIFICATION
NO POSTING PHOTOS ON SOCIAL MEDIA (BAN CELL PHONES AT THE VENUE).
WRITE UP A DRESS CODE (LOOK INTO CLOTHES BEFOREHAND).
HOLD AN EXPLANATORY SESSION FOR PARENTS BEFOREHAND. CREATE A MANUAL OF THE DOS AND DON'TS AND DRESS CODE FOR THE EVENT. ENTRANCE INSPECTION AT THE EVENT VENUE.
ORGANIZING AND MONITORING EVENT TRANSPORT. MAINTENANCE SYSTEM.
CHECK ID AT RECEPTION?
WON'T THIS CAUSE MORE TROUBLE?
NO EXPLANATORY SESSION
UPLOAD THE MATERIALS ON THE WEBSITE
LOOK FOR CUTE STUFF AND CREATE A LINEUP!
LENDING VENDORS WILL MAKE MONEY!
IF THE CATERING IS ORDERED FROM LOCAL BUSINESSES,
STRICTLY!
OFFICIAL PHOTOGRAPHER ON-SITE, NO PURCHASING
EXPLAIN DRESS CODE TO REGULAR GUESTS
CAN WE EVEN DO THAT? ACTUALLY IMPOSSIBLE (^)
IS THERE ANY POINT TO THAT? I DON'T GET IT... (^)
NOPE!!
IF YOU USE LACKEYS, IT'LL BE OKAY! TOBE-SENPAI WILL WORK FOR FREE!!
COMPLETELY WHOLESOME EVENT? REQUIRES SCHEDULE ADJUSTMENT!

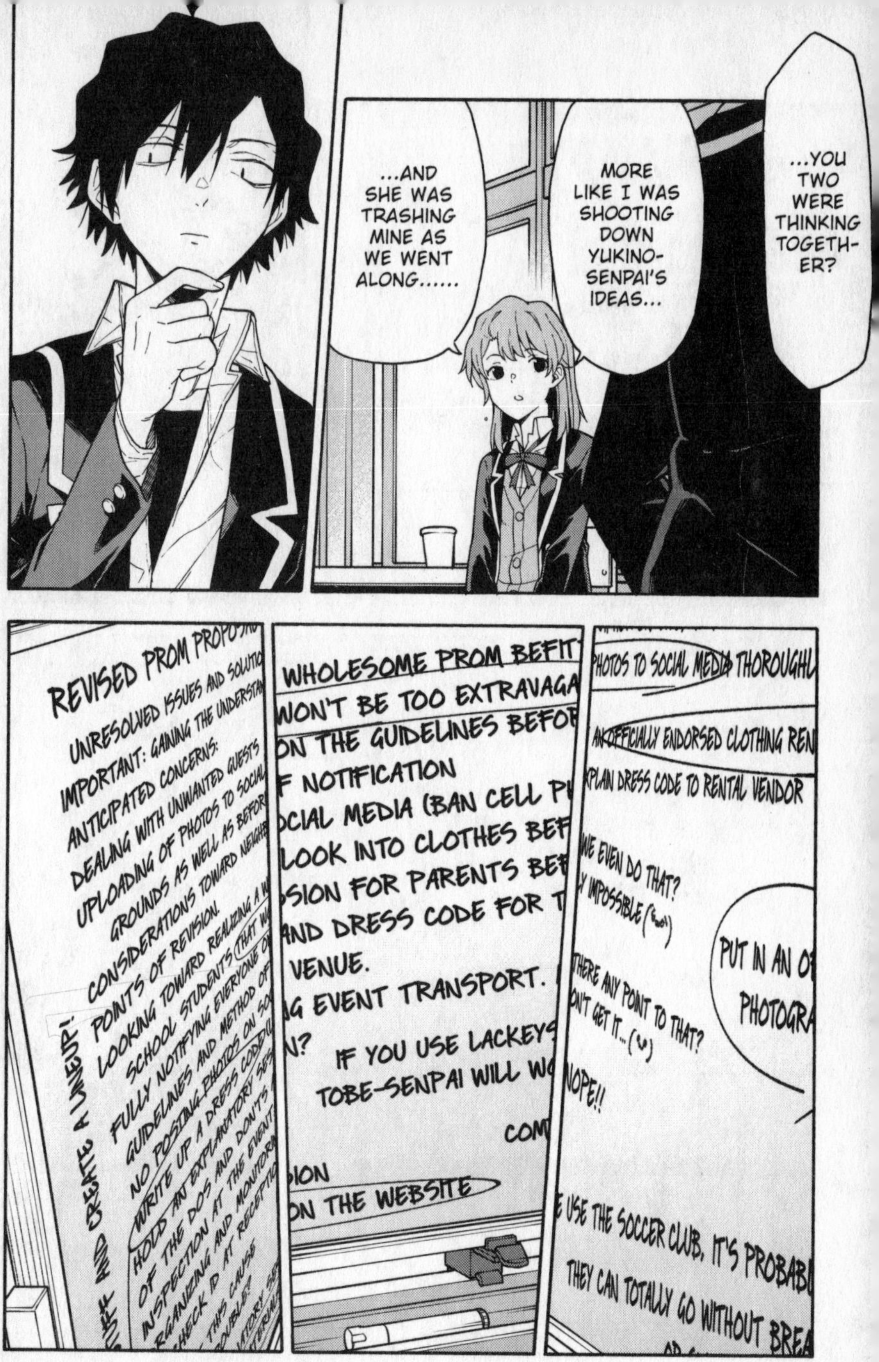
...YOU TWO WERE THINKING TOGETH-ER?
MORE LIKE I WAS SHOOTING DOWN YUKINO-SENPAI'S IDEAS...
...AND SHE WAS TRASHING MINE AS WE WENT ALONG......
PHOTOS TO SOCIAL MEDIA THOROUGHL
AN OFFICIALLY ENDORSED CLOTHING REN
XPLAIN DRESS CODE TO RENTAL VENDOR
WE EVEN DO THAT?
IMPOSSIBLE
PUT IN AN O
PHOTOGRA
THERE ANY POINT TO THAT?
ON'T GET IT...
NOPE!!
E USE THE SOCCER CLUB, IT'S PROBAB
THEY CAN TOTALLY GO WITHOUT BREA
WHOLESOME PROM BEFIT
WON'T BE TOO EXTRAVAGA
ON THE GUIDELINES BEFO
F NOTIFICATION
OCIAL MEDIA (BAN CELL P
LOOK INTO CLOTHES BEF
SION FOR PARENTS BE
AND DRESS CODE FOR T
VENUE.
G EVENT TRANSPORT.
N?
IF YOU USE LACKEYS
TOBE-SENPAI WILL WO
COM
SION
ON THE WEBSITE
REVISED PROM PROPOS
UNRESOLVED ISSUES AND SOLUTIO
IMPORTANT: GAINING THE UNDERSTAN
ANTICIPATED CONCERNS:
DEALING WITH UNWANTED GUESTS
UPLOADING OF PHOTOS TO SOCIAL
GROUNDS AS WELL AS BEFOR
CONSIDERATIONS TOWARD NEIGH
POINTS OF REVISION.
LOOKING TOWARD REALIZING A W
SCHOOL STUDENTS THAT W
FULLY NOTIFYING EVERYONE OF
GUIDELINES AND METHOD OF
NO POSTING PHOTOS ON SO
WRITE UP A DRESS CODE
HOLD AN EXPLANATORY SES
OF THE DOS AND DON'TS
INSPECTION AT THE EVENT
RGANIZING AND MONITORI
CHECK ID AT RECEPTIO
THIS CAUSE
DOUBLE?
AND CREATE A LINEUP!

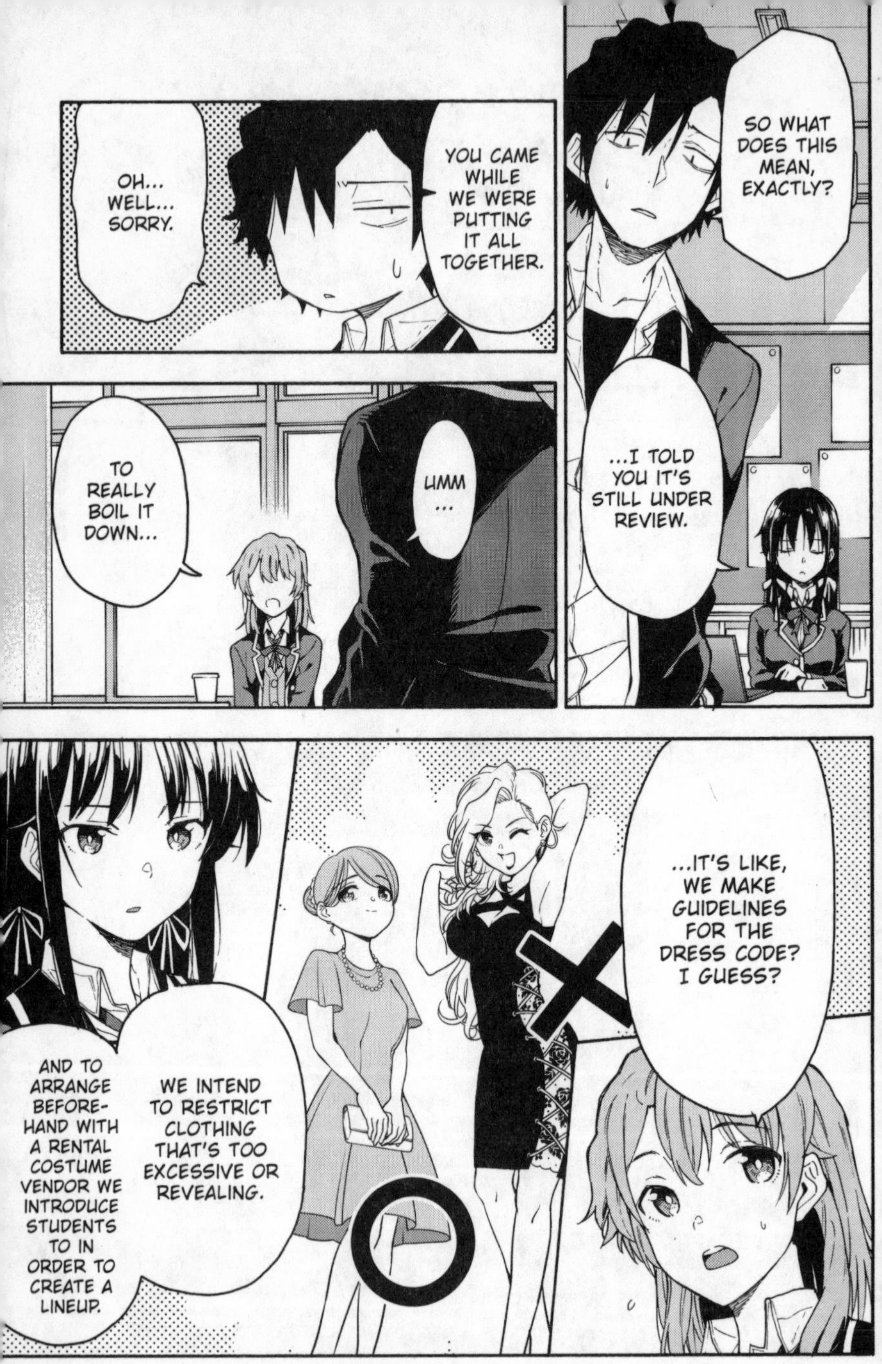
SO WHAT DOES THIS MEAN, EXACTLY?
...I TOLD YOU IT'S STILL UNDER REVIEW.
YOU CAME WHILE WE WERE PUTTING IT ALL TOGETHER.
OH... WELL... SORRY.
UMM ...
TO REALLY BOIL IT DOWN...
...IT'S LIKE, WE MAKE GUIDELINES FOR THE DRESS CODE? I GUESS?
WE INTEND TO RESTRICT CLOTHING THAT'S TOO EXCESSIVE OR REVEALING.
AND TO ARRANGE BEFORE-HAND WITH A RENTAL COSTUME VENDOR WE INTRODUCE STUDENTS TO IN ORDER TO CREATE A LINEUP.

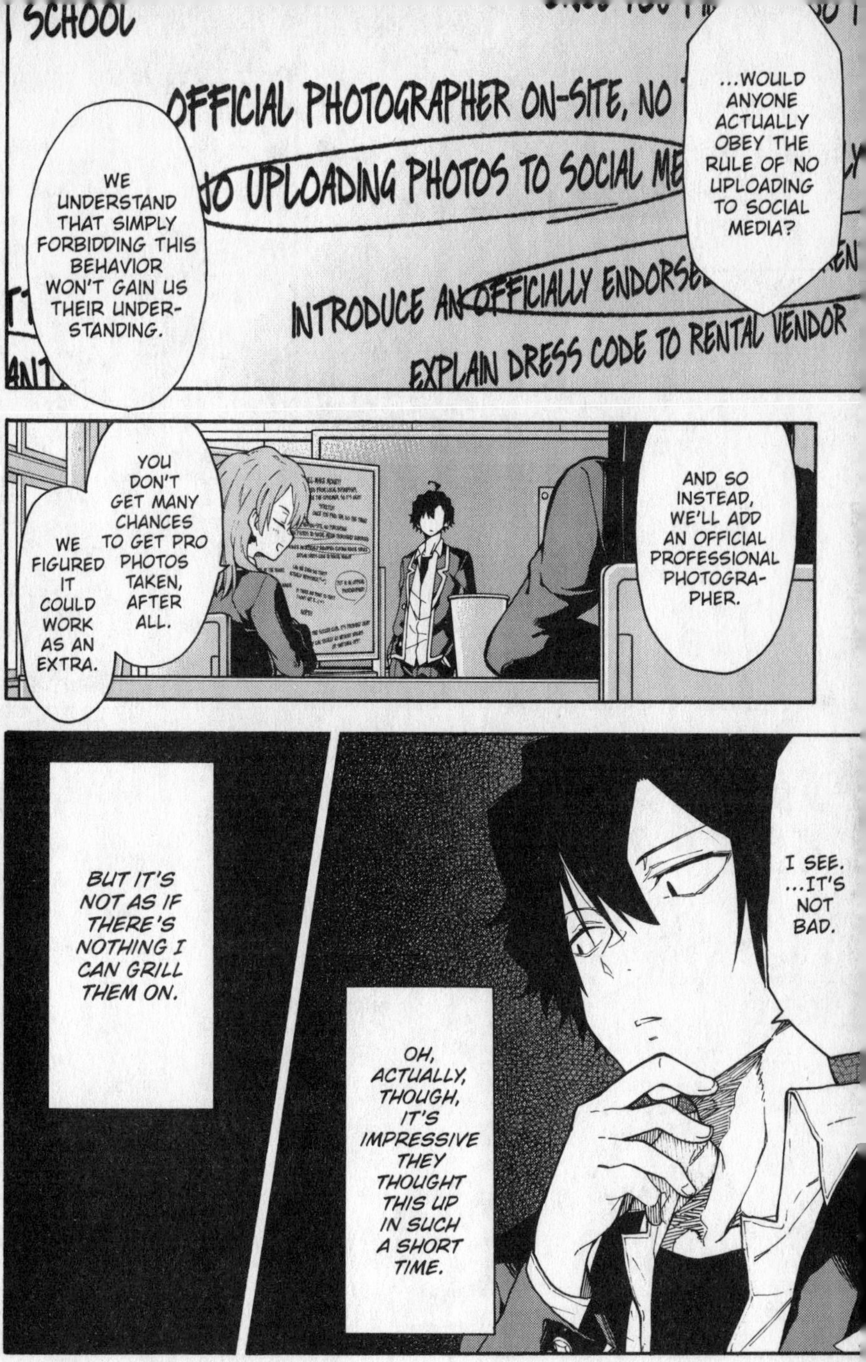
SCHOOL
OFFICIAL PHOTOGRAPHER ON-SITE, NO
UPLOADING PHOTOS TO SOCIAL ME
INTRODUCE AN OFFICIALLY ENDORSE
EXPLAIN DRESS CODE TO RENTAL VENDOR
...WOULD ANYONE ACTUALLY OBEY THE RULE OF NO UPLOADING TO SOCIAL MEDIA?
WE UNDERSTAND THAT SIMPLY FORBIDDING THIS BEHAVIOR WON'T GAIN US THEIR UNDER-STANDING.
AND SO INSTEAD, WE'LL ADD AN OFFICIAL PROFESSIONAL PHOTOGRA-PHER.
YOU DON'T GET MANY CHANCES TO GET PRO PHOTOS TAKEN, AFTER ALL.
WE FIGURED IT COULD WORK AS AN EXTRA.
I SEE. ...IT'S NOT BAD.
OH, ACTUALLY, THOUGH, IT'S IMPRESSIVE THEY THOUGHT THIS UP IN SUCH A SHORT TIME.
BUT IT'S NOT AS IF THERE'S NOTHING I CAN GRILL THEM ON.

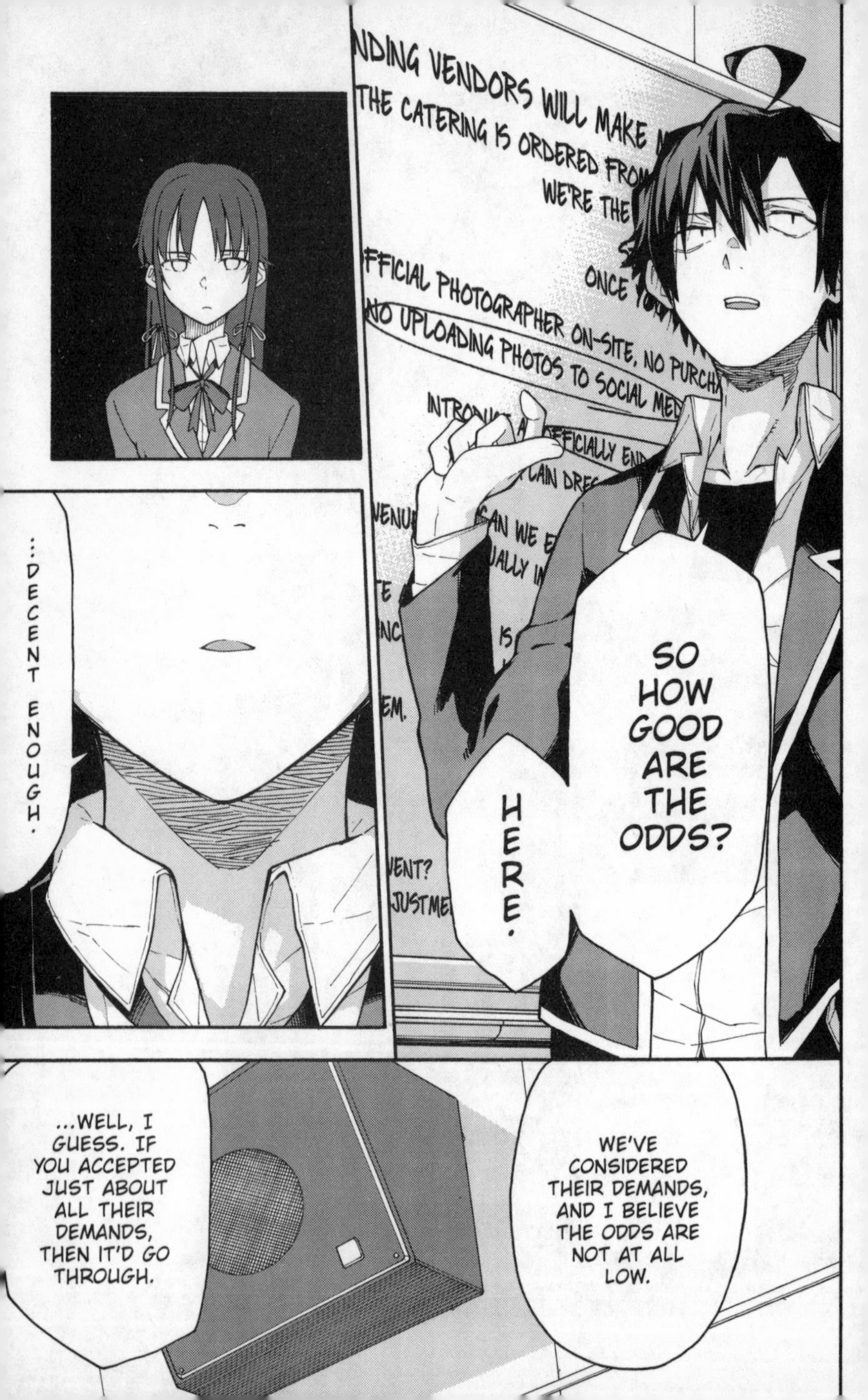
NDING VENDORS WILL MAKE
THE CATERING IS ORDERED FROM
WE'RE THE
ONCE
FFICIAL PHOTOGRAPHER ON-SITE, NO PURCHA
NO UPLOADING PHOTOS TO SOCIAL MED
SO HOW GOOD ARE THE ODDS?
HERE.
...DECENT ENOUGH.
WE'VE CONSIDERED THEIR DEMANDS, AND I BELIEVE THE ODDS ARE NOT AT ALL LOW.
...WELL, I GUESS. IF YOU ACCEPTED JUST ABOUT ALL THEIR DEMANDS, THEN IT'D GO THROUGH.

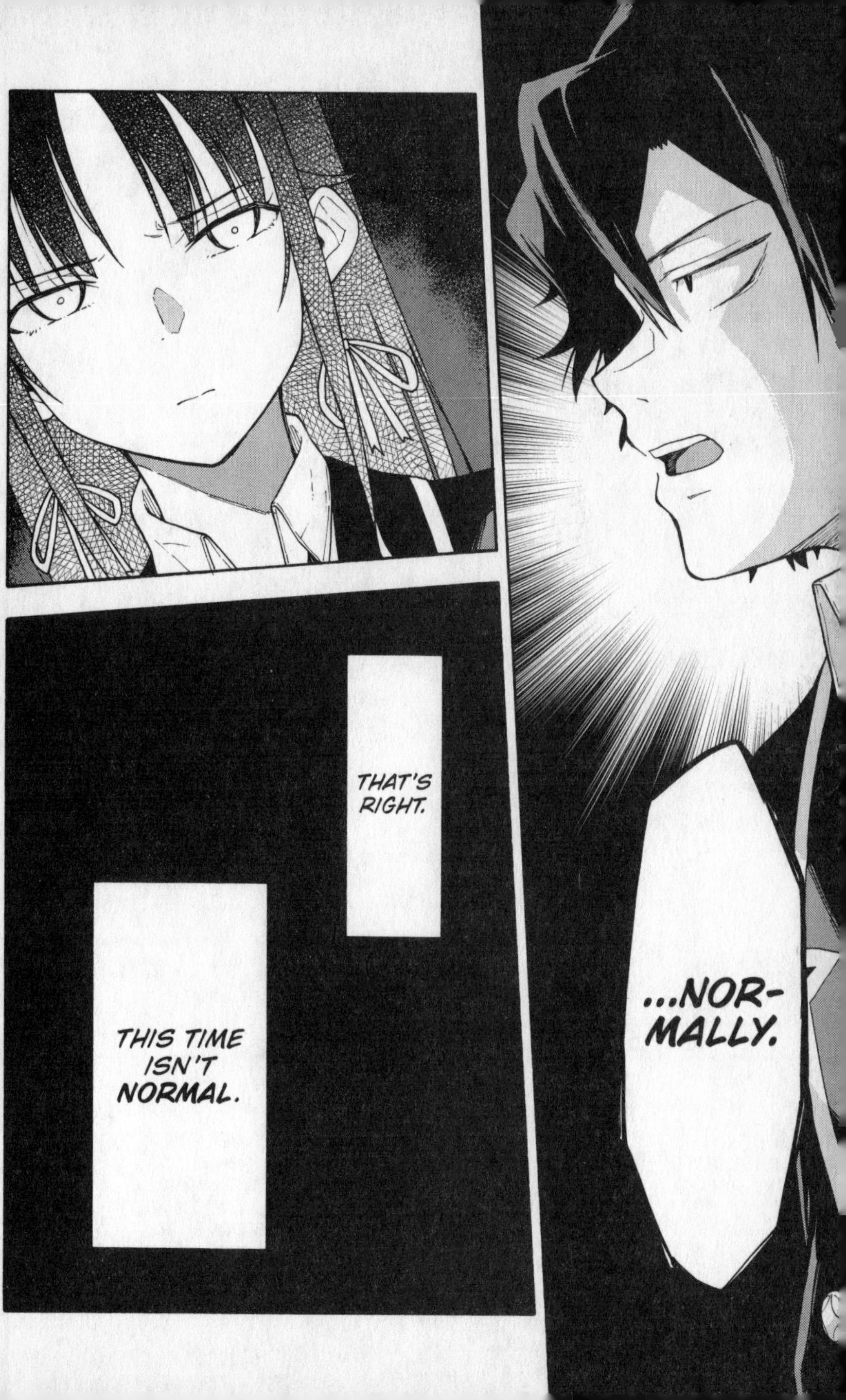
...NOR-
MALLY.
THAT'S RIGHT.
THIS TIME ISN'T NORMAL.

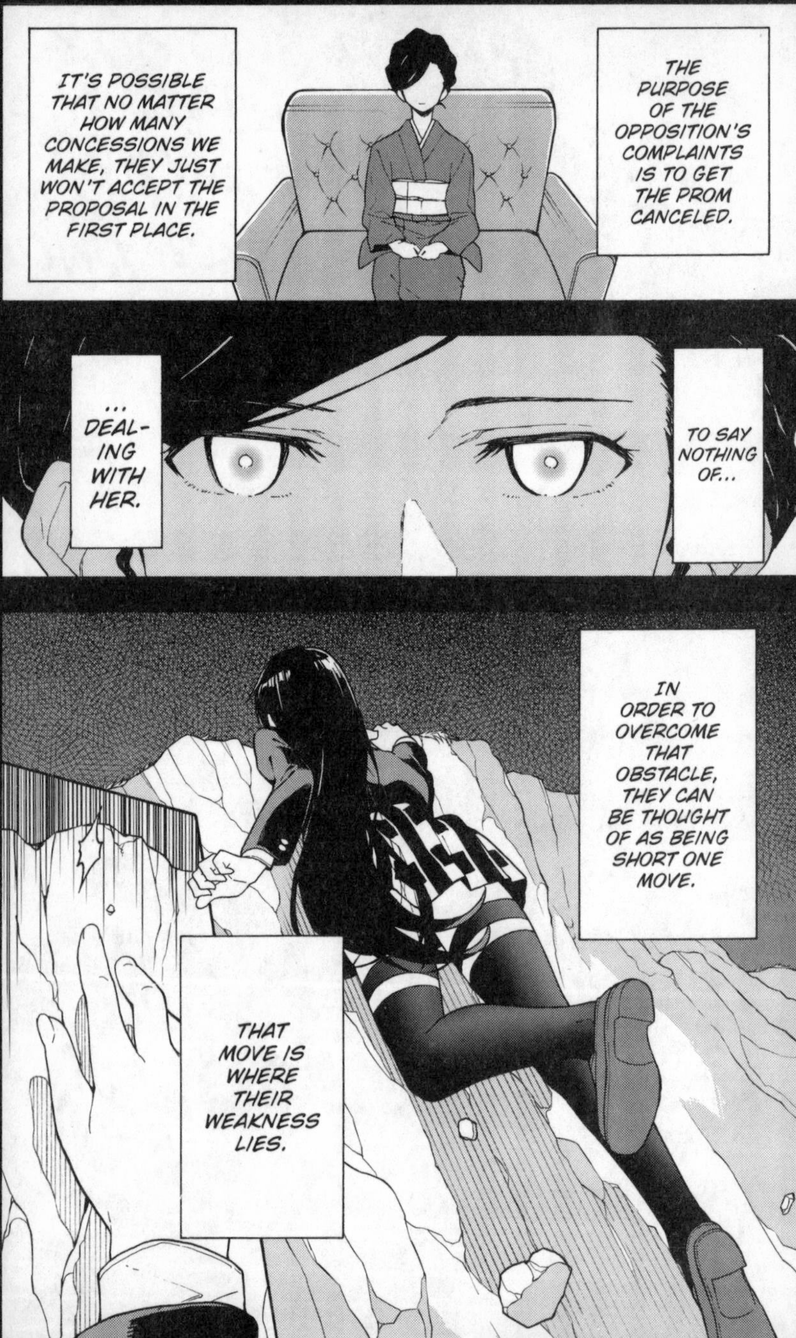
THE PURPOSE OF THE OPPOSITION'S COMPLAINTS IS TO GET THE PROM CANCELED.
IT'S POSSIBLE THAT NO MATTER HOW MANY CONCESSIONS WE MAKE, THEY JUST WON'T ACCEPT THE PROPOSAL IN THE FIRST PLACE.
TO SAY NOTHING OF...
...DEALING WITH HER.
IN ORDER TO OVERCOME THAT OBSTACLE, THEY CAN BE THOUGHT OF AS BEING SHORT ONE MOVE.
THAT MOVE IS WHERE THEIR WEAKNESS LIES.

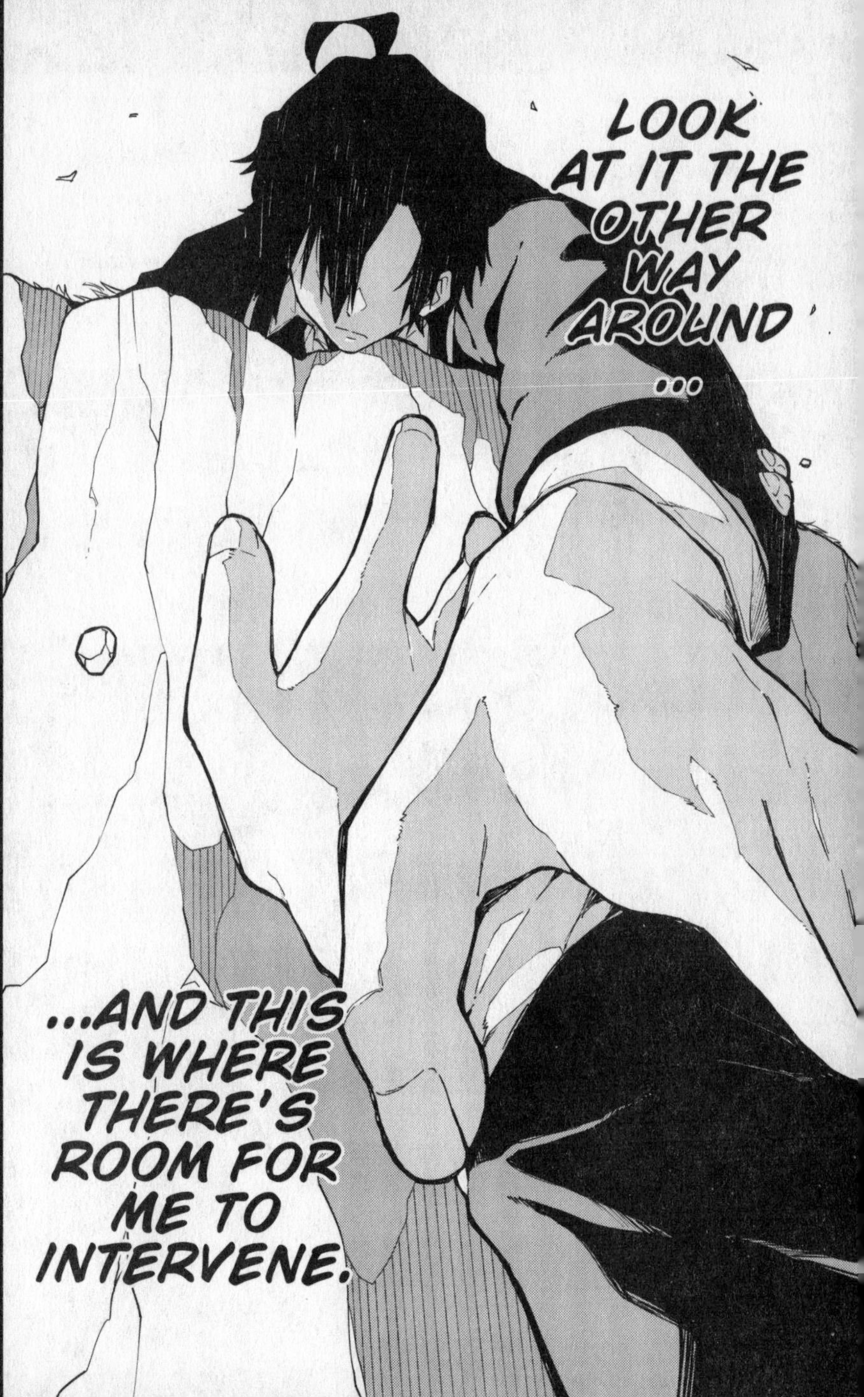
LOOK AT IT THE OTHER WAY AROUND ...
...AND THIS IS WHERE THERE'S ROOM FOR ME TO INTERVENE.

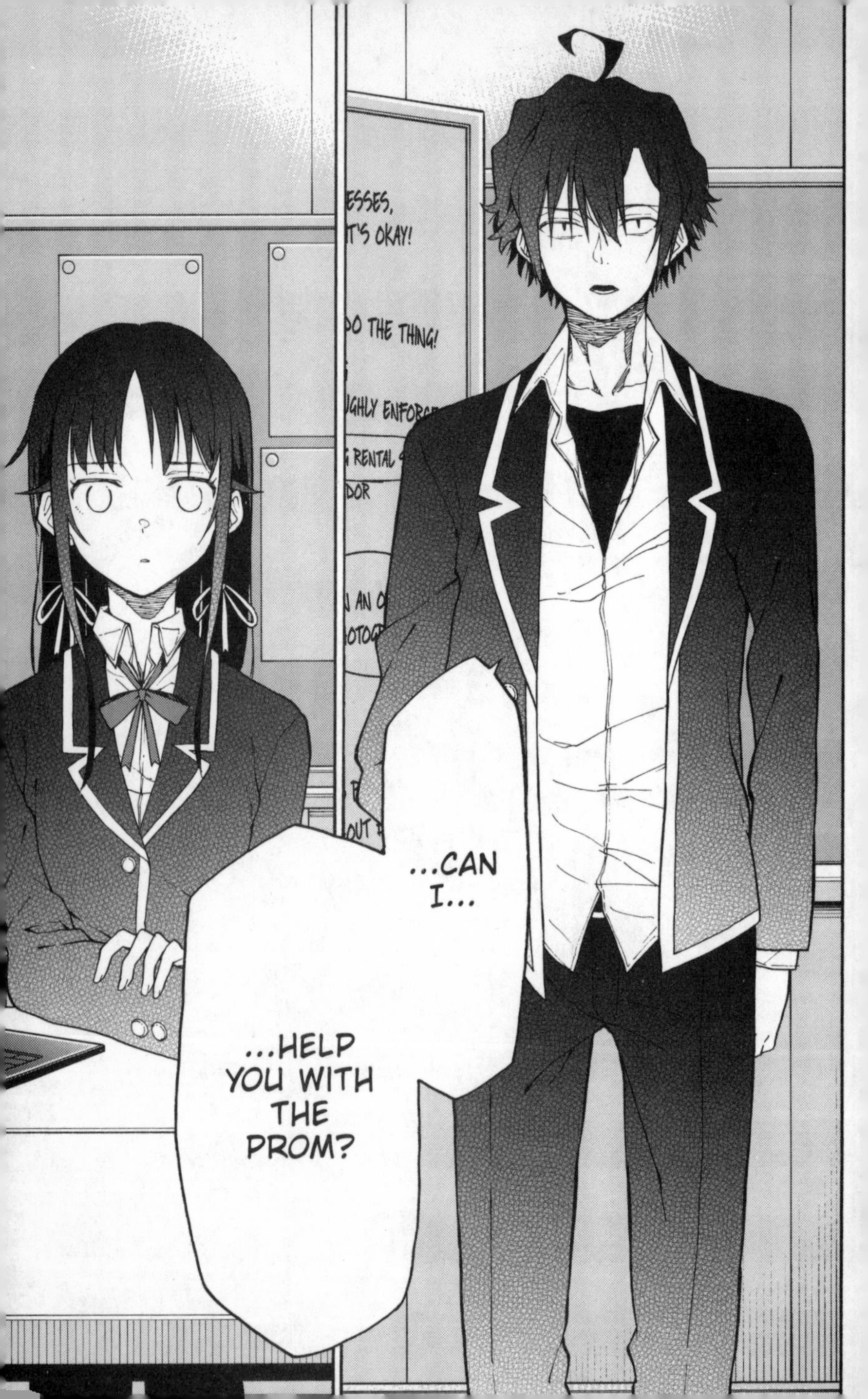
...CAN I...
...HELP YOU WITH THE PROM?

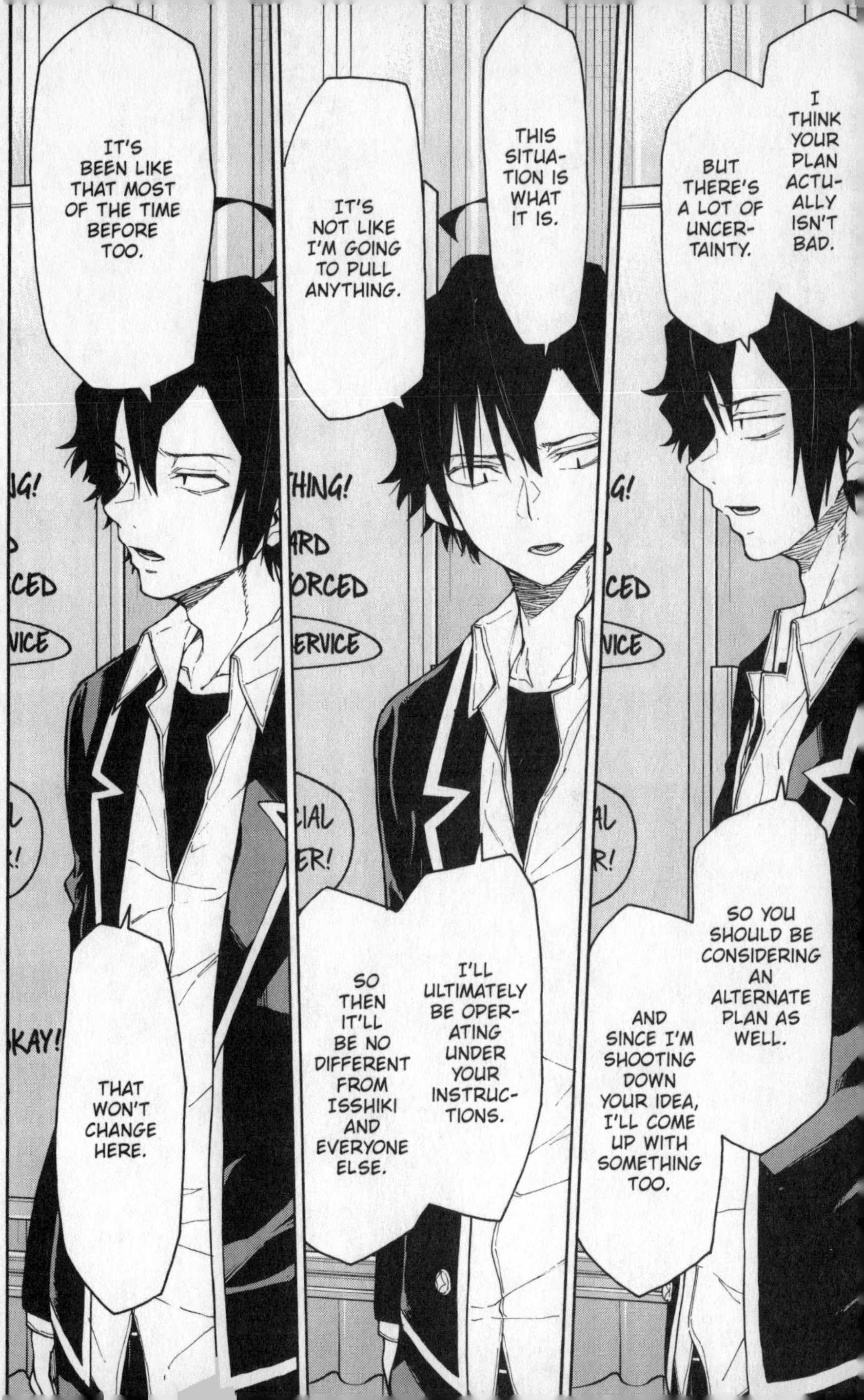
I THINK YOUR PLAN ACTUALLY ISN'T BAD.
BUT THERE'S A LOT OF UNCERTAINTY.
SO YOU SHOULD BE CONSIDERING AN ALTERNATE PLAN AS WELL.
AND SINCE I'M SHOOTING DOWN YOUR IDEA, I'LL COME UP WITH SOMETHING TOO.
THIS SITUATION IS WHAT IT IS.
IT'S NOT LIKE I'M GOING TO PULL ANYTHING.
I'LL ULTIMATELY BE OPERATING UNDER YOUR INSTRUCTIONS.
SO THEN IT'LL BE NO DIFFERENT FROM ISSHIKI AND EVERYONE ELSE.
IT'S BEEN LIKE THAT MOST OF THE TIME BEFORE TOO.
THAT WON'T CHANGE HERE.

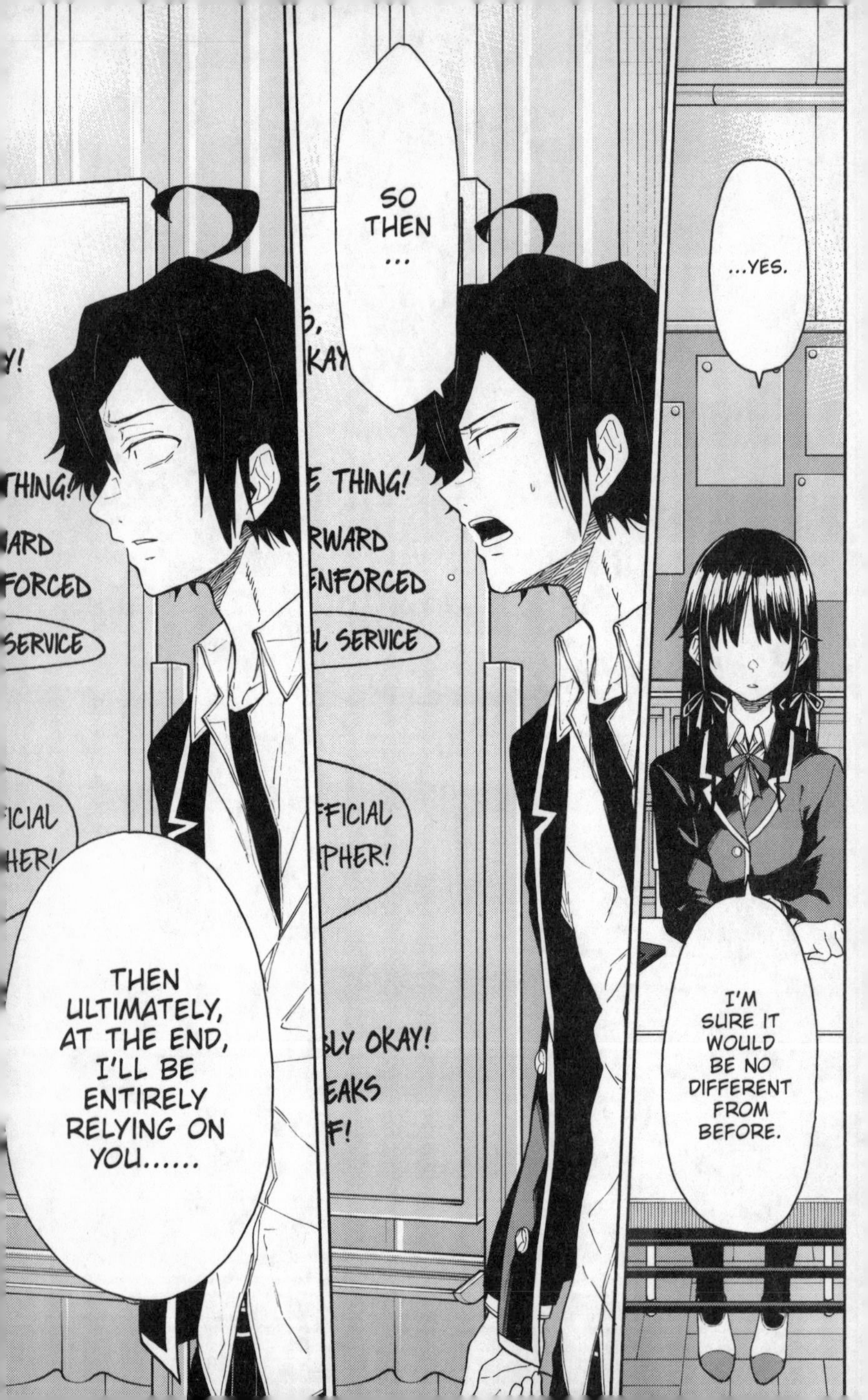
...YES.
I'M SURE IT WOULD BE NO DIFFERENT FROM BEFORE.
SO THEN ...
THEN ULTIMATELY, AT THE END, I'LL BE ENTIRELY RELYING ON YOU......

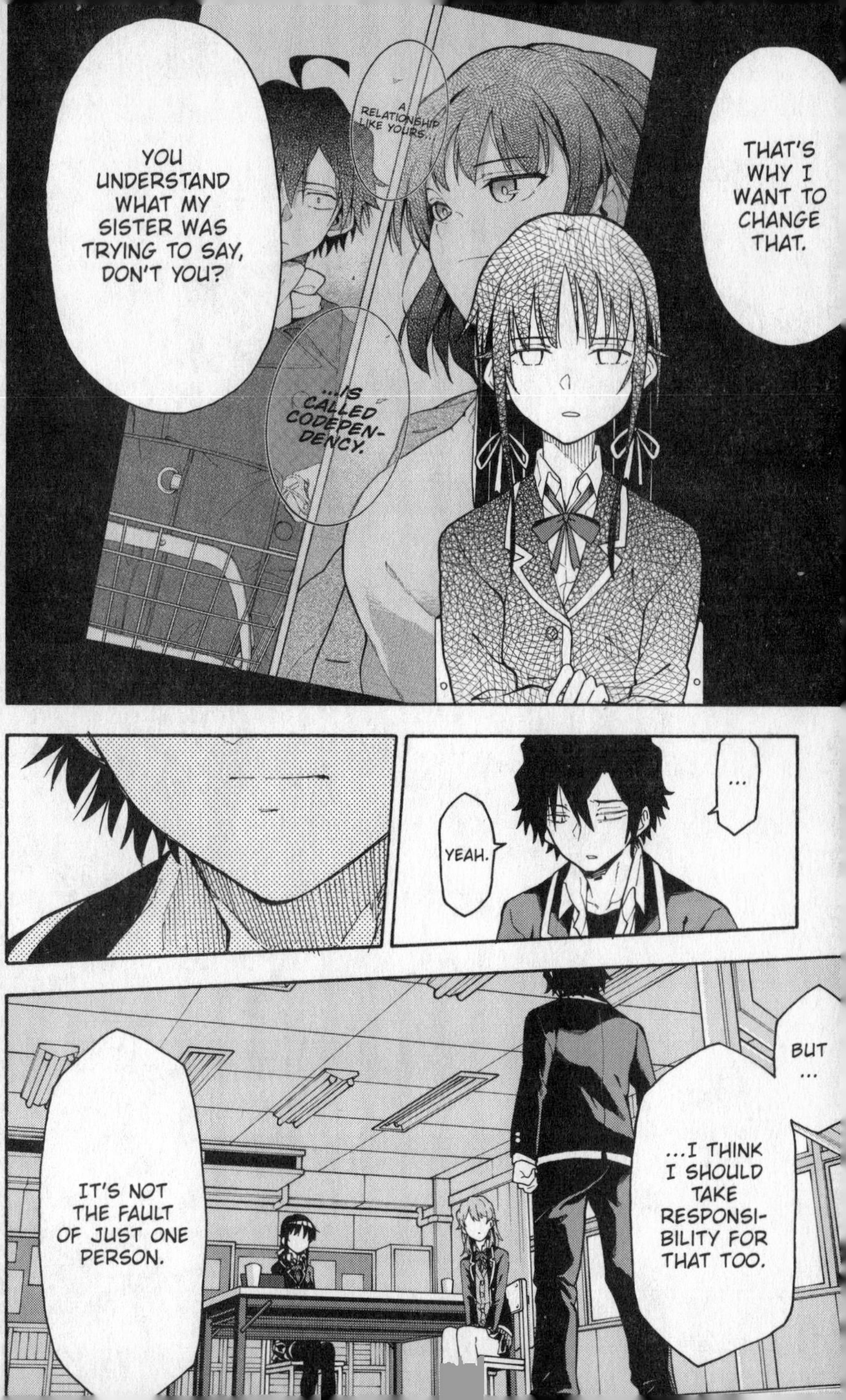
YOU UNDERSTAND WHAT MY SISTER WAS TRYING TO SAY, DON'T YOU?
A RELATIONSHIP LIKE YOURS...
...IS CALLED CODEPENDENCY.
THAT'S WHY I WANT TO CHANGE THAT.
...
YEAH.
BUT...
...I THINK I SHOULD TAKE RESPONSIBILITY FOR THAT TOO.
IT'S NOT THE FAULT OF JUST ONE PERSON.

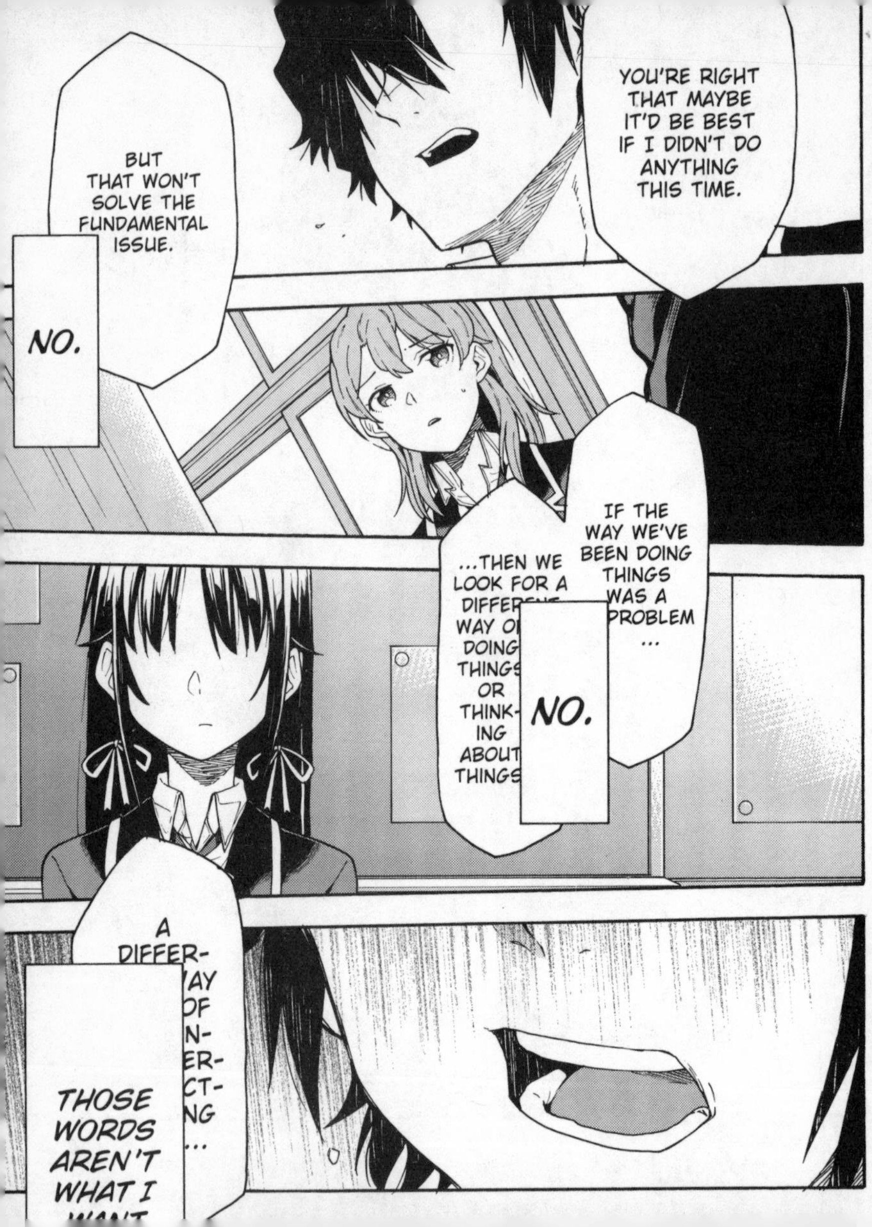
YOU'RE RIGHT THAT MAYBE IT'D BE BEST IF I DIDN'T DO ANYTHING THIS TIME.
BUT THAT WON'T SOLVE THE FUNDAMENTAL ISSUE.
NO.
IF THE WAY WE'VE BEEN DOING THINGS WAS A PROBLEM...
...THEN WE LOOK FOR A DIFFER WAY O DOING THING OR THINK- ING ABOUT THINGS
NO.
A DIFFER- AY OF N- ER- CT- NG...
THOSE WORDS AREN'T WHAT I

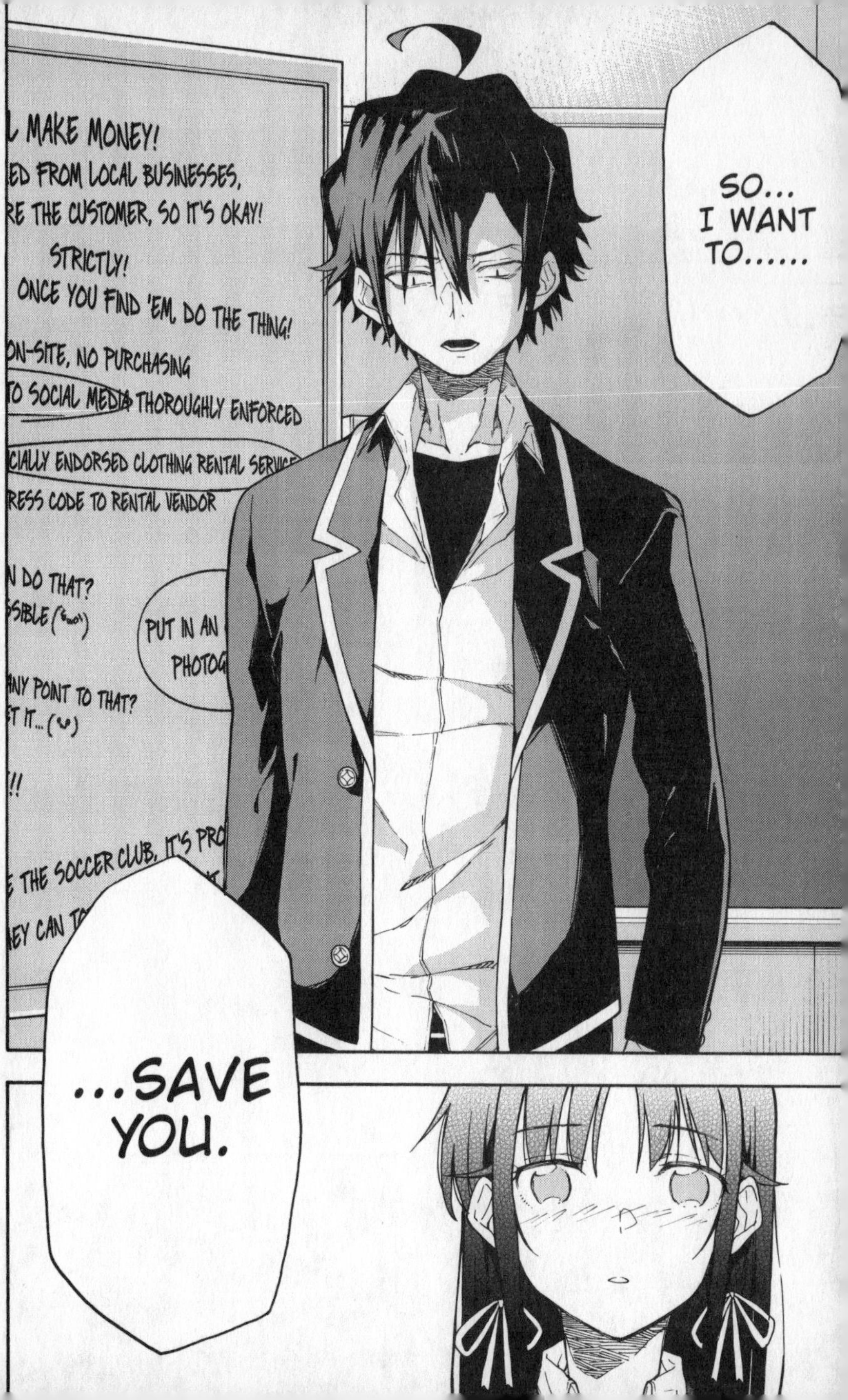
SO... I WANT TO......
L MAKE MONEY!
ED FROM LOCAL BUSINESSES,
RE THE CUSTOMER, SO IT'S OKAY!
STRICTLY!
ONCE YOU FIND 'EM, DO THE THING!
ON-SITE, NO PURCHASING
TO SOCIAL MEDIA THOROUGHLY ENFORCED
CIALLY ENDORSED CLOTHING RENTAL SERVIC
RESS CODE TO RENTAL VENDOR
N DO THAT?
SSIBLE
PUT IN AN
PHOTOG
ANY POINT TO THAT?
T IT...
!!
THE SOCCER CLUB, IT'S PRO
EY CAN T
...SAVE YOU.

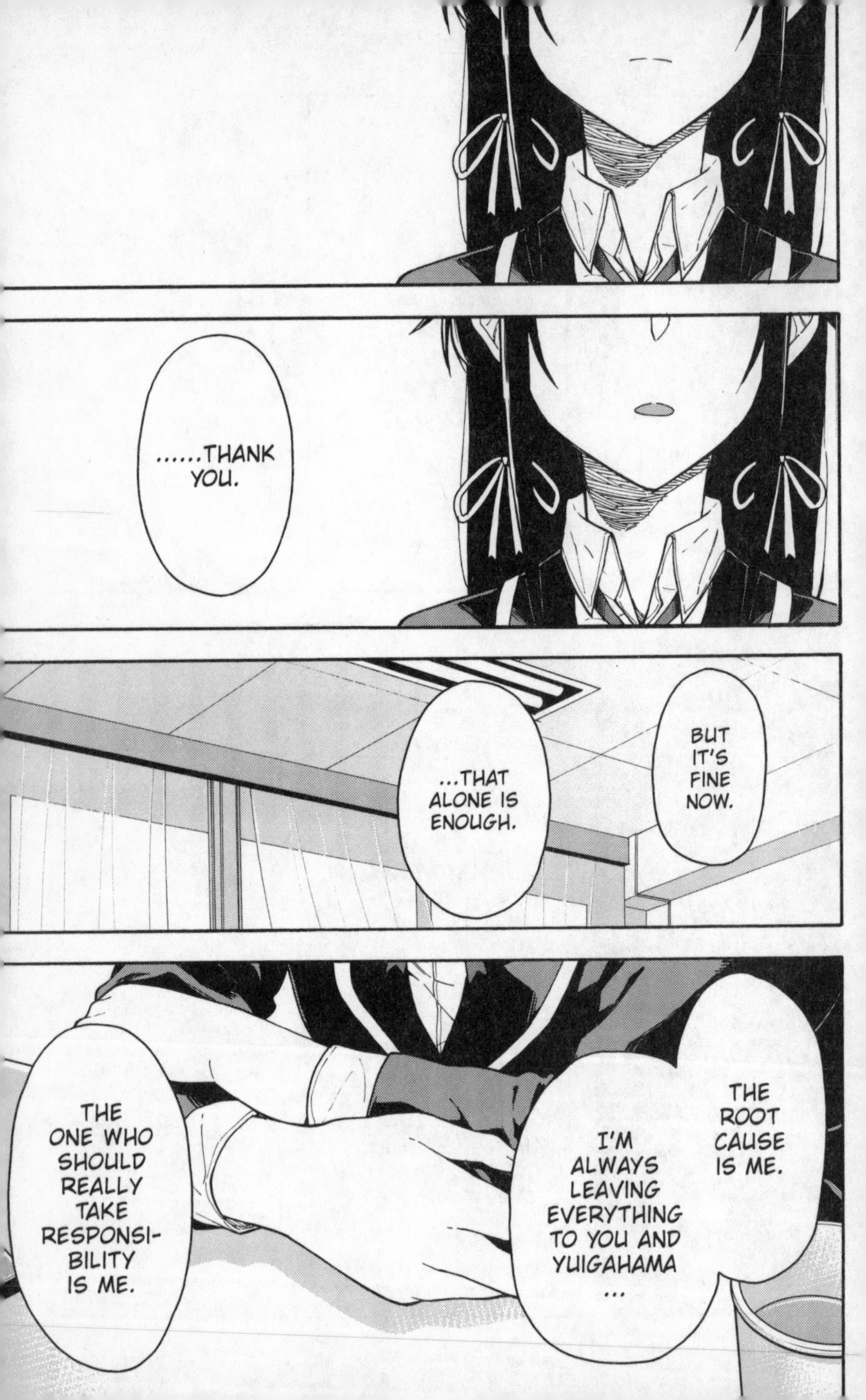

......THANK YOU.
BUT IT'S FINE NOW.
...THAT ALONE IS ENOUGH.
THE ROOT CAUSE IS ME.
I'M ALWAYS LEAVING EVERYTHING TO YOU AND YUIGAHAMA ...
THE ONE WHO SHOULD REALLY TAKE RESPONSI-BILITY IS ME.

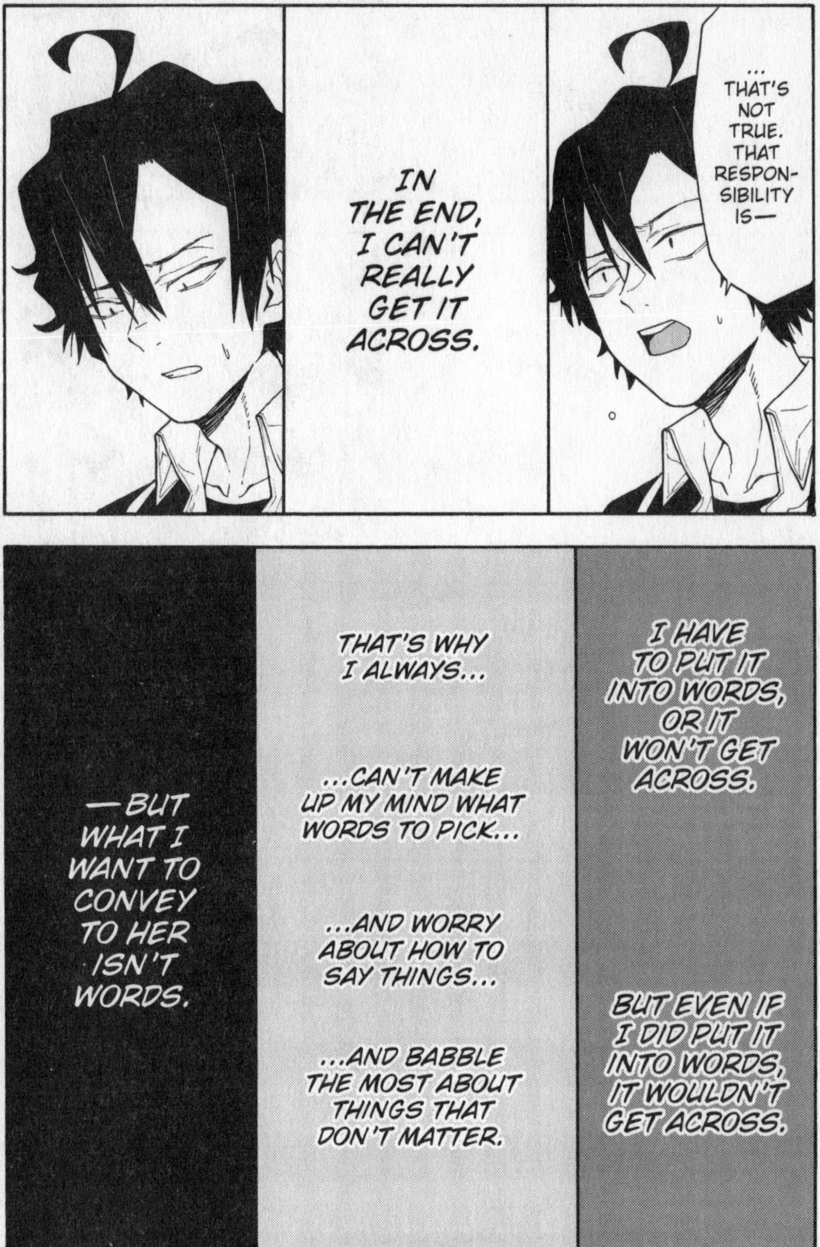
... THAT'S NOT TRUE. THAT RESPON-SIBILITY IS—
IN THE END, I CAN'T REALLY GET IT ACROSS.
I HAVE TO PUT IT INTO WORDS, OR IT WON'T GET ACROSS.
BUT EVEN IF I DID PUT IT INTO WORDS, IT WOULDN'T GET ACROSS.
THAT'S WHY I ALWAYS...
...CAN'T MAKE UP MY MIND WHAT WORDS TO PICK...
...AND WORRY ABOUT HOW TO SAY THINGS...
...AND BABBLE THE MOST ABOUT THINGS THAT DON'T MATTER.
—BUT WHAT I WANT TO CONVEY TO HER ISN'T WORDS.

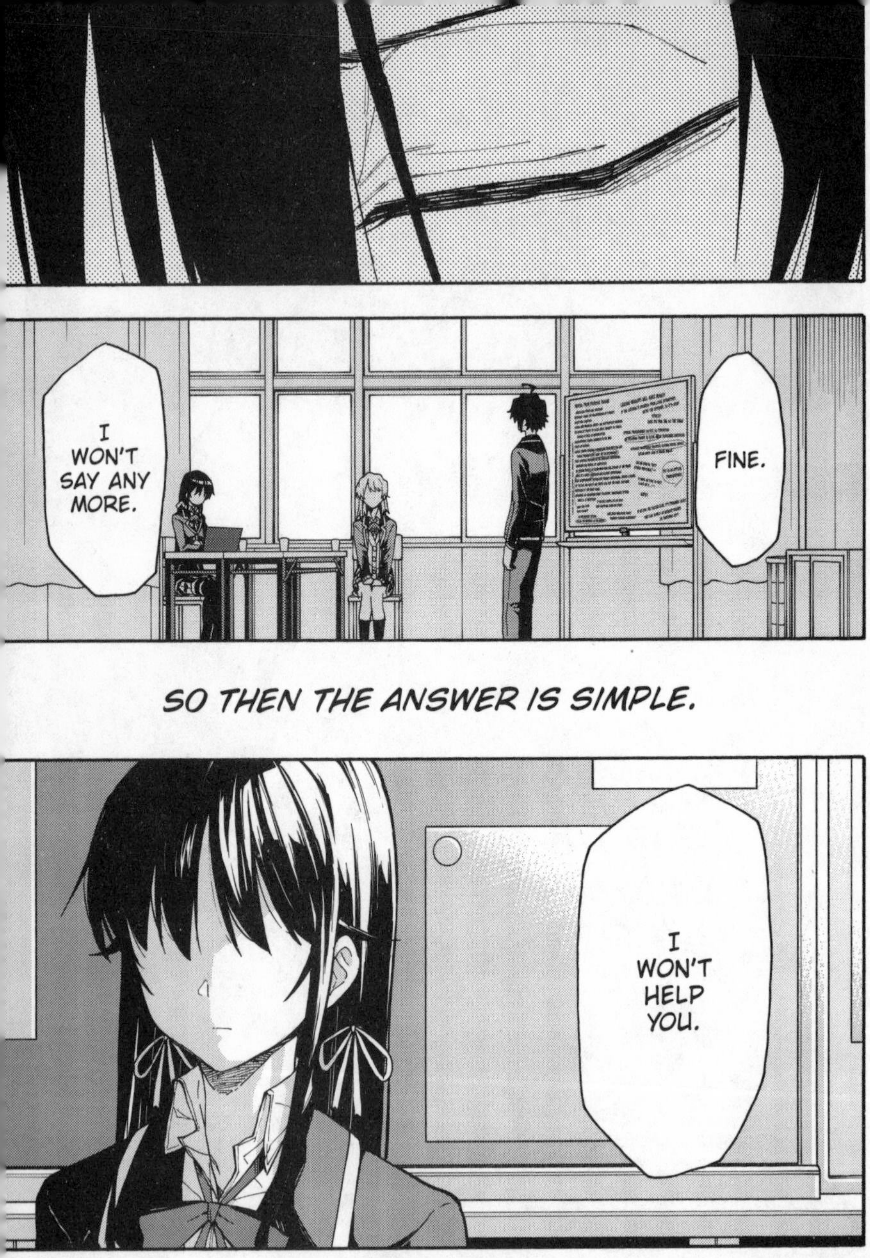
FINE.
I WON'T SAY ANY MORE.
SO THEN THE ANSWER IS SIMPLE.
I WON'T HELP YOU.
I HAVE MY WAY OF DOING THINGS—OUR WAY OF DOING THINGS.

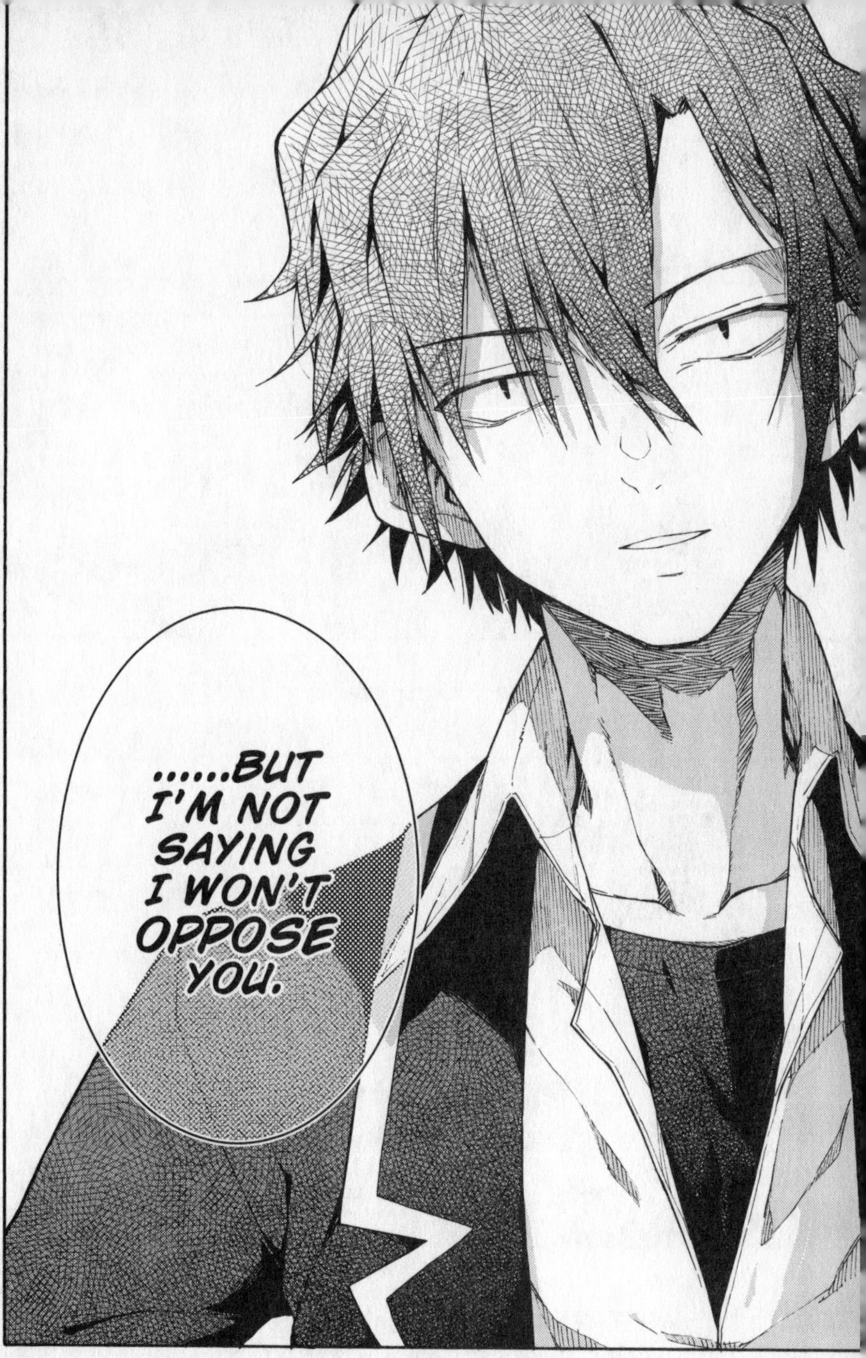
......BUT I'M NOT SAYING I WON'T OPPOSE YOU.

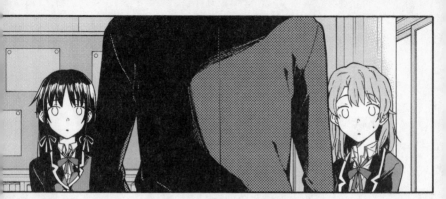

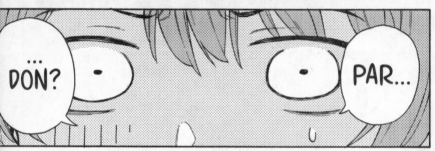

DÖN? PAR...

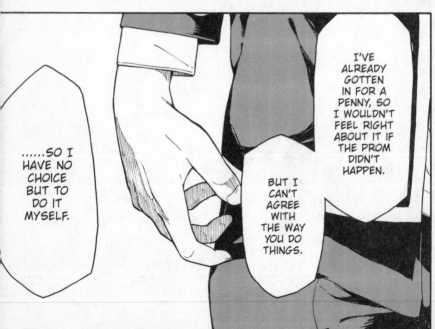

I'VE ALREADY GOTTEN IN FOR A PENNY, SO I WOULDN'T FEEL RIGHT ABOUT IT IF THE PROM DIDN'T HAPPEN.

BUT I CAN'T AGREE WITH THE WAY YOU DO THINGS.

......SO I HAVE NO CHOICE BUT TO DO IT MYSELF.

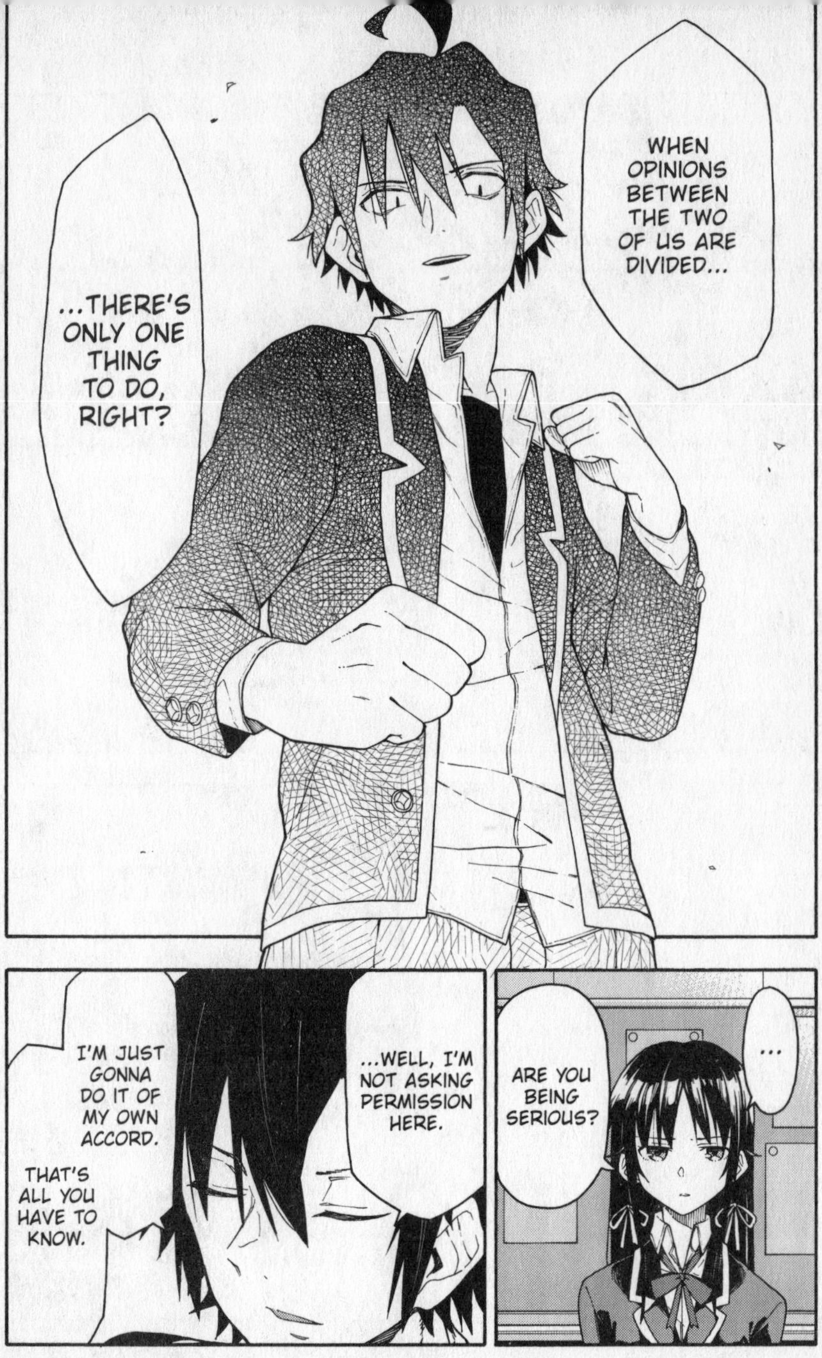
WHEN OPINIONS BETWEEN THE TWO OF US ARE DIVIDED...
...THERE'S ONLY ONE THING TO DO, RIGHT?
...
ARE YOU BEING SERIOUS?
...WELL, I'M NOT ASKING PERMISSION HERE.
I'M JUST GONNA DO IT OF MY OWN ACCORD.
THAT'S ALL YOU HAVE TO KNOW.

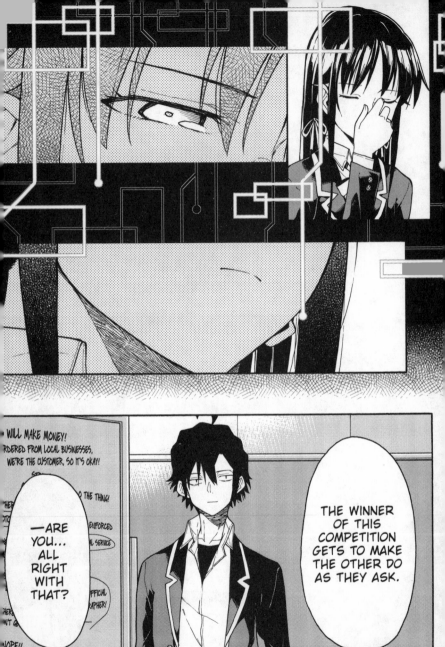

WILL MAKE MONEY!
RDERED FROM LOCAL BUSINESSES,
WE'RE THE CUSTOMER, SO IT'S OKAY!

O THE THING!

HE ENFORCED

AL SERVICE

—ARE YOU... ALL RIGHT WITH THAT?

OFFICIAL
RAPHER!

HER

N'T GO

NOPE!!

E USE THE SOCCER CLUB, IT'S PROBABLY OKAY!!
THEY CAN TOTALLY GO WITHOUT BREAKS
OR SWITCHING OFF!

THE WINNER OF THIS COMPETITION GETS TO MAKE THE OTHER DO AS THEY ASK.

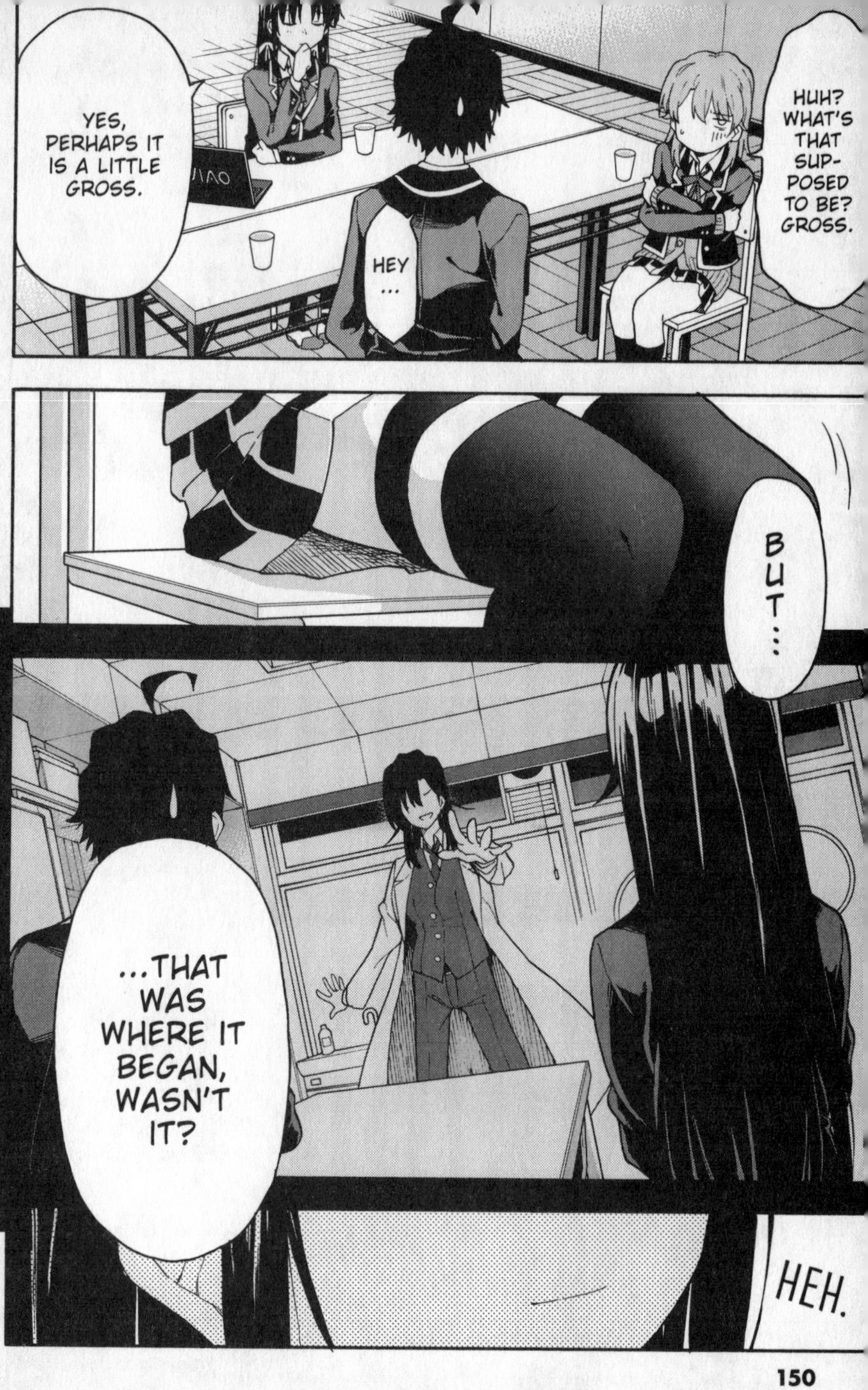
HUH? WHAT'S THAT SUP-POSED TO BE? GROSS.
HEY ...
YES, PERHAPS IT IS A LITTLE GROSS.
BUT...
...THAT WAS WHERE IT BEGAN, WASN'T IT?
HEH.

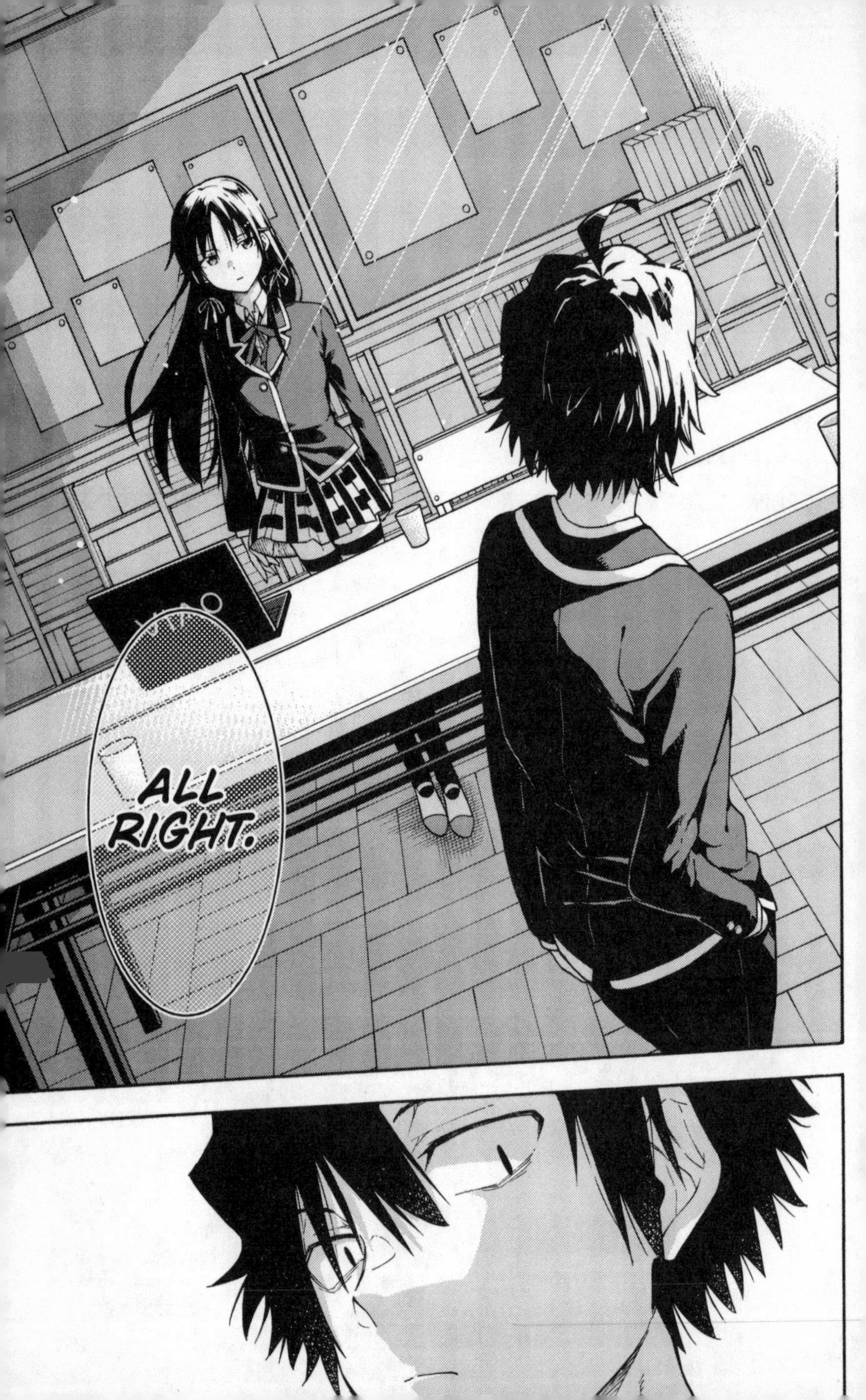
ALL RIGHT.

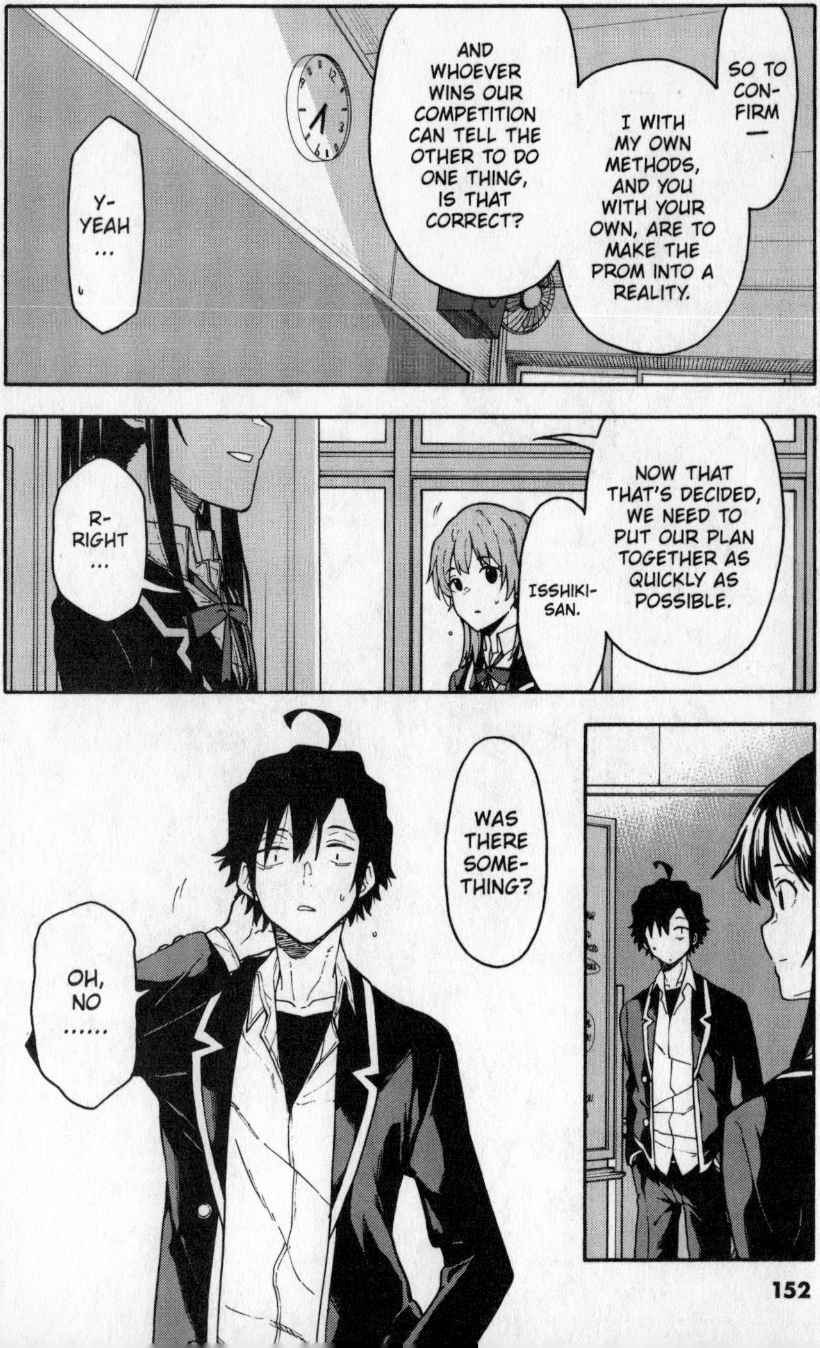
SO TO CON-FIRM—
I WITH MY OWN METHODS, AND YOU WITH YOUR OWN, ARE TO MAKE THE PROM INTO A REALITY.
AND WHOEVER WINS OUR COMPETITION CAN TELL THE OTHER TO DO ONE THING, IS THAT CORRECT?
Y-YEAH...
NOW THAT THAT'S DECIDED, WE NEED TO PUT OUR PLAN TOGETHER AS QUICKLY AS POSSIBLE.
ISSHIKI-SAN.
R-RIGHT...
WAS THERE SOME-THING?
OH, NO......

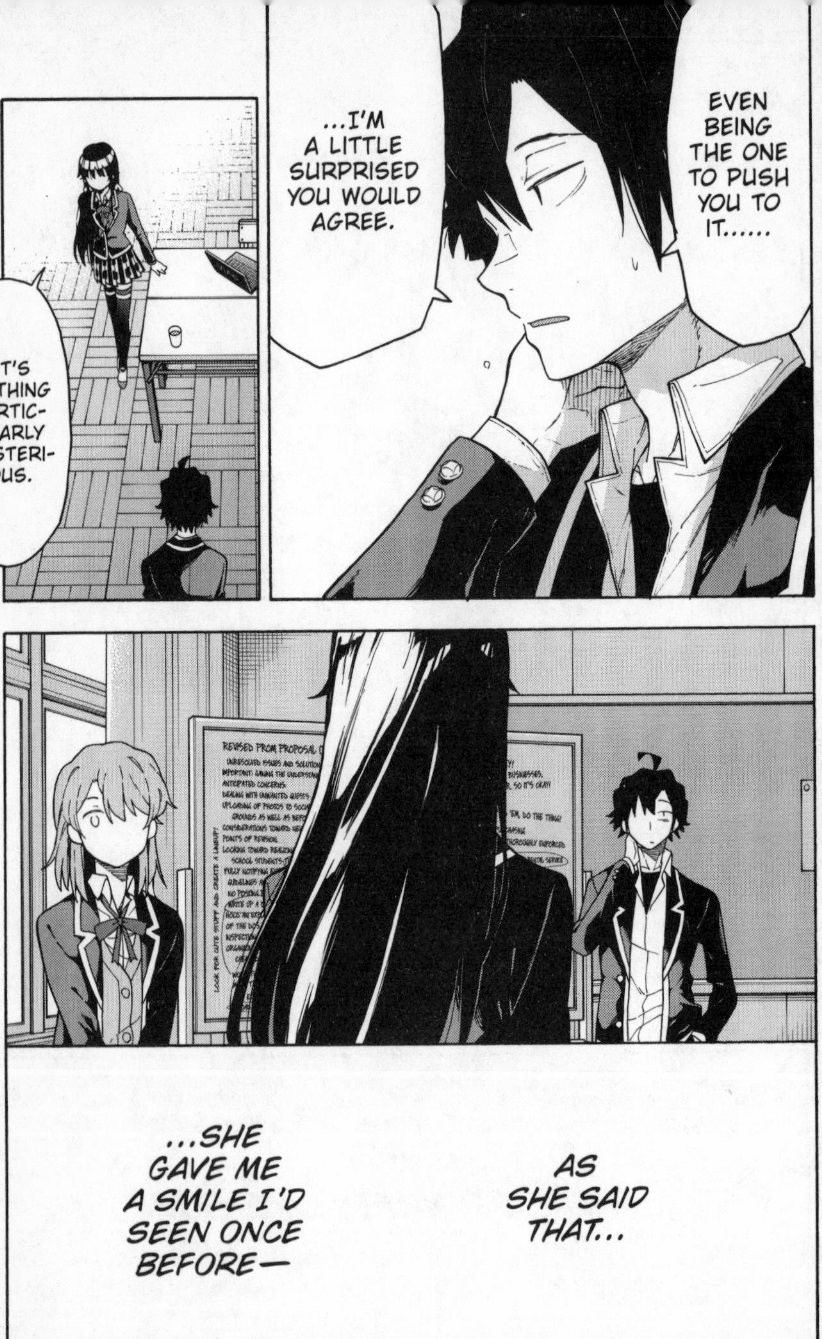
EVEN BEING THE ONE TO PUSH YOU TO IT......
...I'M A LITTLE SURPRISED YOU WOULD AGREE.
IT'S NOTHING PARTICULARLY MYSTERIOUS.
AS SHE SAID THAT...
...SHE GAVE ME A SMILE I'D SEEN ONCE BEFORE—

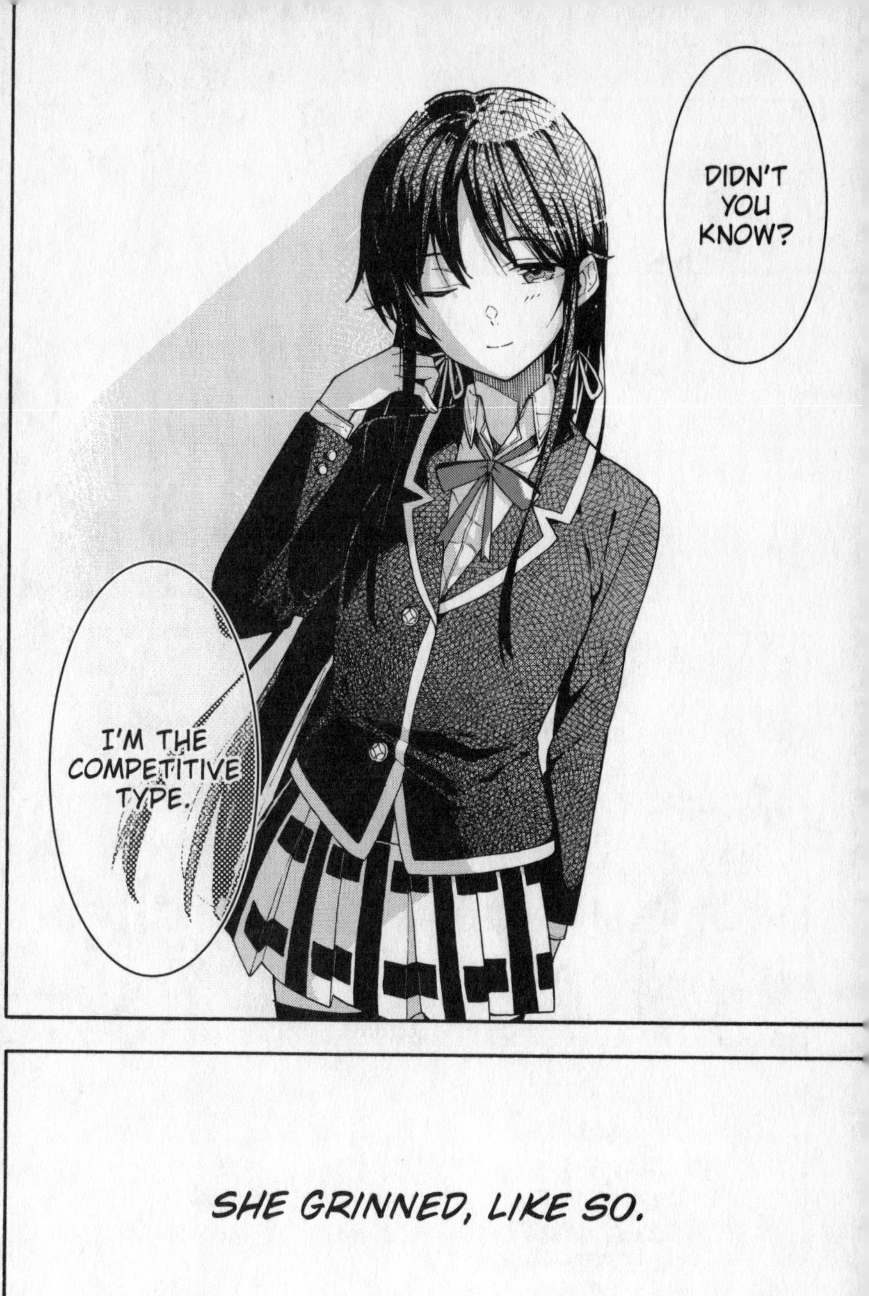
DIDN'T YOU KNOW?
I'M THE COMPETITIVE TYPE.
SHE GRINNED, LIKE SO.

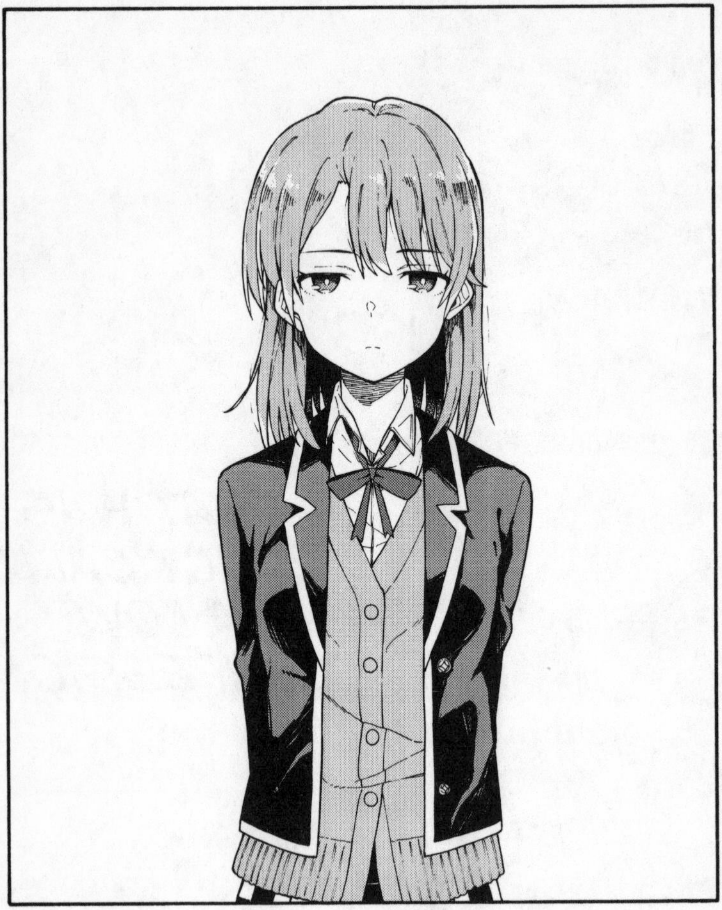

CHAPTER 96.5 ··· INTERLUDE IROHA ISSHIKI.

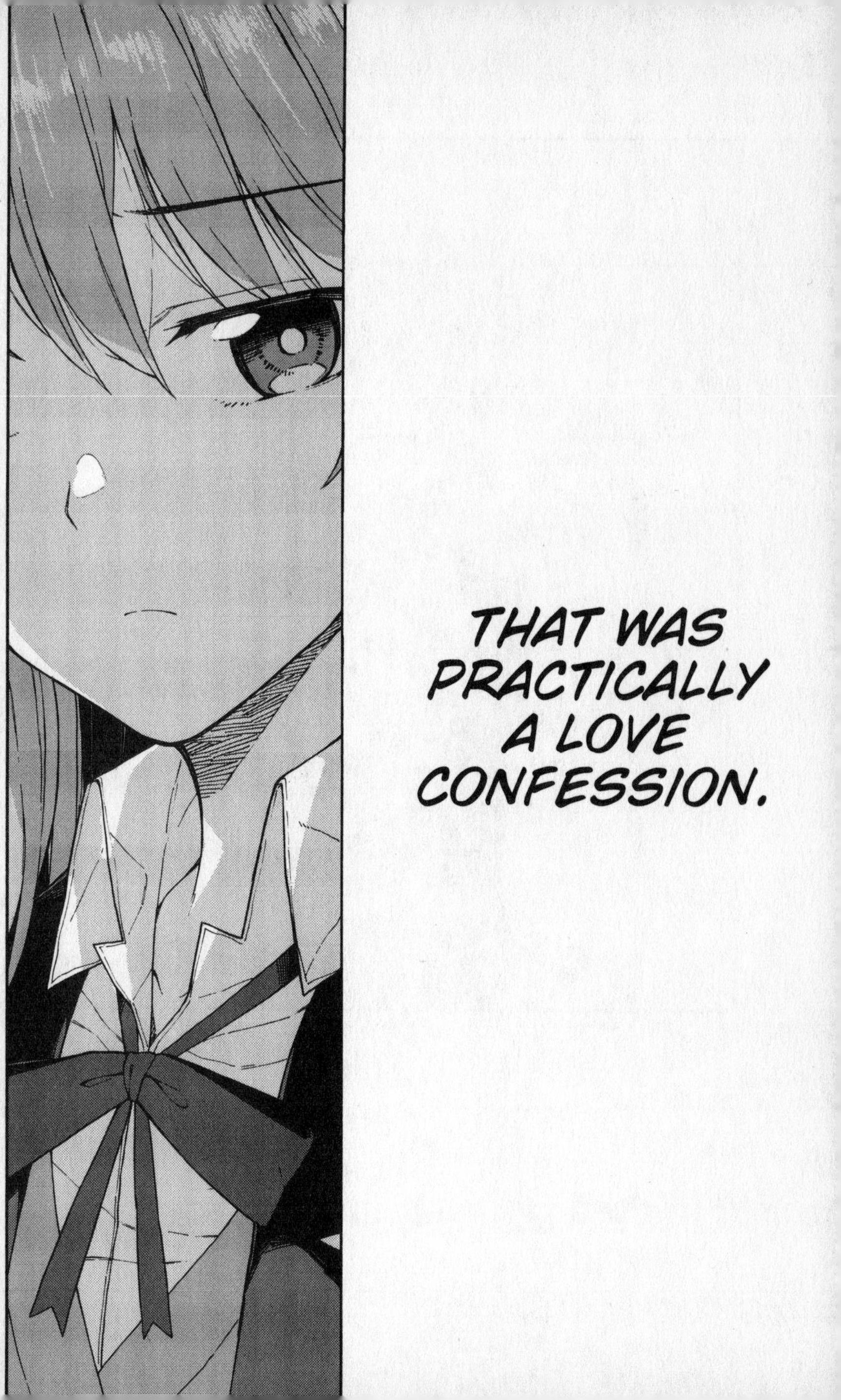
THAT WAS PRACTICALLY A LOVE CONFESSION.

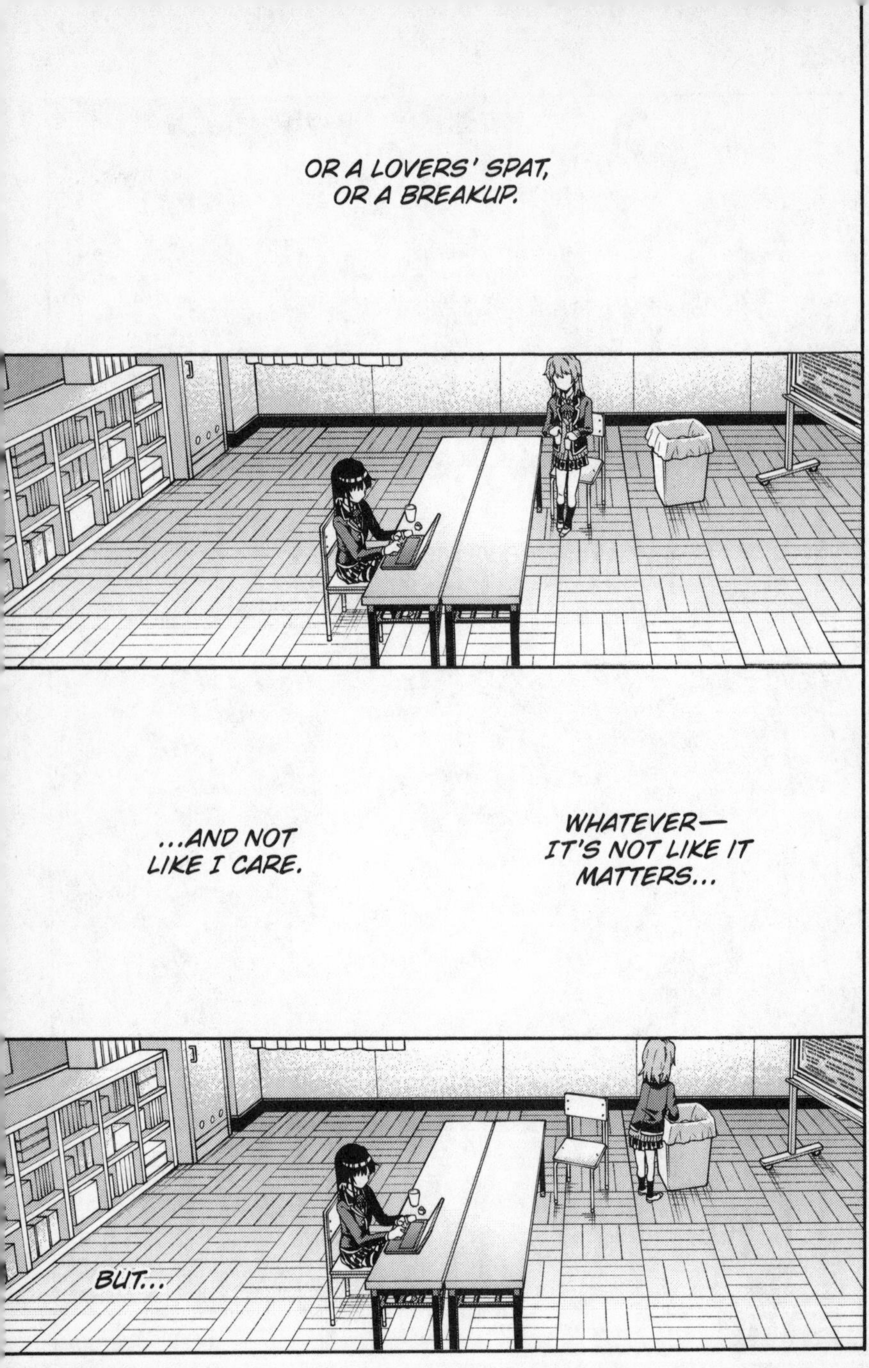
OR A LOVERS' SPAT, OR A BREAKUP.
WHATEVER— IT'S NOT LIKE IT MATTERS...
...AND NOT LIKE I CARE.
BUT...

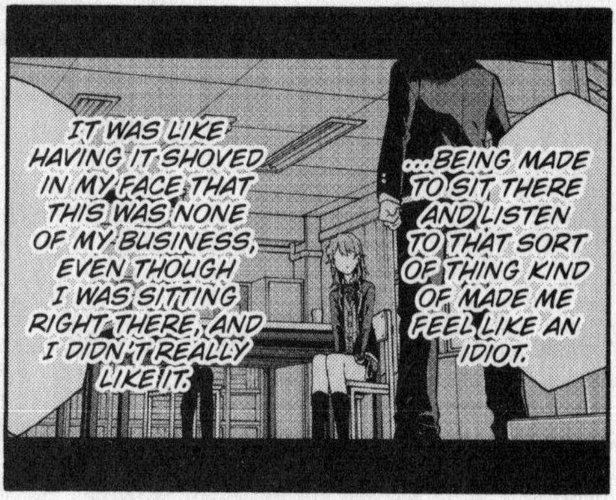
...BEING MADE TO SIT THERE AND LISTEN TO THAT SORT OF THING KIND OF MADE ME FEEL LIKE AN IDIOT.
IT WAS LIKE HAVING IT SHOVED IN MY FACE THAT THIS WAS NONE OF MY BUSINESS, EVEN THOUGH I WAS SITTING RIGHT THERE, AND I DIDN'T REALLY LIKE IT.

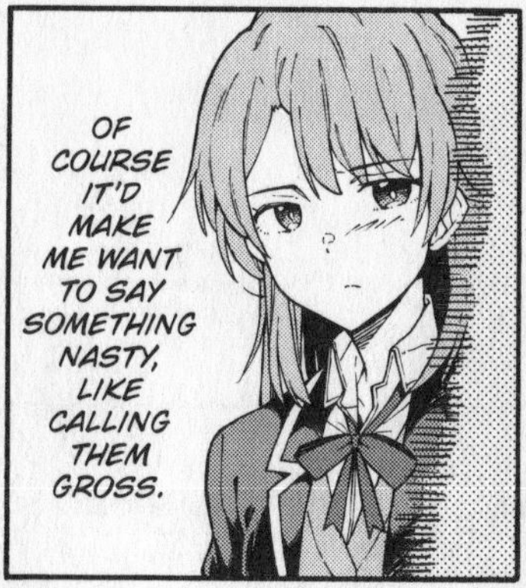
OF COURSE IT'D MAKE ME WANT TO SAY SOMETHING NASTY, LIKE CALLING THEM GROSS.

I HONESTLY WANT PROPER RESPONSIBILITY TO BE TAKEN.

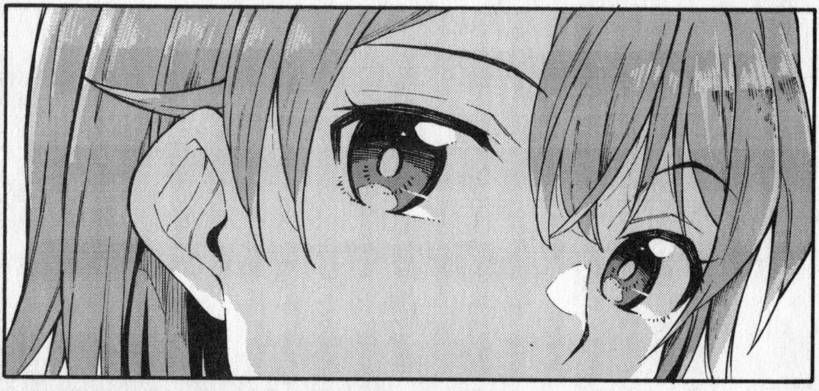

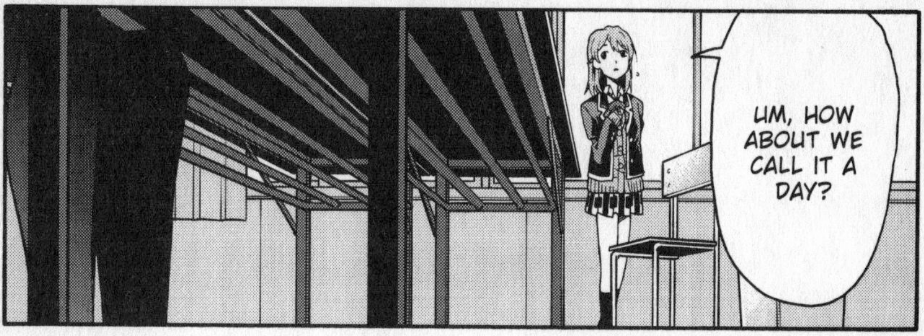
UM, HOW ABOUT WE CALL IT A DAY?

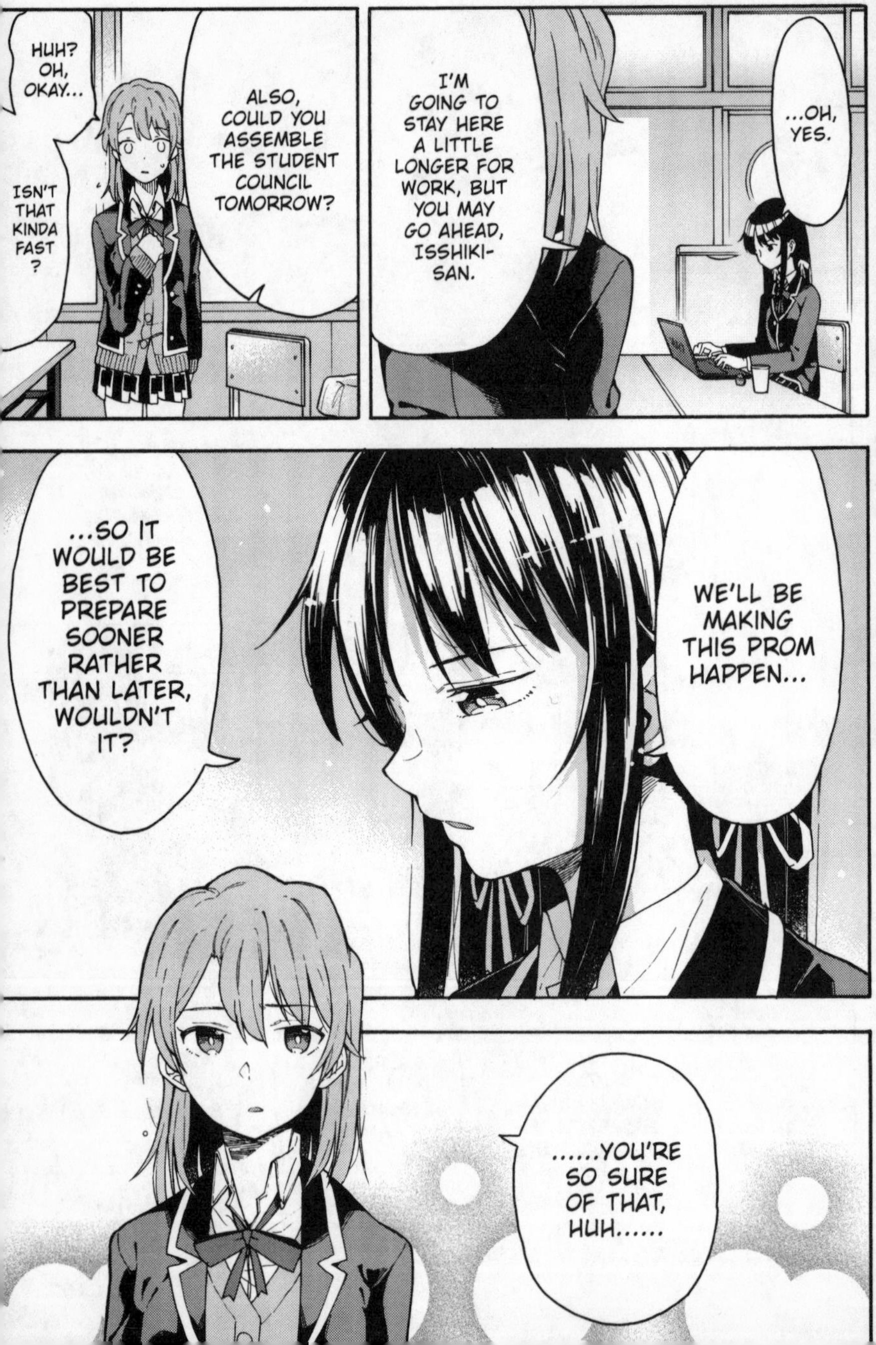
...OH, YES.
I'M GOING TO STAY HERE A LITTLE LONGER FOR WORK, BUT YOU MAY GO AHEAD, ISSHIKI-SAN.
ALSO, COULD YOU ASSEMBLE THE STUDENT COUNCIL TOMORROW?
HUH? OH, OKAY...
ISN'T THAT KINDA FAST?
WE'LL BE MAKING THIS PROM HAPPEN...
...SO IT WOULD BE BEST TO PREPARE SOONER RATHER THAN LATER, WOULDN'T IT?
......YOU'RE SO SURE OF THAT, HUH......

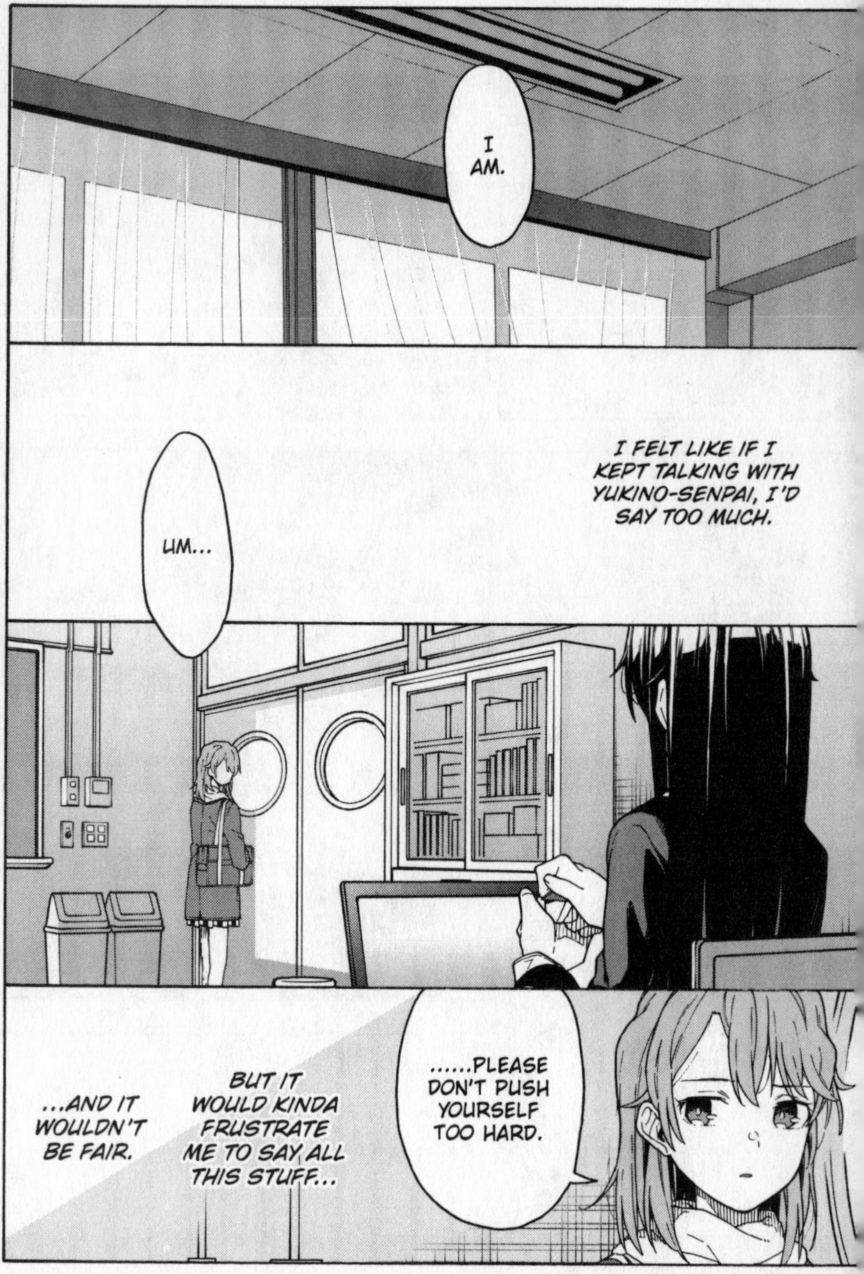
I AM.
I FELT LIKE IF I KEPT TALKING WITH YUKINO-SENPAI, I'D SAY TOO MUCH.
UM...
......PLEASE DON'T PUSH YOURSELF TOO HARD.
BUT IT WOULD KINDA FRUSTRATE ME TO SAY ALL THIS STUFF...
...AND IT WOULDN'T BE FAIR.

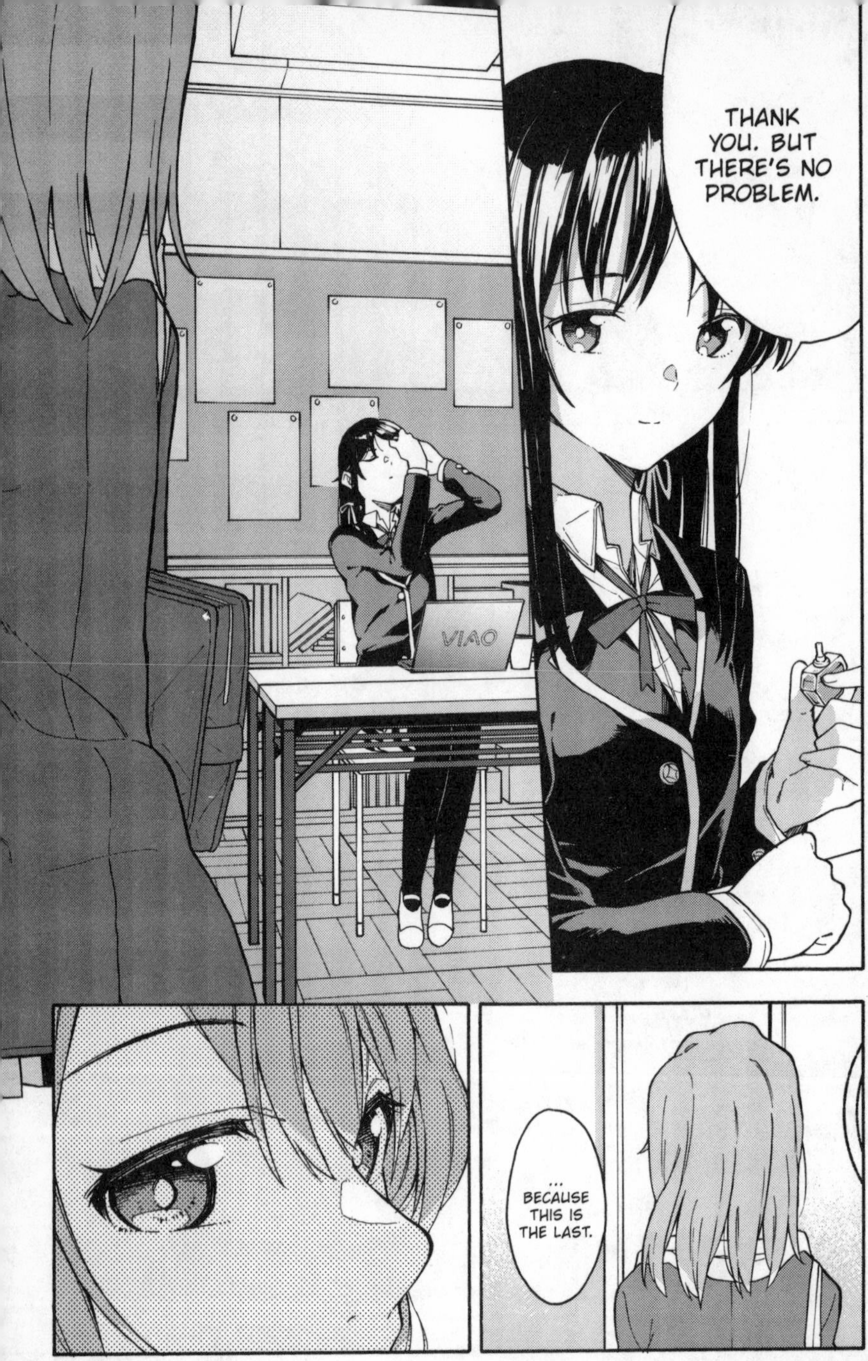
THANK YOU. BUT THERE'S NO PROBLEM.
... BECAUSE THIS IS THE LAST.

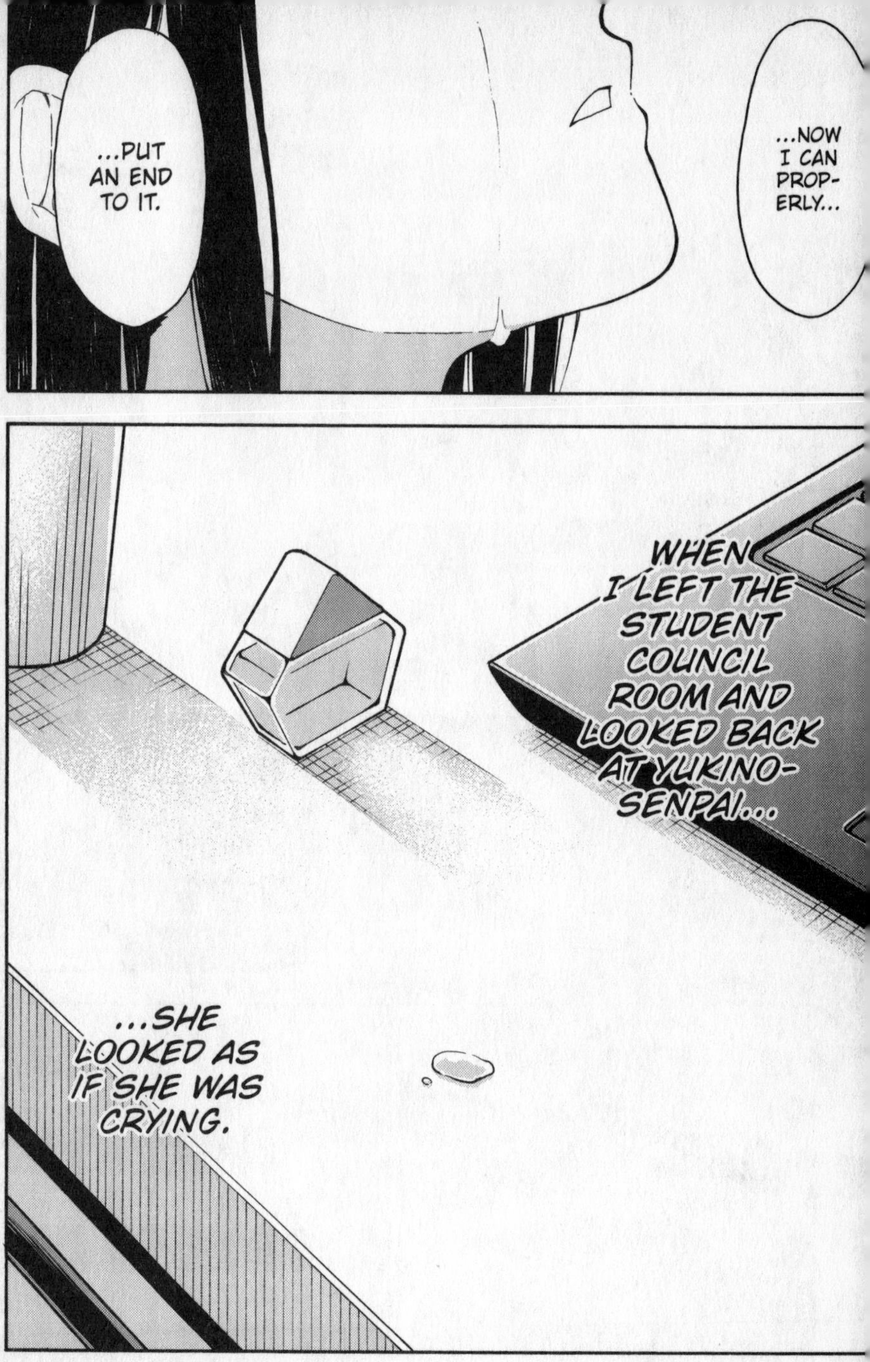
...NOW I CAN PROPERLY...
...PUT AN END TO IT.
WHEN I LEFT THE STUDENT COUNCIL ROOM AND LOOKED BACK AT YUKINO-SENPAI...
...SHE LOOKED AS IF SHE WAS CRYING.

TRANSLATION NOTES

Page 10
IKEO is a parody of the Swedish furniture store chain IKEA, which indeed has stores in Japan as well.

Page 55
The **Imo-Kin Trio** was a group of three boys from a variety show who formed a pop combo in the mid-1980s and performed comedic songs. Their motif was that one kid was a nerd/prep type, one was a delinquent, and one was very average.

Page 58
Aion Marinria is a parody of an actual shopping mall in Chiba called Aeon Marinpia.

Page 71
The lines that Hachiman is writing are from the classic short story "The Moon over the Mountain" by Japanese author Atsushi Nakajima. Taking inspiration from an old Tang dynasty Chinese legend, Nakajima's story is about a failed poet named Zheng Li who is unable to make a living off poetry and attempts to return to a government job. However, his arrogance and jealousy toward his colleagues turn him into a man-eating tiger. Ultimately, Li's greatest regret is that he was too cowardly and prideful to test himself or learn from others, and thus he sabotaged his own career in poetry.

The **Tianbao era** took place during the Tang dynasty in China.

Page 111
"Oh-hooo? Verily so?" (*Ee, hontou ni gozaru kaa?*) is a quote from the character Sasaki Kojirou, an Assassin in Type Moon's Fate franchise. It is officially translated as "Oh? Is that true?" but this book uses a different approach to emphasize how odd it's supposed to sound in normal speech.

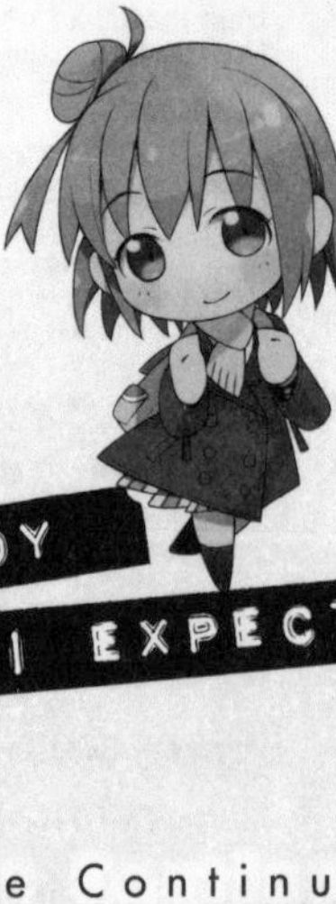

MY YOUTH ROMANTIC COMEDY IS WRONG, AS I EXPECTED

...To Be Continued.

MY YOUTH ROMANTIC COMEDY IS WRONG, AS I EXPECTED @COMIC ⑰

Original Story: Wataru Watari
Art: Naomichi Io
Character Design: Ponkan⑧
ORIGINAL COVER DESIGN/Hiroyuki KAWASOME (Graphio)

Translation: Jennifer Ward

Lettering: Bianca Pistillo

YAHARI ORE NO SEISHUN LOVE COME WA MACHIGATTEIRU.
@COMIC Vol. 17 by Wataru WATARI, Naomichi IO, PONKAN⑧
© 2013 Wataru WATARI, Naomichi IO, PONKAN⑧
All rights reserved.
Original Japanese edition published by SHOGAKUKAN.
English translation rights arranged with SHOGAKUKAN through Tuttle-Mori Agency, Inc., Tokyo.

Yen Press
150 West 30th Street, 19th Floor
New York, NY 10001

Visit us at yenpress.com
facebook.com/yenpress
twitter.com/yenpress
yenpress.tumblr.com
instagram.com/yenpress

First Yen Press Edition: January 2022

Yen Press is an imprint of Yen Press, LLC.
The Yen Press name and logo are trademarks of Yen Press, LLC.

The publisher is not responsible for websites (or their content) that are not owned by the publisher.

Library of Congress Control Number: 2016931004

ISBN: 978-1-9753-3963-0

10 9 8 7 6 5 4 3 2 1

WOR

Printed in the United States of America